# Ford Madox Ford's
# *The Good Soldier*

*Centenary Essays*

*Edited by*

Max Saunders
Sara Haslam

BRILL
RODOPI

LEIDEN | BOSTON

Cover illustration: Alfred Cohen, 'Ford Madox Ford', charcoal drawing with gouache, 12.5 x 9 inches, 1991. © The Estate of Alfred Cohen and by permission of the Alfred Cohen Art Foundation. Back cover image: Nauheim, Germany.

Series title page illustration: Ford c.1915, pen and ink drawing. © The Estate of Alfred Cohen and by permission of the Alfred Cohen Art Foundation.

Frontispiece: Dust-jacket of the UK first edition of *The Good Soldier*, London: John Lane, the Bodley Head, 1915. Reproduced with the permission of Sotheby's.

The stills from the television adaptation of *The Good Soldier* reproduced on pp. 108-10: © ITV/Rex.

Excerpts from the letters of David Jones quoted on pp. 243-4: © The David Jones Estate. Quoted by permission of the Estate.

Library of Congress Control Number: 2015941193

For information about the Ford Madox Ford Society, please see the website at:
http://www.fordmadoxfordsociety.org
Or contact: Dr Sara Haslam, S.J.Haslam@open.ac.uk. Department of Literature, Open University, Walton Hall, Milton Keynes, MK7 6AA, UK
Or: max.saunders@kcl.ac.uk

IFMFS is a peer-reviewed annual series. Guidelines for contributors, including a full list of abbreviations of Ford's titles and related works, can be found by following the links on the Society's website.

ISSN 1569-4070
ISBN 978-90-04-29916-0 (hardback)
ISBN 978-90-04-29917-7 (e-book)

MIX
Paper from responsible sources
FSC® C109576
www.fsc.org

Printed by Printforce, the Netherlands

I had never really tried to put into any novel of mine *all* that I knew about writing [. . . .] But I have always been mad about writing—about the way writing should be done and partly alone, partly with the companionship of Conrad, I had even at that date made exhaustive studies into how words should be handled and novels constructed.

So, on the day I was forty I sat down to show what I could do—and the *Good Soldier* resulted.

Ford, 'Dedicatory Letter to STELLA FORD' (1927), in *The Good Soldier,* ed. MAX SAUNDERS,
Oxford: Oxford University Press, 2012, pp. 3-6 (p.3).

∴

Front cover of the original dust-jacket of the UK first edition of *The Good Soldier*
(London: John Lane, The Bodley Head, 1915), © Sotheby's.

# CONTENTS

## SECTION 2: MIND/BODY, CARE, TREATMENT

## SECTION 3: CONTEXTS AND CONTRASTS

# LIST OF ILLUSTRATIONS

# GENERAL EDITOR'S PREFACE

## Max Saunders

Ford Madox Ford was a major presence in early twentieth-century literature, and he has remained a significant – if sometimes controversial – figure in the history of modern English and American literature for over a century. Throughout that time he has been written about, not just by critics, but often by leading novelists and poets, such as Graham Greene, Robert Lowell, William Carlos Williams, Anthony Burgess, A. S. Byatt, Julian Barnes, Edmund White and Colm Tóibín. His two acknowledged masterpieces have remained in print since the 1940s. *The Good Soldier* – the subject of this collection – has long been acknowledged a modern classic, and increasingly figures in studies of modernism and on syllabuses. *Parade's End* has been more gradually gaining recognition as comparably important. Malcolm Bradbury called it 'a central Modernist novel of the 1920s, in which it is exemplary'; and for Samuel Hynes it is 'the greatest war novel ever written by an Englishman'. The five-part television adaptation of *Parade's End*, dramatized by Tom Stoppard for the BBC and HBO, and directed by Susanna White, with an outstanding cast led by Benedict Cumberbatch and Rebecca Hall, was broadcast worldwide in 2012 and 2013 to excellent reviews. It has proved a watershed, introducing Ford's work to millions of viewers.

During the last few decades, there has also been a striking resurgence of critical interest in Ford and in the multifarious aspects of his work. As befits such an internationalist phenomenon as Ford himself, this attention has been markedly international, manifesting itself not only in the United Kingdom and the USA, but in Continental Europe and elsewhere. Many of his works have not only been republished in their original language, but also translated into more than a dozen others.

The founding of this series, International Ford Madox Ford Studies, reflected this increasing interest in Ford's writing and the wider understanding of his role in literary history. Each volume is normally based upon a particular theme, issue, or text, and relates aspects of Ford's work, life, and contacts, to broader concerns of his time. Previous volumes have focused on ideas of modernity, history, the city, culture and change, the places he lived in and wrote about, and his complex engagements with several generations of literary movements.

This fourteenth volume is only the second to focus on a specific work, joining volume 13, which took *Parade's End* as its subject. Yet *Parade's End* is a vast work, running to over 800 pages, and comprising four individual novels. Here, the subject is a single, relatively short, novel. *The Good Soldier* has been the most widely read, studied and written about of all Ford's four-score books. When IFMFS was established at the start of the new millennium, Ford appeared at risk of being remembered as a one-book writer – or at least as the author of a single memorable book. In conjunction with Carcanet Press's laudable programme of bringing back into circulation a wide range of his work, the central aims of the series were to encourage attention to the diversity of his *oeuvre*, and to explore the complexity of his relations to other writers – whether his precursors, contemporaries or successors. Now, with the Carcanet 'Millennium Ford' edition running to some twenty volumes; with the rediscovery of *Parade's End*; and with the prospect of Oxford University Press's project to produce critical editions of Ford's complete works, the situation for twenty-first century Ford looks very different. It is from this perspective that the present volume takes the opportunity offered by the centenary of the first publication of *The Good Soldier* to look again at this remarkable novel; at its significance not only for Ford, but for modern literature.

Most of the essays included here began as papers given at the Ford Madox Ford Society's conference organized by Geraint Evans at the University of Swansea from the 12th-14th September 2013.

The series is published in association with the Ford Madox Ford Society. Forthcoming publications will be announced on the Society's website, together with details of whom to contact with suggestions about future collections or contributions. The address is:

    http://www.fordmadoxfordsociety.org/

# INTRODUCTION: *The Good Soldier* at 100

## Max Saunders

When Frank Kermode wrote a Foreword over a decade ago for the second volume in this series, *Ford Madox Ford's Modernity*, he registered a hesitation about Ford's standing:

> The claims to canonical status of *The Good Soldier* and the tetralogy *Parade's End* [. . .] have been made more or less confidently ever since their publication, but over the years one has been conscious of an element of uncertainty about the higher claims made for Ford. He has somehow hovered on the threshold of immortality.

And he closed the Foreword by quoting a similar observation by Roger Poole, one of the contributors to that volume who made the – certainly – high claim for Ford as (in Kermode's words) 'technically at least the equal of James, Conrad and Joyce'; yet went on to lament that nonetheless Ford 'even now remains a figure in the shadows, off-stage, waiting'. 'This splendid collection may well change all that' Kermode concluded: 'Ford is now close to centre stage, and lit with increasing brilliance'.

The centenary in 2015 of the first publication of *The Good Soldier* seems the right moment to ask to what extent this situation has changed. Claims for Ford's centrality and canonicity continue to be made, regardless of modern critical skepticism about centres and canons. Such claims continue to focus on *The Good Soldier* and *Parade's End* – though perhaps with the latter now figuring more prominently, thanks to that version of canonicity conferred by television adaptations. Tom Stoppard was reported in the *Guardian* as hoping that 'the BBC2 drama will restore Ford's reputation, placing him alongside authors like DH Lawrence and Evelyn Waugh in the pantheon of early 20th century greats'.[1]

To judge whether this has happened or not, we would need to know who keeps the keys for such a pantheon. Does a BBC or HBO badge now gain you admission? If the currency is media current-ness, journalists and bloggers certainly felt more pressure to write about Ford in 2012 than they felt shame in confessing to not having read

*Parade's End.* Nonetheless, the filming of the tetralogy has certainly drawn a new generation of readers to Ford, and it is to be hoped that they will continue to read and enjoy his work after the impact of the adaptation dissipates, and the First World War centenaries have passed. His longer-term presence in cultural memory will be partly in the hands of teachers in schools and universities. Here too the signs are auspicious, and perhaps more international. Ford's work has been on more syllabuses, and more widely translated, in recent years. *The Good Soldier* might justly be called a global text now. There are versions of it not just in French, German, Italian, and Spanish, but also in Portuguese, Japanese, Hungarian, Polish, Hebrew, Swedish, Finnish, Turkish, and doubtless other languages. It has also been noticeable that younger scholars have been turning their attention to Ford, who has been figuring increasingly in studies of modern literature focusing on multiple authors.

This greater cultural presence also reflects the fact that the seventy-year term of copyright expired at the end of 2009 (for all his work published in the UK during his lifetime, and for most of it – mainly work published before 1923 – in the US). This has unleashed a wave of new editions – especially of *The Good Soldier*.

The most significant of these – and the one which is having the greatest impact on twenty-first century discussions of the novel – is Martin Stannard's magnificent Norton Critical Edition, first published in 1995 (during the a brief window during which Ford came out of UK copyright while the term was still fifty years after an author's death, then went back in when the term was extended to harmonize with EC legislation), and reissued in a revised edition in 2012. Though earlier Ford scholarship had discussed the manuscript revisions of the novel, Stannard's critical apparatus makes the evidence fully and more generally available. His is also the most fully annotated edition, containing fascinating material about Nauheim at the time Ford and Violet Hunt were there in 1910-11; and it includes an authoritative discussion of the development of the novel, which is particularly illuminating about some of the key questions discussed in essays here, such as the reliability of the narrator, John Dowell; and the inconsistencies in the chronology he advances for the events in the story.

Since the publication in 1962 of David Dow Harvey's trailblazing bibliography on Ford, as the American New Critics had just discovered Ford, there have probably been some three hundred essays, chapters and books discussing *The Good Soldier*, taking criticism of the novel into all the new critical areas of the period: psychoanalysis, feminism, Marxism, poststructuralism, new historicism, postcolonialism, textual theory, modernist magazine studies, the new modernist studies and the like. That they are all revisited in this collection testifies to their continuing productiveness in approaching this rich and multiplicitous novel.

But the sign that Ford is now being accorded a different kind of attention – both broader and more sophisticated – is that the prime difference between the kind of discussion his work receives now, and many of these earlier studies, is demonstrated in the greater awareness of the range of his work, and the interconnections between its different parts. This is standard expectation elsewhere in literary studies. An account of T. S. Eliot's more metaphysical poetry would be inadequate without considering Eliot's critical writing on metaphysical poets, and his posthumously published lectures and letters relating to the topic. But the combination of Ford's uncertain status, and the vastness of his *oeuvre*, has meant that those of his works that have received attention – and especially *The Good Soldier* – have too often been treated in isolation from his other writings. Nowadays the greater availability of much of his work, together with a thriving critical community discovering its interest, has begun to explore the interrelatedness of his *oeuvre*. An analysis of the technical complexity of *The Good Soldier* is more likely now to be informed by his criticial writing – not only in his periodical essays, but in books like his memoir of collaborating with Conrad, or his literary-historical *summa*, *The March of Literature*. Studies of *The Good Soldier*'s debts to writers like Conrad or James will refer to Ford's pioneering books on either writer. Discussion of the Englishness of *The Good Soldier*'s 'English people' is likely to draw upon his trilogy devoted to *England and the English*; and also his wartime propaganda books contrasting English culture with those of Germany and France, where *The Good Soldier* is also set. Conversely, his use of an American narrator might be compared with his writings about the US and Americans in his reminiscential books (including *New York is Not America*). Indeed, Ford's use of an unreliable reminiscential narrator is itself hard to separate from his own attraction towards fictionalizing reminiscence. The period covered by his first book of autobiography, *Return to Yesterday*, is from the 1890s to the First World War – exactly the time-frame of *The Good Soldier*. The sense of the past which saturates *The Good Soldier* is more likely to be connected with Ford's historical fiction: its heady clash between Protestantism and Catholicism with his trilogy of novels about Henry VIII, *The Fifth Queen*; its references to the Troubadours and the chivalric tradition with Ford's medieval novels such as *Ladies Whose Bright Eyes* or *The Young Lovell* – as well as with his late genre-defying book of cultural history, reminiscence and travel writing, *Provence*.

Ford is thus both a highly intertextual writer, and one who often returns to the same preoccupations in different works in different genres. If that's true of many writers, it's perhaps more familiar in modernist poets such as Eliot or Pound. Students of prose are sometimes less attuned to this essentially poetic effect, when a novel seems to condense a lifetime's thought about a series of topics.

Two further areas deserve mention, where new scholarship on Ford and his circle has changed how we read *The Good Soldier*. One comes under the heading of biographical research. Not just the several biographical books devoted to Ford which have appeared since 1970, by Arthur Mizener, Thomas Moser, Alan Judd, and myself; but also the plethora of other publications that have added to our biographical knowledge of him. These include the publication of his correspondence with crucial figures such as Ezra Pound, Stella Bowen, and Caroline Gordon; as well as the biographies and letters of numerous of Ford's contacts, from well-known writers like Lawrence, Conrad, and Rhys to less familiar figures who are equally important to Ford's life, such as Olive Garnett, or Jeanne Foster. We now have a much fuller picture of Ford's literary and social life, as indeed of his personal life, and how they bear upon *The Good Soldier*.

How intensely fraught a time it was for Ford and his circle as he was beginning the novel is still becoming apparent. To take one example: thanks to the work of Moser and Stannard,[2] we knew that the opening of the novel had been dictated to Brigit Patmore. She had a reputation as a beauty, was unhappily married, and had been taken up by Ezra Pound and his friends. Ford's relationship with Violet Hunt had come under increasing strain as his wife, Elsie Hueffer, continued to refuse a divorce. Ford had been living in Giessen in Germany, trying to obtain German citizenship so as to be able to divorce her in Germany; and he and Hunt claimed this had enabled them to marry on the continent. In fact we now know the citizenship was refused.[3] They may have married regardless, which would have opened Ford to a charge of bigamy; or they may have decided simply to pretend their union had been legitimized. When a newspaper, the

*Throne*, described Violet in print as 'Miss Violet Hunt (Mrs. Ford Madox Hueffer)', Elsie decided to sue the paper, and the resulting libel trial caused a scandal that damaged Ford's reputation in Britain for at least a decade, and brought on a recurrence of the nervous collapse he'd suffered in 1904. They lay low in France for three months. It was when they returned that Hunt invited Patmore to stay with them at her Sussex cottage at Selsey. She may have thought – as Dowell imagines Leonora thinking about Maisie Maidan in *The Good Soldier* – that if there were signs that her man was beginning to stray, it was better to try to exercise some form of control over the distraction. The evidence for whether or not Ford and Patmore had a consummated affair is conflicting. She denied it later; whereas Hunt wrote in her diary that Patmore had 'succumbed from the flattery of his suit—his plausibility . . .'[4] – which sounds physical, but may have been more emotional. It was while she was at Selsey that Ford wrote one of his best poems, 'On Heaven', dedicated to Hunt, but clearly imagining Patmore in the role of the beloved, as 'my young love', 'very tall and quaint / And golden, like a *quattrocento* saint'.[5] The poem's longing for a romantic escape from a failed relationship maps onto both Ford's marriage to Elsie and (quasi-)marriage to Violet; but also onto Edward Ashburnham's sentimental adulteries in the novel:

> Well, you see, in England
> She had a husband. And four families –
> His, hers, mine, and another woman's too –
> Would have gone crazy. (*Selected Poems* 102)

The poem, like the novel, plumbs the depths of English renunciation, as well as the renunciation of that renunciation, or the dream of renouncing it:

> But one is English,
> Though one be never so much of a ghost;
> And if most of your life have been spent in the craze to relinquish
> What you want most,
> You will go on relinquishing,
> You will go on vanquishing
> Human longings, even
> In Heaven.
>
> God! You will have forgotten what the rest of the world is on fire for—

> The madness of desire for the long and quiet embrace,
> The coming nearer of a tear-wet face;
> Forgotten the desire to slake
> The thirst, and the long, slow ache,
> And to interlace
> Lash with lash, lip with lip, limb with limb, and the fingers of the hand with
> the hand
> And . . . (*Selected Poems* 101)

However confidently a biographer might read such poetry or fiction as coded autobiography, it is still startling to find confirmation of the kind offered by Violet Hunt's diary for 1914, when it appeared in the public domain in 1995.[6] Ford began *The Good Soldier* in the second half of 1913: he said on his birthday, 17 December, though Mizener contested that, placing it in the summer at Selsey. However, Hunt's diary accords with Ford's dating. She has Patmore's husband coming to collect her on the 12th April 1914 – long enough after December 1913 for Patmore to have been able to complete her work on the manuscript.[7] Hunt added that she assumed he knew what Brigit 'had been up to'. This possible complicity or connivance suggests a parallel with the married women Ashburnham takes up with – Maisie Maidan or Mrs Basil. But what happened next is much closer to Ashburnham's last passion, for his wife's ward Nancy Rufford, and his fatal attempt at renunciation. The following Spring, Hunt wrote in her diary entry for 16 April 1914 that Ford 'went to Conrads / his idea of a rest cure & get over Bridgit [*sic*]. He stayed in lodgings near Capel. I think he really was trying to give her up'. The diary doesn't just confirm his infatuation with Patmore – that has never been in doubt. Nor does it just confirm his attempt to renounce that passion. It also gives a striking insight into their lives while Ford was writing the novel. On 8 May 1914 Hunt wrote: 'Brigit came & went? Is this the day they sat & cried all day silently & I left them alone'.

'On Heaven' was first published in the Chicago magazine *Poetry* in June 1914. It's just possible the passage about 'The coming nearer of a tear-wet face' was written after 8 May (or, quite probably, given her compulsive revising of her diaries, that Hunt had got the date wrong, wondering about the event in a later retrospective addition). There's no corresponding scene in *The Good Soldier*. On the contrary, Nancy's departure for Ceylon is public – on a station platform, with Dowell as unofficial chaperone – and terrifyingly devoid of any expression of feeling. But the force of that suppression testifies to the strength not only of their passion but the sadness of their situation. If Ford and Patmore sat crying silently all day, they too must have felt they were living out the saddest story. And it's hard not to feel that that sense of sadness, and silent communion, gets into the novel's language of extreme sadness, as well as Dowell's imagination of a 'silent listener' (*GS* 44):

> So I shall just imagine myself for a fortnight or so at one side of the fireplace of a country cottage, with a sympathetic soul opposite me. And I shall go on talking, in a low voice while the sea sounds in the distance and overhead the great black flood of wind polishes the bright stars. (*GS* 18)

That curious image of the 'black flood of wind', set against the sound of the sea, is also in 'On Heaven':

> And the voice that called from depth in her to depth
> In me . . . my God, in the dreadful nights,
> Through the roar of the great black winds, through the sound of the sea!
> (*Selected Poems* 102)

It is not surprising that poem and novel arise from the same period of fraught intensity. The juxtaposition brings out the lyrical impulse in both; but also enables us to see the differences. The narrator of 'On Heaven' is also the sentimental lover. In *The Good Soldier* Ford splits the roles: the novel ironises Ashburnham's sentimental impulses: 'all good soldiers are sentimentalists — all good soldiers of that type' (*GS* 28). But it narrates them with a lyricism that – as here – seems to arouse the very sentiments it is holding at a distance.

Returning to Hunt's diary, one also can't help wondering how she knew Ford and Patmore had sat crying silently all day if she left them to it. Was she keeping them under surveillance nonetheless, at least intermittently? Or had they told her? In her memoir, *The Flurried Years*, she certainly seems as aware as Brigit's husband, Deighton Patmore, of what had been going on:

> I confess I had thought of the ultimate cataclysm as, alone in the mornings while the dictation was going on, I wandered round one or other of the three beaches of Selsey [. . . .][8]

'I would come in late sometimes for lunch', she wrote, 'and I would meet the poet rushing, hatless, down the village street, wanting to know if I had committed suicide'. She hadn't, 'yet', she noted, but then goes on to describe the 'poison ring' that she wore, and implies that she was near to using it, as Dowell's wife Florence uses hers in the novel.[9] Was there a suggestion here of wishful thinking on Ford's part, beneath the apparent concern – a desire to put into her head the very thought he was acting to prevent? From another point of view, though, if Ford told her both about his passion for Patmore and his attempt to renounce it, isn't there also a suggestion that the sadness had already become a story? – That, even as he was living out the scenario, he was imagining how it would narrate; turning it into words? According to that perspective, it isn't just that fiction draws upon experiences people have lived, but that writers might live out situations with a feel for the stories they will transform them into.

The second significant shift in ways of approaching Ford in general, and *The Good Soldier* in particular, is to do with a revival in the fortunes of the concept of impressionism in literature. From the *fin-de-siècle* to the Second World War, the language of 'impressions' and 'impressionism' abounds, nowhere more than in Ford's work. As he makes clear in his fine memoir *Joseph Conrad: A Personal Remembrance*, with its account of their technical deliberations into how novels should be written, Ford's apprenticeship period as Conrad's collaborator was deeply concerned with the rendering of impressions. Ford described this book as '*the writer's impression of a writer who avowed himself impressionist*', and explained:

> We accepted without much protest the stigma 'Impressionists' that was thrown at us [. . . .] we saw that Life did not narrate, but made impressions on our brains. We in turn, if we wished to produce on you an effect of life, must not narrate but render impressions.[10]

Ford had used these terms himself before 1913. But it was then, as he was poised to write *The Good Soldier*, that he began to define himself explicitly as an impressionist, in two major essays. The first, 'Impressionism – Some Speculations' was published in *Poetry* and revised into the preface to his 1913 *Collected Poems*, which was admired by Pound and, though him, exerted influence on English poetics.[11] The other, 'On Impressionism', was primarily concerned with prose, and gives a virtuoso practical demonstration of how a novelist might construct a character's stream of consciousness, or provoke uncertainty about the reliability of a narrator – both topics of fundamental importance to *The Good Soldier*.

The writers and artists of this period did not describe themselves as modernists in the way that they are now described. Instead, they used the labels of more distinct, more fissile movements: Imagism, Imagisme, Impressionism, Futurism, Vorticism, Cubism, and Surrealism. Though the terms 'modern', and even 'modernist' were sometimes used to describe them, they weren't used in the sense now familiar, to describe a whole self-conscious and international movement. 'Modernism', as many have recognized, is a retrospective category. But it has been such a dominant one that it eclipsed impressionism, at least in literature. Ford's previous account (first published in 1920, well before the *annus mirabilis* of modernism saw *Ulysses, The Waste Land*, and *Jacob's Room* all published in 1922) of his collaboration with Conrad sounds modernist enough in its emphasis on form:

> For I think we both started out with at least this much of a New Form in our heads: we considered a Novel to be a rendering of an Affair. We used to say [. . .] that a Subject must be seized by the throat until the last drop of dramatic possibility was squeezed out of it. I suppose we had to concede that much to the Cult of the Strong Situation. Nevertheless, a Novel was the rendering of an Affair: of one embroilment, one set of embarrassments, one human coil, one psychological progression. From this the Novel got its Unity [. . . .] the whole novel was to be an exhaustion of aspects, was to proceed to one culmination, to reveal once and for all, in the last sentence, or the penultimate; in the last phrase, or the one before it, the psychological significance of the whole.[12]

Yet the kind of writer Ford saw as impressionist, reaching for this new sense of form, along with Conrad and himself, ranged widely from late nineteenth-century figures like Flaubert, Maupassant, James, and Stephen Crane (all often associated with realism or Naturalism) to twentieth-century figures (now seen as canonical modernists) such as Lawrence, Pound, Hemingway and even Joyce. Fordian impressionism is thus an elastic category; too much so for modernist scholars invested in the idea of a decisive fracture in literary history separating modernism from what preceded it.

Conversely though, one advantage of the notion of literary impressionism is precisely that it registers the continuities in developments from the nineteenth into the twentieth centuries, and from realism to modernism. Recent scholarship has recovered the importance of impressionism in the period; and Ford has been a central figure in its reinvestigation. Thomas Moser, in his 1980 psychobiography, *The Life in the Fiction of Ford Madox Ford*, pointed the way, arguing for the significance of literary impressionism to Ford and *The Good Soldier*. If his relating of the method to Ford's agoraphobia seemed too restricted to individual pathology, he nonetheless sketched out what a history of the category might look like. More recently, Jesse Matz in *Literary Impressionism and Modernist Aesthetics* (2001), and Tamar Katz in *Impressionist Subjects* (2000), have mapped the terrain (including *The Good Soldier*) in finer detail.

The result has been to recover a coherent set of aesthetic practices from the late nineteenth century to the mid twentieth, which precedes, influences and runs in parallel with modernism. Stannard's Norton edition of *The Good Soldier* too has done much to secure Ford's place in this new literary history, as it includes a forty-five page selection of criticism headed 'Literary Impressionism'. Ford's own essays 'On Impressionism' and 'Techniques' are reprinted there, together with excerpts from the Conrad memoir, headed 'Developing the Theory of Impressionism with Conrad'. It is clear even from this selection that Ford is a major theorist of literary impressionism. But his critical writing is still unfamiliar (or under-researched) enough for most modernist scholars to know little other than this selection, along with perhaps one or two other works. What hasn't yet been recognized in modernist studies, though it will as Ford's criticism is edited and republished, is how he is the outstanding, as well as the most prolific, critic writing about impressionism: the pioneer who first defined the entire field for twentieth-century literature.

Ford's bravura use of first-person narration in *The Good Soldier* has perhaps obscured the importance of his impressionism. It is a rare device in his novels: the three collaborations with Joseph Conrad are the only others to use it. The effect, nowhere more than in *The Good Soldier*, is to give us a double-articulated impressionism: Ford's impression of Dowell giving his impressions. This has inevitably drawn criticism of the novel towards the question of the reliability or otherwise of its narrator.

The essays in this collection are striking for the fresh light they shed on this topic; as well as on the related issues of the book's chronology (one of the main areas in which Dowell's reliability appears compromised), and its genre (should we trust the teller's valuation of it as 'the saddest story', or read it as the comedy of his misunderstanding of his own experience?). These questions of narrator, chronology and genre provide the bases for the first section of this volume. Where Ford's critics have tended to place *The Good Soldier* as a work of classic modernism in its foregrounding of the technique of narration, Catherine Belsey's essay reads it instead as 'Ford's Postmodern Novel'. Drawing upon Jean-François Lyotard's identification of a strain of postmodernism *within* modernism, she brings out the ways in which it is a narrative which 'not only refuses to deliver consoling certainties but also challenges the rules of representation'.[13] Melba Cuddy-Keane gives a contrasting account of Dowell's chronological tangle, advancing the original argument that the outbreak of war on the 4th August – a date that Ford had already coincidentally written into the plot – displaced an earlier conception in which the 4th July would have been prominent, with all its connotations – especially for an American narrator – of independence; of national freedom from Britain. Eyal Segal offers another kind of account of the workings of unreliability in the novel. His narratological reading differs from those which have tended to take Dowell's presentation of himself as imagining himself *speaking* the narration to a sympathetic listener at face value. Instead, Segal builds on Dowell's other portrayal of himself as *writing* the story, arguing rigorously for the importance of 'Compositional (Un)reliability' as distinct from narratorial – thereby complicating the assumption on which much previous criticism of the novel has rested, that the novel is Ford's composition, giving form to Dowell's chaotic telling. Composition, according to this reading, is double-articulated too; the rules of representation less clear-cut than they might appear.

Isabelle Brasme's essay is another which addresses Dowell's narratorial disconnectedness and (un)reliability. But rather than interpreting these as providing insight into the character, or his author, her emphasis falls more on history. Ricoeur's thought on narrative and temporality is invoked to illuminate the ways in which *The Good Soldier* interrogates what narrative does to historical events, and how history is written. Rob Hawkes's chapter is concerned with Dowell as a guide not to fact but to genre; with his reliability as to register and tone. He uses Dowell's comment about the melodramatic nature of his story to bring out a crucial division. The plot summary, with its abundance of deception, suicide, death, and madness, certainly reads like the stuff of melodrama. But Dowell's tone of sadness, and his sympathy, pull the narration toward an elegiac or even tragic register, while his irony and flashes of humour suggest something more comic. Hawkes argues for the modernity of melodrama, and for Dowell's recourse to it as a way of narrating events without having to make sense of them. From this point of view, though conventional melodrama seeks to impose moral certainties, however inadequate, on an unintelligible world, Dowell's appropriation of the melodramatic works in the opposite way, making the characters and events seem absurd. Melodrama in *The Good Soldier* might thus be seen as a further strategy by which Ford engineers a postmodern refusal of consolation even for extreme sadness.

Janet Harris' essay approaches the question of genre through the practice of 're-mediation':[14] the turning of novels into screenplays into television drama. Her analysis of the 1981 Granada TV production of *The Good Soldier*, starring Jeremy Brett (as Ashburnham) and Robin Ellis (as Dowell), concentrates on the mode of narration too, but in terms of how narration differs in a more visual medium; how the *mise-en-scène* can convey understanding instead of, or at odds with, the words; though she also notes how the ability of film to give us images floating free of interpretation (comparable to Hawkes's account of melodrama) offers the perfect analogue for this novel in which Dowell's habitual response to his experience is to give us an impressionistic picture, and then refuse us the consolation of understanding. She argues that the novel's modernism lends itself to this modern medium, while noting how the adaptation elicited some comparably challenging modernist techniques in the editing, such as the presentation of the same event from different perspectives – a concern, as we shall see, of essays in the third section.

Dividing such essays about a single work into groups is often a somewhat arbitrary operation. All the chapters in this volume read the novel closely, attending to its narrator and its narrative. But the remaining essays are gathered into two further sections. The second concentrates, as the characters in the novel seem to do, on the body: its relation to the mind and the feelings; its weaknesses and illnesses; and the regimes of treatment or observation imposed. Sara Haslam's essay takes recent research on the neurotransmitter dopamine as a stimulant to rethinking Dowell's personality, his motivation or rather lack of it. Where earlier and especially male critics (described surgically but memorably by Belsey as 'presumably testosterone-fuelled Lawrentians') have sometimes denigrated what they perceive as Dowell's sexual inadequacy, it's his cognitive deficiencies that strike Haslam. Dopamine is associated with the excitement of acquiring information;

but just as Dowell diagnoses himself as lacking 'the seeing eye', so he seems lacking as an information-gatherer. Haslam explores the concept of 'bodily plot' in the novel: the way events are shaped by physiology or neurology. Her argument brings out intriguingly the importance to the novel, as to Ford's writing in general, of 'the hour between dog and wolf': the dusk; the time when perceptions become unreliable, metamorphoses occur, desire is aroused.

Max Saunders (as he calls himself) traces the trajectory of the word 'case' through *The Good Soldier*, arguing that it brings out another aspect of the uncertainty as to how to interpret or place the novel. The term 'case' hovers between the medical, the psychological, the sexological, the criminological, the legal, or the moral-philosophical. The chapter connects these discourses of the 'case' to the profuse imagery of cases running through the novel (in particular the image of Ashburnham's profusion of leather cases), arguing that what is at stake is precisely the relation between form and content; how a narration can frame, and thus seek to contain, its subjects.

Elizabeth Brunton focuses on the novel's medical discourse: its central thematics of heart trouble, whether actual illness, supposed illness, feigned illness, or heartbreak. She argues that Ford, like his characters, subverts the gender-norms for heart patients. By contrast with Joyce's Paddy Dignam, whose heart attack is associated with hard-drinking masculinity, or Woolf's Clarissa Dalloway, whose illness leaves her pale and frail, Edward Ashburnham's and Florence Dowell's feigned conditions concealing their passions enables them to conduct adulterous affairs and thus realise a subversive sexuality. Barry Sheils approaches the novel's presentation of life in a medical establishment from the perspective not of the 'patients' but their 'nurses'. Prompted by Dowell's description of his role as like that of a nurse, Sheils observes the sustained language of 'professional care' throughout the novel, drawing out the implicit parallels between nurse, narrator, and novelist. He compares Ford's novel with Florence Nightingale's handbook *Notes on Nursing*, not just for the way the writer, like the nurse, must observe the pathological subject; but for the way the nurse, like the writer (whom Nightingale was convinced misrepresented illness) must describe the symptoms; must become a (better) writer.

The subject of Paul Skinner's essay is 'breeding': the sexual acts that, with their concealment, drive the plot; procreation, or the lack of it (he notes that neither the Ashburnhams nor the Dowells have children); and the assigning of biological value to individuals of the species. He registers the density in the novel of the language of eugenics in vogue throughout the Edwardian period, exploring how far Ford's 'good people' might represent a criticism of eugenicist pseudoscience rather than its reflection. The dark side of eugenics, notoriously realised by the Nazis, is the willingness to contemplate the murder of those deemed 'degenerate': the mentally impaired, the underclass, the sexually non-normative, the disobedient. Venetia Abdalla's essay approaches the medical, the bodily, and the morbid through the theme of poison – prominent in *The Good Soldier* via the ring in which (as we have seen) Florence hides the prussic acid she uses to commit suicide; but also, as Abdalla demonstrates, pervasive in Ford's work, as in that of the woman he was living with when he wrote the novel, Violet Hunt. Abdalla reads the novel as 'A Tale of Poison', posing a parallel between the destructive effects of passion, as of toxins; and drawing out the complex cultural associations of poison.

Comparative criticism, placing Ford's novel against texts by other writers, or contrasting different movements, versions, genres, or media, has already figured in the chapters of the first two sections. They are all sharpened by the awareness of the novel's contexts and affiliations. But comparison becomes the dominant method of the final section, which combines original work on some familiar Fordian double-acts, and inaugurative comparisons with less expected figures. Harry Ricketts takes John Bayley's quip that *The Good Soldier* read like 'early Kipling told by Henry James' as a spur to investigate Ford's debt to Kipling. Ashburnham emerges from his chapter as a recognizably Kiplingesque character – understandably, given that Kipling's fiction must have provided Ford with much of his know-ledge of the Indian background for the novel. In Julian Preece's chapter it is the German background that is at issue. His approach to the use of the 4th August date in *The Good Soldier* is to read it as implying the war as the story's tacit context. This turns the book into an oblique form of historical and political novel. Preece examines not only the geographical context of the Germany Ford had been living in for a couple of years before starting the novel, and what he had been writing about it; but also the German heritage he had acquired since childhood from his German father and cosmopolitan education; and in addition the little-noted German context he gives Dowell too. The chapter considers the novel in relation to a range of German fiction, much of which Ford knew, by figures such as Goethe, Schnitzler, and Mann – as well as to modernist contemporaries he doesn't mention, such as Musil, and, most surprisingly, Kafka.

Cara Chimirri compares Ford with David Jones. Jones's master-piece (at least in his writing, as opposed to his other art, painting) *In Parenthesis*, his complex modernist long poem about the First World War, might suggest comparison primarily with *Parade's End*; Jones's service in the Royal Welch Fusiliers with Ford's in the Welch Regiment. (Indeed, it's characteristic of the work in this volume that it opens up such new vistas for future research.) Instead, Chimirri sets Jones's epic layering of modern war over mythological wars against Dowell's invocation of devastation, when he places himself among 'human beings who have witnessed the sack of a city or the falling to pieces of a people' (*GS* 12). Ford too sets the break-up of his micro-cosm of 'good people' against the backdrop of wars, revolution, and religious conflict from the Middle Ages to the Boer War and the outbreak of WW1. One effect of such chronological collages, akin to what Cuddy-Keane calls 'palimpsestic plots', is to turn time into space. Chimirri traces comparable preoccupations with the spatiality of recollection in both writers, and in particular their exploration of liminal spaces.

The chapters by Nagihan Haliloğlu and Peter Marks both con-cern the policing of social mores by middle-class society. Haliloğlu compares Ford with Jean Rhys, noting a parallel between the concern with respectability both of the 'good people' in Ford's novel and of the characters in Rhys's *Quartet* (modelled, of course, on Rhys and Ford themselves, and on their partners) – Rhys including as an epigraph Cheever Dunning's poem 'Good Samaritan'. Where Ford's – or at least Dowell's – attitude to the goodness of his 'good people' may appear ironic, *Quartet*'s take is more cynical: bourgeois respectability is (self-)satisfied so long as its indiscretions don't become public. It is the monitoring of society that provides Marks's subject. He uses recent surveillance theory to bring out the extent to which the worlds of Bad Nauheim (and by extension Hampshire or Connecticut) are self-policed through obsessive observation. The comparative axis here is the relation between Ford and H. G. Wells. Starting from Ford's response to Wells's *A Modern Utopia*, Marks identifies the longing for utopian tranquility that motivates Dowell. Drawing on Ford's representations of surveillance in his other work, such as the court spying of the *Fifth Queen* trilogy, Marks shows both how the neurotic compulsion to monitor in order to avoid risk can actually prove the engine of catastrophe; and also the ways in which surveillance is what authors as well as characters do. After all, it isn't just conspirators but also novelists who engage in plotting.

Omar Sabbagh offers a different reading of *The Good Soldier* in relation to the idea of the 'quartet', setting Ford alongside Lawrence Durrell. The relativism of *The Alexandria Quartet* is compared to Ford's 'four-square coterie', and Dowell's attempt to make us see not just his own perspective but those of the other major characters (if tellingly minus that of his wife, Florence). As he puts it:

> At any rate, I think I have brought my story up to the date of Maisie Maidan's death. I mean that I have explained everything that went before it from the several points of view that were necessary—from Leonora's, from Edward's and to some extent, from my own. You have the facts for the trouble of finding them; you have the points of view as far as I could ascertain or put them. (*GS* 143)

Here too, the comparison is a fertile one, suggesting other parallels also worth future investigation: notably with Ford's own quartet of *Parade's End*, and its moving between the viewpoints of its central characters – Christopher and Mark Tietjens, Sylvia Tietjens, and Valentine Wannop; but also the relativistic presentation of morality in the Tudor trilogy about Henry VIII, Thomas Cromwell and Katharine Howard; and novels of doubling and identity-exchanges of Ford's last decade, especially *The Rash Act* and *Henry for Hugh*. Ford's memoir of Conrad is relevant here too, not merely for its indispensable reflections on how to create points of view, and the impressions of dramatized consciousnesses; but for its unparalleled sounding of a process in which the point of view of the author is itself multiple. Sabbagh's analysis of Durrell's use of a single narrator to construct multiple points of view returns us to the concerns of the first section, with narrative, narrators, and their limitations, their reliability or otherwise.

It also reminds us of the influence Ford's work – and especially *The Good Soldier* – has had on other writers. Rebecca West, whose own *The Return of the Soldier* (1918) owes much to Ford's novel, said she thought it had 'set the pattern for perhaps half the novels which have been written since'.[15] If Durrell was evasive about his knowledge of Ford's work, many other novelists have written explicitly about him, whether in the form of reminiscence or criticism, or even fiction drawing on Ford or his work, ranging from contemporaries mentioned here – Conrad, Wells, Hunt and Rhys – to other contemporaries discussed in earlier volumes in this series (Pound, Hemingway, William Carlos Williams, Graham Greene and others); and to later generations of admirers, such as Anthony Burgess, A. S. Byatt, Julian Barnes, Ruth Rendell, Tom Stoppard, Mary Gordon and Richard Ford.

To conclude: the essays collected here strikingly light up new aspects of a book we may have thought we knew well. They not only provide new and compelling readings of familiar issues – unreliable narration, chronological inconsistency, tonal and generic instabilities, Ford's relation to other writers; but also take the criticism into a number of new areas: medical humanities and nursing studies, neurocriticism, surveillance studies, adaptation studies. One distinct strand brings out the novel's power to unsettle boundaries – between mind and body, authority and unreliability, sexuality and respectability, masculine and feminine, seeing and understanding; between different genres, representations, perspectives, judgements, diagnoses. The essays are testimony to this extraordinary novel's power still to get under the skin of its readers a century after its first appearance.

## NOTES

1 See http://www.guardian.co.uk/media/2010/jul/29/tom-stoppard-bbc.
2 Ford, *The Good Soldier*, ed. Martin Stannard, second edition, New York and London: W. W. Norton, 2012, p. 189.
3 See Saunders, 'Introduction: Edwardian Ford?', *The Edwardian Ford Madox Ford*, IFMFS 12, ed. Laura Colombino and Max Saunders, Amsterdam and New York: Rodopi, 2013, pp. 13-34 (p. 21).
4 Hunt, entry for 20 April 1917: *The Return of the Good Soldier: Ford Madox Ford and Violet Hunt's 1917 Diary*, ed. Robert and Marie Secor, Victoria, BC: University of Victoria, 1983, p. 57. Quoted in Ford, *The Good Soldier*, ed. Max Saunders, World's Classics, Oxford: Oxford University Press, 2012 – henceforth *GS*; p. xx.
5 Ford, 'On Heaven', in *Selected Poems*, ed. Max Saunders, Manchester: Carcanet, 1997, pp. 99-110 (p. 99).
6 The diary was auctioned at Christie's, King Street, London, on 6 November 1995, and is now in the Ford collection of the Carl A. Kroch Library, Cornell University. It is quoted here from my Oxford World's Classics edition of the novel; *GS* xxi.

7   'On Heaven' also supports the dating of the affair as taking place during the
    winter rather than the summer. The lovers make their pledges 'in your Sussex
    mud, /Amongst the frost-bound farms by the yeasty sea'; *Selected Poems* 102.
8   Violet Hunt, *The Flurried Years*, London: Hurst and Blackett, 1926, pp. 216-17.
9   Hunt, *The Flurried Years*, p. 217. An anonymous poem appeared in *Poetry*, 5:1
    (October 1914), at the end of the editorial note titled 'Our Contemporaries' (42-5),
    headed 'A Comment', p. 45. Here it is in its entirety:

    *By the Other Woman in Hueffer's poem On Heaven in Poetry for June 1914*

    For those who have won earthly love
    Immortal joys are spread;
    Kind God, hush thou my soul to sleep
    When I am dead.

    It seems likely it was written by Hunt herself, or a friend of hers siding with her in
    her exasperation at Ford; though the combination of the first two lines, with their
    comparability to Ford's *Mister Bosphorus and the Muses*, and the last two, with
    their echo of one of Ford's favourite poets, Christina Rossetti, could conceivably
    have been written by Ford himself. In any of these cases, the lines suggest a
    suicidal mood that may well have been Hunt's at the time. I'm grateful to Ashley
    Chantler for drawing my attention to this poem, not previously noticed by Ford
    scholars.
10  Ford, *Joseph Conrad: A Personal Remembrance*, London: Duckworth, 1924, p.
    182.
11  See Saunders, 'Imagism vs. Impressionism: Ezra Pound and Ford Madox Ford', in
    *Imagism: Essays on its Initiation, Impact and Influence*, ed. John Gery, Daniel
    Kempton, and H. R. Stoneback, New Orleans: University of New Orleans Press,
    2013, pp. 93-106.
12  Ford, *Thus to Revisit*, London: Chapman and Hall, 1921, p. 44. This chapter was
    first published in the *Dial*, 69 (August 1920), 132-41.
13  See p. 33 below.
14  See Jay David Bolter and Richard Grusin, *Remediation: Understanding New
    Media*, Cambridge, MA: MIT Press, 2000.
15  See Seamus O'Malley, '*The Return of the Soldier* and *Parade's End*: Ford's
    Reworking of West's Pastoral', *Ford Madox Ford's Literary Contacts*, IFMFS 6,
    ed. Paul Skinner, Amsterdam and New York: Rodopi, 2007, pp. 155-64; and
    David Ayers, *English Literature of the 1920s*, Oxford: Oxford University Press,
    2004, p. 59. West, 'Unlucky Eccentric's Private World', *Sunday Telegraph* (17
    June 1962), 6.

# THE GOOD SOLDIER: FORD'S POSTMODERN NOVEL[1]

## Catherine Belsey

**Abstract**

Jean-François Lyotard distinguishes between two versions of modernism. The first laments the inevitable loss of realism and the impossibility of telling the truth in fiction; the second, which Lyotard calls the postmodern, celebrates the liberation this entails and the freedom to keep the reader guessing. Postmodernism gleefully refuses the reassurance promised by realism that the world is just as we thought it was. *The Good Soldier* creates the illusion that it is a realist novel, but in practice keeps us guessing throughout about exactly what happened and how we should interpret it. As the story unfolds, the novel doubles back on what it has previously encouraged us to assume, inviting readers to reassess the events, the characters and the relationships between them. The narrative voice equivocates. In the process, it promotes reflection on what we take to be the behaviour of the fictional figures, our own assumptions about the world, and the nature of the language that frames both.

## I

According to a distinction proposed by Jean-François Lyotard, *The Good Soldier* is formally and thematically a postmodern novel. This classification has been put forward before[2] but I want to pursue its implications in some detail. To avoid misunderstanding, I should perhaps make clear that my design here is not to revive the moribund debate about the definition of postmodernism, but to draw on distinctions Lyotard makes in order to single out features of Ford's text. Once the label coined to identify a difference supplants the text itself as an object of debate, the label becomes an obstacle to criticism. We have probably heard enough about postmodernism as a category, and if any other term offered itself, I would gladly adopt it. But this is the word Lyotard used in 1982 to specify a particular version of modernism itself and I gratefully borrow it as a frame for a reading of the novel. In my view, *The Good Soldier* breaks rules and poses questions without laying claim to either a deeper truth or new answers. Instead, it asks its reader to reflect on the wayward behaviour not only of human beings but also of the language that both defines and delimits their options – and ours.

When Lyotard published 'Answering the Question: What is Postmodernism?' in the French journal *Critique*, the essay appeared with a footnote, deleted from the English translation, that described it as a very personal *'texte de combat'*.[3] Because this engaged and combative intervention takes no prisoners, it spells out, perhaps more sharply than usual, what is at stake, as far as Lyotard is concerned, in postmodernist art. His target is the retreat from experimentation, the slide back into the reassuring lap of realism – and by way of my own personal combative contribution to the discussion, I would add that, even after thirty years, the distinctions he makes in this essay are no less relevant to us now in the clutches, as we apparently are in the UK, of the pallid 'literary novel'. Ford, I suggest, was way ahead of our current favoured and prize-winning practitioners.

Lyotard's objection to realism was its propensity to protect consciousnesses from doubt. Whether in visual art or in writing, he argued, realism assumes that we recognize – or can be coaxed to recognize – an already existing reality. Perspective painting stabilizes the object depicted, places it in such a way that it is intelligible to the spectator from a given point of view, and invests it with a significance that is – or can be made – evident to everyone. The realist novel similarly invites recognition of a world seen as given. Appealing implicitly or explicitly to 'what we all know', invoking Roland Barthes's 'code of reference',[4] classic realism reproduces a syntax and a vocabulary that permit readers to make sense not only of the text but at the same time of the world it depicts as familiar. By this means, Lyotard continues, realism encourages the reader to arrive without difficulty at a validation of his or her own identity in the course of experiencing the gratifying confirmation of an understanding shared with others. Communication takes place: heads nod. However surprising the events or the characters may be, however desolate the outcome, the perceiving subject and the objects perceived are in their proper places as evidence that the world depicted is possible, plausible, convincing as a replica of reality, the actuality we know as our own. Such art, such writing is 'therapeutic', Lyotard complains.[5] Even if the story introduces us to new vistas, even though the tale makes us sadder or wiser, realism leaves the perceiving subject and consensus on the objects of perception in the same relation as before. 'Yes, that's it, that's how it is!'

Modernism, meanwhile, responds, he says, to 'the withdrawal of the real',[6] a twentieth-century breakdown of confidence in what passes for actual. But the emphasis varies. Modernism, Lyotard proposes, either regrets what is lost or takes advantage of the freedom scepticism confers. In the first case, the work, nostalgic for the missing certainties, preserves the pleasures offered by good form; the second, which Lyotard identifies as the postmodern *in modernism*, refuses that solace and seeks out new modes of presentation, proceeds without regulations in order to uncover after the event the rules of 'what *will have been done*'.[7]

## II

To my mind, *The Good Soldier* not only refuses to deliver consoling certainties but also challenges the rules of representation. To begin with, attempts to reduce the story to consistency or locate a coherent theme seem doomed to disappointment. Whatever, for example, are we to make of a novel where the death of the protagonist – or the figure named in the title as the protagonist, since that too is open to discussion – is related in an afterthought? 'It suddenly occurs to me that I have forgotten to say how Edward met his death' (*GS* 168). And what is the genre of this final episode? Tragedy? Melodrama? Or a bleak form of comedy? The understatement of the final sentences perfectly encapsulates the pervading irony: 'I trotted off with the telegram to Leonora. She was quite pleased with it' (169).

This fatal telegram, delivered to Edward, who promptly takes out his little penknife – as unheroic an instrument of death as it is possible to name – seems to be (and cannot be) the same as the one read out at a hitherto quiet dinner by Leonora only six pages earlier (*GS* 163). But the temptation to document dates and places is as irrelevant as it is irresistible: that's not where the energy of the story lies.[8] It is impossible to tell how many of the inconsistencies are due to oversight in a novel where one recurring strategy is definition and redefinition by contradiction. From the beginning *The Good Soldier* unfolds its story only gradually – and then backtracks: the life of the foursome was a minuet, they knew the steps, they were perfectly at ease with each other (11); on the contrary, it was a prison, 'full of screaming hysterics' (12); Florence was never out of the sight of her husband – and yet she must have been (12); an ideal couple, the Ashburnhams never spoke a word to each other in private (13). These conflicting observations come hard on each other's heels, foregrounding enigma. Other affirmations are not undermined until many pages later: Edward specializes in sentimental novels (26): he has literary tastes (97). There is a great deal of prolepsis, as the narrator contrasts the dismal present with the seeming innocence of the past, but some of these forward glimpses are misleading: the narrator repeatedly hints that Nancy is dead (55, 87, 90, 91). Was her madness a still grimmer afterthought or are we to understand insanity as a figurative death? Dowell alludes to some of this, justifying it in the name of a deeper realism:

> One remembers points that one has forgotten and one explains them all the more minutely since one recognises that one has forgotten to mention them in their proper places and that one may have given, by omitting them a false impression. (*GS* 125)

Is this a cover for carelessness? Or does Ford's literary impressionism distrust as improbable the prodigious memories of conventional first-person narrators? Is Dowell's layered commentary legitimately naturalized as record of his dawning awareness? Does his story mimic life in its subsequent revelation of new meanings for what seemed straightforward events? Or is the novel designed to mislead?

If some of the precise details of the plot are elusive, the themes are just as hard to pin down. What is this novel about, I wondered, as I read it for the first time? Desire, obviously, and there are some extraordinary observations on the nature of desire as a craving for confirmation, implicating the object of desire in the fundamental psychic life of the desiring subject (*GS* 82-3). All the characters want what they can't have; no one gets what they most want (158). At the same time, there is nearly as much talk of hate as there is of love. Edward intermittently hates Leonora: 'whatever she did caused him to hate her. [. . .] Hatred hung in all the heavy nights and filled the shadowy corners of the room' (121). Leonora sporadically hates Edward (25, 137, 140). Above all, Dowell hates Florence to the point where he would gladly see her damned: 'I hate Florence with such a hatred that I would not spare her an eternity of loneliness' (55).

If love and hate are opposite sides of the same coin, passion is also closely allied with power. Henry James makes his influence felt here, as elsewhere. Florence controls Dowell by means of her 'heart'; she has a hold over Leonora because she has seen through the façade; she has a hold over Edward, because he feels an obligation to her. Dowell has an unwitting power over Florence, who cannot face the possibility that he will learn about Jimmy. Above all, when Leonora takes command of Edward's income, he cannot implement the generosity that is his defining virtue – can't be who he most is.

All this I grasped – if slowly – but I had the dissatisfied sense that none of it took me to the core of the novel. Would an ethical reading give me a place to stand, I asked myself. The strategy is always available as a last resort to anyone brought up in the vague aura of piety that characterized English studies in the 1970s and is still faintly perceptible among those who turn to literature to learn how to live. Besides, the novel from *Tom Jones* to *Lord Jim* has traditionally offered moral footholds, if not prescriptions. These may then be called into question: if we know how we value American innocence in *The Portrait of a Lady*, we might not be so clear when it comes to *The Golden Bowl*. Even in late James, though, it is possible to identify the terms of the debate about love and power.

But if *The Good Soldier* allows us to glimpse a virtue, it so often goes on to undermine its own proposition. Who, for example, are the culprits?[9] There seems nothing to be said in favour of Florence, but Florence is not the precipitating agent of the final tragedy, if tragedy it is. 'The girl' is clearly not to blame: she is an innocent abroad in an unintelligible world. Leonora? She is surely as much victim as perpetrator. Dowell – Do-well? A previous generation of male critics, presumably testosterone-fuelled Lawrentians, took the line that the failure of his marriage was his own fault: apparently, he could have sorted Florence out by asserting his manhood. I'm not sure what anxieties these commentators were projecting onto Ford's unoffending narrator: let's hope that feminism was already beginning to frighten them. In any case, I don't think that line would persuade many people now.

How, then, are we to regard Edward, 'an excellent magistrate, a first rate soldier, one of the best landlords, so they said, in Hampshire, England' (*GS* 14)? In Ford's novel that interpolated 'so they said' might – or might not – speak volumes. Is Ashburnham presented as a hero at the mercy of a repressive society, or a villain who follows his own will whatever the cost? He doesn't apparently pursue his desires when it comes to Nancy, and yet for a romantic, if that's what he is, reciprocal renunciation has its own pleasures. What he wants more than her body is her love and he kills himself when she tells him she's having a 'rattling good time' without him (169). Meanwhile, is he a capable landlord if his serial philanthropy risks bankrupting the estate? And is he a good soldier? He is certainly a heroic one: he saves his comrades when they're in trouble much as he means to come to the aid of distressed servant girls on trains; he earns the DSO and is twice recommended for the VC.

And yet, aren't heroics too called into question in this deeply ironic novel? What are we to make of the Red Sea voyage as conveyed by Dowell but from Leonora's point of view? Where exactly is the irony to be located?

> One of their bitterest quarrels came after he had, for the second time, in the Red Sea, jumped overboard from the troopship and rescued a private soldier. She stood it the first time and even complimented him. But the Red Sea was awful, that trip, and the private soldiers seemed to develop a suicidal craze. It got on Leonora's nerves; she figured Edward, for the rest of that trip, jumping overboard every ten minutes. (*GS* 118)

Is the *Boys' Own* bravery named here to Edward's credit, and to Leonora's corresponding discredit, since she fails to respect chivalry, or is it continuous with the extravagant support of family retainers and the maintenance of expensive subscriptions he can't afford? Was the chivalric version of soldiery already in question when the First World War began?

In 1927 Ford claimed that he had named the book *The Good Soldier* in 'hasty irony' and that he had never ceased to regret it (*GS* 6). Perhaps. Earlier versions bear out his claim that he wanted to call it *The Saddest Story*. But doesn't the existing title perfectly condense the questions prompted by this novel? What are the values it asks us to recognize and share? What is there here to stabilize the object of knowledge, invest it with a consensual significance, or protect consciousnesses from doubt?

## III

Among all the uncertainties, one feature of this text is clear. It's a page-turner. The recurrent prolepsis, the repeated deferrals, kept me on the edge of my chair. Far from the relaxed listener in a country cottage of Dowell's imagination (*GS* 15, 124), I found myself all alert concentration, anxious to make my way through the 'maze' he also calls his tale (124). The strategy of writing about the past from the present builds suspense by keeping two (or more) distinct temporal orders in view. The puzzle is how to find a path from one to the other(s), not least when these distinct temporalities so often seem to belong to different genres. The novel opens on what looks like a comedy of manners: deracinated Americans find refuge with a model English couple, their companionable lives measured out in restaurant tables, concerts, visits to the baths. But within two pages, the narrator speaks from another time and in a different vocabulary: 'Permanence? Stability! I can't believe it's gone. I can't believe that that long tranquil life ... vanished in four crashing days' (11). Who is 'the girl' (21)? And why is Edward now to be thought of as having been in 'Absolute, hopeless, dumb agony such as passes the mind of man to imagine' (21)? And above all, how are we to resolve the contradictions? Ford insisted that the primary consideration of the author must be his tale: 'the first thing he has to consider is his story and the last thing that he has to consider is his story, and in between [. . .] he will consider his story'.[10] In *The Good Soldier* that story engages the reader in wanting to make sense of the information presented in an order that is apparently rambling and in practice (probably) anything but random.

Classic realism similarly keeps the attention of the reader by setting up enigmas on the basis of information withheld: the narrator writing from the present knows all along who committed the murder or who married the heroine. But Ford takes that strategy to an extreme, since what follows often directly overrides the apparent proposition. On the first page of *The Good Soldier* Dowell confides at the mention of Bad Nauheim, 'You will gather from this statement that one of us had, as the saying is, a "heart", and, from the statement that my wife is dead, that she was the sufferer' (*GS* 9). Thus prompted, I did – and I was wrong: not everything we are encouraged to 'gather' is the case. The pattern is consistent. The aptly named Mrs Maidan, whose love affair with Edward was chaste on account of her 'heart', is first reported to have died 'quite quietly – of heart trouble' (42). This is the truth but not the whole truth, since it will later emerge, in one of the novel's characteristic touches of dark comedy, that her body is found upside down in a trunk with her feet in the air (58), perhaps echoing the strange, apparently unmotivated, upturned cow on the way to M[arburg] (36).[11]

On a second reading some of the difficulties dissolve when with hindsight it becomes clear that we are to take many of the narrator's statements as ironic. 'Poor dear Florence' is now evidently not dear at all. 'She seemed to dance over the floors of castles and over seas and over and over the salons of modistes and over the *plages* of the Riviera – like a gay tremulous beam, reflected from water upon a ceiling'

(*GS* 17). The first, innocent reading is likely to attract us to the striking image of the dancing, trembling reflected light. Only the second time round does the full disparity become obvious between castles and seas, on the one hand, and dressmakers' showrooms on the other.

The identification of irony is always a pleasure: it puts the reader in the know; the stability of the referent is restored again, reassuring doubtful souls. But *The Good Soldier* does not always deliver such easy gratification. What, for example, are we to make of another early comment on Florence? 'I don't believe that for one minute she was out of my sight, except when she was safely tucked up in bed' (*GS* 12). 'Tucked up' is not quite how we shall later imagine her in bed with Edward or, for that matter, Jimmy, but the comment certainly resonates differently on a second reading. Is this ironic or isn't it? Irony is hard to be sure of; it may reside in the eye of the reader. The only guarantee that *A Modest Proposal* is ironic is a supposed intention we have no certain access to. Everything we know about Swift, including his predilection for irony, goes to indicate that he was not seriously inciting the Irish to eat their babies. At the same time, it is difficult to demonstrate from the text alone that the shocked readers who took *A Modest Proposal* at face value were wrong.

If Ford's irony is elusive, perhaps it is better defined as equivocation. Tucked up or not, Florence *is* in bed much of the time she's out of her husband's sight, but not in the sense that the reader is initially invited to suppose. 'You will gather [. . .] that my wife was the sufferer' evades the question of whether or not Florence really has a bad heart. Nor is the equivocation confined to isolated sentences. The play on 'heart' and heart is structural: there is nothing wrong with Florence's 'heart' but her heart is missing, presumed dead; Edward's physical organ does not need spa treatment but his emotional one is susceptible to a damage that will eventually prove fatal. Meanwhile, the record of the crisis at M[arburg], when Florence lays her finger on Edward's wrist, also palters with us in a double sense. In the first place, it is and is not a climactic moment in the novel. The vocabulary insists that a cataclysmic event has occurred and yet the episode apparently ends in bathos:

> I was aware of something treacherous, something frightful, something evil in the day. I can't define it and can't find a simile for it. It wasn't as if a snake had looked out of a hole. No, it was as if my heart had missed a beat. It was as if we were going to run and cry out; all four of us in separate directions, averting our heads. In Ashburnham's face I know that there was absolute

> panic. I was horribly frightened and then I discovered that the pain in my left
> wrist was caused by Leonora's clutching it. (*GS* 38)

'Treacherous', 'evil' are strong terms and the panic is not Dowell's
alone. And yet all this psychic energy is apparently dissipated when
Leonora attributes her loss of control to Florence's comments on Irish
Catholics. The explanation, Dowell notes, 'gave me the greatest relief
that I have ever had in my life' (39).

In this instance, religious allegiances both are and are not
what's at stake. The Protest Florence has taken them there to see,
signed by Luther and others, *was* an important moment in the
emergence of the Protestant ethic, just as Florence says it was, though
its exemplar in the novel is her own Philadelphia-Quaker husband, not
Edward, as she claims; in England the Reformation *was* the time when
divorce became an option, although not for Irish Catholics like
Leonora, even if that was what she wanted;[12] religious loyalties *are*
critical in the relationship between Leonora and Edward, not to
mention Florence and the Misses Hurlbird. And yet the treachery that
has been brought out into the open, despite the elaborate façade
constructed to conceal it, is Florence's affair with Edward, and from
this moment on we simultaneously know this and don't know it for
sure. And we both know and don't know that Dowell and Leonora
know it but can't yet trust each other to confirm the fact. So when
Leonora offers an alternative account of her outburst, Dowell
gratefully represses what he has perceived, replicating the all-too-
human practice of concealing from consciousness what consciousness
can't bear to acknowledge, equivocating *with himself*. The façade is
restored and his 'ignorance' remains 'absolute', he claims, for another
seven or eight years (*GS* 73), as it must for the sake of the story, while
the reader remains in suspense about the precise implications of the
event until the novel revisits the issues nearly a hundred pages later
from Leonora's perspective (126-9) and then Nancy's (147) – and
perhaps beyond that.

## IV

I would suspect my psychoanalytic reading as anachronistic,
inappropriately post-Freudian, were it not for Dowell's own comments
in a quite different context on his unforeseen declaration, in the state
of shock produced by Florence's death, that now he can marry 'the
girl':

Now that is to me a very amazing thing – amazing for the light of possibilities that it casts into the human heart. For I had never had the slightest conscious idea of marrying the girl ['conscious' is Ford's own revision in the manuscript]; I never had the slightest idea even of caring for her [. . . .] It is as if one had a dual personality, the one I being entirely unconscious of the other. I had thought nothing; I had said such an extraordinary thing. (*GS* 75)

Unconscious wishes unexpectedly make themselves known to consciousness in speech.[13] The founder of 'the talking cure' himself could not have put it better.[14] And Dowell adds reflectively, 'I don't know that the analysis of my own psychology matters at all to this story' (75), prompting the knowing reader to exclaim, if not in so many words, 'yes, it matters; it explains your role throughout; the ego censors what it can't afford to acknowledge. In rapid succession you felt nothing at all about being a deceived husband and you felt everything, especially hatred (54-5).[15] There's no contradiction between such contrary states, thanks to what you will go on to call "that mysterious and unconscious self that underlies most people" (76)'.

As if to confirm the possibility of a knowledge held on what Freud calls that other scene,[16] Dowell explains in very similar terms his lack of surprise when Bagshawe reveals Florence's relationship with Jimmy: 'I suppose that my inner soul – my dual personality – had realized long before that Florence was a personality of paper' (*GS* 86). If psychoanalysis undermines 'the old stable ego of the character'[17] by adding a further self concealed from the ego itself, it also transforms the possibility of certainty into a new kind of doubt by destabilizing the meanings that make truth an option. When Dowell and Leonora agree to 'accept the situation' at M[arburg] (53), it is a different situation that each is formally accepting. From then on Leonora was to take it for granted – both rightly and wrongly – that Dowell 'had permitted all that she had permitted' (75). Language itself proves duplicitous – without the least intention to deceive – when involuntary equivocation dislodges the old stable referent of the sign as the guarantee of accurate communication. Words can't be trusted – and not only because people tell lies but because they speak in the same words of what might or might not be different things. Meanings are held in a suspense that may never be resolved.

What holds for exchanges between the characters also obtains in the relationship between Dowell and his listener, or the text and its reader. Even when it seems at its most transparent, the narrative often provokes a sense that there's more at stake than meets the eye. In the event, the confirmation that Edward and Florence have been lovers comes for the reader a few pages after the trip to M[arburg] and entirely without emphasis, as if in passing, no more than a subordinate clause in a plea for pity for 'that poor wretch' Edward. 'I have the right to say it, since for years he was my wife's lover . . .' (*GS* 41-2). On the one hand, the revelation flatters the reader, who has obliquely been led to expect it and is now encouraged to feel perceptive. Here *The Good Soldier* mimics the strategies of nineteenth–century classic realism, taking to a logical extreme the device of teasing the reader by alternately hinting and confirming. On the other hand, the conventional classic-realist novel is finally resolved by the delivery of knowledge (we learn who dunnit, who is wicked or trustworthy, who will marry the heroine) and this offers the reader the reassurance Lyotard names: there is, in spite of everything, justice, moral worth, true love – or perhaps despair; at least there is a truth of the story, even if sometimes that truth is nihilistic. *The Good Soldier*, however, distances itself from such resolution with characteristic irony:

> Well, that is the end of the story. And, when I come to look at it I see that it is a happy ending with wedding bells and all. The villains – for obviously Edward and the girl were villains – have been punished by suicide and madness. The heroine – the perfectly normal, virtuous and slightly deceitful heroine – has become the happy wife of a perfectly normal, virtuous and slightly-deceitful husband. She will shortly become the mother of a perfectly normal, virtuous, slightly-deceitful son or daughter. A happy ending, that is what it works out at. (*GS* 166-7)

But if we are not to believe this – and we're self-evidently not – the problem remains that we cannot count on getting at the truth of the story simply by reversing these propositions.

The inconsequential confirmation that Edward was Florence's lover, to return to that for the moment, marks the fact as oddly incidental, as if this is not the real issue. Again and again, the revelations in *The Good Soldier* are – or can be seen as – beside the point: *that*, we are entitled to feel, is not, after all, what we wanted to know. And indeed, Florence's infidelity as such is not what Dowell cannot face. After a year or two of marriage, long before the trip to M[arburg], there was, he later tells us, no longer any question for him of loving her; Florence had become a burden, an obligation (*GS* 68). And Dowell is exhausted – by, he still later confides, 'twelve years of the repression of my instincts [. . .] twelve years of playing the trained poodle' (86). Instead, the threat at M[arburg] is to the quartet, to the minuet they tread jointly; the fear Dowell names is that 'we were going to run and cry out; all four of us in separate directions, averting our heads'. In some unspecified way, he needs the Ashburnhams: 'I do not believe that I could have gone on any more without them. I was getting too tired' (53).

But what exactly does that imply about their role in Dowell's psychic economy? Does their civilized, easy façade simply offer him relief by providing new addressees for Florence's unremitting chatter, or does he have a more personal investment in either or both of the Ashburnhams? What exactly is his relationship with the beautiful Leonora, whom he says he loves but not sexually, while resenting her marriage to Rodney Bayham (*GS* 157, 167)? And how are we to understand the place of Edward – his rival, or role model (as he says, 157, 168), or even unconscious object of desire (as he doesn't exactly say)? Explanations are postponed, deferred to a future place in the narrative, or withheld altogether. There is no sense of a final reckoning, a moment when the reader is invited to look back through the story and make sense of all that was mysterious at the time.

And the desire of the reader is maintained in the process, because what we are incited to want is resolution of the enigmas the novel builds. We are to be held by the desire for presence, for these people and their emotions made present and transparent to our understanding. But that is the one thing the duplicitous, equivocating signifier cannot be counted on to deliver, so that *The Good Soldier* has the power to sustain desire beyond its last page, even when all the 'facts' have apparently been laid bare. Facts themselves don't satisfy: as Conrad's Marlow points out in a different context, they 'are so often more enigmatic than the craftiest arrangement of words'.[18]

This observation itself equivocates, of course: in a novel there are no facts as such, but only ever an arrangement of words. It's surely safe to say that their arrangement in *The Good Soldier* is among the craftiest. Bleak in its account of human relations but jubilant in its power to exploit the possibilities of the signifier, the novel dramatizes what Lyotard would call the postmodern condition, in the grip of unconscious imperatives we cannot be sure we are aware of and held by an equivocating signifying system we cannot rely on as a ground of certainty.

**V**

But what about chronology? Surely a novel begun in 1913 cannot by definition be postmodern; it has to be modernist. This is where Lyotard's distinctions may be seen as most suggestive. In his account, dates are not the issue. Instead, what distinguishes the postmodern is the attitude it displays to the withdrawal of the real. On the one hand, there is nostalgia for lost presence, as we find in Proust and, arguably, Lawrence; on the other, we see a celebration of the possibilities released by the fact that presence is no longer an option, as, for instance, in Virginia Woolf's *Orlando*. The first suspects the pleasure of the text as a snare and a delusion; the second divorces pleasure from therapy, locating it in a challenge to orthodoxy. Duchamp and Joyce are in this sense postmodern, and Lyotard adds, 'The nuance which distinguishes these two modes may be infinitesimal; they often coexist in the same piece ... and yet they testify to a differend . . . between regret and assay'.[19]

*The Good Soldier* is not *Ulysses* but it does refuse the solace of conventional form. While it depicts a culture on the verge of collapse, it does not retreat into nostalgia for a past wholeness; nor does it campaign for an alternative future. If it implies that civilization has invented ideals for us to live by that are incompatible with the things we are, it does not make any demands for the emancipation of the desire it defines so closely. Instead, the novel poses questions. At the beginning these take the form of fairly crude oppositions: 'Am I no better than a eunuch or is the proper man [. . .] a raging stallion forever neighing after his neighbour's womenkind?' (*GS* 15). Critics who answer yes to either of these options are, to my mind, closing off the issues prematurely. Later, the text moves on to more open-ended questions: 'what should these people have done?' (155). Is there some sort of earthly paradise where people get what they want, or are all lives 'broken, tumultuous, agonised' (158)? This is where literary impressionism comes into its own: Dowell does not have to know the answers. Instead, he passes the responsibility on to the reader (his imagined listener): 'Perhaps you can make head or tail of it; it is beyond me' (158); 'I can't make out which of them was right. *I leave it to you*' (my emphasis, 163).

Given that 'there is nothing to guide us' (*GS* 15), we are put on the spot. Moralists and sex therapists may be eager to supply the missing contents: our job, in my view, as critics, is to note what is not there. And if there is no rule of conduct by which the characters are

found wanting, no big idea that might put things right, there are no
pre-established rules that ought to govern storytelling, except that the
author 'must learn to suppress himself'.[20] Giving absolute priority to
the story itself, *The Good Soldier* discovers its own rules as it goes
along, evading the prescriptions of genre, while playing fast and loose
with the classic-realist promise that, although red herrings are fine, the
narrator will not misinform the reader. Ford tells a tale that is sad,
absurd, comic, and inconsequential by turns. Refusing to answer its
own questions, the novel destabilizes objects and values, withholding
the therapy that protects consciousnesses from doubt. And yet it gives
pleasure, not least by exploiting the potential duplicity of the signifier.
Far from reiterating the familiar lament that language falls short of the
whole truth, *The Good Soldier* demonstrates that the signifier can be
full of meaning and at one and the same time quite withhold
intelligibility. This might be easy to say: it is less easy to sustain
across the course of a narrative without antagonizing readers. Desolate
though its outcomes are, the clever, witty, disconcerting text of *The
Good Soldier* gives the firm impression of enjoying itself. 'Just look',
it seems to say, 'at what fiction can do!'

## NOTES

1   I modified my views in the course of discussions at *The Good Soldier* Centenary
    Conference, Swansea University, 2013. I am grateful to all the participants and, in
    particular, Harry Ricketts, Sara Haslam, Paul Skinner, Renée Dickinson and
    Elizabeth Brunton.
2   Eugene Goodheart, 'What Dowell Knew' (1986). Reprinted in Ford Madox Ford,
    *The Good Soldier*, ed. Martin Stannard, New York: W. W. Norton, 2012, 382-91,
    (p. 382). All references to *The Good Soldier* (henceforth *GS*) are to this edition
    and page numbers are cited in the text. Other materials from this edition are cited
    as 'Stannard'.
3   Jean-François Lyotard, 'Answering the Question: What is Postmodernism?', trans.
    Régis Durand, *The Postmodern Condition: A Report on Knowledge*, Manchester:
    Manchester University Press, 1984, 71-82. '*Réponse a la question: qu'est-ce que
    le postmoderne?*, *Critique* 419 (April, 1982), 357-67, (p. 357).
4   'It was one of those evenings ...'; 'She was the kind of woman who ...' The code
    of reference appeals to a collective and anonymous wisdom. See Roland Barthes,
    *S/Z*, trans. Richard Miller, London: Jonathan Cape, 1975, pp. 18, 24, 25 and
    *passim*.
5   Lyotard, 'What is Postmodernism?', p. 74.

6   Lyotard, 'What is Postmodernism?', p. 79.
7   Lyotard, 'What is Postmodernism?', p. 81.
8   See Vincent J. Cheng. 'A Chronology of *The Good Soldier*' (1986), reprinted in Stannard, 391-5.
9   The question of culpability is raised but not resolved on pp. 113-14.
10  Ford, '[Developing the Theory of Impressionism with Conrad]', Stannard, 288-99, (p. 296).
11  Carol Jacobs, '[The Passion for Talk]' (1992), reprinted in Stannard, 354-61, (p. 356).
12  Later, when she persuades Leonora to explain Mrs Brand's divorce case, Nancy will remember 'Henry VIII and the basis upon which Protestantism rests' (*GS* 147).
13  Cf. Edward: 'It was as if his passion for her hadn't existed; as if the very words that he spoke, without knowing that he spoke them, created the passion as they went along. Before he spoke, there was nothing; afterwards, it was the integral fact of his life' (*GS* 83).
14  It was Anna O. who called her treatment a 'talking cure'. See Sigmund Freud and Josef Breuer, *Studies on Hysteria*, ed. Angela Richards, London: Penguin, 1974, p. 83.
15  See also *Some Do Not . . .*, where 'A tramp who had had his leg cut off by a train had told him that he had tried to get up, feeling nothing at all .... The pain comes back though . . .': Ford Madox Ford, *Parade's End*, London: Penguin, 2012, p. 122.
16  *The Standard Edition of the Complete Psychological Works of Sigmund Freud*, vol. 5, (1900-1901): *The Interpretation of Dreams (Second Part) and On Dreams, i-iv*, London: The Hogarth Press and the Institute of Psycho-analysis, 1953, pp. 535-6.
17  James T. Boulton ed., *The Selected Letters of D. H. Lawrence*, Cambridge: Cambridge University Press, 1997, p. 78.
18  Joseph Conrad, *Lord Jim: A Tale*, ed. J. H. Stape and Ernest W. Sullivan II, Cambridge: Cambridge University Press, 2012, p. 256
19  Lyotard, 'What is Postmodernism?', p. 80. 'Differend' is my translation. It denominates a difference that cannot be debated or legislated away and where 'One side's legitimacy does not imply the other's lack of legitimacy' (Jean-François Lyotard, *The Differend: Phrases in Dispute*, trans. Georges Van Den Abbeele, Manchester: Manchester University Press, 1988, p. xi).
20  Ford, '[Developing the Theory]', p. 296.

# JULY 4 TO AUGUST 4: PARADIGMATIC AND PALIMPSESTIC PLOTS IN *THE GOOD SOLDIER*

## Melba Cuddy-Keane

**Abstract**

The well-recognized problems in the chronology of *The Good Soldier* can be readily explained once we recognize the palimpsestic date, in the novel, of July 4. The masking of the Declaration of Independence by the imperialist and nationalist violence that erupted, for Britain, on August 4 emerges, in a broad paradigmatic way, as the vital tension underwriting the overt plot. The contest between freedom and fatality constitutes a dynamic struggle not only in the composition of this novel but in the compositional efforts of the narrator-protagonist John Dowell as well. The plot of narration (as opposed to the plot of action) reveals Dowell's longing for an emotional human relation that would free him from his repetitive and convention-bound life. This palimpsestic interior text emerges through his employment of empathetic and embodied Free Indirect Discourse, until his glimpsed freedom is again overwhelmed by the inexorability of external forces. Ultimately, the novel encompasses three conflicting discursive modalities: the Protestant-Enlightenment narrative of independence, the determinist, mechanistic narrative of modernity, and the ironic plot of modernist ethics that requires inhabiting two different positions at the same time.

---

Situation One: A man, convinced that his wife has a heart condition that precludes any kind of sexual activity or indeed emotional excitement, believes he is fulfilling the role of a virtuous, supportive husband by devoting himself to a life of platonic care. They meet another couple, and their seemingly perfect friendship relieves his loneliness. But in 'four crashing days', nine years and six months after their momentous meeting, he discovers that his wife was deceiving him; his closest friends were deceiving him, and he has been deceiving himself. Has truth then replaced falsehood, or does the disclosure shatter the paradigm of epistemological certainty, including the viability of making true/false distinctions, with the multiple realities of layered simultaneous and contradictory perceptions?

Situation Two: Critics reading Ford Madox Ford's *The Good Soldier* (1915) interpreted the novel's obsessively repetitive placement of events on August 4 as a covert reference to the real-world events on August 4, 1914, the day German troops invaded Belgium and England declared war. Approximately fifty years after the publication of Ford's novel, editorial work on the early drafts of Ford's novel exposed a reference to August 4 in a portion of the text apparently written before August 4, 1914.[1] Did this discovery then correct a false reading with a true, exposing the arbitrariness of the seemingly portentous date? Or does Ford's pre-war planning merely add another layer to this complicated text? Are we left with an uncanny parallel between John Dowell's attempts to unravel his life history and our critical attempts to unravel the mysteries of the text's composition and the numerous and contradictory interpretations it has produced?

## A Palimpsestic Chronology

To begin to tackle these questions, I return once more to the perplexing labyrinth of the novel's hopelessly muddled chronology.[2] I follow the conjecture of most of *The Good Soldier*'s textual scholars: that Ford used the date August 4 before August 4, 1914, but that after the entrance of Britain into the European conflict, he heightened the emphasis on this day as a pivotal date. What I do further, however, is to take seriously an early, but later revised, reference to July in the manuscript, and the indirect, but still evident, allusions to July that remain in the published text. Just possibly, I suggest, the published text is haunted by an earlier plotting that involved the contrasting paradigm of a different date.

On two occasions, Dowell emphasizes the uncanny calendrical coincidences in his wife Florence's life: she is born (1874), she embarks on a world cruise (1899), she begins an affair with her cousin Jimmy (1900), she marries Dowell (1901), she begins an affair with Edward Ashburnham (1904), and she dies (1913) – all on August 4. The first of these summaries (minus her death) appears in the apparent first draft of the novel, but since the relevant passage is in an undated carbon copy typed by Ford (Stannard 203), the date of its composition is impossible to determine, based on material evidence alone. The second complete summary is a later addition to H. D.'s [Hilda Doolittle's] script, made in Ford's hand (206).[3] Stannard correctly observes that it is impossible to date Ford's marginal insertion; however, H. D.'s husband Richard Aldington wrote, in a letter dated by his editor 4 July 1914, that Hilda was breaking down 'through working too hard with Hueffer on his novel'.[4] Since the page in question appears in the first of the three portions in H. D.'s hand, less than half way through the total number of pages she transcribed, and approximately one third of the way from the point where her handwriting begins to where it ends, there is ample evidence that this crucial page substantially predates the war.[5] As Stannard notes, the passage includes the detail that Florence was seen coming out of Jimmy's room on 'the 4th of August, 1900', but Dowell's accompanying comment, we should note further, more significantly indicates Ford's plan. The full passage in H. D.'s hand goes on to present Dowell's view that the incident precipitated Florence's suicide, likely because 'the date was too much for her superstitious personality' (*GS* 96).[6] Dowell thus clearly identifies August 4th as the day of Florence's death, indicating that coincidences on this date were planned by Ford from the start. Indeed, the comment about Florence's 'superstitious personality' best makes sense if we assume the first summary (65) had already been written at this point.

But neither summary includes an occurrence remembered (or mis-remembered) by Dowell elsewhere: that the two couples first met on August 4, 1904 (24; 69). Yet Dowell and Florence could not have made the acquaintance of Leonora and Edward Ashburnham on August 4, 1904 when Dowell also unequivocally places another event, Maisie Maidan's death, on August 4, 1904, coincident with the beginning of Florence's and Edward's affair (65). Since he also claims that he and Florence 'saw plenty' of Maisie Maidan for a month before her death (45), and Maisie accompanied the Ashburnhams, they must all have been acquainted in July. In the manuscript, the month for their meeting is indeed first given as 'July,' inserted in ink by Brigit Patmore, Ford's first amanuensis in the spring of 1914,[7] and only later revised to August 1904, in pencil, by Ford himself (Stannard 197).[8]

If we restore a date in July for the beginning of the Dowell-Ashburnham friendship, then some of the chronological puzzles begin to make sense. Right from the earliest draft, Dowell claims that his fantasy of a 'long tranquil life' dissolved nine years and six months minus 'four crashing days' after it began. If the establishment of the foursome 'roundtable' took place on July 4 rather than August 4, then nine years and six months brings us to January 4. And if Leonora's narration of a whole history of which Dowell has been unaware took four days, then the 'four crashing days' would be January 1-4. Since Leonora's first allusion to Florence's suicide takes place in the evening, placing her revelation on New Year's Eve, her full story presumably commenced at midnight (or thereabouts). Fittingly, for a novel so concerned with portentous dates, the moment when Leonora

Ashburnham initiates a total revolution in Dowell's world system marks the turn of the New Year.

Furthermore, this dating helps to explain another peculiarity in the chronology. Just before she tells Dowell of Florence's suicide, Leonora says: 'Edward has been dead only ten days and yet there are rabbits on the lawn' (86). But later in the novel, Dowell states that Leonora 'kept it up jolly well' until 'eight days after Edward's funeral' (187). Why would the funeral take place two days following death, rather than the normal three-day interval? If Leonora's revelation takes place on January 1, then Edward died, ten days earlier, on December 22. To avoid a funeral mass on December 25 (a requirement by law in the Roman Catholic Church and by custom in the Anglican Church), the funeral would have been held on December 24, 1913. Juxtaposing Edward's funeral next to the day of Christ's birth also adds further to the ironies and ambiguities surrounding Edward's suffering and 'martyrdom'.

But why set the initial meeting specifically on the fourth of the month, if the initial choice of the date had nothing to do with the outbreak of war? If the August dating was originally used merely as relational to a July dating, then – particularly considering that the Dowells are American – the allusion is most likely to another momentous date in political history, the fourth of July. The American 'War of Independence' is mentioned only once in the novel, in Dowell's comment that Florence's family was on 'the losing side' (67); but he employs the analogy of the French Revolution in the opening chapter, and his metaphors, including 'the sack of a city or the falling to pieces of a people' (12), establish at the outset a correlation between individual life and the world stage. The adoption by the United States Congress of the Declaration of Independence on July 4, 1776 thus offers one plausible explanation for Ford's use of the fourth of the month.[9] Ford's own testimony about the novel's composition is that he had the story 'hatching' within him for a decade. My supposition is that he initially devised a chronology around July 4, later abandoning the date but not altering the references to years, months, and days that remain as that date's trace. Like Faulkner's *Absalom, Absalom!*, *The Good Soldier* seems to be a novel in which, at some point, the novelist changed his plotting and didn't entirely clear away old tracks.[10]

## A Palimpsestic Narrative

If my speculations about this palimpsestic date clear up some of the novel's chronological mysteries, the fourth of July poses further complexities given Dowell's ambivalent stance toward American independence. Dowell's loyalties are – or at least were in the past – decidedly mixed. He is, on the one hand, an anglophile and conservative monarchist: he is impressed by Ashburnham's ties to 'the Ashburnham who accompanied Charles I to the scaffold' (12); he prefers, with the Hurlbirds, the British General Braddock from the Seven Years' War over George Washington from the War of Independence (67), and he likens the collapse of his safe world to the sacking of Versailles by the French revolutionary mob (13). On the other hand, in response to Leonora's defensive assertion that she is an Irish Catholic, Dowell – a Quaker from Philadelphia – claims 'the liberty of a free American citizen to think what I please about your co-religionists' (57). Dowell here aligns with the Protestant Reformation and the American values of liberty and democratic freedom against the combination of rigidity and manipulative secrecy he identifies with the older Irish or English Catholic regime. His conflicted loyalties, however, reflect the fundamental difficulty of choosing any one side. Freedom can be liberating and empowering but destructive if it gets out of hand; external authority (in the form of dogma, convention, or political regimes), can ensure safety and order but can be coercive and crippling as well. The tension between inner freedom and outer authority is present in Dowell himself.

In addition to being a tension *within* Dowell, a conflicted relation to freedom creates a further tension *between* the Dowells of past and present. *The Good Soldier*, as is well known, is a classic example of what James Phelan calls dual focalization,[11] in which the *narrator*-I (the Dowell of the present) struggles to understand not only the other characters, but also the perceptions – or failures in perception – of the *character*-I (the Dowell of the past). The relation of the two focalizations is primarily one of contrast, as the obtuseness and conventionality of the character-Dowell's perceptions are overwritten with the narrator-Dowell's increasing grasp of the emotional complexities and ethical ambiguities of his tale. Yet the relation is not as simple as pure opposition: fluctuations in both modes of perception (seeing in terms of conventionalities and seeing in terms of complexities) occur on *both* levels. The simplicity-prone character-Dowell occasionally pierces the veils of deception around him, so that in a moment of blinding perception he reads his wife's act of laying her finger on Edward Ashburnham's wrist as a clear sexual invitation. In reversing but similarly unstable fashion, the complexity-prone narrator-Dowell frequently reverts back to his protective shell or stubbornly hugs the shore of his outraged victimization. The experiencing-I and the narrating-I thus *both* exhibit perceptual instability, giving the two Dowells a confusing tendency to blur. Yet the outcome of instability in each plot line follows a different path. In the past-time plot of *action*, Dowell immediately represses his emotional insight, covering his knowledge with the protective layer of good form. Contrastingly, in the present-time plot of *narration*, Dowell's sensory, emotional, intuitive self begins to develop and expand. Although his narration reveals a war among different voices struggling for expression, with many twistings and reversions in its course, the emergence of an uninhibited, positive emotional voice offers potential for change. It is the fate of that voice and its bid for freedom that constitutes, I suggest, the palimpsestic plot.

The plot of narration – a term first used by Wayne Booth – has been well recognized in studies of women's writing, where the act of writing itself frequently affirms a positive agency countering the subjection of identity pervading the woman's life. And in *The Good Soldier*, I suggest, the plot of narration adumbrates something almost entirely absent in the plot of action: a man on the verge of making his own personal declaration of independence. Judged by events alone, Dowell is almost a cipher for the lack of personal freedom. Finally released, by his wife's death, from his role as self-sacrificing guardian of her supposedly delicate heart, he nonetheless catapults back into the duties of nursemaid once more. Nancy Rufford, the young woman whom he had hoped to marry, but who, it turns out, was Edward's final, ultimate, but absolutely forbidden love, goes mad when she learns of Edward's suicide, and there is only Dowell left to care for her ruined shell. In the narrated *action*, Dowell thus appears to end where he began. My interest here, however, is less in that fatalistic outcome than in the taste of freedom that, in the narrative of *consciousness*, offers, like July 4, a palimpsestic text.

By entertaining the possibility of Dowell's development, I am drawing on the vein of criticism proceeding from Samuel Hynes rather than Mark Schorer – the two early critics of this novel who, Stannard notes, 'laid the foundation for most [subsequent] debate' (xi).[12] The view of Dowell as '*incapable* of passion' (Schorer vii; my emphasis) acquires support both from the behaviour of the character-Dowell in the past and indeed from much of the commentary offered by the narrator-Dowell in the present; nonetheless, there is also strong evidence that, in the process of his narration, Dowell, as Hynes asserts, 'learns the reality of Passion' (61). Yet I do not think, with Hynes, that 'Convention' in itself is responsible for Passion's demise. Dowell's final capitulation to a passionless existence is not merely because society must ultimately win in the end or because he is 'ill-equipped for [his] knowledge' (Hynes 61), but rather because a brutalist external fatality overwhelms and destroys the potential for individual freedom. On both the personal and historical stage, August 4 trumps the fourth of July.

The palimpsestic plot resides in Dowell's multiple voices, each one implying a different relation of the author to his materials. While in Ford's fiction, Dowell is narrator and character, in Dowell's autobiography, he subsumes the role of author as well. However unreliable he may be as Ford's narrator, Dowell's narration reliably reflects his self-authoring at any given moment in time, and such self-authoring helps to determine the nature of his autobiographical tale. The way an author creates a persona, the way that persona is characterized by voice, and the way that voice implies attitudes, beliefs, and values are significant factors informing our understanding of the overall meaning of the work. Dowell's changing voice, however, reveals a competition among personae, leaving in doubt the kind of storyworld that he is in. By turns, his voice is objective and historical; defensive and denying; romantic and sentimental; bitter and accusatory; fatalistic and ironic; and at times, I suggest, unguarded and passionate. These variations, however, do more than introduce character instability. Dowell's voice – the stance he takes toward his materials – is the primary indicator of how he conceives the genre of his life. In effect, there are multiple storyworlds in Dowell's tale, offering contending constructions of reality.[13] The deeper significance of the variation bears on whether we live in a comic, tragic, absurd, or ironic world.

The voice I have described as unguarded and passionate, the voice that could indicate we are living in a humanely meaningful world, is generally the most overlooked, possibly because it is fleeting, possibly because it emerges in subtleties of tone and style. It is most strongly evidenced in two key scenes, through Dowell's movement between objective narration and subjective focalization. Dowell's potential for sensory, emotional perception is first strongly hinted in a passage in which he reflects on Edward's love for Nancy (III: 1). At first, Dowell summarizes what Edward has told him: 'He assured me'; 'He said'; 'He realized'; 'He swore' (90). Dowell then universalizes to 'a man's' experience, but also intensifies by shifting into the present tense: 'He wants to get'; 'He wants to hear'; 'he wants to see' (92). The passage builds up an escalating intensity through repetition, compression, and acceleration: 'He desires to see with the same eyes, to touch with the same sense of touch, to hear with the same ears, to lose his identity, to be enveloped, to be supported.' Then, for one sentence, Dowell makes a significant pronoun shift: 'We are all so afraid, we are all so alone, we all so need from the outside the assurance of our own worthiness to exist' (93). Universalizing emotions, Dowell testifies to their continuing existence; relocating them in the present tense, he testifies, at least momentarily, to the informative role of his own emotions in constructing his tale. Contrary to some interpretations, Dowell is not, in this passage, dismissing sexual desire: rather, he avows that sex is so certainly and always present that it hardly needs mention, further betraying the intimate knowledge that desire can be aroused by such tiny details as an the 'turn of the eye-brow' or an 'untied shoelace' (92). But he goes beyond sexual desire to articulate a desire for existential intimacy. If his confession appears somewhat maudlin, we might consider the distance he has come from his opening claim that the story is one he 'heard' (implying, about others) to his recognition here that he is telling a story about himself.

The second, and more definitive, emotional disclosure comes in Dowell's use of free indirect discourse, or FID. As numerous critics have argued, the significance of FID lies in the structural indeterminacy of its dual voicing;[14] a narrator slips into the mind of another yet, referring to the other in the third person (he/she), simultaneously retains the presence of the narrating–I. Also, since the narrator is projecting into the other's mind, FID relies on the imaginative and empathetic resources of the narrating mind. Dowell's employment of FID emerges most dramatically in an extended passage in Part IV of the novel, in which he shifts from recording and reflecting on the past to imagining and reconstructing it. Dowell is narrating the experience of Nancy Rufford at the point when she first discovers her love for Edward; but unlike Edward's explanation about his love for Nancy, there is no indication that Nancy ever spoke to Dowell about her experience. Even assuming some transmission

through Leonora, Dowell's narration goes well beyond any information that he could possibly have heard. His employment of FID, that
is, involves a process of imaginative reconstruction, much like, to
draw again upon *Absalom, Absalom!,* the process of Quentin-Shreve's
reconstruction of the voices of Henry Sutpen and Charles Bon.
Similarly, Dowell's voice slips into being Nancy's voice, but for
Dowell to be able to perform such narration, he must draw upon his
formerly repressed resources – his capacity for sensory and emotional
knowledge – or, in other words, the interior palimpsestic text that has
been struggling to emerge.

The passage as a whole enacts a complex shifting through
multiple voicings, varying from the most distanced and monistic to the
most imbricated and complex. 'So these matters presented themselves
to Nancy's mind' (167) evidences Dowell in the role of external
narrator, in his distanced, objective reporting function, in contrast to
passages where he focalizes through Nancy's mind, offering what
Dorrit Cohn termed psycho-analogies for thoughts:[15] 'She remembered someone's love for the Princess Badrulbadour; she remembered
to have heard that love was a flame, a thirst, a withering up of the
vitals,' with the objective Dowell adding 'though she did not know
what the vitals were' (170). In a more complex shifting, he moves
rapidly from objective description ('Her heart beat painfully; she
began to cry'), to character focalization ('She asked God how He
could permit such things to be'), to FID: 'Perhaps, then, Edward loved
some one else. It was unthinkable' (168). Dowell's struggle toward
empathetic projection is even more dramatically enacted when he
begins with character focalization ('And suddenly Nancy found that
she was crying'); shifts to objective description ('She was crying
quietly; she went on to cry with long convulsive sobs'); returns to
character focalization ('It seemed to her that everything gay,
everything charming, all light, all sweetness, had gone out of life');
and then powerfully renders Nancy's own voice through FID:
'Unhappiness; unhappiness; unhappiness was all around her' (171).

These variations, I submit, represent not just different narratorial voices, but different relations between the narrator and his
character-subject – positions I would define as *interested* in external
narration, *sympathetic* in character focalization, and *empathetic* in
FID. In distinguishing between sympathy and empathy in this way, I
am drawing on the commonly cited distinction in their German roots
between Mitfühlung (sympathy) or 'feeling with' and 'Einfühlung'

(empathy) or 'feeling in or into' – the distinction that Suzanne Keen explains as separating sympathy as 'feeling for' someone and empathy as '[m]irroring what [another] person might be expected to feel in [a particular] condition or context' (208).[16] But to clarify empathy's specific application to FID, I turn as well to cognitive philosophers Allison Barnes and Paul Thagard, who argue that empathy is distinguished by an essential doubleness in response, defining it as a mode of projecting out into the other that retains a sense of the other's difference.[17] They quote Lauren Wispe: 'In empathy the self is the vehicle for understanding, and it never loses its identity. Sympathy, on the other hand, is concerned with communion rather than accuracy, and self-awareness is reduced rather than enhanced.' (79).[18] The doubleness inherent in this particular understanding of empathy is crucial for the sense of empathy that we must engage here, where we are concerned not with the effect of empathetic narrative on the reader (the more usual focus), but with its effect on the narrator. Empathetic narration as employed in Dowell's use of FID functions as a mode of knowledge that is both knowledge of the other and knowledge of the self. As Dowell-as-narrator moves toward empathetic ways of knowing when he describes Nancy's realization of Edward's love for her and hers for him, he releases a hidden depth in himself that the earlier Dowell-as-character has never known.[19] Expanding from a re-creative to a creative role, he reveals enhanced abilities for empathetic understanding and the emotional openness that such empathy requires.

In narrative terms, one of the strongest indicators of Dowell's new approach is his ability to project into what I term embodied FID. Embodied FID involves narrating the bodily experience of others as they experience it, but – like FID – casting it in a third-person point of view. In proposing this particular rhetorical form, I follow those theorists, like Brian McHale and Stefan Oltean, who allow a functional role for FID beyond strict grammatical or syntactic definition.[20] FID can appear more generally, as Oltean phrases it, in third person representation with first person deixis or, even more broadly, in representations of the experience of another from the inside while the context preserves a sense of the other's separateness and difference. Embodied FID can thus be a site for intercorporeal relations—that is, co-ordinations and interactions between our own experiences of embodiment and the embodied experiences of others – and, as such, it has a revolutionary potential for instigating cognitive change.

I am not suggesting that all embodied FID necessarily creates, from intercorporeality, a dynamic result. Embodiment makes available potentialities and affordances but does not determine what we do with them. But for Dowell, it seems, embodied projection brings him to a threshold of opportunity for expanding his emotional reach. Dowell describes Nancy's listening to the voice of Edward, in an exterior room, speaking on the telephone, and as Edward's words become a caress for her ear, Dowell imagines her transposing the caress of sound to the caress of touch she so longs for on her body: 'She moved her hand over the bareness of the base of her throat, to have the warmth of flesh upon it and upon her bosom' (176). It is, I think, an amazing sentence to have come from Dowell's pen; the action's multiple displacements – Edward's voice by Edward's hand, Edward's hand by Nancy's hand; Nancy's body by Dowell's (projected) body – lead us to ask, just who is touching whom? In order to write Nancy's longing, Dowell draws on his own longing; or, perhaps, imagining and writing Nancy's longing helps him to realize his own. However it occurs, the intensity of embodied experience yields an emotion very different in quality from such self-pitying, maudlin declarations as the earlier, 'I only know that I am alone – horribly alone' (14). Although we are unable to separate Nancy's emotion from Dowell's emotion, we can hear, emergent in the narrative voice, the possibilities of a new Dowell – one who has dropped his defensive barriers and is 'in touch' with himself and his world.

Unfortunately, perhaps tragically, Dowell's new-found potential for development is cut short. Nancy goes mad, he becomes her nursemaid, and his narratorial voice reverts to an earlier mode. At the beginning of his narrative, Dowell frequently expresses his disillusion-ment by distancing himself from emotion, often beginning an after-thought with a sardonic 'Well' and countering a moving description with its dry, sarcastic counterpart: 'Well, she was a good actress' (43) or 'Well, that was Edward Ashburnham' (29). Even in his empathetic description of Nancy's feelings, Dowell employs belittling deflation to keep his burgeoning lyricism in check: after evocatively describing a tune in Nancy's head 'in which major notes with their cheerful in-sistence wavered and melted into minor sounds as, beneath a bridge the highlights on dark waters melt and waver and disappear into black depths,' he retracts, 'Well, it was a silly old tune' (170). But in the portion of the narrative written *after* the eighteen-month hiatus during which Dowell has brought his ruined Nancy back to England, the deflationary afterthought not only becomes more frequent; it acquires

a new tone. Whereas the narrative up to this point is written in
response to his discovery of Florence's adultery with Edward, this
latter part responds to the trauma of Nancy's collapse, juxtaposed to
Leonora's success. Whereas the deflationary afterthoughts in the first
part are characterized by anger and bitterness, in the final two chapters
the tone changes to tiredness and resignation: 'Well, there it is. I am
very tired of it all' (179). For Dowell not only returns to his former
role; he now also perceives the inevitability of that return. Not
knowing why he 'should always be selected to be serviceable,' he
accedes to his loss of freedom and possibility: 'what I wanted mostly
was to cease being a nurse-attendant. Well, I am a nurse-attendant'
(181). Possibly character has helped to determine his fate – it would
not accord with his ethics to refuse to take on Nancy's care. But, just
as the outbreak of WWI changed the lives of so many around the
world, so the fatality of circumstance conspires to end any possibility
of Dowell's having a choice.

The palimpsestic plot, however, reminds us of what, in a
different world, might have been – reminds us, that is, of the dreams
and illusions that reality destroys. And it thus reinforces the ironic
vision that is Dowell's final world-view. Dowell returns to a life
guided by conventional forms, but not this time in repressive self-
protection: he now holds two parallel worlds at bay. He abandons his
attempt to resolve simultaneously conflicting ethical beliefs:
Leonora's confirmed view of Edward's selfishness versus Edward's
agonized commitment to sacrificial restraint. And he acknowledges
two contradictory plots: one guided by the heart; the other, by the
head. The latter is populated by the fittest who survive; the former, by
the passionate who are destroyed. The latter (which Dowell dislikes)
proceeds according to the determinism that prevails; the former
(which has all his sympathies) is motivated by the fragile hope of
human freedom and possibility. Dowell's claim to know nothing is, in
effect, the knowledge of such irreconcilabilities, the knowledge of
simultaneous and contradictory perceptions. As author, Dowell ends
his narrative in the ironic mode.

## A Palimpsestic Authorial Hand
A palimpsestic text of human freedom thus appears in the ghostly
traces of July 4 in the novel's chronology, and in the creative
potentials of empathetic projection, adumbrated in Dowell's use of
FID. A yet further palimpsestic trace haunts the composition of the

novel itself, although its driving motif is not freedom but fatality. If Dowell's attempt to tell his story can be read as a struggle among multiple voices, the composition of the novel records the work of multiple historical authors. Given that Ford claimed the germ for his novel came to him 'fully a decade' before he wrote it, its conception occurred during the time of his collaborative relation with Joseph Conrad. And if Ford was, at least to some extent, an invisible authorial hand in the composition of *Nostromo* (1904), Conrad's presence is yet more detectable in *The Good Soldier*.[21] A narrator struggling with his relation to a double (Dowell-Ashburnham) is a distinctive Conradian trope, while Dowell's ironic vision of parallel incompatible worlds owes a good deal to characters like Marlow and Dr. Monygham. But the hand of another author appears in Ford's novel as well – Gavrilo Princip, Kaiser Wilhelm, Sir Edward Grey – name it as you will. For while, in the first stages of Ford's composition, August 4th may have signified no more than a month after the fourth of July, the subsequent eruption of world war precluded the possibility of ever again reading that date in an innocent way. A real-world social catastrophe – one impossible to envision when Ford conceived the novel a decade earlier – inserted itself into Ford's plot.

If an external catastrophe plays a determining role in the genesis of Ford's novel, however, Ford still made the choice not to remove, and perhaps even to heighten, his use of the August 4th date. Ford, that is, exercised authorial agency when he acknowledged the influence of an intervening real-world event on the intended implications of his work. Similarly, John Dowell preserves a tenuous hold on self-determination in his final emotional commitment to the overly passionate against his intellectual recognition of the survival of the fittest in the world's scheme, and in his ethical act of going to India to bring Nancy home. The paradigmatic plots of freedom and fatality conjoin in an intertwined dynamic struggle for both the author of the tale and the author within it. But there is yet a third implicit plot here, one that I identify with the double-voicedness, the double positioning inherent in the empathetic mode of FID. Both Ford and Ford's Dowell respond to one of modernism's greatest challenges, especially following the Great War: how to think in an era overwhelmingly destructive of life and idealism and yet act simultaneously in an ethical way. We don't know and yet we must *do*: ultimately, July 4 and August 4 combine in the seemingly impossible plot of inhabiting two different positions at the same time.

## NOTES

1   The first critic to address the appearance of 'August 4' in the manuscripts concluded that 'the manuscripts do not resolve beyond doubt the question when Ford selected the August 4th date' (149). Charles G. Hoffman, 'Ford's Manuscript Revisions of *The Good Soldier*,' *English Literature in Transition*, 9:4 (1966), 145-52. Hoffman nonetheless opened up a debate that persists to the present time.

2   See Ford *The Good Soldier*, Oxford World's Classics, ed. Max Saunders, Oxford: Oxford University Press, 2012 – henceforth *GS*; Appendix C, for a full explanation of its confusions: pp. 214-24.

3   Stannard reproduces this manuscript page. Norton Critical Edition, ed. Martin Stannard, New York and London: W. W. Norton & Company, 1995, p. 178.

4   Richard Aldington, Letter to F. S. Flint [4 July 1914]. *Richard Aldington: An Autobiography in Letters,* ed. Norman T Gates, University Park, Pa.: Pennsylvania State University Press, 1992, pp. 10-11.

5   H. D.'s handwriting begins on MS 141 and ends on MS 253; the page in question is MS 180. Stannard also points to evidence that her transcription extended further, in pages 'scrapped' by Ford's typed revision of her continuing holograph (208). Ford himself claimed that his 'American poetess' amanuensis 'fainted' three times while he 'was dictating the most tragic portion of [his] most tragic book' (*IWN* 241). Even allowing for exaggeration, his remark indicates that they were well past MS180 by July 14, 1914.

6   All subsequent page references to the novel refer to Saunders' Oxford World's Classics edition.

7   Patmore left the Hunt-Ford residence and returned to her husband on April 12, 1914 (*GS* xxi).

8   The penciled change to August is indeed incorporated into the portion of the novel published in the issue of *Blast* dated 20 June 1914, and released on July 2 (92). Ford had already changed the meeting of the Dowells and Ashburnhams from July to August *before* the war, creating confusion, however, as he did so. He may have hastily made this change when he realized he has the Dowells arrive in Nauheim in July (11) and that, at the time of the meeting, Dowell claims that Florence has been taking the baths for a month (24). But Ford then allowed the inconsistency that places the meeting with the Ashburnhams on the same day as Maisie Maidan's death. If he realized he was in trouble with his dating, he may have counted on Dowell's inconsistencies to 'cover' the impossible time frame.

9   By strange coincidence, July 4 is another uncanny date. Although the Declaration of Independence is dated July 4, 1776, and Thomas Jefferson, John Adams, and Benjamin Franklin all claimed they signed it on this date, signing of the official parchment copy did not begin until August 2. Three US Presidents died on July 4 (John Adams, Thomas Jefferson, and James Munroe); another (Calvin Coolidge) was born on this date. By further coincidence, it is also the date of Aldington's letter cited above.

10  Robert Dale Parker reads the numerous chronological discrepancies in Faulkner's novel as a disinterest or disbelief in facticity that serves to suspend us in the realm of fictionality. See Robert Dale Parker, 'The Chronology and Genealogy

of *Absalom, Absalom!*: The Authority of Fiction and the Fiction Of Authority', *Studies in American Fiction*, 14:2 (1986), 191-198.

11  See James Phelan, *Living to Tell About It: A Rhetoric and Ethics of Character Narration*, Ithaca: Cornell University Press, 2005.

12  See Mark Schorer, 'An Interpretation,' Ford, *The Good Soldier*, ed. Mark Schorer, New York: Random House, 1955: pp. v-xv and Samuel Hynes, 'Ford Madox Ford: a. The Epistemology of The Good Soldier,' in *Edwardian Occasions: Essays on English Writing in the Early Twentieth Century*, London: Routledge and Kegan Paul, 1972: pp. 54-62.

13  A distinction might be drawn here between Ford's tale, which orchestrates multiple perceptions of and attitudes toward Dowell within a single storyworld and Dowell's authorial shifts between different and conflicting storyworlds.

14  For an account of experiments testing readers' perceptions of FID's dual voice, see Joe Bray, 'The "dual voice" of free indirect discourse: a reading experiment', *Language and Literature*, 16:1 (2007), 37–52.

15  See Dorrit Cohn, *Transparent Minds: Narrative Modes for Presenting Consciousness in Fiction*, Princeton, New Jersey: Princeton University Press, 1978.

16  Suzanne Keen, 'A Theory of Narrative Empathy,' *Narrative*, 14 (2006), 207-36.

17  Allison Barnes and Paul Thagard, 'Empathy and Analogy,' *Dialogue: Canadian Philosophical Review*, 36 (1997), 705–20.

18  Lauren Wispe, *The Psychology of Sympathy*, New York: Plenum Press, 1991.

19  I differ here somewhat from Hynes, who sees Dowell's empathetic identification with Edward as the sign of his growth.

20  See Brian McHale, 'Unspeakable Sentences, Unnatural Acts: Linguistics and Poetics Revisited,' *Poetics Today*, 4:1 (1983), 17-45 and Stefan Oltean, 'A Survey of the Pragmatic and Referential Functions of Free Indirect Discourse,' *Poetics Today* 14:4 (1993), 691-714.

21  Even Xavier Brice, who attributes Ford's claim to have written some of *Nostromo* to exaggeration, concludes that Ford was nonetheless a 'vital collaborator'. Inadvertently supporting Conrad's influence on *The Good Soldier*, one piece of evidence Brice presents to argue for Conrad's authorship of some disputed pages in *Nostromo* is Decoud's use of FID (87). See Xavier Brice, 'Ford Madox Ford and the Composition of *Nostromo*', *The Conradian*, 29:2, *Nostromo*: Centennial Essays (2004), 75-95.

Bad Nauheim: Kurhaus (Assembly Rooms) and Spa fountain in 1900.

# *THE GOOD SOLDIER* AND THE PROBLEM OF COMPOSITIONAL (UN)RELIABILITY

## Eyal Segal

**Abstract**
The notion of unreliability entails the reader's perception of a split between two communicative levels: one that includes the narrator, who communicates directly with his/her addressee, and one that includes the author, who communicates indirectly with the reader, sending him/her messages that differ from those the narrator seems to be responsible for. In most cases of assessing the tensions or discrepancies between these communicative levels, the critics' main interest lies in epistemological and ethical issues; this essay, however, focuses on the *compositional* level, an aspect much less often dealt with in this context. I believe *The Good Soldier* constitutes a particularly powerful instance of what may be termed 'compositional unreliability': the narrative is told by an 'amateurish' narrator in a seemingly rambling, associative, and unorderly manner, while at the same time the text is perceived by the reader as highly planned, structured, and organized. The positing of Dowell as a compositionally unreliable narrator is integral to Ford's modernist-impressionist poetics, helping him achieve two of his major aesthetic goals: a strong mimetic illusion and *progression d'effet*.

The problem I would like to address in this essay is related to the familiar issue of unreliable narration, but can, I hope, shed some light on it from a new angle, with regard to both the general phenomenon and Ford's novel. Basically, the notion of unreliability entails the reader's perception of a split between two communicative levels: one that includes the narrator, who communicates directly with his/her addressee, and one that includes the author, who communicates indirectly with the reader, behind the narrator's back, so to speak, sending him/her messages that differ from those the narrator seems to be responsible for.[1]

Critical discussions of 'unreliability' amount, in most cases, to assessing the tensions or discrepancies between these two communicative levels. Usually, the critics' main interest lies in epistemological and ethical issues – that is, the ways in which the narrator's understanding, interpretation, and evaluation of the facts reported by him differ from those of the (reliable) author; the narrator is perceived as someone who does not comprehend the full implications of what he is telling, because he is not smart enough, or sensitive enough, or suffers from a certain 'blind spot' in his vision of the world, and so forth. The critical history of *The Good Soldier* is, indeed, very rich in discussions pertaining to this issue, with varying verdicts on Dowell's degree of (un)reliability.[2]

An aspect which is much less often dealt with in this context, but that in my opinion is highly relevant to the same critical and interpretative framework, relates to what may be termed the *compositional* dimension of the text. That is, the question of the tensions that exist between the author and the narrator regarding this dimension: to what extent does the narrator share with the author the responsibility for this aspect of the text, and to what extent do the two part company – either because the narrator is perceived as lacking aesthetic or rhetorical control over the discourse, or because his control is perceived as directed to other ends than those of the author; in other words, how 'compositionally (un)reliable' is the narrator?

The following observation by David Lodge, who uses *The Good Soldier* as a typical example of a modernist novel (in its suppression or displacement of the author), should give an immediate sense of the kinds of effects on the reader – and some of the interpretative problems – involved here:

> The Narrators of modernist novels – e.g. the teacher of languages in Conrad's *Under Western Eyes*, or Dowell in Ford's *The Good Soldier*, must pretend to be *amateur* narrators, disclaiming any literary skill even while they display the most dazzling command of time shift, symbolism, scenic construction, etc.[3]

Lodge's response to Ford's novel reflects a kind of dual quality, or effect, which is indeed very prominent in the text. On the one hand, the novel creates the impression of being told in a very rambling, associative, and unplanned manner – a sort of stream of consciousness on the level of narration. But on the other hand, the novel also leaves an impression of being highly planned, structured, and organized. Lodge's formulation suggests that he considers this duality as a kind of 'cheating' by Ford; I would prefer to view Ford's novel as a particularly powerful instance of what I have termed 'compositional unreliability'. That is, I believe that essentially, the way we are supposed to react to the double effect of the novel is to hold Dowell, the narrator, responsible for the 'unordered' aspect of the text, while perceiving Ford as responsible for its ordered aspect,[4] which is disguised – or mimetically motivated – by the nature of Dowell's narration.

Let me demonstrate this claim by looking at a highly strategic point in the text – namely, its ending. Toward the end of the novel, there appears a kind of summing up by Dowell which seems to lead the text to its natural close. Dowell tells us about the current situation at the time of his writing, and refers to the latest events in the chronology of the story: his buying of, and living in, the Ashburnhams' estate, his looking after Nancy in her insane condition, and Leonora's marriage to Rodney Bayham. In the following passage (which begins with a reference to Nancy), he explicitly announces that he has reached the end of his story:

> It is very extraordinary to see the perfect flush of health on her cheeks, to see the lustre of her coiled black hair, the poise of the head upon the neck, the grace of the white hands – and to think that it all means nothing – that it is a picture without a meaning. Yes, it is queer.
>
> But, at any rate, there is always Leonora to cheer you up; I don't want to sadden you. Her husband is quite an economical person of so normal a figure that he can get quite a large proportion of his clothes ready-made. That is the great desideratum of life, and that is the end of my story. The child is to be brought up as a Romanist.[5]

Note the use of the present tense, which indicates that Dowell has reached the (chrono)logical end of the story – the moment of narration. However, as it turns out, this is not the actual end of the *novel*, because Dowell continues his narration, saying: 'It suddenly occurs to me that I have forgotten to say how Edward met his death' (*GS* 161); and there follows a report of the last time in which Dowell saw Edward alive, immediately before the latter's suicide, after receiving Nancy's telegram from Brindisi.

Throughout the novel, Dowell tells us several times that his discourse flashes backward and forward because he has forgotten something. Specifically, the phrase 'It occurs to me' occurs two more times: in Chapter 3 of Part I ('And it occurs to me that some way back I began a sentence that I have never finished' [*GS* 23]) and at the beginning of Part II ('It occurs to me that I have never told you anything about my marriage' [*GS* 57]). This constitutes one of many signals in Dowell's discourse that are instrumental in creating an impression of spontaneous flow of the narration – of Dowell freely digressing and changing the subject of his narration in midcourse without any apparent planning, in a way which reminds one more of the associative logic of 'live' speech or conversation than of writing.[6] And this effect, I would maintain, is particularly powerful when a phrase like 'it suddenly occurs to me' appears at the end of the novel, because the strategic importance of the ending in any narrative makes it a moment where the expectation of planning or calculation by the narrator is particularly strong, and therefore its apparent absence particularly surprising, even disturbing.

But for this very reason, the reader has a powerful motivation to look for some other guiding hand, some agency to whom the idea of ending the narrative with how Edward met his death did not 'suddenly occur' as if he had forgotten to tell us about it in its 'proper' place, but who has rather planned in advance to end the narrative in this very way, in order to achieve some definite rhetorical goals. And this is, of course, no other than the *author* Ford Madox Ford, who is perceived as responsible not only for the creation of the story-materials, but also for their manner of presentation by a narrator-character such as Dowell.[7] If we look further, beyond these general considerations, for specific rhetorical goals which might have led Ford to conclude the novel in this manner, one which stands out is the alignment of the reader's sympathies with Edward and against Leonora. The tendency of making Edward Ashburnham more compelling, increasing by degrees the reader's interest in – and sympathy for – his passions and sentimentalism, is noticeable in the later parts of the novel.[8] In an important respect, it reaches its peak at the end with both the heart-rending description of that terrible moment in Edward's life, which leads to his suicide, and the description of Leonora's reaction to Nancy's telegram, the direct cause of Edward's suicide, in the very last words of the novel – 'she was quite pleased with it' (*GS* 162) – words which put the final seal on the impression that Leonora's 'cheerful' fate as described at the end, is achieved only at the price of Edward's life and Nancy's sanity.

I believe that the kind of double effect on the reader I have just described as taking place in the final paragraphs, reflects in miniature a split characterizing the novel as a whole: between Dowell's 'free', associative style of narration and Ford's firm and calculated control of the discourse for various aesthetic and rhetorical ends, with the former supplying a systematic mimetic disguise for the latter. Let me now illustrate this claim in detail with regard to a longer textual segment – Chapters 4 and 5 of Part I.

Most of Chapter 4 deals with the trip that the Dowells and the Ashburnhams take to the town of M— (Marburg), during which Florence acts as a tour guide. She points out the Protest document, and lays a finger on Edward's wrist. At that moment Leonora realizes they are having, or are on the verge of having, an affair; Dowell, however, does not perceive that at the time, although he is aware of something treacherous and evil going on. Leonora rushes out of the room, and Dowell follows her. She is extremely upset, claiming that 'that' is the cause of sorrow in the world. However, when she sees that Dowell does not comprehend her meaning, she reestablishes her composure and says that she was offended by Florence's comments because she is an Irish Catholic.

Thus ends Chapter 4, in which the narration is quite chronologically straightforward. But then, in Chapter 5, the narration becomes considerably less linear, a change which involves a switch in perspective as well – from that of the experiencing-I during the narration of the trip to M. to the more knowledgeable one of the narrating-I. Beginning with a comment about the enormous relief that Leonora's words have given him, Dowell moves on to a series of descriptive generalizations about the nature of his relationship with Florence, particularly with regard to his role as a male nurse. Among other things, he notes that both Florence and Leonora were good actresses, probably in the sense that they managed to mislead him (though it is not fully clear about what) – and then, following a description of Leonora's attitude to his usual talk about heart patients, he lashes out in what seems like a sudden burst of anger, saying that there really was nothing the matter with Edward's heart.

From this point on begins a long series of digressions, many of which deal with matters related to Edward's various love affairs and his marriage to Leonora at a period prior to their acquaintanceship with the Dowells, an acquaintanceship which up to this point seemed to be the narrative's main topic. After noting that Edward did not really suffer from a heart disease, Dowell mentions that he has given up his commission and left India in order to follow a woman (who really was a heart patient) to Nauheim, and that it shows what a 'sentimental ass' Edward was, since the Ashburnhams needed to live in India in order to economize. Dowell goes on to note that at the time he had 'never heard of the Kilsyte case' (*GS* 40) and then summarizes this case, in which Edward got into trouble after kissing a servant girl in a railway train. This transition may create the (false) impression that the Ashburnhams' financial troubles were caused by the Kilsyte case.

Dowell goes on to say that the Kilsyte case made Edward leave servants alone but turned him all the more loose among women of his own class, giving Maisie Maidan as an example; this leads him to elaborate on Maisie and her relationship with Edward, interjecting at a certain point that he wishes 'Florence [unlike Edward] had left her alone' (GS 41); he goes on to mention that Edward eventually left Maisie because of Florence, and that this had to do with Maisie's death; then, contrasting Florence with Leonora, Dowell says that the latter behaved better toward Maisie, since she just boxed her ears – hitting her in an uncontrollable rage outside Edward's room, an event which led to the intimacy that sprang up between Leonora and Florence. This is a good example of how Dowell's narration leads, seemingly by chance and through an associative chain that appears as if it might have led in many other directions, to the telling of a very important event: the first meeting between Leonora and Florence. This meeting turns out to have preceded the one between the two couples (narrated earlier, in Chapter 3), and now sheds a new light on that (chronologically) later meeting.

But the meeting between Leonora and Florence is not narrated in a linear fashion either. Explaining how the incident between Maisie and Leonora has led to this meeting, Dowell tells us that Florence, walking in the hotel's corridor, saw Leonora slapping Maisie. He then begins to clarify why Leonora behaved in this manner – since she was very upset, having just discovered that Edward was paying a blackmailer. But mentioning the blackmail leads Dowell to shift his focus to the Ashburnhams' financial troubles, elaborating on Edward's two affairs which cost him money – those that took place in Monte Carlo and India, the latter succeeding the former. This, in turn, leads Dowell to make a general claim about Edward's love affairs (or 'passions') – that they were 'quite logical in their progression upwards' (GS 45). Next, the women involved in Edward's love affairs are contrasted with Leonora, whose marriage to Edward was arranged by his parents. There follows a series of generalizations about her married life with Edward, leading to her description as relatively happy during their voyage back from India, since their economic situation has improved and she felt that Edward was under control, his relations with Maisie being of a kind she could tolerate. Leonora's attitude to Maisie is characterized in this context as motherly and this leads, again seemingly by chance, to the completion of the narration of how Leonora came to slap Maisie when she thought the latter has just spent time with Edward in the privacy of his room ('And that [motherly] attitude of Leonora's towards Mrs Maidan no doubt partly accounted for the smack in the face. She was hitting a naughty child who had been stealing chocolates at an inopportune moment' [*GS* 49]) – and of how this incident, witnessed by Florence, led Leonora to the idea of keeping the latter 'under observation' (*GS* 51) until she could prove to her that she was not jealous of Maisie. (An idea which, in turn, led to the meeting between the Ashburnhams and the Dowells later that day in the hotel's dining room.)

At this point Dowell recalls that Maisie died at the same day of the trip to M—, enabling him to fix the day exactly.[9] And it is only here, toward the end of the chapter, when Dowell finally returns to the topic of this trip in a manner which seems merely coincidental, that he continues the report of his conversation with Leonora from the point at which he left it at the end of the previous chapter: 'At any rate [a phrase which is supposed to bridge a gap of thirteen pages!] the measure of my relief when Leonora said that she was an Irish Catholic gives you the measure of my affection for that couple' (*GS* 51). From this point on, Dowell's report of his conversation with Leonora continues until the end of Chapter 5 (even though the end of this conversation is delayed until the next chapter, which – following another long digression, relating to Florence's affair with Edward – ends with the account of Maisie's death and how it was discovered by Leonora after her return from M—).

Let me draw attention to two important aspects of how Ford's compositional control over the novel is disguised by the manner of Dowell's narration, as illustrated by the sequence of Chapters 4-5:

1. Despite the piecemeal and associative impression often produced by the narration, the continuity of the plot lines established as the main narrative axes is eventually preserved – though, as far as Dowell is concerned, apparently not by design. The main axis in the sequence I have examined is the story of the trip to Marburg; and the apparent lack of design concerns not only Dowell's return toward the end of Chapter 5 to his conversation with Leonora after a long series of digressions, but also how he begins to relate the story in the first place. Although it turns out to be one of the most important events in the acquaintanceship of the Dowells and the Ashburnhams, the trip is introduced, seemingly by chance, as an example of one of a series of generalizations made by Dowell at the beginning of Chapter 4 about the relations between the two couples ('I can give you a rather

extraordinary instance of this [...]' [*GS* 32]). Dowell's initial inability to fix the date of the trip also blurs at first its unique status within the chain of events, whereas his recollection toward the end of Chapter 5 that the trip occurred on the day of Maisie's death helps (though apparently unintentionally, as far as Dowell is concerned) reorient the reader in the story's sequence after the long series of digressions. A similar dynamic of (delayed) continuity-as-if-by-chance operates with regard to the story of how Florence and Leonora have come to know each other, which itself appears as a digression.

2. Nearly all the pieces of information mentioned as if without design in the course of the various digressions turn out, when the focus shifts elsewhere in later parts of the novel, to play an important role in other stages of the plot. Thus, the information about the married life of Edward and Leonora (particularly the period preceding their meeting with the Dowells), which during Chapter 5 of Part I is perceived as digressive in relation to the story of the trip to Marburg, becomes part of the main focus of interest in Part III of the novel. And apart from preparing the ground for later stages of the novel's sequence,[10] some of the 'incidental' digressive materials in Chapter 5 also shed a new light on events narrated earlier – as when the revelation of the circumstances of the first meeting between Florence and Leonora leads to a new understanding of the meeting between the two couples which took place later the same day.

The positing of Dowell as a compositionally unreliable narrator is integral to Ford's modernist-impressionist poetics, and helps him achieve some of his major aesthetic aims. Examining Ford's critical writings, which sometimes serve as manifestoes,[11] we can identify two major poetic tenets or principles, from which his more specific 'rules' or judgments concerning writing are derived: the first is realism (though of a decidedly subjective-impressionist nature), and the second is the need to always keep the reader's interest in the story alive. As a result, we can usually find for any rule or advice concerning writing given by Ford two kinds of explanations, or justifications: in terms of being true to life and in terms of being interesting.

For example, in his book on Joseph Conrad, when describing the principles developed by Conrad and himself for writing novels during their literary cooperation, Ford states that they arrived at the conclusion that when reporting a character's speech, one should not report verbatim everything s/he said, but rather provide 'just a salient or characteristic phrase or two, and a mannerism of the speaker',[12] making 'use of indirect locutions, together with the rendering of the effects of other portions of speech' (*JC* 186). This principle is justified, first of all, by being true to life: a salient phrase or two, together with a general impression, is supposedly the most a person can remember from a conversation, even a relatively short time after its occurrence. (Let us note that Ford's explanation of why this way of reporting speech is true to life, and of how it prevents the reader from wondering how the author or the narrator can possibly remember every word of a long speech that he has heard, illustrates very well the subjective-impressionist slant of Ford's conception of 'realism'. This is to a large extent realism of perception: Ford is interested, first and foremost, not in the full reproduction of the represented object itself – namely, the speech – but rather in reproducing the way it is *perceived* by human consciousness.) But the principle of reporting speech is also justified as being more *interesting* and suggestive than a fuller, non-selective transcription of a complete conversation – a way to get 'a great deal more into a given space' (*JC* 186-7).

The same double motivation, of achieving both realism and narrative interest, accounts for the nature and style of Dowell's narration. On the one hand, this narration – which is associative, digressive, and does not move 'straight forward' in a linear chronological order – is, according to Ford, true to life, since it reflects the way stories are really told as they are remembered, as well as the way in which a person gets acquainted with the life-stories of other people he meets:

> For it became very early evident to us [Ford and Conrad] that what was the matter with the novel, and the British novel in particular, was that it went straight forward, whereas in your gradual making acquaintanceship with your fellows you never do go straight forward. (*JC* 129)

> The novelist from, say, Richardson to Meredith thought that he had done his job when he had set down a simple tale beginning with the birth of his hero or his heroine and ending when the ring of marriage bells completed the simple convention. But the curious thing was that he never gave a thought to how stories are actually told or even to how the biographies of one's friends come gradually before one.[13]

Interestingly, the reasons which lead Ford to this privileging of deformations of chronological order in the telling of a story are almost the exact opposite of those that lead the Russian Formalists – and Viktor Shklovsky in particular – to the same preference, at about the same period. For Shklovsky, such deformations reflect the artificial and anti-realistic nature of literature, while for Ford, as I have mentioned, they constitute an index of realism. For Shklovsky, the value of such deformations lies in the aesthetic effect of estrangement they create with regard to the story [*fabula*] materials; according to him, the more such deformations are 'realistically' motivated, the more their estranging effect is weakened and their artistic value diminished.[14] For Ford, on the other hand, such realistic (and, more specifically, psychological) motivations constitute a crucial part of the very artistic logic of chronological deformations, since they reflect the subjective order in which reality is perceived and remembered. Thus, Dowell's associative manner of narration is employed by Ford as a global device to achieve realism.[15]

But at the same time, the many deformations of the story's linear order, stemming from Dowell's style of narration, operate at the service of a more covert and purely rhetorical goal, which highlights the split between the two communicative levels of Dowell as narrator and Ford as author. The chronological deformations supply Ford with almost unlimited opportunities for manipulating the reader's narrative interest (as has been illustrated above), especially in accordance with the principle he terms *progression d'effet*. This principle is formulated in his book on Conrad as follows: 'We [Ford and Conrad] agreed that every word set on paper [. . .] must carry the story forward and that, as the story progressed, the story must be carried faster and faster and with more and more intensity' (*JC* 210). *The Good Soldier* may be seen as exemplary in achieving this kind of effect, largely due to the digressive and piecemeal nature of the narration; it allows Ford to provide a very gradual exposure of the full scope and meaning of the 'saddest story' told in the novel, revealing a progressively devastating picture of human blindness, suffering, and misery. Yet, it is important for Ford to disguise (rather than flaunt, Shklovsky-fashion) the workings of this construction; the author's rhetorical art with the narrator's mimetic artlessness.

I would like to end by discussing a passage from the novel which seems to problematize everything I have said so far. It appears at the beginning of the fourth and final part, where Dowell reflects on his act of narration:

> I have, I am aware, told this story in a very rambling way so that it may be difficult for anyone to find their path through what may be a sort of maze. I cannot help it. I have stuck to my idea of being in a country cottage with a silent listener, hearing between the gusts of the wind and amidst the noises of the distant sea, the story as it comes. [Here Dowell refers back to what he said at the beginning of the novel's second chapter, in another meta-narrative passage, about imagining himself at one side of a fireplace of a country cottage, with a sympathetic soul opposite him.] And, when one discusses an affair – a long, sad affair – one goes back, one goes forward. One remembers points that one has forgotten and one explains them all the more minutely since one recognizes that one has forgotten to mention them in their proper places and that one may have given, by omitting them, a false impression. I console myself with thinking that this is a real story and that, after all, real stories are probably told best in the way a person telling a story would tell them. They will then seem most real. (*GS* 119-20)

This passage is not atypical in the sense that Dowell appears throughout the novel as a self-conscious narrator, who makes a considerable number of comments and observations pertaining to his ongoing act of narration. However, it is striking how much Dowell sounds here 'like an impressionist critic or novelist', as Max Saunders puts it in his introduction to the Oxford Classics edition of the novel[16]; the difference between Dowell's and Ford's relation to the discourse, which I have made such an effort to emphasize, seems to disappear, and Dowell's meta-narrative comments might appear as a direct and reliable reflection of Ford's poetic principles. Note, in particular, how the end of the passage gives an impression of Dowell as being highly conscious of the effects of his narration, when he justifies himself in terms that are explicitly rhetorical – 'They will then *seem* most real' (the word 'seem' indicating that he is talking about manipulating the reader's perceptions).

I suggest viewing this passage as an attempt by Ford to help the reader as much as possible to understand and appreciate the innovative poetic principles on which the novel is based, through the voice of his narrator-character.[17] I would like to emphasize the phrase *as much as possible* in the previous sentence, which means that Ford is careful, even here, to maintain the mimetic illusion he has worked so hard to establish by still separating himself from Dowell and keeping the latter's statement 'in character' – which is the character of an *amateur* narrator (to use David Lodge's phrase quoted above), and not of a professional author. Note, for example, that Dowell's tone is highly apologetic; the key phrase here is 'I cannot help it'. He turns realist

almost against his will, presenting the manner in which he has told his
story as something which forced itself upon him rather than as a
conscious poetic choice.[18]

In order to illustrate the importance of this distinction, let me
quote more fully a passage from Ford's book on Conrad to which I
have already referred. The narrative style of this book is also
associative and non-linear; but it is a historical text (although in his
preface Ford calls it 'a novel': *JC* 6),[19] where, in contrast to *The Good
Soldier*, the narrator is identical with the author, so there is no split
between two communicative levels. In the following passage, we are
also presented with an explanation of the book's method of narration:

> It will be as well to attempt here some sort of chronology. This is a novel ex-
> actly on the lines of the formula that Conrad and the writer evolved. For it be-
> came very early evident to us that what was the matter with the novel, and the
> British novel in particular, was that it went straight forward, whereas in your
> gradual making acquaintanceship with your fellows you never do go straight
> forward. You meet an English gentleman at your golf club [. . . .][20] To get
> such a man in fiction you could not begin at his beginning and work his life
> chronologically to the end. You must first get him in with a strong impression,
> and then work backwards and forwards over his past. . . . (*JC* 129-30)

Here, unlike in *The Good Soldier*, we hear the voice of Ford himself,
which is the voice of a professional author (note how he refers to
himself as 'the writer'), who is far from apologetic about his method
of narration, and who justifies it by an argument relating to literary
history – one which makes clear that his method of narration is a
matter of a conscious aesthetic choice. And note that in addition to the
claim that his method is true to life ('in your gradual making acquaintanceship with your fellows you never do go straight forward'), Ford
raises, toward the end of the passage, considerations which relate
directly to his second major poetic principle, namely, narrative interest
('You must first get him in with a strong impression [. . .]') – thereby
emphasizing the purely rhetorical dimension of his writing, and the
narrator-author's control over his discourse. By contrast, Dowell's
explanation of his method of narration does *not* include any reference
to such considerations, which would have highlighted too much, for
Ford's purposes, his image as a rhetorician; Dowell consoles himself
by saying his story will seem more real, not more interesting.

We can see, therefore, that even at the point where Ford seems
to let Dowell become his aesthetic spokesman, he still takes care to

separate himself from his character: full aesthetic consciousness and compositional reliability are the author's alone.


## NOTES

1   This view of unreliable narration is already inherent in Wayne C. Booth's groundbreaking definition and treatment of the phenomenon in *The Rhetoric of Fiction*, Chicago: University of Chicago Press, 1961, but is developed most clearly and systematically by Tamar Yacobi in 'Fictional Reliability as a Communicative Problem', *Poetics Today*, 2, 2 (1981), 113-26; 'Narrative and Normative Pattern: On Interpreting Fiction', *Journal of Literary Studies*, 3 (1987), 18-41; and 'Package-Deals in Fictional Narrative: The Case of the Narrator's (Un)Reliability', *Narrative*, 9 (2001), 223-9.

2   For a sampling, see the following two early influential essays: Mark Schorer,'*The Good Soldier*, an Interpretation', in *Ford Madox Ford: Modern Judgments*, ed. Richard A. Cassell, London: Macmillan, 1972 [1951], pp. 63-9, and Samuel Hynes, 'The Epistemology of *The Good Soldier*', in *Ford Madox Ford: Modern Judgments*, ed. Richard A. Cassell, London: Macmillan, 1972 [1961], pp. 97-105; as well as the following later discussions: Vincent J. Cheng, '"All the devices of the prostitute": Sincerity and the Authorial Personae of Ford Madox Ford', *Journal of Modern Literature*, 15 (1989), 532; C. Ruth Sabol, 'Reliable Narration in *The Good Soldier*', in *Literary Computing and Literary Criticism*, ed. R. G. Potter, Philadelphia: University of Pennsylvania Press, pp. 207-23; Jon Skinner, 'Ford Madox Ford's *The Good Soldier*: A Narratological Cas Limite', *Journal of Narrative Technique*, 19 (1989), 287-99 – henceforth 'Skinner'; Karen A. Hoffman, '"Am I no better than a eunuch?': Narrating Masculinity and Empire in Ford Madox Ford's *The Good Soldier*", *Journal of Modern Literature*, 27, 3 (2004), 30-46; and Paul McCormick, 'Claims of Stable Identity and (Un)reliability in Dissonant Narration', *Poetics Today*, 30 (2009), 325-33 – henceforth 'McCormick'.

3   David Lodge, 'Mimesis and Diegesis in Modern Fiction', in *After Bakhtin: Essays on Fiction and Criticism*, London: Routledge, 1990, p. 41.

4   Though ultimately, Ford – as the creator of Dowell, a narrator-character with a certain style of narration – is responsible, of course, for both aspects.

5   Ford, *The Good Soldier*, ed. Martin Stannard, New York: Norton, 1995, p. 161 – henceforth *GS*.

6   Even though Dowell is depicted as writing the text down – he mentions his act of writing several times throughout the novel, starting almost from its very beginning: 'From there [the Ashburnhams' place], at this moment, I am actually writing' (*GS* 11).

7   A similar point with regard to the novel's ending is made in McCormick 327, though in a somewhat different context.

8   For a perceptive analysis of how the manner in which Edward is presented to the
    reader changes throughout the novel see David Eggenschwiler's 'Very Like a
    Whale:The Comical-Tragical Illusions of *The Good Soldier*', *Genre*, 12 (1979),
    405-10, as part of his general thesis that the novel turns from a sexual farce in its
    first half to a romantic tragedy in its second half.
9   Dowell began his recounting of the trip by saying that he cannot remember
    whether it occurred in the first or second year of the two couples at Nauheim (*GS*
    32). This recollection of the date in midcourse contributes to the unplanned,
    associative impression left by the narration.
10  By 'preparing the ground' I mean not only supplying information that is simply
    expanded upon later, but also conveying information in a manner which creates
    misleading impressions, thus setting up later surprises. A good example is the
    passage that has been mentioned briefly above about the progression of Edward's
    passions. Dowell makes the claim that these were 'quite logical in their
    progression upwards': 'They began with a servant, went on to a courtesan and
    then to a quite nice woman, very unsuitably mated [...] And after this lady came
    Maisie Maidan, and after poor Maisie only one more affair and then – the real
    passion of his life' (*GS* 45-46). This passage may help orient the reader in what is
    becoming a confusing array of love affairs involving Edward by enumerating
    them in chronological order, but it also contains a significant element of
    misdirection. Retrospectively, it becomes clear that the phrase 'only one more
    affair' refers to Florence and 'the real passion of his life' to Nancy. But since at
    this stage of the sequence the reader still does not know who Nancy is, whereas
    his attention has been repeatedly drawn to the relationship between Edward and
    Florence, it is very likely that Florence would be viewed at this point as the
    climax of Edward's upward 'progression' of passions, rather than as the affair
    indifferently mentioned by Dowell right before that. This and the retrospective
    patterning which follows in later stages of the textual sequence are part of a
    surprising global shift in the novel's focus of interest from Florence (in its first
    half) to Nancy (in its second), with the former brushed quite contemptuously
    aside.
11  Particularly the essays 'On Impressionism' (1914), 'Techniques' (1935), and
    passages from *Joseph Conrad: a Personal Remembrance* (1924).
12  Ford, *Joseph Conrad: a Personal Remembrance*, London: Duckworth, 1924 –
    henceforth *JC*; p. 186.
13  Ford, 'Techniques', in *Critical Writings of Ford Madox Ford*, ed. Frank
    MacShane, Lincoln: University of Nebraska Press, 1964, p. 59.
14  This becomes especially clear in Shklovsky's praise of Laurence Sterne for
    avoiding such realistic motivations in *Tristram Shandy*, by laying bare the
    technique of the time shift. See 'Sterne's *Tristram Shandy*: Stylistic
    Commentary', in *Russian Formalist Criticism: Four Essays*, translated by Lee T.
    Lemon and Marion J. Reis, Lincoln: University of Nebraska Press, 1965 [1921],
    p. 30.
15  For a mapping of Ford and Shklovsky's contrasting approaches within a broader
    framework, see Meir Sternberg's extensive discussion of the concept of
    'motivation' in 'Mimesis and Motivation: The Two Faces of Fictional
    Coherence', *Poetics Today*, 33 (2012), 329-483.

16  Max Saunders, 'Introduction', in *The Good Soldier*, Oxford: Oxford University Press, 2012, p. xiii – henceforth 'Saunders'.

17  Such self-pointing of a work to its innovative poetic principles, particularly toward its end – as if in a final attempt to help the reader's comprehension – is far from rare in modernist literature. See Meir Sternberg's discussion of this phenomenon in several major modernist novels – James Joyce's *Ulysses*, Virginia Woolf's *Mrs Dalloway* and William Faulkner's *Light in August*. (Though with a different principle involved – that of the foregrounding of analogical patterning against the background of weak causality.) 'The Compositional Principles of Faulkner's *Light in August* and the Poetics of the Modern Novel' [in Hebrew], *Ha-Sifrut*, 2 (1970), 532.

18  And see, in this context, the characterization of Dowell's attitude to his act of narration as 'apprehensive' in contrast to the 'facetious' attitude of Tristram Shandy, another well-known self-conscious narrator (in Skinner 293). As noted in Saunders xvi, Ford's revisions to the manuscript show him adjusting the balance between Dowell 'as a mouthpiece [of Ford]' and 'as a fully-realized character', excising some of Dowell's comments about novels so as to make him sound less literary. A major example of such an excised comment is the alternative beginning of Chapter 2 in part I, where Dowell considers how it is best to tell the story: 'I have asked novelists about these things but they don't seem able to tell you much. They say it comes […]' (*GS* 196). The final version of this passage, by contrast, highlights the emotional (rather than consciously 'artistic') aspect of Dowell's considerations – his need to imagine 'a sympathetic soul' opposite him (*GS* 15).

19  By this I mean that the text has a historical truth claim, even if it is not considered entirely reliable factually.

20  This 'English gentleman' whose characterization is provided in the segment I have omitted here is, in fact, very reminiscent of Edward Ashburnham, which makes it likely that Ford was thinking, at least in part, of *The Good Soldier* as an example of the 'formula' he is explaining.

Bad Nauheim: the Sprudelhof (Spa Inn) and spa today.

# FROM DISFIGURED TO TRANSFIGURED PAST: MEMORY AND HISTORY IN *THE GOOD SOLDIER*

## Isabelle Brasme

**Abstract**

Narration in *The Good Soldier* has been most noted for its disconnectedness and deliberate unreliability. Dowell not only comes out as an undependable story teller, but repeatedly highlights his own untrustworthiness through the novel. I wish to argue that Ford uses this flawed narrator as a tool to investigate the process of storytelling. Given the historical framework of the novel and the relentless focus on the Fourth of August date, the question of storytelling itself may be also considered as leading to a larger interrogation of the way in which history is written. My perspective is mainly informed by Ricœur's analysis of the relationship between time and narration, and between memory and history. It may indeed appear that Dowell in *The Good Soldier* establishes and explores a phenomenology of memory. In *Time and Narrative*, Ricœur examines the 'refiguration' of time via narration. This chapter contends that the unavoidable refiguration of the past, whilst it may initially appear as disfiguring truth, may ultimately be construed as a transfiguration which is in no way inferior to the original event. Ford intimates to us that in the awareness of the limits of recapturing time past through memory, which is key to his theory of literary impressionism, also lies an updated ethics of the narrative.

Narration in *The Good Soldier* has been most noted for its disconnectedness and deliberate unreliability. Dowell not only comes out as an undependable story teller, but repeatedly highlights his own untrustworthiness. I wish to argue that Ford uses this flawed narrator as a tool to investigate the process of storytelling and question the authority of the narrative stance, not only in the traditional novelistic genre inherited from the nineteenth century, but perhaps also in modernist fiction. Given the historical framework of the novel and the relentless focus on the 4th August date, the question of storytelling itself may also be considered as leading to a larger interrogation of the way in which history is written. My perspective will be mainly informed by Paul Ricœur's analysis of the relationship between time and narration, and between memory and history. It may indeed appear that Ford in *The Good Soldier* establishes and explores a phenomenology of memory. In *Time and Narrative*, Ricœur examines the 'refiguration' of time via narration. This chapter contends that the unavoidable refiguration of the past, whilst it may initially appear as disfiguring truth, may ultimately be construed as a transfiguration which is in no way inferior to the original event. Ford intimates to us that in the awareness of the limits of recapturing time past through memory, which is key to his theory of literary impressionism, also lies an updated ethics of narrative.

## History and Narrative

Ford's involvement in history and history writing is well established. Some of his novels were unambiguously conceived as historical fiction, such as the *Fifth Queen* trilogy, or are directly steeped in historical events, such as *Parade's End*, the genesis of which Ford explained in these terms: 'I wanted the novelist in fact to appear in his really proud position as historian of his own time'.[1] Some of his non-fiction works are also explicitly presented as historical surveys, such as *A History of our Own Times*, or *The Cinque Ports*, whose subtitle is 'A Historical and descriptive record'.[2] I wish to examine the way in which *The Good Soldier*, whilst less openly historical and primarily concerned with narration – its subtitle and Ford's original title, which later became the first sentence of the novel, both describe it as a 'tale' and a 'story' – has in fact as much claims to being considered as a historical novel: a work not only on history, but also and perhaps more importantly, on history writing.

*The Fifth Queen* aims at an impressionist rendering of the innermost feelings of historical figures and of the private background behind public events. We might consider *The Good Soldier* as taking the reverse route: using private figures and individual drama with public events acting as a meaningful, albeit silent backdrop. Ultimately, however, the aim in both novels is the same. Ford's vision of history writing is of course an impressionist one, building up layer upon layer of features, epiphenomena, personalities, that all participate in the big picture – and contribute to its eventual collapse in the case of the pre-war era described in *The Good Soldier*. In the International Ford Madox Ford Studies volume on History and Representation, Elena Lamberti reminded us that Ford 'wanted to render "the spirit of an age, of a town, of a movement", something that, Ford tells us, cannot be done with "facts", but with "impressions"'.[3] The object of Lamberti's essay was Ford's explicitly historical work in *A History of Our Own Times*. Our focus here shall be on the historiographical dimension of *The Good Soldier*, and of its consequences on narration.

It is significant that Florence in the narrative displays erudition not only about history, but about major history writers, as she reads various classic historians before the visit to Marburg Castle: Ranke, Symonds, Motley, Luther.[4] Interestingly, Florence herself is likened to Mrs Markham, who was known for writing a bowdlerised version of history. The question of how history is written thus becomes very early on a theme of the narrative. The characters are not only agents, but writers of history, and questionable writers at that. Significantly, soon after patronizingly likening Florence to Mrs Markham, Dowell denies his own competence as historian, confessing: 'I am not an historian' (*GS* 35).

The mingling of public history and private narrative is highlighted from the beginning of the novel. This is manifest from the very first pages, as Dowell likens the two couples to a 'minuet de la cour' (*GS* 11) on the eve of the French Revolution: 'The mob may sack Versailles; the Trianon may fall, but surely the minuet – the minuet itself is dancing itself away' (11). The intermingling of public and private history is made particularly salient when Dowell relates the visit to Marburg castle, as Florence insists on Henry VIII's private life as placing an inordinate weight on public affairs. Public and private history have a mutual influence upon one another: on the one hand, history imparts a fateful backdrop to the events, as is clear in the passage just mentioned since this visit to Marburg Castle marks a crucial step in the two couples' relationship. On the other hand, whilst the First World War is not directly referred to, it is however constantly in our minds, because of the time when *The Good Soldier* was published, of its title (fortuitous though Ford claims it to be in his dedicatory letter) and through the continual reference to the 4th August.

Beyond the story, the chronology of the narrative itself is significant in terms of its mingling with History: Dowell starts writing it six months after he arrived in England (in the first page of the narration, he tells us: 'Six months ago I had never been to England'; *GS* 9), which was in September 1913, around a month after Florence's suicide on August 4th 1913: 'The fourth of August 1913, the last day of my absolute ignorance – and, I assure you, of my perfect happiness' (71). He thus started writing around March 1914. Further along the text, Dowell tells us he has been 'writing away at this story for now six months' (120), meaning we are now in the late summer of 1914, with the historical weightiness that this implies. Dowell then halts his writing for eighteen months, as is made clear in the fifth chapter of part IV when he resumes his narration: 'I am writing this now, I should say, a full eighteen months after the words that end my last chapter' (149). This eighteen-month interval means Dowell should now be writing in the spring of 1916; so that the ending of this 'saddest story' is supposed to take place a year after the novel was even published, in March 1915.[5] What can we construe of this anticipated bleak ending as regards Ford's view of his own time? Perhaps that he was despairing of the state of that civilisation to which Dowell keeps referring; that he believed the grounds of disaster for humanity were lying deeper than the war, and didn't stop there. This is also apparent in his later novel, *Parade's End*, where the framing of chapters or volumes concerned with the war by passages occurring pre- and post-war emphasizes the fact that the fate of the characters, and more largely of the civilisation they are steeped in, cannot be entirely determined by the war.

Beyond Dowell's attempt – and failure – at deciphering the events leading to his own 'saddest story', we may say that Ford thus also explores the circumstances in which World War One broke out. Ford's refusal explicitly to mention current events within his novel may indicate that he merely strives to approach the present peripherally, to render the impression of Edwardian England and Europe, without claiming to know whether the war was a cause of civilisation's collapse, or a symptom of a civilisation already collapsing.

Historian Paul Veyne argued about the process of history writing as similar to that of story-telling:

> History does not explain, in the sense that it cannot deduce and foresee [. . .]; its explanations are not the referral to a principle that would make the event intelligible, but are the meaning that the historian gives to the account.[6]

> The problem of causality in history is a survival of the paleoepistemological era [. . . .] The physicist goes back from the phenomenon to its principle; he deduces from a more general theory the behaviour of a more limited system, for the explanatory process goes from top to bottom. The historian, on the other hand, confines himself to the horizontal plane.[7]

The interest for *The Good Soldier* is twofold: firstly, according to Veyne, history belongs more to the field of storytelling than to that of science. Events cannot be accounted for in the way physical phenomena can. Historians just tell events, and as soon as an event is being told, point of view enters into play. Secondly, Veyne insists on the absence of causality, or at least on the impossibility to delineate accurate and exhaustive causes for an event. Veyne thus distances himself from historicist tradition. It appears to me that this process is precisely the one Ford adopts in *The Good Soldier*, having Dowell undertake and eventually give up the task of travelling through the past to ascertain the causes of what happened. The 'Post hoc ergo propter hoc' tenet is thus exposed as a fallacy.

This argument can be related to Linda Hutcheon's position that there has been a recent 'shift from VALIDATION to SIGNIFICAT-ION'[8] in postmodernist historiography. In *A Poetics of Postmodernism*, Hutcheon argues that:

> Historiographic metafiction refutes the natural or common-sense methods of distinguishing between historical fact and fiction. It refuses the view that only history has a truth claim, both questioning the ground of that claim in historiography and asserting that history and fiction are discourses; human constructs, signifying systems [. . . .] The past is 'archaeologized' [. . .] but its reservoir of available materials is always acknowledged as a textualized one.[9]

Veyne's work was considered as daringly novel when it was published in the 1970s; Hutcheon's work is even more recent, and focuses on postmodernism. However, exactly the same arguments can be found in Ford's thoughts on history. In his essay 'Creative History and the Historic Sense', written in 1903-04, Ford argues that 'History conceived as an exact Science is an impossibility'.[10] His impressionist technique aims at proposing a new epistemology, one that sets history and fiction on the same footing. The essay concludes thus:

> In their really high manifestations History and Fiction are one: they are documented, tolerant, vivid [. . . .] Fiction indeed, so long as it is not written with a purpose, is Contemporary History and History is the same thing as the Historic Novel, as long as it is inspired with the Historic Sense.[11]

This bears an uncanny resemblance to Hutcheon's equating of history and fiction as discourses, and invites us to ponder whether Ford wasn't ahead of his contemporaries in his reflection on history: his arguments sound much closer to a postmodern analysis than to those developed at the beginning of the twentieth century.

The question for *The Good Soldier* is whether Dowell himself can be considered as being 'inspired with the Historic Sense'. This is where conjuring up Ricœur's analysis of the relationship between memory and history may prove fruitful.

**A Phenomenology of Memory**

In *Time and Narrative*, Volume II, Ricœur argues that narrative action is the means for man of dealing with time, which otherwise only exists as a non-signifying, inexpressible, inhuman reality – something that we cannot grasp. Ricœur talks here of a 'fictive experience of time'[12] as our only possible approach of the past. Although Ricœur conjures a variety of thinkers and modes of thinking, the phenomenologist approach is openly favoured. Dowell himself is a clear advocate of phenomenology when he argues:

> If for nine years I have possessed a goodly apple that is rotten at the core and discover its rottenness only in nine years and six months less four days, isn't it true to say that for nine years I possessed a goodly apple? (*GS* 12)

This comes early on in the narrative, and may sound programmatic of his epistemological posture in the novel. Additionally, Dowell's seemingly irrelevant mention of the 'black and white cow land[ing] on its back in the middle of a stream', which he is the only one to see through the train window on his way to Marburg castle, is perhaps also an echo of Forster's presentation of phenomenology in the opening pages of *The Longest Journey*, published in 1907. Forster's novel begins with the following dialogue:

> 'The cow is there', said Ansell [...].
> 'You have not proved it', said a voice.
> 'I have proved it to myself'.
> 'I have proved to myself that she isn't', said the voice. 'The cow is *not* there'.[13]

Some of Forster's stories were published in *The English Review* at the same time when *The Longest Journey* came out, which does render plausible the hypothesis that Ford had indeed read this novel. The mention of the cow in Dowell's narrative underlines the utter unreliability of his account, but also its absolute irreplaceability, since he is the only witness to tell the events.

In the third volume of his work on *Time and Narrative*, Ricœur describes *The Magic Mountain* as 'a novel about time, a novel about illness, and a novel about culture'.[14] This description – and indeed, Ricœur's whole analysis of *The Magic Mountain* – may apply to *The Good Soldier*. Like *The Magic Mountain*, *The Good Soldier* is a novel where the experience of time has a structural impact on the narration. Narration allows a 'refiguration' of time into a graspable entity. The question, however, is whether Dowell's work as a narrator enacts a 'configuration' or 'refiguration' of time, to take up Ricœur's phrasing, or whether his storytelling only achieves a disfiguration of the past.

In one of his latest works, *Memory, History, Forgetting,* Ricœur goes on to re-examine and somewhat qualify his thoughts developed in *Time and Narrative,* addressing in particular the flaws inherent in the representation of the past available through a memory that is always inevitably at a distance from it – if not openly mistaken or defective. Ricœur chooses to revisit and revalidate Bergson to differentiate between the two kinds of memory. Bergson, in *Matière et Mémoire,* argues that 'Spontaneous recollection is perfect from the outset; time can add nothing to its image without disfiguring it'.[15] Bergson's ideas were highly favoured among English intellectuals in the early 1910s, and his theories on time and memory do help understand *The Good Soldier* better.[16] Bergson (and Ricœur in his wake) favour the process of *mneme,* spontaneous memory, as it appears closer to the original event on what Ricœur calls the 'gradient of distanciation';[17] conversely, *anamnesis,* which corresponds to the more active, self-conscious process of remembering, appears as twice removed from the past. Ricœur argued that 'the interference of the pragmatics of memory [. . .] has a jamming effect on the entire problematic of veracity'.[18]

In *The Good Soldier,* Dowell is unwilling (or at least unable, as in states of post-traumatic stress disorder, which might be another interesting perspective to adopt) to gain access to the past otherwise than through painstaking retrospection, or what Ricœur termed 'laborious recollection' ('rappel laborieux'), as opposed to 'spontaneous recollection'. Dowell keeps resisting the fact that he as a subject is faced with a flux of data that are forever changing and reconfiguring. He tries for instance to decompose past duration through well-defined phases and steps. This perception of time, however, is a construct, and as such, pushes the actual past event even further away. This is highlighted by the many flaws of Dowell's apparently precise reconstitution of the past. The most significant errors concern those related with the fateful 4th August. On the day Florence dies, that is to say 4 August 1913, Dowell remarks to Leonora that their acquaintance started 'on that day, exactly nine years before' (*GS* 69). The two couples are said to have met in the evening (23). However, 4 August 1904 is also referred to as the day when Maisie Maidan dies: 'The death of Mrs. Maidan occurred on the 4th of

August 1904' (57). This is supposedly also the day when Florence takes the foursome to Marburg Castle in the afternoon: 'That enables me to fix exactly the day of our going to the town of M—. For it was the very day poor Mrs Maidan died' (51). This excursion was prepared several days ahead on the part of Florence, and implied an already settled relationship between the Ashburnhams and the Dowells.[19] The more precise Dowell attempts to be, the more mistakes he makes, and the more befuddling his narration is for the reader. The 'interference of the pragmatics of memory' does have the 'jamming effect' described by Ricœur.

Dowell's obsession with keeping track of time, which is made evident through his compulsive counting of days, months, or years all along the narrative, can be related with his 'habit of counting [his] footsteps', which is mentioned at the beginning of the novel (*GS* 22). Dowell boasts of his perfect memory of distances: 'I know the exact distances' and proceeds to give us the exact number of steps leading from one place to another in Nauheim:

> From the Hotel Regina you took one hundred and eighty-seven paces, then, turning sharp, lefthanded, four hundred and twenty took you straight down to the fountain. From the Englischer Hof, staring on the sidewalk, it was ninety-seven paces and the same four hundred and twenty, but turning lefthanded this time. (*GS* 22)

Similarly, Dowell keeps mentioning specific dates in order to claim accuracy, to the point that some passages are written 'in a diary form':

> Thus: on the 1st of September they returned from Nauheim [. . . .] By the 1st of October they were all going to meets together [. . . .] About the 6th of that month Edward gave the horse to young Selmes [. . . .] On the 20th she read the account of the divorce case [. . . .] On the 23rd she had the conversation with her aunt in the hall. Her aunt's coming to her bedroom did not occur until the 12th of November. (*GS* 142)

The tone and rhythm of this passage, with its short, matter-of-fact sentences, is strikingly similar to the passage where Dowell charts the town of Nauheim through the number of his footsteps.

Simultaneously, and within the same page, however, Dowell admits the unfeasibility of this kind of exact cartography of the past:

> I have been casting back again; but I cannot help it. It is so difficult to keep all these people going. I tell you about Leonora and bring her up to date; then about

> Edward who has fallen behind. And then the girl gets hopelessly left behind. (*GS* 142)

Dowell here keeps mentioning memory in terms of space: 'back', 'going', 'fallen behind', 'left behind'. This is precisely why the kind of reconstruction that Dowell hopes for, cannot work: he tries to summon up the past by rendering time through space. This handling of time, however, is a construct, as Bergson underlines, and as such, pushes the actual past even further away. According to Bergson, the difference between life and this kind of reconstruction is a difference between the temporal plane and the spatial plane. Dowell's endeavour may seem as bound to fail because he cannot, or will not, embrace a Bergsonian approach to memory.

However, one of Ricœur's main points in *Memory, History, Forgetting* is that this imperfect reconstruction of time is our only way to the past:

> We have no other resource, concerning our reference to the past, except memory itself. To memory is tied an ambition, a claim – that of being faithful to the past. In this respect, the deficiencies stemming from forgetting [. . .] should not be treated straight away as pathological forms, as dysfunctions, but as the shadowy underside of the bright region of memory, which binds us to what has passed before we remember it. If we can reproach memory with being unreliable, it is precisely because it is our one and only resource for signifying the past-character of what we declare we remember. No one would dream of addressing the same reproach to imagination.[20]

This admission that memory, albeit flawed, is our only access to the past, is very much akin to what we the readers may be led to conclude on reading Dowell's meandering narrative. As Samuel Hynes pointed out in his remarkable essay on 'The Epistemology of *The Good Soldier*':[21]

> the factors which seem to disqualify Dowell – his ignorance, his inability to act, his profound doubt – are not seen in relation to any norm; there is neither a 'primary author' nor a 'knower' [. . . .] There is only Dowell.[22]

The narrator's limitations in *The Good Soldier* have been time and again highlighted and analysed: sometimes as deliberate, at other times as unintentional on the part of Dowell. Ultimately, beyond Dowell's own constant feeling of failure, these limitations *are* Ford's own narrative goals. By choosing a blatantly limited narrator as our only access to the story, Ford wishes to emphasize the vanity of any form of reconstruction of events. In the essay 'Techniques', Ford stresses the unreliability of the narrator as a major device of his impressionism, one that was inspired by Maupassant:

> The novel must be put into the mouth of a narrator – who must be limited by probability as to what he can know of the affair that he is adumbrating [. . . .] The narration is thus a little more limited in possibilities [. . . .] A narrator, that is to say, being already a fictional character, may indulge in any prejudices or wrong-headedness and any likings or dislikes for the other characters of the book, for he is just a living being like anybody else.[23]

The phrase 'limited in possibilities' finds a striking echo in Ricœur's conclusion to Volume III of *History and Narrative*:

> It ought not to be said that our eulogy to narrative *unthinkingly* has given life again to the claims of the constituting subject to master all meaning. On the contrary, it is fitting that every mode of thought should verify the validity of its employment by taking an exact measure of the limits to its employment.[24]

In *The Good Soldier* indeed, it may appear that Ford is pushing the same kind of reasoning to its ultimate point by using a blatantly unreliable narrator, in order to demonstrate the way in which memories, remembered impressions, are better than nothing at all – are valid because they exist. The interest of Dowell's narration does not lie in its validity or absence thereof; it is, therefore it has some legitimacy. This is where the layering of narrative instances in *The Good Soldier* comes into play. An alternative narrative emerges beyond that of Dowell's; a narrative that is effected between Ford and his reader, and that may vary with each reading.

To take up again Hutcheon's phrasing, Dowell's endeavour can definitely be termed as 'archaeological', trying to dig out layer upon layer of memories. His problem is that he doesn't seem to accept the fact that this 'reservoir' is inevitably 'textualized'. The aporia is Dowell's, not Ford's.

This may help confirm the idea that Ford's works not only encompass modernist aesthetics, but also prefigure what later came to be considered as postmodernist views, especially in terms of deconstructionism. Instead of offering an alternative, satisfying artwork to the witnessed chaos of the world, as other modernists did, Ford leaves us with a mere adumbration and a variety of possible ways to redefine the world. His means of representation is ultimately a gesture forever suspended *towards* representation.

## NOTES

1  Ford Madox Ford, *It Was the Nightingale* (1933), Manchester: Carcanet, 2007, p. 180.
2  The International Ford Madox Ford Studies volume *History and Representation in Ford Madox Ford's Writings*, ed. Joseph Wiesenfarth, IFMFS 3, Amsterdam: Rodopi, 2004, focused on Ford's status as 'historian of his own time'.
3  Elena Lamberti, 'Writing History: Ford and the Debate on 'Objective Truth' in the Late 20th Century', *History and Representation in Ford Madox Ford's Writings*, p. 99.
4  Ford Madox Ford, *The Good Soldier*, Norton Critical Edition, ed. Martin Stannard, New York and London: W. W. Norton & Company, 1995, p. 34; henceforth *GS*.
5  For more detail about the narrative's chronology, see George Letissier, 'Fatalité des dates et chronologie déboussolée' in *Synthèse d'une œuvre: The Good Soldier*, Paris: Editions du Temps (2005), pp. 118-123; and Max Saunders' appendix to the Oxford World's Classics edition of *The Good Soldier*, Oxford: Oxford University Press, 2012, pp. 214-24.
6  Paul Veyne, *Writing History: Essay on Epistemology*, trans. Mina Moore-Rinvolucri, Manchester: Manchester University Press, 1984, p. 90. Original text: 'L'histoire n'explique pas, en ce sens qu'elle ne peut déduire et prévoir [. . .]; ses explications ne sont pas le renvoi à un principe qui rendrait l'événement intelligible, elles sont le sens que l'historien prête au récit'. Paul Veyne, *Comment on écrit l'histoire, Essai d'épistémologie* (1971), Paris: Éditions du Seuil, 1996, p. 127.
7  *Ibid.*, p. 91. Original text: 'Le problème de la causalité en histoire est une survivance de l'ère paléo-épistémologique [. . . .] Le physicien remonte du phénomène à son principe ; il déduit d'une théorie plus générale le comportement d'un système plus limité ; le processus explicatif va de haut en bas. L'historien se cantonne au contraire dans le plan horizontal'. Paul Veyne, *op. cit.*, p. 128).
8  Linda Hutcheon, *A Poetics of Postmodernism*, New York: Routledge, 1988, p. 90.
9  *Ibid.*, p. 93.
10  Ford Madox Ford, 'Creative History and the Historic Sense', in *Critical Essays*, ed. Max Saunders and Richard Stang, Manchester: Carcanet, 2002, p. 5.
11  *Ibid.*, p. 13.
12  In Part III, Chapter 4: 'expérience temporelle fictive'.
13  E. M. Forster, *The Longest Journey*, London: Penguin, 2001, p. 3.
14  '[U]n roman du temps, un roman de la maladie et un roman de la culture': Paul Ricœur, *Temps et Récit 2*, Paris: Éditions du Seuil, 1984, p. 219. Translation: *Time and Narrative, volume 2,* trans. Kathleen McLaughlin, Chicago: University of Chicago Press, 1990, p. 116.
15  'Le souvenir spontané est tout de suite parfait; le temps ne pourra rien ajouter à son image sans le dénaturer'. Bergson, *Matière et Mémoire* (1896), quoted by Ricœur in *La Mémoire l'histoire, l'oubli*, Paris: Seuil, 2000, p. 31. Translation Nancy Margaret Paul and W. Scott Palmer, London: George Allen, 1911, p. 95.
16  'Quand nous nous remémorons des faits passés, quand nous interprétons des faits présents, quand nous entendons un discours, quand nous suivons la pensée d'autrui et quand nous nous écoutons penser nous-mêmes, enfin quand un système

complexe de représentations occupe notre intelligence, nous sentons que nous pouvons prendre deux attitudes différentes, l'une de tension et l'autre de relâchement, qui se distinguent surtout en ce que le sentiment de l'effort est présent dans l'une et absent de l'autre. Le jeu des représentations est-il le même dans les deux cas?' (Bergson, *L'Énergie spirituelle* [1919], in *Œuvres*, Paris: PUF, 1963, p. 930).

17  Paul Ricœur, *Memory, History, Forgetting*, translated by Kathleen Blamey, Chicago: University of Chicago Press, 2006, p. 25. Original text: 'gradient de distanciation', Paul Ricœur, *La Mémoire, l'histoire, l'oubli*, Paris: Seuil, 2000, p. 30.

18  Paul Ricœur, *Memory, History, Forgetting*, p. 4. Original text: 'l'interférence de la pragmatique de la mémoire [. . .] exerce un effet de brouillage sur la prétention de la mémoire à la véracité.' Paul Ricœur, *La Mémoire, l'histoire, l'oubli*, Paris: Seuil, 2000, p. 4.

19  This discrepancy is noted by Thomas Moser in *The Life in the Fiction of Ford Madox Ford*, Princeton: Princeton University Press, 1980, pp. 161-2.

20  Paul Ricœur, *Memory, History, Forgetting*, p. 21. Original text: 'Nous n'avons pas d'autre ressource, concernant la référence au passé, que la mémoire elle-même. A la mémoire est attaché une ambition, une prétention, celle d'être fidèle au passé; à cet égard, les déficiences relevant de l'oubli [. . .] ne doivent pas être traitées d'emblée comme des formes pathologiques, comme des dysfonctions, mais comme l'envers de l'ombre de la région éclairée de la mémoire, qui nous relie à ce qui s'est passé avant que nous en fassions mémoire. Si l'on peut faire reproche à la mémoire de s'avérer peu fiable, c'est précisément parce qu'elle est notre seule et unique ressource pour signifier le caractère passé de ce dont nous déclarons nous souvenir. Nul ne songerait à adresser pareil reproche à l'imagination'. Paul Ricœur, *La Mémoire, l'histoire, l'oubli*, Paris: Seuil, 2000, p. 26.

21  Samuel Hynes, 'The Epistemology of *The Good Soldier*', *Sewanee Review* 69:2 (Spring 1961), pp. 225-35; reprinted in the Norton edition of *The Good Soldier*, pp. 310-17.

22  Samuel Hynes, 'The Epistemology of *The Good Soldier*', *GS* 312.

23  'Techniques', 1935, *GS* 298.

24  Paul Ricœur, *History and Narrative III*, trans. Kathleen Blamey, Chicago: Chicago University Press, 1990, 274. Original text: 'La pertinence de la réplique du récit aux apories du temps diminue d'un stade à l'autre, au point que le temps paraît sortir vainqueur de la lutte, après avoir été tenu captif dans les filets de l'intrigue. Il est bon qu'il en soit ainsi: il ne sera pas dit que l'éloge du récit aura sournoisement redonné vie à la prétention du sujet constituant à maîtriser le sens. Il convient au contraire à tout mode de pensée de vérifier la validité de son emploi dans la circonscription qui lui est assignée, en prenant une exacte mesure des limites de son emploi.' (*Temps et Récit 3*, Paris: Seuil, 1985, p. 488). '[. . .] *Il ne sera pas dit, non plus, que l'aveu des limites du récit, corrélatif de l'aveu du mystère du temps, aura cautionné l'obscurantisme*; le mystère du temps n'équivaut pas à un interdit pesant sur le langage; il suscite plutôt l'exigence de penser plus et de dire autrement' (p. 489).

# 'IT IS MELODRAMA; BUT I CAN'T HELP IT': DOWELL'S MELODRAMATIC IMAGINATION

## Rob Hawkes

**Abstract**

While much discussion of *The Good Soldier* has focused on the question of its genre, little attention has been paid to what I describe as Dowell's 'melodramatic imagination'. This chapter argues for the recognition of melodrama as an important aspect of the novel's generic fabric. As critics such as Peter Brooks and Ben Singer underscore, melodrama is an acutely modern form, having emerged in the aftermath of the French Revolution and being marked by the tendency to articulate whilst simultaneously mitigating the uncertainties and contradictions of modernity. In emphasising the significance of Dowell's melodramatic imagination, I compare *The Good Soldier* to Ford's *Mr. Fleight* (1913) which also draws heavily on melodrama's dramatic apparatus. For Dowell, I argue that the melodramatic mode becomes a powerful narrative resource, allowing him to negotiate a series of apparently incomprehensible events by adopting a form that circumvents the necessity to make sense.

For all its narrative intricacy and bewildering chronological complexity, the plot of *The Good Soldier* revolves around just a small number of key incidents. Many of these events take place on 4 August and, of course, Dowell famously describes several incompatible events as having occurred on 4 August 1904: the very first meeting of the Dowells and the Ashburnhams in 'the dining-room of the Hotel Excelsior'[1] and the death of Maisie Maidan following the 'protest scene' at Marburg castle. For the purposes of this essay, though, I want to begin with another of these red-letter days: 4 August 1913. This date marks what is arguably the novel's most significant turning point: the fateful evening on which Edward Ashburnham suddenly declares his passion for his ward Nancy Rufford and is overheard by Florence Dowell, who commits suicide in response to what she hears and thus brings to an end her nine-year affair with Ashburnham. It is this event, furthermore, that destroys John Dowell's 'long, tranquil life, which was just stepping a minuet' (*GS* 11) by revealing the duplicity of both his best friend and his wife and sets in motion the series of events leading to Ashburnham's own suicide and to Nancy's mental collapse. The scene which precipitates all of this is described by Dowell as follows:

> Anyhow, there you have the picture, the immensely tall trees, elms most of them, towering and feathering away up into the black mistiness that trees seem to gather about them at night; the silhouettes of those two upon the seat; the beams of light coming from the Casino, the woman all in black peeping with fear behind the tree-trunk. It is melodrama; but I can't help it. (*GS* 80)

The 'woman all in black' is, of course, Florence, poised to run back to her hotel room and poison herself. What interests me here is Dowell's description of the scene as melodrama and, even more intriguingly, as melodrama that *can't be helped*. A common complaint about modernist novels is that 'nothing happens' in them, but this accusation can hardly be levelled at Ford's masterpiece. It is packed with incident: betrayals, love affairs, storms on the high seas, violence, suicide and madness; and if one simply considers the stripped-down series of events that make up the tale – which Vincent Cheng was kind enough to provide in 1986[2] – then it does indeed come across as a work of high melodrama. And yet, this is not what a great many readers are struck by when first encountering the text. Instead, discussions of the novel often focus on its technical achievement, or on the problem of Dowell's unreliable narration and the epistemological questions it raises. Furthermore, although a significant part of the critical discussion surrounding *The Good Soldier* has focused on the question of its genre, what hasn't been discussed in depth is what I will describe here as Dowell's 'melodramatic imagination'.[3] Indeed, I will argue that melodrama needs to be acknowledged as an important aspect of *The Good Soldier*'s generic texture, while asking why Dowell might want to view his adoption of the melodramatic mode as something that he 'can't help'.

Ever since Mark Schorer first described *The Good Soldier* as 'a comedy of humor' in 1948, the debate has raged among critics as to whether the novel should be read as essentially a comic or a tragic vision.[4] If we turn our attention to the novel itself, it becomes apparent that the seeds of this contention, over which generations of critics have argued, are rooted in Dowell's own language and in his perplexed attempts to provide shape and structure to his tale:

> I call this the Saddest Story, rather than 'The Ashburnham Tragedy', just because it is so sad, just because there was no current to draw things along to

> a swift and inevitable end. There is about it none of the elevation that accompanies tragedy; there is about it no nemesis, no destiny. Here were two noble people – for I am convinced that both Edward and Leonora had noble natures – here, then, were two noble natures [. . . .] And they themselves steadily deteriorated. And why? For what purpose? To point what lesson? It is all a darkness.
>
> There is not even any villain in the story [. . . .] (*GS* 113–14)

Here, Dowell is characteristically vague about the criteria by which his story may or may not be understood as a 'tragedy'. Nevertheless, whatever the requirements, Dowell appears certain that sadness alone is not enough. A series of qualities are evoked that would, it seems, apply to tragedy, but which Dowell believes to be absent from the story of the Ashburnhams: inevitability, elevation, nemesis, destiny. The sense of nobility, conversely, is present in the tale, but since the deterioration of these 'two noble natures' is not accompanied by a sense of purpose, or a lesson, it remains outside Dowell's definition of tragedy. The final ingredient that 'the Saddest Story' lacks, for Dowell, is a villain. Although none of these terms is explored or explained by Dowell, readers with even the most rudimentary understanding of Aristotelian poetics are bound to find at least some of them familiar.

In the final stages of the novel, as Dowell begins to grasp ever more desperately for shape and stability, he turns his previous assertion on its head and claims that Leonora 'took on the complexion of a mad woman; of a woman very wicked; of the villain of the piece' (*GS* 159).[5] No sooner has this allegation of villainy been lodged, though, it too is reversed as Dowell attempts to conclude his narrative with something approaching finality:

> Well, that is the end of the story. And when I come to look at it I see that it is a happy ending with wedding bells and all. The villains – for obviously Edward and the girl were villains – have been punished by suicide and madness. The heroine – the perfectly normal, virtuous and slightly deceitful heroine – has become the happy wife of a perfectly normal, virtuous and slightly deceitful husband. (*GS* 166–7)

The fact that Dowell's efforts here to impose order onto the events he narrates seem increasingly frantic and untrustworthy is an indication of the degree to which the reader's faith in Dowell, as narrator, is persistently destabilised as *The Good Soldier* draws to a close. The bitter irony with which he declares the 'obviousness' of Edward's and Nancy's villainy further undermines his claim to have discovered a 'happy ending' for the saddest story. However, the contortions to which Dowell seems determined to subject his tale can be read as a belated and somewhat vexed attempt to place the narrative within a recognisable and meaningful generic framework, thus prefiguring the problems critics have come up against when seeking to identify a specific genre for the text.

What I find particularly striking about Dowell's struggle in this regard are his difficulties in making judgements of an ethical nature. Despite his betrayal at the hands of his best friend and wife, Dowell is reluctant to identify a villain in his tale and when, eventually, he tries to do so he is uncertain as to whether either Leonora or Edward and the girl are the true villains. In *The Political Unconscious*, Fredric Jameson argues that, to function properly, tragedy must lack such an ethical dimension, describing it as 'in a special sense "beyond good and evil"':

> The ethical opposition is [. . .] wholly absent from tragedy, whose fundamental staging of the triumph of an inhuman destiny or fate generates a perspective which radically transcends the purely individual categories of good and evil. This proposition may be demonstrated by our feeling, when, in something that looks like a tragedy, we encounter judgements of a more properly ethical type (re-emergence of 'heroes' and 'villains'), that the text in question is rather to be considered a melodrama, that is, a degraded form of romance.[6]

As we have seen, *The Good Soldier* presents Dowell struggling to negotiate with this very set of distinctions, at one moment rejecting the notion that either 'an inhuman destiny or fate' or a 'villain' might be identified within his tale, only to make quite opposite assertions a few pages later. In *The Melodramatic Imagination*, Peter Brooks attempts to rescue the terms 'melodrama' and 'melodramatic' from their habitual usage as derogatory expressions, aptly demonstrated here by Jameson. While acknowledging that melodrama 'generally operates in the mode of romance', Brooks refuses to dismiss it as a degraded form, demonstrating the fundamental importance of the melodramatic mode to the very development of the novel, and to Honoré de Balzac and Henry James in particular.[7] Furthermore, for Brooks, melodrama 'appears to be a peculiarly modern form':

> The origins of melodrama can be accurately located within the context of the French Revolution and its aftermath. This is the epistemological moment which it illustrates and to which it contributes: the moment that symbolically,

> and really, marks the final liquidation of the traditional Sacred and its representative institutions (Church and Monarch), the shattering of the myth of Christendom, the dissolution of an organic and hierarchically cohesive society [. . . .] We may legitimately claim that melodrama becomes the principal mode for uncovering, demonstrating, and making operative the essential moral universe in a post-sacred era. (Brooks 14–15)[8]

In his fascinating study of American 'blood-and-thunder' melodrama in the late nineteenth and early twentieth centuries, Ben Singer also considers the intimate connection between melodrama and modernity:

> Many recent scholars [. . .] have interpreted melodrama's insistence on moral affirmation as a symptomatic response to a new condition of moral ambiguity and individual vulnerability following the erosion of religious and patriarchal traditions and the emergence of rampant cultural discontinuity, ideological flux, and competitive individualism within capitalist modernity. Melodrama expressed the anxiety of moral disarray and then ameliorated it through utopian moral clarity.[9]

The appeal of melodrama's moral polarisation, then, as represented by the virtuous heroes and caped villains of the popular stage, lies in its ability to administer to the needs once provided for by 'the traditional Sacred'. Melodrama, that is to say, provides an image of an ethically intelligible world in a post-sacred era.

In recognising the importance of Dowell's melodramatic imagination in *The Good Soldier*, it is useful to note that significant traces of melodrama can be found elsewhere in Ford's oeuvre. For example, *Mr. Fleight* (1913), published two years before *The Good Soldier*, relies heavily on the dramatic apparatus of melodrama. The novel focuses on the eponymous hero's quest for political and social advancement. Early in the novel, Fleight complains that, despite having 'pots of money', he is 'nobody': 'Society being what it is, I feel that I ought to be Prime Minister, or a Privy Councillor at least'.[10] To this end he enlists the help of Mr Blood, 'the last mastodon', who, a hundred years ago, 'would have represented the Englishman and the gentleman' (*MrF* 14, 8). Blood, we are told, 'cared even less' than 'a halfpenny whether the nation was going to ruin', and we first meet him 'counting the motors against the horse traffic' from the window of his club as a gauge of encroaching modernity (*MrF* 8, 2). Fleight appeals to this sense of ironic enjoyment of the degradation of society in attempting to gain Blood's assistance:

> I know you're too lazy even to mock at Society, let alone to hit it or destroy it.
> But say I'm the fox with the tail on fire that you could set going into the corn.
> If you heartened up a chap like me to becoming a duke and hereditary
> standard-bearer – and heaven knows I'm rich enough – you'd laugh. It would
> be just as funny as watching the cabs on the Embankment. (*MrF* 4)

Blood agrees, advising his new friend that if he wishes 'to go up at all
fast as a climber' he will need to take up politics, become a
constituency MP (at a cost of 'about £2 per vote per annum'), run a
daily paper 'to boom yourself with the general public' and 'a serious
monthly or weekly to advertise you to thinking people', and acquire
'an expensive wife for the society side of things', all of which will
amount to '£150,000 a year for sheer bribery' (*MrF* 21). Thus Fleight
becomes a candidate for parliament and sponsors a literary magazine
called the *New Review*, which forms the second strand of the novel's
plot-line. The novel draws to a close at a lavish party to celebrate the
launch of the *New Review*. The election, at this stage, appears lost, but
the sudden news that Fleight's opponent has died 'of a cold in his
head' conveniently secures him the parliamentary seat.

As Max Saunders notes, *Mr. Fleight*'s 'plot draws on fairy-tale
in charting Fleight's path from unprepossessing outsider to ruler'.[11]
There is certainly a strange sense of fantastical providence about the
story's abrupt resolution, which turns on the promise that Augusta
Macphail – another social climber and the *New Review*'s editor –
makes to Blood: 'If your Fleight can point to any single instance of
real luck happening to him from this day on, I'll marry him' (*MrF*
295). Moments later, the vow becomes more specific: she'll marry
Fleight if he wins the forthcoming bye-election. However, as Blood
protests, this is 'absolutely impossible': 'Nothing but a miracle could
get him in now' (*MrF* 296). Within a page we discover that just such a
'miracle' has occurred, and within a few more the novel has ended. As
Brooks points out, such plot devices are very much a part of the
melodramatic repertory:

> melodramatic vows and pacts are always absolutes; there is never a thought of
> violating them. The same is true of the inexorable deadlines that force a race
> against the clock [. . . .] We are not encouraged to investigate the psychology
> of the vow or the logic of the deadline but, rather, to submit to their drama-
> turgy, their functioning as mechanism. (Brooks 31)

If, therefore, we regard Augusta's promise as a specifically melodramatic device, recognising it for its overt theatricality, then we stand

to gain in our appreciation of the novel's generic texture. When Augusta commits to marrying Fleight if he wins, we are not invited to question the plausibility of this act in the context of the story or of her character, or to ask whether or not the promise will be honoured. Similarly, we are not invited to question the appropriateness of the narrative device and the suddenness with which it concludes the tale.

Another aspect of the conclusion to *Mr. Fleight* that bears fruitful comparison with the conventions of melodrama is the extremely fortuitous death of Fleight's election rival due to 'a cold in his head'. Singer highlights the prevalence of chance events in both stage and screen melodrama:

> Chance wreaks havoc on the lives of the protagonists, accentuating their vulnerability within an unpredictable world. But, conventionally, it is also chance, rather than causal action on the part of the protagonists, that brings about the villain's demise and saves the day. The villain might be struck by a bolt of lightning, or fall into a grain silo, or be buried under an avalanche [. . . .] (Singer 136)

Like vows, pacts, and deadlines, chance occurrences are convenient plotting devices since they are not required to satisfy any logic of narrative progression, of cause and effect. However, chance events also serve to reinforce melodrama's moral framework. By chance, heroes are rewarded and villains punished, thus affirming 'the certainty of a kind of cosmic moral adjudication' (Singer 137). Clearly most readers do not take Fleight's luck 'seriously' in this sense. That is, we do not take him to have been rewarded for his virtues by divine providence, and neither do we feel that his rival has been punished for villainy when we learn of his pathetic demise from a head cold. By the same token, we do not question the likelihood of the rival's death coming at such an opportune moment. We do not ask ourselves whether or not we believe that the government would have selected a parliamentary candidate with such a weak constitution. We do not, furthermore, ask whether it is possible to die from a head cold, and, if we do decide that the cause of death is less than plausible, we do not suspect that a more sinister explanation of the death (and therefore the election victory) is more so. We are invited, nonetheless, to 'submit' (in Brooks' terms) to the 'dramaturgy' of these unlikely events and even to take pleasure in their excessive nature. What I am suggesting, then, is that the question of plausibility is highly dependent on generic context, and that certain generic conventions function either to suppress any sense of implausibility, or to exaggerate it for dramatic and/or comic effect.

This observation brings me back to *The Good Soldier* and, in particular, to a controversial reading of the novel put forward by Roger Poole. Poole reads the novel as a disguised murder mystery in which Dowell and Leonora have conspired to kill Edward, Florence, and Maisie Maidan. Dowell's apparent confusion over the facts of his tale is, for Poole, an elaborate smokescreen intended to throw the reader off the scent. Nevertheless, according to Poole, Ford leaves clues throughout the text as to the novel's 'real plot line'. One of the mainstays of Poole's argument is the *implausibility* of Dowell's version of events. For example, Poole argues that Ashburnham's affair with La Dolciquita 'simply reeks with improbability':

> The incident of 'the mistress of the Grand Duke, La Dolciquita' is so utterly unlikely, is described in such a melodramatic and dissonantly 'false' tonality, that it can only be offered as a test of the reader's gullibility. Would an officer and a gentleman like Ashburnham fall hopelessly in love with a whore, give her excessively generous gifts, feel obliged to her and dependent upon her, and finally get too drunk to recognise her?[12]

Similarly, Poole argues that Florence's alleged affair with Jimmy, which began during her expedition with her Uncle Hurlbird, is ludicrously far-fetched: 'It is inconceivable that in the 1890s a young lady from Society would be "accompanied" in that sense by a male lover in a trip round the world with her uncle' (Poole 411). These challenges to the reader's faith (or 'gullibility' for Poole) call into question the very supposition that Edward and Florence were adulterers in the first place. The story of the affair between them – for which, Poole believes, there is 'no textual evidence at all' (Poole 416) – along with the stories of all their previous affairs, is all part of Dowell's deception, explaining and justifying their deaths while distracting the reader from the possibility that they were murdered. Surely, Poole reasons, we cannot be expected to believe the version of events Dowell gives in the face of the glaring implausibility of so many of its details.

My aim here is neither to endorse nor to discredit Poole's interpretation. However, Poole's reading should, I think, be recognised as a demonstration of the lengths to which some readers are prepared to go, and the amount of effort they are prepared to expend, in attempting to cope with *The Good Soldier*'s narrative instability. In this instance, I am insisting, the *generic* instability of Ford's novel radically undermines the reader's ability to decide what is or is not likely, conceivable, or plausible. Interestingly, Poole argues that the description of Ashburnham's affair with the courtesan is unbelievable because its tone is 'melodramatic', and as we know melodrama is, precisely, a category within which logic and likelihood are of much diminished importance. It is, furthermore, yet another of the categories to which Dowell explicitly alludes as he tries to provide shape to his narrative. Let us return to Dowell's description of the scene of Ashburnham's declaration of passion for Nancy:

> there you have the picture, the immensely tall trees [. . .]; the silhouettes of those two upon the seat; the beams of light coming from the Casino, the woman all in black peeping with fear behind the tree-trunk. It is melodrama; but I can't help it. (*GS* 80)

What is particularly intriguing about this version of events is that it is, as Dowell openly admits a few pages later, 'only conjecture' (*GS* 83). Dowell was not present at the scene – he 'pieced it together afterwards' – and the only first-hand account he has received is from Ashburnham 'in his final outburst' (*GS* 79). Since we are told that Ashburnham was unaware of Florence's presence, since Florence died almost immediately afterwards, and since Nancy, the only other potential witness, has lost her mind, there is no verifiable 'evidence' (as Poole might have put it) that such a scene took place at all. My concern is not to establish whether or not one might 'prove' the accuracy of Dowell's description of the scene. However, acknowledging the possibility that the scene is purely a product of Dowell's imagination – and recognising it, furthermore, as a specifically *melodramatic* imagination – is essential.

Why, we might ask, does Dowell remark that the melodrama of the scene is something that he 'can't help'? This comment would cause the reader very little trouble if it could be read as an affirmation that the scene 'really' happened in this way (i.e. it 'really' was melodramatic), and so the atmosphere of melodrama cannot be avoided. However, since we have already established that we, like Dowell, cannot be certain of the accuracy of his description, we are forced to work harder to interpret this brief aside. I would like to start by acknowledging the anxiety over melodrama's lowly status implied by the assertion that it *can't* be helped. Dowell, that is to say, seems aware that melodrama is regarded as a 'degraded' form, and seems to recognise the connotations of artificiality complained of by Poole, its inappropriateness for the purposes of a serious narrator telling a 'real story'. Does this mean, however, that Dowell's moments of over-wrought, melodramatic narration represent nothing other than a temptation, to which he guiltily succumbs at various points in his tale, but which he really ought to have avoided? I would argue, on the contrary, that Dowell's embarrassment over the appropriateness of the mode may well mask its usefulness as a narrative resource.

For a narrator like Dowell, who struggles to make sense of his own tale (that is, if we discount Poole's reading), it is not difficult to see the attraction of a narrative form which circumvents the necessity to make sense. Like his other gestures towards generic stability, Dowell's adoption of the melodramatic mode provides a glimpse of the intelligibility that constantly threatens to elude him. At times, this is the ethical intelligibility sought via the identification of heroes and villains. At others, melodrama provides an essential narrative function, allowing inexplicable events to be narrated. Poole may be right to highlight the implausibility of Ashburnham's affairs, their incompat-ibility with the role of gentleman, magistrate, good soldier, and so on, for this is precisely the problem that Dowell encounters in attempting to tell the tale. The fact that Dowell lapses into melodrama at moments when the events he describes appear to make very little sense – Leonora's outburst at the 'protest' scene, Edward's liaison with the courtesan, Florence's sudden appearance in the hotel lobby and sub-sequent death – may be an indication of the very usefulness of a genre that depends on the submission of its audience to the 'dramaturgy' of the unlikely event. Faced with the task of narrating events that exceed his capacity to understand, Dowell 'can't help' but turn to 'the mode of excess' (Brooks iii).

## NOTES

1   Ford, *The Good Soldier*, second edition, ed. Martin Stannard, New York: Norton, 2012 – henceforth *GS*; p. 23. For further discussion of 4 August and *The Good Soldier*'s time-scheme, see Rob Hawkes, *Ford Madox Ford and the Misfit Moderns: Edwardian Fiction and the First World War*, Basingstoke: Palgrave Macmillan, 2012, pp. 93–7.

2   See Vincent J. Cheng, 'A Chronology of *The Good Soldier*', *English Language Notes*, 24:1 (September 1986), 91–7. Max Saunders also provides a chronology of the novel in the recent Oxford World's Classics edition. See Ford, *The Good Soldier*, ed. Max Saunders, Oxford: Oxford University Press, 2012, pp. 214–24.

3   Joseph Wiesenfarth's discussion of the gothic in *Parade's End*, however, touches on the question of melodrama. See his *Gothic Manners in the Classic English Novel*, Madison: University of Wisconsin Press, 1988, pp. 161–84.

4   Mark Schorer, '*The Good Soldier*: An Interpretation', in Richard A. Cassell (ed.), *Ford Madox Ford: Modern Judgements*, London: MacMillan, 1972, p. 68. See also John A. Meixner, *Ford Madox Ford's Novels: A Critical Study*, Minneapolis: University of Minnesota Press, 1962, pp. 152–3; David Eggenschwiler, 'Very Like a Whale: The Comical-Tragical Illusions of *The Good Soldier*', *Genre* 12:3 (Fall 1979), 401–14; and Avrom Fleishman, 'The Genre of *The Good Soldier*: Ford's Comic Mastery', *Studies in the Literary Imagination*, 13:1 (Spring 1980), 31–42.

5   At this stage Dowell also appears to overturn his previous statement as to the most appropriate title for the tale, referring to it, precisely, as 'the Ashburnham tragedy' (*GS* 158).

6   Fredric Jameson, *The Political Unconscious: Narrative as a Socially Symbolic Act*, London: Routledge, 2002, p. 102. Jameson argues that the 'categories' of comedy 'are also quite distinct from romance, and more resolutely social: the classical conflict in comedy is not between good and evil, but between youth and age' (p. 102).

7   Peter Brooks, *The Melodramatic Imagination: Balzac, Henry James, Melodrama, and the Mode of Excess*, New Haven: Yale University Press, 1995 – henceforth Brooks; p. 30.

8   Significantly, given its status as a pivotal moment in the onset of modernity, Dowell refers to the French Revolution in the opening chapter of *The Good Soldier*: 'The mob may sack Versailles; the Trianon may fall, but surely the minuet – the minuet itself is dancing itself away into the furthest stars' (*GS* 11).

9   Ben Singer, *Melodrama and Modernity: Early Sensational Cinema and Its Contexts*, New York: Columbia University Press, 2001 – henceforth Singer; p. 46.

10  Ford, *Mr. Fleight*, London: Howard Latimer, 1913 – henceforth *MrF*; p. 3.

11  Max Saunders, *Ford Madox Ford: A Dual Life*, 2 vols, Oxford: Oxford University Press, 1996, I, p. 378.

12  Roger Poole, 'The Real Plot Line of Ford Madox Ford's *The Good Soldier*: An Essay in Applied Deconstruction', *Textual Practice*, 4:3 (1990) – henceforth Poole; 397. Poole elaborates his contentious reading of *The Good Soldier* in 'The Unknown Ford Madox Ford', in Robert Hampson and Max Saunders (eds), *Ford Madox Ford's Modernity*, International Ford Madox Ford Studies 2, Amsterdam and New York: Rodopi, 2003, pp. 117–36.

# SCREENING *THE GOOD SOLDIER*

## Janet Harris

**Abstract**

As a reader I took *The Good Soldier* at face value, accepting its opening statement that 'This is the saddest story I have ever heard,' and thought the television adaptation was about silence and what was not said or heard. However, from the point of view of a television director, it soon became clear that many of the factors which make this novel a modern novel and many of the techniques which make it a great novel also make it eminently suitable for television.

   In this chapter I argue that Ford understood that to see was not to know, and like a camera Dowell 'sees' events, but has no knowledge of them. The camera might witness events, but without context or history, both personal and general, the events are just pictures. We see them, but don't understand them.

   Television enables the visual enhancement of Ford's portrayal of a rigid society governed by an imposed and self-inflicted discourse of societal propriety and Victorian morality, but the camera also becomes another voice in addition to that of Dowell and the protagonists. It takes on the modernist premise of Ford that there is no one reality to an event, but that reality is different to each interpretation and shows how sight itself can influence an interpretation.

In 2012 I was asked whether I might be interested in presenting a paper on the 1981 television adaptation of *The Good Soldier* (directed by Kevin Billington). I am a documentary director but had spent my early television career in BBC series and serials working on television dramas. I then joined the BBC documentary unit and went freelance in 2002. John Grierson called making documentaries 'the creative treatment of actuality',[1] and the translation of real life onto the screen and its construction into a story that is understandable and watchable is a craft that draws on the skills of any director. I was therefore very intrigued by the proposition.

   In writing about a television adaptation of a book there is the temptation to get drawn into the debate about fidelity, authenticity and to what degree the television version is 'successful' in extracting the essence of the fictional text.[2] However, as Imelda Whelehan points out, this would also entail a discussion about 'appropriate' textual readings, the intentions, experience and identities of both viewers and readers.[3] I acknowledge the theoretical debates about whether the television series can be a version of the original or an adaption,[4] but side with Barthes who writes that 'the text is a fabric of quotations resulting from a thousand sources of culture',[5] and believe that the text, that is the television series, should be considered an adaptation, which 'contains the fundamental parts of the novel',[6] but that it is also a text in its own right.

As a documentary director I might be said to 'adapt' reality to television. I take the fundamentals of what I observe; that which Cardwell suggests 'represents the cluster of its essential properties'[7] and adapt it to the medium of television. I know what works on television and what doesn't, and I start from the acknowledgement that two different media require different tools by which to communicate. Although I am writing this essay from the point of view of both a reader, and a viewer, I also write as someone who works in television, and it is this view that I will foreground, although of course, one cannot exclude the other responses to the texts.

After reading the book, I thought that the thrust of my argument would be about silence, and how the television adaptation dealt with what was being said, or not said. The book opens with the famous sentence 'This is the saddest story I have ever heard'[8] and as a reader I read and listened to Dowell as he narrated this story. The telling of the story was not simple or linear, with scenes being retold through varied voices. I read and heard the understated reported speech of the era, and I was much struck by the poetry and austerity of the words. It was what was *not* said which first struck me as being difficult to adapt to television.

How could you convey this description on television? Ashburnham's face 'expressed nothing whatever [. . . .] neither joy nor despair, neither hope nor fear; neither boredom nor satisfaction' (*GS* 26) and 'How is it possible to have achieved nine years and to have nothing whatever to show for it?' (*GS* 34).

How could you convey such negatives, or the lack of conversation between Leonora and Edward other than being told of it by a narrator, as in the book? How could you convey the complexity of the prose, and the beauty of the description? For example, Dowell tells us that 'the whole world for me is like spots of colour in an immense canvas' (*GS* 19). This suggests so much, but also suggests the opposite, which again is not said, that is that things outside of Dowell's known world are perceived as a monochrome canvas.

In a book you can describe character and interior monologue, you can have moments when nothing actually happens; more silences; and you can have a page of explanation which gives you a fuller understanding of a character. For example, Ford takes a whole page to describe what love means to Dowell:

> it is impossible to believe in the permanence of man's or woman's love [. . . .] a love affair [. . .] is something in the nature of a widening of the experience [. . . .] the craving for identity with the woman he loves [. . . .] we all so need from the outside the assurance of our own worthiness to exist. (*GS* 92-3)

You come to understand what love means to Dowell through his own narrated history and experience.

Then there was the problem of Ford's use of flash forwards, and flash backs, of his use of three tenses in one sentence. His chronology follows the logic of the mind, not of temporal development, and the moment is present and past. Julian Barnes writes: 'Dowell goes backwards, forwards, sideways, switching times and tenses. He even comes up with an "impossible tense", beginning a sentence like this: "Supposing that you should come upon us sitting together . . ." – as if such a coming-upon were still possible'[9].

The mind of a reader can slip nine years and two continents in a sentence, but the television viewer cannot. The complexity of the novel presents difficulty for a simple more traditional television narrative structure, which is beginning, middle and end, and you cannot change locations, costumes and years in seconds without confusing the audience and making them dizzy.

> The adapter must at once resign himself to the sacrifice of dozens of ambiguities and implications, for they are made possible by purely novelistic means – in this instance, by the taste of the narrator for seeming irrelevance, for digressions that do not digress, for missing apparently obvious connections and for insisting hysterically upon others that look imaginary and without point...[10]

Television thus has its limitations. The major one is the time constraint. *The Good Soldier* series was reduced to 105 minutes, in three episodes. The book contains just over 75,000 words, and would take over six hours to read aloud. In the television series there is not time or place for lengthy description. We do not get the lengthy description of what love means to Dowell, as stated above. When Dowell is talking to Leonora about Nancy he says: 'I love her very much you know . . .'.

Leonora replies 'Leave it a year.' And John answers 'Oh all right then'[11] and that's it.

You don't get the sense as you do in the novel that love is a mirror that constructs and is needed to hide Dowell's emptiness; again there is a silence within Dowell, the depth of which would seem to be impossible to convey on screen. Major scenes are also left out in the television adaptation, such as Dowell's elopement with Florence, Leonora's Irish Catholic childhood and the problems of her mixed marriage, Edward Ashburnham's gambling, and Nancy Rufford's drunken mother,

However, as a television director I was immediately conscious of Ford's ability to present a visible picture, a technique mentioned by Whelehan when writing about adaptation.[12] She points out that many authors who write about adaptation mention the filmic nature of the text under scrutiny. She quotes Conrad's claim in his novel *The Nigger of the 'Narcissus'*, that that his aim was to make the reader 'see',[13] which is held up as the key link between the modernist novelists and the film maker. Ford collaborated with Conrad on three works, although White writes that it was one of Ford's greatest regrets that Conrad did not have much respect for his work.[14] Another author of historic backgrounds, Leo Tolstoy, was an admirer of cinema:

> this swift change of scene, this blending of emotion and experience – it is much better than the heavy, long-drawn-out kind of writing to which we are accustomed. It is closer to life. In life, too, changes and transitions flash by before our eyes, and emotions of the soul are like a hurricane. The cinema has divined the mystery of motion.[15]

Ford could thus be said to be a part of this modern group. However I argue that Ford's use of filmic techniques in the book go beyond the purely visual. Ford understood that to see was not to know, and like a camera Dowell 'sees' events, but has no knowledge of them. The camera might witness events, but without context or history, both personal and general, the events are just pictures. We see them, but don't understand them. It is only when we have the knowledge, as for example Dowell's knowledge that Florence was having an affair with Edward, that the scene once shown, takes on a completely different meaning, and the vision changes

It was the viewing of the television series which emphasised that the book is not just primarily about silence, that is, in lack of communication, although there is that. It is actually about sight, about perception, and about the relationship between seeing, knowing and understanding. It is thus a serious contender for adaptation.

As indicated above, writers have pointed to the filmic qualities of novels of this time, and Bender writes that many of the narrative conventions valued by Ford appear to be prototypes for the cinema, which:

> creates its art by distortion through eccentric point of view, fluid time utilizing flash back and flash forward, manipulation of focus and partially obscured vision, framing devices, montage and similar techniques.[16]

I will examine these issues in detail, but first look at how the television can enhance the seemingly more simple descriptive passages in the book.

Ford is a very visual writer and television can obviously visualise the descriptive passages. In a single shot we see Nauheim, but not only do we see the hotel and the gardens described by Ford, but the theatrical direction and placing of the characters tells us more about the place. From the placing of the four protagonists on the steps you get an idea of the stuffiness of the place, the restriction of the clothes and how the imposed order affects events. In his review of the adaptation for *The London Review of Books* Frank Kermode writes that the photography 'catches wonderfully the extraordinary elegance of the spa where the central action takes place, while the direction equally well suggests that we are in a maximum security prison'.[17]

Television as the 'quintessence of postmodern culture'[18] utilises intertextuality to a large degree. It does not just express or enhance meaning, but makes reference to other art works, and other television programmes. Barthes writes that images are 'polysemous', that is they have many meanings and interpretations which are anchored by the use of language.[19] However, Kress and Van Leeuwen reject this order of meaning, and state that all texts are multimodal.[20] Language and image work together, and visual signs have meaning potential that can be realised through their combination with other signs, so they can have meaning without reference to any language.[21] Television can thus elicit understanding from the spoken words, but also connotation and denotation from the images.

Thompson writes of visual motifs which 'become emblematic of an important idea',[22] and this theatrical motif is repeated in the sets and positioning of the characters throughout the series. British television drama in the 70s was criticised for its theatricality, but this sense of stillness and of an external direction creates a strong visual motif, that is Ford's portrayal of a rigid society governed by an imposed and self-inflicted discourse of societal propriety and Victorian morality.

05'04" (Scene on steps with Grand Duke)

Television's primary means of communication is visual. Sontag writes that:

> photographs are a way of imprisoning reality, understood as recalcitrant, inaccessible, of making it stand still. Or they enlarge a reality that is felt to be shrunk, hollowed out, perishable, remote.[23]

So, a translated description in the book does not just set a scene on screen, as in the introduction above, but as seen can convey much more. In the scene above which is at the beginning of the series, the location is established, and here the Grand Duke of Nassau Schwerin and his entourage are descending the stairs where they encounter Dowell, and he talks to him about racing. The rigid nature and hierarchy of society are emphasized in the theatricality of the descending order of persona, and their location centre stage. The performative nature of the society is also hinted at, where the discourse of order and propriety is materialized in the choreography of the actors.

The camera is never neutral. If I film someone walking to me, or away it suggests a point of view. How you film something has meaning. Hitchcock used the close-up to great effect by showing the amputated finger in *The 39 Steps*. Likewise, a close-up and hold on Florence by the camera conveys much without saying anything. In the book, Dowell describes Florence: 'Yes, that is how I most exactly remember her, in that dress, in that hat, looking over her shoulder at me so that the eyes flashed very blue – dark pebble blue . . .' (*GS* 25).

In the series, Florence is portrayed in a mid-shot, asking: You'll come for me at eleven John?

Dowell: 'Of course my dear' (04'54").

The shot is held so the audience can also remember her, and recognise that the coquettish glance (04' 58") with a hint of the sexual double entendre is a character portrayal of Florence. All this is conveyed in the one sequence. Film and television are capable of mirroring not only physical activities but mental processes. Films can recreate the activities of the mind: the focusing of attention on one object or another (by means of a close up), the recalling of memories or projecting of imaginings (by means of a flashback, flash forward, or 'mind-screen'), the division of interest (by means of the cross-cut).[24]

Eric Ambler writes an essay about the turning of a book into a film and quotes a passage from the author:

> You know that bit in the book where the girl about to marry thinks of the lover she has killed? It took me three pages to describe what she was thinking. He does it in one shot of her looking down at a cup of water and then slowly letting the water dribble away into the sand. I wish I'd thought of that.[25]

The polysemic nature of television enriches the reception of *The Good Soldier*, but Ford's writing also seems ideally to utilise the different levels of television. The varied voices and layers of understanding are factors in both forms. The first layer is that which you see. For example the scene with the Grand Duke; but, as also mentioned, other knowledges come to mind. Viewing the scenes involves a negotiation of meaning; of television knowledges, of ideologies, and of the knowledge of similar television genres. Neale writes of the systems of orientations, expectations and conventions that circulate between industry, text and subject.[26]

In the knowledge of what costume drama brings to your understanding of the scene you come to the screen with the expectation of 'proper' upper class behaviour, for example from *Upstairs Downstairs*[27] and *Brideshead Revisited*.[28] It is this assumption of how the people of this age and class should be that the television version of *The Good Soldier* so dramatically overturns.

Although Dowell is the narrator in *The Good Soldier*, he states 'I have explained everything that went before it from the several points of view that were necessary – from Leonora's, from Edward's and to some extent, from my own' (*GS* 143). Dowell is the narrator, but Ford replays scenes from other points of view so we gradually understand what the reality is. In the question and answer session held in 2012 with Susanna White, the director of Ford's other televised series, *Parade's End*, Max Saunders spoke of his view that the hardest thing for anyone playing Christopher Tietjens was 'projecting thoughtfulness', but that Benedict Cumberbatch 'staring thoughtfully into middle distance' gave a convincing impression of Christopher working through mathematical equations in his head.[29]

Ford understood how perceptions can be manipulated, and television can manipulate very effectively. A viewer will see what he expects to see. Cumberbatch could have been thinking about the week's shopping list, but Saunders interpreted what he saw from his knowledge of the book, and believed that Cumberbatch was performing Tietjens.

As in real life, what at first appears to be happening is just that, an appearance. The unfolding of the knowledge is eminently televisual. In most television, seeing is also believing. In this adaptation, as in the book, it is not. Scenes are run twice, the first time as the innocent and inexplicable, the second take from a different knowledge or from a different aspect. The relationship is far more complex. It is the relationship between perceiving and understanding, of knowing and coming to knowledge, and of the many voices which contribute to that knowledge.

The striking similarity between the book and the tools of television are further manifest in the book's use of the replay of scenes. This is reminiscent of the way television can be viewed, where scenes can be replayed again to establish something missed, or not understood. The importance of performance is also evident. In the book, how people are perceived to behave and their performance is paramount. For example Dowell's assumption 'The given proposition was, that we were all "good people"' (*GS* 33) who ate 'slices of thin, tepid, pink india rubber' (*GS* 34), drank brandy and had cold baths in the morning. The characters act in front of each other, directed by a self-imposed audience of moral adjudicators, and the actors act for an unseen television audience under the instructions of Kevin Billington.

In the book you have the voices of the protagonists and that of the reader who brings her own knowledge and interpretation to the text. In television you not only have the viewer and the text, but the voices of the actors. You read the book in your own voice, and imagine scenes, costumes and places from your own knowledge. Kellner writes of the contradictions in television which are agents of polysemy, and are central to television's ability to appeal to a diversity of social agents.[30] On television people speak in different voices and do things which fall outside your imagination, so the conflicts in society remain or are exaggerated. The success of television, Kellner writes, is based on the fact that it cannot iron out differences in society.[31] The character of Dowell is perhaps more like a reader than a viewer. He accepts what people say to him without listening to the different accents or seeing what was behind the different characters.

It is not just characters, but narratives which can be contradicted. Barthes refers to such narratives: the marriage, the meeting, the seduction, where events are encoded and decoded according to our cultural knowledge of these narratives. You visualise ways of seeing a meeting, or a seduction, but the television can show you the different and contradictory ways these are conducted. However, the richness is not just supplied by a reference to other texts, as noted by Barthes; there is another layer. It is not just similar events in costume drama that these narratives are compared to, but events in the 'real world'.

As a narrative tool the visual nature of Dowell's narration makes him a camera to events. He sees them at their first showing and, like a camera, he sees only a certain appearance of events. However, in the television adaptation, the camera becomes another voice in addition to that of Dowell and the protagonists. It takes on the modernist premise of Ford that there is no one reality to an event, but that reality is different in each interpretation and shows how sight itself can influence an interpretation.

For example, taking the scene from the adaptation where the quartet visits Marburg:[32] we the audience and Dowell are ignorant of what is going on, but with the flight from the room by Leonora and Dowell, the camera shows us that Leonora clearly knows something that we do not. In the adaptation we flash forward to after Edward's death and learn about Florence being Edward's mistress in a conversation Dowell has with Leonora. The scene is shown again, but this time it is shot from a different point of view, from that of the narrator in the diegetic present.[33] We the audience know what is happening, Leonora knows, but Dowell still doesn't.

Ford constructs this drama of unfolding in the book. In a similar way the camera enhances the tension of the drama unfolding. There is a trio of participants; the actor, the camera, and the audience. To keep suspense one of these participants has to be ignorant of what is going on. It is the drama of the finding out by the ignorant player which holds the viewer, whether it is the viewer who wants to know, or the suspense of knowing when a player will know what is going on.

Ford's layering of time is also a feature which is eminently suitable for television. The broadcast nature of television means that as a medium it has a 'peculiar relationship with real-life time'.[34] Dienst writes that television engenders an 'absolute mechanical present tense, always occurring elsewhere first'.[35] Thus Barnes's noting of the tenses that Ford uses as quoted above, 'Supposing that you should come upon us sitting together . . .'[36] where the past and present collide, can be encompassed on television. We accept that the story is being told to us in the now, as events are unfolding now on the screen, but we understand that some events took place at different times, when the narrator saw them, or when they were recorded, and we accept that this does not occur necessarily in chronological order.

The 'nowness' of television also makes suspense seem more real, and invites the viewer to 'live' the experience of solving the enigma rather than be told the process of its achieved and recorded resolution. Television engages the viewer more intensely because its enigmas appear to be unresolved and the viewer is invited to experience their resolution, not merely to learn it.[37] Gitlin writes that in a book the reader knows that the end has already been written and will eventually be revealed to them, but that the viewer 'writes' his script alongside the one that is revealed, thus enhancing the suspense. This also plays well into the essence of the novel that the script, and thus understanding and perception, changes with knowledge gained from each passing scene.

I have not ventured into a critique of the adaptation itself as this is not a study of the production. However, some of the issues which arise from this particular version perhaps do have an impact on the reading of how well this novel is suited to television. I mentioned the impact of the different layers of understanding that television brings to viewing, and when viewing the recording, the other roles played by the actors also affects this knowledge. Watching the DVD in 2013 I could not divorce Jeremy Brett who played Edward Ashburnham from Sherlock Holmes, the character he played in the Granada series which was made between 1984 and 1994. The Granada adaptation of *The Good Soldier* was made earlier, in 1981, so this would not have been a consideration for the television viewers at that time. Likewise, Robin Ellis *was* Poldark, from the eponymous BBC Series made between 1975 and 1977. His American accent slipped at times, which was disconcerting. These issues will be different for each viewer, but obviously should be taken into account when examining the adaptation of a novel into a television series. Many commentators also mentioned the unsuitability of the choice of actor for the character of Jimmy, played by John Ratzenburger, who later became famous for his role as Cliff Claven in *Cheers* (NBC) which was made between 1982 and 1993. Obviously, these comments are made in retrospect, but show some of the perils of adaptation.

In conclusion I thus acknowledge the complexity of the adaptation, but would argue that many of the factors which make this novel a modern work and many of the techniques which make it a great novel also make it eminently suitable for television, which thus perhaps contribute to its claim to modernity. The visual nature of Ford's description, and the multiple tenses are all television tools, but above all the book, like television can show us that the nature of seeing and knowing, of seeing and coming to understanding are not the same. Ford describes the process of how seeing becomes understanding, but on television we actually go through the process ourselves, seeing what Dowell sees, seeing what the camera sees, and so gradually we come to some understanding.

# NOTES

1   John Grierson, 'The First Principles of Documentary', in Forsyth Hardy, ed., *Grierson on Documentary*, London: Faber & Faber, 1966.
2   Imelda Whelehan, 'Adaptations: The contemporary dilemmas' in *Adaptations: From Text to Screen, Screen to Text*, ed. Deborah Cartmell and Imelda Whelehan, London and New York: Routledge, 2002, pp. 3-28 (p. 3).
3   *Ibid.*
4   Sarah Cardwell, *Adaptation Revisited: Television and the Classic Novel*, Manchester and New York: Manchester University Press, 2002.
5   Roland Barthes, 'The Death of the Author', ed. and trans. S. Heath, in *Image, Music, Text*, London: Fontana, 1968, pp. 49-56 (p. 53).
6   Cardwell, *op. cit.*, p. 26.
7   *Ibid.*, p. 26.
8   Ford Madox Ford, *The Good Soldier*, ed. Max Saunders, Oxford: Oxford University Press, 2012 – henceforth *GS*; p. 11.
9   Julian Barnes, 'The Saddest Story', *Guardian* (7 June 2008): http://www.theguardian.com/books/2008/jun/07/fiction.julianbarnes (accessed 10 January 2014).
10  Frank Kermode, 'Frank Kermode Writes about Granada Television's Version, Broadcast on 15 April, of Ford Madox Ford's *The Good Soldier*', *London Review of Books*, 3:9 (21 May–3 June 1981), 15.
11  *The Good Soldier,* dir. Kevin Billington, ITV, 15 April 1981 (DVD).
12  Whelehan, *op. cit.*
13  *Ibid.*, p. 4.
14  Edmund White, 'The Panorama of Ford Madox Ford', *New York Review of Books* (24 March 2011), 29-32.
15  Alan Spiegel, *Fiction and the Camera Eye: Visual consciousness in film and the modern novel*, Charlottesville: University Press of Virginia, 1976, p. 162.
16  Todd. K. Bender., *Literary Impressionism in Jean Rhys, Ford Madox Ford, Joseph Conrad and Charlotte Bronte*, New York and London: Garland Publishing Inc., 1977, p. 53.
17  Kermode, *op. cit.*, p. 15.
18  Jim Collins, 'Postmodernism and Television' in R. Allen, ed. *Channels of Discourse, Reassembled*, 2nd edn, London: Routledge 1992, p. 327.
19  Roland Barthes, *Image-Music-Text*, ed. and trans. S. Heath, Glasgow: Fontana/Collins 1977.
20  Gunther Kress, and TheoVan Leeuwen, *Reading Images – The Grammar of Visual Design*, London: Routledge, 1996.
21  David Machin and Adam Jaworski, 'The use of film archive footage to symbolise news events', *Visual Communication*, 5:3 (2006) 345-66 (p. 361).
22  KristenThompson, *Storytelling in Film and Television*, Cambridge, MA: Harvard University Press, 2003, p. 23.
23  Susan Sontag, *On Photography*, New York: Farrah, Straus and Giroux, 1977, p. 163.
24  'A mindscreen presents the audiovisual field of the mind's eye ... [it] offers the cinema a first-person mode of discourse, presenting matters as a character or some

other narrative agency (even the self-conscious narrative system itself) sees them'. Bruce Kawin, 'Dorothy's Dream: Mindscreen in *The Wizard of Oz*' in *Selected Film Essays and Interviews*, London: Anthem Press, 2013, p. 167.

25 Eric Ambler, 'The Film of the Book', *Penguin Film Review*, 9 (1949), 22-5 (p. 24).

26 Steve Neale. 'Genre and cinema', *Popular Television and Film*, ed. T. Bennett, S. Boyd-Bowman, C. Mercer and J. Woolacott, London: BFI Publishing, 1981, pp. 6-25. (p. 19).

27 *Upstairs Downstairs* ITV 1971, dir. Raymond Menmuir and Derek Bennett.

28 *Brideshead Revisited* ITV 1981, dir. Charles Sturridge and Michael Lindsay-Hogg.

29 The discussion was part of the conference 'Ford Madox Ford and Parade's End', at the Institute of English Studies, 27-9 September 2012. See also: Max Saunders. *Adapting Parade's End* (The Arts and Humanities Festival at Kings College London 11-25 Oct 2013) http://kingsahfest.wordpress.com/2012/09/24/adapting-parades-end/ [accessed 10 January 2014).

30 Douglas Kellner, *Media Culture: Cultural Studies, Identity and Politics between the Modern and the Post-modern*, London: Routledge, 1994.

31 *Ibid.*

32 *The Good Soldier* ITV 1981 Act II 29'30" (DVD).

33 *The Good Soldier* ITV 1981 Act II 43'00" (DVD).

34 Cardwell, *op. cit.*, p. 85.

35 Richard Dienst, *Still Life in Real Time: Theory after Television*, Durham: NC, Duke University Press, 1994, p. 18.

36 Barnes, *op. cit.*

37 T. Gitlin, *Inside Prime Time*, New York: Pantheon, 1983, p. 97.

# DOWELL AND DOPAMINE:
# INFORMATION, PLEASURE AND PLOT

## Sara Haslam

**Abstract**

Ford's first substantial foray into the territory that became *The Good Soldier* (two pages of *The Spirit of the People* (1907), provide the germ of the story) proves his claim to Stella Bowen that he had it 'hatching within' him for around a decade.[1] The verb relates to his famous description of the novel earlier in the dedicatory letter as his Great Auk's 'egg', his swan-song before leaving the creative stage clear for '*les jeunes*'. Its use three paragraphs later still snags the attention: that combination of biological and creative graft, work and care, underlining the re-discovered value of the result to himself, as well as to her. Like an egg, *The Good Soldier* is both vital and supremely strong (there are still so many ways to interpret and unpack it, while some elements remain impregnable), and simultaneously fragile (all those contradictions). More importantly, though, Ford's choice of image conjoins the life of the mind and the life of the body: both combined to produce the work he has re-visited and is now dedicating to her. Things are not so simple for his narrator, and in this chapter I explore how and why. I begin with discussion of the 'suffering' reader, and author, assessing to what extent Ford may have been susceptible to the idea of a 'bodily plot'. Extending this to consider Dowell's relationship with time, and his plot, I use neuroscience to explore key elements of Ford's presentation of his doubtful, hesitant and uncertain narrator. The pleasure of information is a key driver, or motivator, for the human subject. The key related neuromodulator is dopamine. Information itself makes us happy, but not as happy as looking for it, or, perhaps, trying to put it into words. Where is Dowell's pleasure in information? Is this more or less significant than what he actually knows or does not know? How does this affect his relationship to his story and the structure that he creates for it? These questions are addressed in the chapter that follows.

## Introduction

When Ford most obviously experimented with the story of *The Good Soldier*, in *The Spirit of the People*, published in 1907, there was no problem with plot. The narrating 'I' saw, and knew, all: a summer guest, observing the inhabitants of a 'house of a married couple' as they desired, repressed and suffered in silence. That watchful 'I' also felt the effects of such suffering. Though he claimed his intense curiosity meant he was not 'very emotional' himself the strain of the final parting of Mr P—— and his ward was enough to give him, rather than them, 'the jumps'. His knowledge, his seeing, became feeling. Mind and body were working together, and Ford's narrative 'I' displays an authorial 'interest' in the most concerned of senses as it engages with a particularly English 'hard case'.[2] The condemnation of repressive silence, and lack of tenderness, to which it leads (this manifestation of Englishness is judged 'almost appalling'), is a rare example of a Fordian moral intervention, and he veers away from it, stung, as though he has surprised even himself after bringing the vignette to a close.[3]

Mind and body do not work together in the narrator Ford finally chose to tell his tale in novel form, and this chapter explores the ways in which the divide becomes apparent, and its effects. What happens to the telling of stories, and to the experience that leads to them (and the need for them), when the two are divided instead? My focus in this chapter is partly the reader: profitable ground considering, for example, late essays by both Ford and Lawrence on the desirability of an emotional (even suffering) readerly response to a novel – especially in the light of Ford's to his own nascent text as outlined above. (Ford's 'jumps' are more nervy than the bodily 'tremble' Lawrence advocates, but the sense of the physical response is strong in each case.)[4] In the main, however, I am interested in what Ford might be saying in this novel about what happens to the mind's relationship to time – to 'plot', effectively, when we are talking about the narrator of a novel – when the body's is, somehow, compromised. Dowell can sometimes sound like a less arch, less articulate, outrider to a Lawrence novel. By the end of the first chapter, he is awash in questions of sexual morality, and plaintively asking if his 'chastity' means he is 'no better than a eunuch'.[5] And his talk of apples, sexuality and knowledge seems impossible to ignore as an influence on *Women in Love*, for example,[6] but I argue that, though Dowell is physically constricted, this is about more than sex. *The Good Soldier* is undoubtedly about the body – about what sustains it, nourishes it, and connects it to other bodies, or fails to – as refracted through Dowell's fragmented, fragmenting narration, but whatever Lawrence might say about the intuitive intelligence that 'arises out of sex and beauty', it's not sex alone that would sort time, and his plot, out for Dowell, as I hope to show here.[7]

Dowell's early question about how it is possible to have 'achieved nine years', 'without anything to show for it' helped to determine my approach (*GS* 31). The time has been 'won', survived, marked off, rather than lived and owned: how does Ford depict this unusual narrative progression, for what purpose, and to what and where else has it brought his narrator? At the end of the novel Dowell says he is 'very much' back where he started (*GS* 157). How true is this? I explore these questions in what follows. Dowell's mis-reading of Florence on the night of her suicide, for example, though he watches her react to the fact he is with Bagshawe (77-8), is only one symptom of his problem with plot. He might have 'achieved nine years' but one of the things he does not have to show for it is the ability to interpret for his reader the things that he sees. And yet, Ford employs him as a first person narrator. Dowell is how he is because Ford has something particular to say about lived experience and its representation in fiction. This is Dowell's plot.

I begin with a chemically sensitive reading of a contemporary first-person narrative in which the relationship between time and body is clearly felt and clearly expressed. The story can be ordered by the mind, narrated, in this case partly because the body is seen to feel it. It's a war text (Ernst Jünger's *In Stahlgewittern* [*Storm of Steel*][8]), and so more accurately describes a collapse in civilisation than Dowell's tale. However, Dowell's story attends to the destructive, fatal, force of certain types of pre-war behaviour, moral codes and hypocrisies on and over the brink of disintegration; and Ford chose to signify the import of his tale with repeated references to August 4th (the extent of the debate around composition this date has provoked means Ford has pulled off an unintentional stunt in making it seem both a pre- *and* a post-war text). The comparison, therefore, seems appropriate enough. I then move to give examples of Ford's earlier, similar understanding of this relationship between mind/body and time, before developing a neurochemical reading of *The Good Soldier*. In the case of Ford's novel, I argue, such a reading must be related to its impressionism: 'Well, those are my impressions' (79), says Dowell, after narrating the whole of his recollection of the days leading to Florence's suicide – which does not amount to much. The impressionism of *The Good Soldier* is, when it is articulated, closer still to pointillism. (Ford relied heavily on dots of all kinds: ellipsis in *Parade's End*, for example.[9]) This visual artistic technique was developed in the belief that the most dramatic spots of contrasting colour would, if seen from the right distance in the right way, be blended in the eye of the observer to produce a desired representative effect.[10] Dowell sees the 'whole world' like 'spots of colour in an immense canvas' (17), and I think that's Ford's way of warning us at the beginning, and with typical circularity reminding us at the end (Dowell is 'very much' back where he started), that Dowell will need his reader more than a narrator normally would. He does not join the dots on his own. Tarascon and Beaucaire are two such dots, or spots: a pair of towns on the Rhone he visited with Florence, one of which Dowell does see again but forgets to tell us, or make sense of the return, despite the fact that the act of seeing in spots is of fundamental importance to his sense of his world (*GS* 155). Dowell's perception, depending as it does on what he is used to, perhaps what he wants or what he expects to see, remains fragmented, unblended, with the dots spaced well apart. If anyone's eye is to mix the colour in order to see, and understand, it is the reader's, though Dowell can be relied on to provide the kind of exaggerated, dramatic contrast that Seurat captured in paint.

## Bodily Plotting

Caroline Patey, among others, has argued for the ways in which Conrad's *Heart of Darkness* is a subtext for *The Good Soldier*: its cardiological obsession mirroring the 'darkness' of Empire.[11] Hearts are dark in *The Good Soldier*; feeling and knowledge are both clouded – but there are other ways of finding and reading the darkness of Dowell's trouble with plot. Research for a recent article on the fiction of the First World War generated an interest in soldier-writers' focus on dusk. The astonishing savagery and drunken excess of Ernst Jünger's memoir *Storm of Steel* is moderated throughout by, for example, a spring ride through what Michael Hofmann's translation renders as the 'gloaming'.[12] 'The clover lay like burgundy cushions on the fields stitched with hawthorn' as Jünger anticipates arrival at the house of a girl he has met. In later accounts of evening walks in May 1917 when the fields are full of flowers, the smell grows 'headier and wilder' in each 24-hour cycle; nature makes the thought of battle almost compelling through its radiant, narcotic blooming (*Steel* 143). It is also in the gloaming that Jünger comes up with just the right sort of drink: a 'fifty-fifty mixture of red wine and advocaat' that helps him to come to terms in his diary with the fact he has been leap-frogged for promotion (*Steel* 182).

This focus on dusk might be explained by the variety it helps to create, showing Jünger as a naturally-inclined romantic, and as a writer, as well as the murderously successful platoon commander he also was. Or perhaps it is down to Jünger's belief that 'day in the trenches begins at dusk' (*Steel* 43), when he is woken from his afternoon sleep to check the sentries and scrutinize no man's land. This is closer to the reason for the focus, because what Jünger is showing us is dusk's character, and the range of its effects on the responsive human subject. It is a time of transformation, of uncertainty, and of possibility. Dusk modifies both sense perception and behaviour. It allows him to see, one evening in June, 1917, 'more and more of my favourite colour, that red which shades into black that is at once sombre and stimulating' (*Steel* 144). Jünger feels himself to be susceptible, responsive and open. Things happen in this, the hour between dog and wolf, and the plot is shaped accordingly as Jünger writes his story.

The phrase 'l'heure entre chien et loup', as Ford probably heard it first, is discussed in detail in Jean Genet's memoir, *Un Captif Amoureux* [*Prisoner of Love*] (1986), here in translation:

> The hour between dog and wolf that is, dusk, when the two can't be distinguished from each other, suggests a lot of things besides the time of day. . . . The hour in which – and it's a space rather than a time – every being becomes his own shadow, and thus something other than himself. The hour of metamorphoses, when people half hope, half fear that a dog will become a wolf. The hour that comes down to us from at least as far back as the Middle Ages, when country people believed that transformation might happen at any minute. [13]

Ford was susceptible to the idea of transformation, and to this hour being its proper time. It is in the 'gloaming' that the city man becomes free on his return to the heart of the country. The transformation is an existential one, akin to a personal epiphany, or moment of self-recognition: the city man 'has shaken off' his identity, he 'cannot be recalled to earth', he 'moves his limbs purposelessly in order to realise to the fullest how a free man feels', Ford writes in *The Heart of the Country* – very shortly before he was experimenting with the plot of *The Good Soldier* (*EE* 115). (In 1911, Ford showed how he felt this freedom in period terms too – the dawn of a new century meant the death of those suffocating Victorian greats and a new era for the artistically inclined.[14]) He displayed his faith as a writer in the possibilities of this hour more than once, though in the pre-war novel *The Young Lovell*, for example, it's the hour before dawn rather than the one before dark in which the protagonist is deeply lost as he sets out on his journey of love-induced transformations, transitions and dream visions. It is the same 'magic hour' as the one that precipitates Ford's own visions of nine-foot long snakes and a 'green, vermilion

spotted lizard' in his Provençal garden.[15] But he names its evening
equivalent as the hour between dog and wolf in the post-war memoir
*It Was the Nightingale*, acknowledging its French roots, using the
phrase to describe his view of his life at its lowest point: 'in the last
days of January [. . . . T]he heavy drag of winter is then at its most dire
and your courage at its lowest as if in a long four o'clock in the
morning of the year. You seem to pass as if you yourself were
invisible in the owl light of the deep streets... Between dog and wolf
they say here. It is a good phrase' (*IWN* 32). Ford's view of his
shadow at this point is a dark one. But in truth the phrase is more
broadly descriptive of the post-war transformation he records in *It
Was the Nightingale*, from a death-fixated ex-soldier into the writer of
*Parade's End*. The literary character, the sensibility and suggestibility
of this transformative hour – the way it can be used to stage a turn, a
change, or understanding – can be chemically read too.

## Time and Biology

The neuroscientist and economist John Coates uses the phrase to title
his widely-reviewed book on the biology of risk: *The Hour Between
Dog and Wolf: Risk-Taking, Gut Feelings and the Biology of Boom
and Bust* (2012). He quotes from Jean Genet epigraphically to set the
scene for his demonstration of the ways in which the human subject
thinks with both body and brain. This 'thought' is related to hormonal
surges that characterise and cause the transformations he is interested
in, which despite the constant movement of global finance across time
zones he still calls 'the hour between dog and wolf' (Coates 9).
Despite his focus on the world of trading floors his story has a 'narrative arc' – a tragic one because of the overconfidence and particular
susceptibilities of risk-takers, leading as they do to periodic financial
crashes. Though this is interesting, of course, and relevant to any
essay about fiction, my attention to his argument is mainly spurred by
his view that 'a story of human behaviour spiked with biology can
lead to particularly vivid moments of recognition' (Coates 11) – which
he himself relates back to Aristotle – in its account of the pleasures
and effects of hormones on the human relationship to information
(whether it is about stock prices or who might be sleeping with your
wife). The 'spikes', the transformative, pivotal hours are central to any
human drama – to war, for example, and quotations from Remarque's
*All Quiet on the Western Front* illustrate Coates' argument. These
'spikes' are widely apparent in the narratives soldier-writers craft

about their experiences in fact, shaping and explaining them. One would think they would command a central place in a novel about a different but still dramatic collapse in (at least one man's view of) civilization: *The Good Soldier*, say.

But do they? Turning first to war fiction and the neuroscientific explanation for moments such as this in Jünger: 'eyes and ears are tensed to the maximum, the rustling approach of strange feet in the tall grass is an unutterably menacing thing. Your breath comes in shallow bursts . . . you tremble with two contradictory impulses: the heightened awareness of the huntsman, and the terror of the quarry' (*Steel* 71); or this in Remarque: 'a tense expectancy suddenly gets into our veins, our hands and our eyes, a readiness, a heightened wakefulness, a strange suppleness of the senses'[16] (the answer is a rush of noradrenaline which enhances alertness and vigilance, and lowers the sensory thresholds so that all that is perceived is perceived more sharply; Coates 125), one is reminded of Tietjens being released temporarily from his mind-bound existence and 'pleased with his body' having rescued a wounded subaltern under fire: '"Thank God for my enormous physical strength!"'.[17] Ford writes the bodily plot here: the narration slows to accommodate every look, every breath, every sensation ('it was slow, slow, slow . . . like a slowed down movie'), as Tietjens is made whole. And so where is the biology of Dowell's fiction? Where is his hour between dog and wolf? If such pivotal moments are indeed absent, in what ways might their lack be claimed as causative factors in both his idiosyncractic form of spaced out impressionism and the structure of the novel's plot?

One obvious place to identify a pivotal hour might be amongst the Connecticut evenings over the course of which the attempted group seduction of Florence takes place. It is evening; Dowell finds he wants Florence. But Ford does not indulge this potential to any degree. He instead makes Dowell humorously oblivious to the competition ('I was as timid as you will, but in that matter I was like a chicken determined to get across the road in front of an automobile'; *GS* 59). This complacency is partly due to arrogance, of course, because although he is not a 'strapping' New Englander, Dowell knows, quietly, that he can give Florence the 'European settlement' she will insist upon (60). It still is humorous. Another obvious possible transformative hour would be the key scene at M[arburg], in which Leonora's face gives him a vision of hell (39). Although he manages to explore the possibility of knowing more about that hell for a number of pages, Dowell arrives instead at self-satisfied 'relief' that he can continue to consider the Ashburnhams as friends (*GS* 53). He achieves this by patronising Florence's anti-Catholic jibes, being nonchalant about his own prejudice, and taking '*two minutes*' [my emphasis] to 'fix' the whole matter of religion (in that location!) with Leonora. Or what, finally, about the night of Florence's suicide: one climax of the 'saddest story' (9, 83)? Do we as readers recognise it as the 'saddest story'? Do we either 'tremble' or get the 'jumps', to go back to the language of affect with which we began? Is Dowell's transformation into a state of knowledge a moment of recognition for him either? I believe the answer is 'no' in each case. And Dowell answers the last question for himself. The generic and affective heights of tragedy are missed by some distance, as he knows: '[i]t is melodrama', he confesses: 'but I can't help it' (80). (I do agree with John A. Meixner, and others, that the *events* of this novel are tragic, but not that they are given this status by Ford in his construction of the plot: this is partly what is so interesting about this novel and its effects.[18]) It therefore remains unclear to readers what drives Dowell, aside from the second-rate pull of melodrama; what gets him from 'a' to 'b', from spot to spot. The structure of *The Good Soldier* suggests a narrator who is not enthralled by his own plot. His form of unreliability, I suggest, demands its own scale.

I want to address briefly three of the most predictable answers as to what might reasonably be expected to drive Dowell, all of which have been introduced above: 1) information; 2) sex; 3) money.

1. Information. Ford wanted to please his readers, and gave considerable thought to how to do so. In 'On Impressionism' (1914), for example, where he considers methods 'of surprise, of fatigue', 'passages of sweetness', and progression by intense contrast as ways of capturing a reader's attention – the aim of which, note, is to 'attain the sort of odd *vibration* that scenes in real life really have' [my italics].[19] Later, in 'Techniques' (1935), he advises the literary technician 'to think about nothing but how to please your reader'.[20] In the 1927 letter dedicating that year's American edition of *The Good Soldier* to Bowen, Ford anticipates her pleasure at hearing from him the stories surrounding the genesis of the novel. He specifies that they are familiar to her, which may not give her as much pleasure as something new.[21] The pleasure of information is a driver, or motivator, for the human subject. The key related

neuromodulator is dopamine. Information itself makes us happy, but not as happy as looking for it, or, perhaps, as happy as trying to put it into words. Coates goes so far as to assert that we are addicted to information (135) (a concept that is increasingly common in this new information age), thanks in part to the way dopamine operates, but we are particularly addicted to novelty. 'Our sensory apparatus' Coates writes, 'has been designed to attend almost exclusively to information. It ignores predictable events but orients rapidly to novel ones' (122). We gradually lose awareness of unchanging stimuli, he goes on to suggest, but new information holds a strange and powerful attraction for us. 'When in its presence', he writes, 'we come alive' (124). Dowell is, supposedly, narratorily fixated with knowledge. It is a short novel, but in it he uses forms of the word over 200 times, often negatively, of course ('I know nothing – nothing in the world – of the hearts of men'; *GS* 12). But his relationship with knowledge, his acquiring of information, is almost exclusively empty of pleasure, even before events become primarily traumatic ones. However, Dowell does enjoy novelty. This is why the farcical M[arburg] cow scene is important. From the beginning of the paragraph when he talks of his anticipation of the M[arburg] expedition, and uses the time to qualify painstakingly the colour green as seen from the train window, we are building to his expression of 'real joy' in watching one cow throw another into a stream (36). This scene displays his capacity to respond to novelty, but also, in its infantile rendering, how much he has been starved, and has starved himself, of the life which it brings. 'Off duty' in his cow-fixated way, he tunes out the grown-up information-competition between the women. Florence is 'imparting information so hard' (36) about Ludwig the Courageous, while Leonora tries to catch her out. Dowell is only interested in the cow. Or, in another example, think of the way seeing Edward for the first time stands out in Dowell's brain, because of the novelty – only a page earlier he has admitted counting the paces from the Hotel Regina to the baths out of bored desperation (22). Dowell is passionately interested by Edward's face, in that moment at least (perhaps helped by the fact that it is twilight, the transformative hour). He works out who he is, and renders his appearance in minute detail (23-4). But he does not get sufficient pleasure from that experience to hunt for further information when he needs it, to get from 'a' to 'b', or to join later dots together on his own.

2. Sex. Probably nearly enough has been said about Dowell and sex. Eugene Goodheart and Arthur Mizener both write back in different ways to Mark Schorer on this subject. Mizener really does not like Schorer's 'Lawrentian conception of human nature' and defends Dowell against Schorer's charge of 'fantastic [sexual] failure'.[22] Mizener also writes that 'the Dowell who is telling the story knows everything that Ford does and thinks all the things that Ford did about human affairs' (265).[23] No, he doesn't. Ford knew about the 'mind quickened by passion', for example, and how it is preferable to the 'mind rendered slothful by preoccupation entirely trivial' - such as counting the steps from the hotel to the hot rooms, perhaps ('OI' 285; *GS* 22)? Let's settle for now with Max Saunders's note in his introduction to the new Oxford World's Classics edition that Dowell's 'trouble with knowledge is inescapably carnal'.[24] More important in the context of this chapter, however, is to acknowledge sex as a prime motivational driver which does not drive our narrator, 'one-minded' as he is when he climbs into Florence's bedroom at one in the morning in order only to 'wake her up'. The oddness of this does not go unremarked on by him. And he is prepared to blame himself for not attempting to seduce her, when she was already awake (of course she was), and therefore for the fact that it was the first and last time he was embraced by a woman with any warmth. 'I fancy that, if I had shown warmth then, she would have acted the proper wife to me, or would have put me back again. But, because I acted like a Philadelphia gentleman, she made me, I suppose, go through with the part of a male nurse', he writes (*GS* 63). His mind was somewhere else, he says. At the same time, it was his body that was not moving him forward out of his physical reticence, from 'a' to 'b'. Dopamine and testosterone are thought to work synergistically (Coates 151), but that is not the case here.

3. Money. It is no surprise that, in Coates's researches on the trading floor, he found that as profits rose, so did testosterone. But he also discovered a direct link between the amount of testosterone in the traders' systems in the morning, and the amount of money they made in the afternoon. In a bull market, when the appetite for risk produced by the hormone increases, so, it seems, does the cash reward. Dowell has no need of a cash reward. Money routinely falls into his lap, even when he does 'not want [it] at all badly' (*GS* 134). It's a philosophical issue, a moral issue, a philanthropy issue

for Dowell, but never one of need. And the other opportunities he
has for creating similarly motivational competition fail because
Edward sees him 'not so much as a man', while Dowell in turn
watches Ashburnham 'face off' against other men in polo, for example (*GS* 27). The information competition between the women
on the way to M[arburg] (cited earlier) has a far more urgent sense
of motivational hormonal surges than anything Dowell brings to
the four-square coterie.

What I have been intending to show in this section is the number of
ways in which the material and chemical drivers one might expect to
motivate Dowell are more or less absent. Their lack does not have to
lead to neurosis, perhaps (though Dowell readily confesses violent
hatred of Florence as a result of repression, and his existence in 'hell';
*GS* 55, 41) but it does inhibit various likely actions and their potential
rewards. These absent drivers can be related to Dowell's class identity, his sense of himself as a Philadelphia gentleman. This identity
cripples his attention to novelty by being performed almost only in
relation to what is *routine* in the circles in which he moves: what good
people do, how they eat their beef and how they take their wine (30).
With Dowell, one might want to go further back, though, to explain
why, in him, the day-time performance is his only performance, thus
separating him from what happens in his fellow protagonists at night,
or behind locked doors and underneath tales of a heart. Maybe his
'animal spirits' were not fully developed. If he was in front of us we
could measure the relative lengths of his index and ring-finger to find
out. These ratios are used to determine how much testosterone a man
has been exposed to in the womb (Coates 174). But Florence does not
need to measure his fingers. She knows from the start that he's the
man she needs him to be (*GS* 60). She anticipates the 'sedulous,
strained nurse' that he becomes (12).

### Dowell's Biology
I have concentrated so far on the world of the novel, on the events that
Dowell describes, discussing both the inhibitors to natural forward
movement and the ability to link those events, understand and engage
with them. Dowell's particular chemical feedback loop seems to be a
negative one, operating for the years of the novel's events in reverse.
The propulsive action that could help produce the hormonal help he
needs to enact his physical existence, including the desire to know, is

not propulsive at all. He becomes increasingly alienated from information, sex, and possibly even money, and therefore from the story in
which he finds himself, as I suggest below. I want to conclude by
exploring briefly the ways in which all this might help us to re-
approach Dowell's unreliability, his relationship to his plot, and ultimately related ways of codifying Ford's philosophical schema in this
novel. Ford made him this way. He built a plot round a man who had
no real interest in driving it.

Dowell may well be naturally lacking certain hormones. The
way Ford sets his story as well as structures his story suggests so.
Those warm spring/summer Connecticut evenings should encourage
Dowell to feel like more than a chicken, because he *wants* Florence.
And because it's the hour between dog and wolf. There is also a calendar point to make here. In humans, testosterone levels rise until the
autumn, and then fall until the spring (the autumnal drop is part of the
reason, Coates suggests, why economic crashes tend to happen in October; 189). But the focus on the hormones in relation to sex should not
obscure focus on what I want to argue is actually a more significant
issue, which is to do with their relation to plot. Ford's interest in the
primacy of the body as played out in this novel is to do with how story
itself cannot properly be understood, shaped, and told without it. It is
impossible to imagine constructing a version of Freytag's Triangle
that could do justice to *The Good Soldier* – another reason why this
novel finds itself closer to melodrama than tragedy. (Gustav Freytag
depicted Aristotle's description of plot as an isosceles triangle, with
rising action leading to the apex and falling action dropping from it.)
Aristotle's description cannot be applied due to the shape of Ford's
novel, as well as its structurally determined ambivalence toward
recognition – Dowell's and by natural extension the reader's.[25]

'A novel is a version of the ways in which a man can know
reality', says Samuel Hynes in his essay on Ford's novel (quoted in
*GS* 327). This might in turn suggest that Dowell's reality is closer to
magic realism, where time and space stretch and twist so that madly
different things sometimes seem to happen on the same day. Or so that
he simply stops knowing, thinking, seeking any kind of information
for months and years on end. 'The death of Mrs Maidan occurred on
the 4th August 1904. And then nothing happened until the 4th of
August 1913' (59). That cannot possibly be true, or, rather, it could
not be true for any other narrator. In the November twilight when he
gets his news from Leonora, Dowell does have some of his dots

joined, looking back to a conversation begun on the night his wife died. He collapses into the same few narrative hours his coming to learn about Nancy, Edward's affair with Florence, Florence's suicide, all while dealing with Edward's recent death (75-7). And yet this produces nothing but a sense of leisure in both him and Leonora, a leisure manifested perfectly by a narrative which is paced strikingly slowly at this point. It is balanced, positively sane.

Dowell cannot shape appropriately what he knows (he cannot avoid melodrama), any more than he could originally seek it in real time. Because his distance from his plot is a physical one, he does not feel its curves, its peaks in anything like the correct relation to one another. Nor does he pass them on – as he confesses in the famous passage about his story going 'back and forward' (124-5). One may go back and forward, but one still does not have to produce a narrative that is as clunky, unbalanced and disorientating as this one. Dowell has not lived his story, in other words, despite his first person narration, and this is the fundamental reason for his 'false impression'. The reader does not feel his interest, even retrospectively, or any sense of purpose in filling in the gaps. The reader feels instead the spots, the dots, and the lack of tragedy in the too-wide space between.

The mind needs the body, I think Ford is saying. Trust in the body, or look what happens when you try to tell a story never mind what happens when you try to live a life. And so perhaps this novel was a conscious intervention into what Edward Said and others have identified as a fictional debate at that time on the subject of the young intellectual.[26] There are none here, after all. This is a novel about the physicality of knowledge, one which challenges the primacy of the mind in the mind/body divide, certainly, but also the concept of the divide itself. (Ford sums up Aristotle's ethics by finding his view of happiness the result of 'equal and harmonious blending of the intellect and animal instincts' and this is one reason he admires him more than Plato.[27]) Does this mean that all the mistakes/tangles that Saunders points out in his chronology are intentional, and intended to be Dowell's?[28] No. Ford was too busy living to iron them all out. But he did deliberately make a monumental mess of it. Dowell experiences a version of the hour between dog and wolf. Edward kills himself late one afternoon. Dowell's shadow, the man he loved because he was 'just himself', the man he followed and watched (166, 176) is dead. He becomes 'unstuck' to the extent that Dowell the cuckold becomes Dowell the author. Do body and mind then begin to work together?

No, because they cannot. We have the brain we do, Coates writes, *because* of our body and the movement of which it is capable. Over time, in humans, the brain became more tightly bound to the body, not less. And the information sent by the body to the brain comes freighted with suggestions (Coates 36-42). Ford knows how fast that can happen. 'At that Leonora screamed out and wavered swiftly towards the closed door. And Nancy found that she was springing out of her chair with her white arms stretched wide' (*GS* 162). (Compare this with Dowell's monumental, yet simultaneously ponderous, admission that 'I have only followed, faintly, and in my unconscious desires, Edward Ashburnham; 157.) But the more of a Philadelphia gentleman (with pointillist proclivities) you are, the less of a body you even think you have, and so the more unreliable you are too. You are beyond the help of the transformational, unifying hour between dog and wolf if you're Dowell, condemned never to join experience to knowledge, or information to pleasure, or to know what it is to be in control of your plot. Whether his reader 'trembles', or 'suffers', to go back to my opening discussion, or whether, rather, they remain frustratedly lost, mired in his plot, is a metatextual question that is still very much part of Ford's point.

Dowell says that he is back very much where he started as the events of the novel come to an end (157). He also says that if the world had been less like spots of colour he would have had more to hold on to. But what he does have to hold on to is Nancy, and the dynamic between them at the end of the novel is a fascinating one, partly because of the way in which he is therefore 'following Edward', triangulating and confusing desire, wanting the same woman Edward wanted, though less incestuously, perhaps. Dowell cannot have her if she stays mad, and so he finds himself in a perfectly choreographed dance of madness and sanity in which his ward reminds him of what it means to want, and at the same time grants him refuge from it. (Nancy will probably never appreciate the meaning of the Anglican marriage service, thereby ensuring he cannot have what he wants; 157). The gaps between the spots of colour have lessened, tightened, because of the closeness of his life with Nancy. But the ability to join them is yet more prescribed. Dowell's sanity is now bound to Nancy's insanity, without, apparently, troubling him very much, because of the way he himself constructs the mind/body divide in the girl. He must observe her from his own very particular distance to render her a beautiful 'picture without a meaning'; callous, voyeuristic, fetishistic even, as he bestows his cool gaze upon the 'perfect flush of health on her cheeks' and 'the lustre of her coiled black hair' (168). Doesn't he, in fact, *only* want her because Edward did? Her 'meaning' is lost in the multiple spaces Dowell opens up.

Nancy is very different from Florence. Her manifested reminder of the costs of wanting make Florence's suffering and suicide look melodramatically cheap in comparison. And her pictorial perfection allows Ford to show Dowell more dramatically mirroring his final female 'partner' and her 'mad desirings', while he disciplines his own. (In one picture of development, according to Adam Phillips, sanity 'is more like an overcoming, a mastery, a disciplining of the mad desirings of childhood.'[29]) The spots on the canvas must stay separate regardless of viewers' distance if the body does not feel its way through its plot.

## NOTES

1   In the dedicatory letter to Stella Ford published in 1927 on the novel's re-issue. See Ford Madox Ford, *The Good Soldier*, ed. Martin Stannard, New York: Norton, 2012, pp. 5, 4.
2   See Max Saunders's essay here for more on such cases.
3   See the account in *The Spirit of the People*, in *England and the English* (comprising *The Soul of London*, *The Heart of the Country* and *The Spirit of the People*), ed. Sara Haslam, Manchester: Carcanet: 2003 – henceforth *EE*; pp. 313-5. In the epilogue to *A Call*, published in 1910, so between *The Spirit of the People* and *The Good Soldier*, he writes that the Impressionist novelist has no business pointing a moral: Manchester: Carcanet, 1984, p. 163.
4   See Ford's review of Sinclair Lewis's Dodsworth in the *Bookman*, 69 (April 1929), 191; and Lawrence's essay 'Why the Novel Matters', published posthumously in 1936 (in Anthony Beale, ed., *Selected Literary Criticism: D. H. Lawrence*, London: Heinemann, 1967, p. 105).
5   Ford Madox Ford, *The Good Soldier*, ed. Martin Stannard, New York: Norton, 2012 – henceforth *GS*; p. 15.
6   See the discussion between Rupert, Hermione and Ursula in chapter 3, 'The Class Room'.
7   In 'Sex Versus Loveliness' (1928), in *D. H. Lawrence: Selected Essays*, Harmondsworth, Middlesex: Penguin, 1950, p. 14.
8   The novel was published in 1920 in a private print run. Sales went into six figures in the 1930s; it was translated into English in 1929.
9   See the Notes on the Text to the Carcanet editions (2010-2011) of the four novels that comprise *Parade's End* for discussions of the importance of ellipsis in Ford's work, as well as, for example, Isabelle Brasme, '"A Caricature of his Own

Voice": Ford and Self-Editing in *Parade's End'*, in *Ford Madox Ford, Modernist Magazines and Editing*, ed. Jason Harding, IFMFS 9, New York: Rodopi, 2010, pp. 243-52.

10 This is *The Good Soldier*'s brand of ellipsis, itself transformed in *Parade's End*, for example.

11 See 'Empire, Ethnology and *The Good Soldier*' in *Ford Madox Ford's Modernity*, IFMFS 2, ed. Robert Hampson and Max Saunders, pp. 83-102.

12 See note 8 above. Ernst Jünger, *Storm of Steel*, tr. Michael Hofmann – henceforth *Steel*, London: Penguin, 2004, p. 68.

13 The translator is Barbara Bray; in John Coates, *The Hour Between Dog and Wolf: Risk Taking, Gut Feelings and the Biology of Boom and Bust*, London: Fourth Estate, 2012 – henceforth 'Coates'; preliminary pages.

14 Ford Madox Ford, *Ancient Lights and Certain New Reflections*, London: Chapman & Hall, 1911, pp. vii-viii.

15 Ford Madox Ford, *It Was the Nightingale*, New York: The Ecco Press, 1984 – henceforth *IWN*; p. 8.

16 Erich Maria Remarque, *All Quiet on the Western Front*, tr. Brian Murdoch, London: Vintage, 1996, p. 38.

17 Ford Madox Ford, *A Man Could Stand Up –*, ed. Sara Haslam, Manchester: Carcanet, 2012, pp. 178, 176.

18 There's a long section on this in Meixner's book (*Ford Madox Ford's Novels: A Critical Study* (1962)), but see the extract in *GS* 334-9.

19 Ford Madox Ford, 'On Impressionism' in *GS*, pp. 271-88 – henceforth'OI'; p. 278.

20 Published in the *Southern Review* (July 1935). In *GS*, pp. 300-15; p. 312.

21 It's important to note here that they are about to part – reasonably amicably – but novelty is replacing familiarity in their relationship at this point.

22 Arthur Mizener, *The Saddest Story; A Biography of Ford Madox Ford*, New York: Carroll & Graf, 1971, pp. 258-9.

23 Mizener, p. 263.

24 Ford Madox Ford, *The Good Soldier*, ed. Max Saunders, Oxford: World's Classics, p. xxxii.

25 See Peter Turchi, *Maps of the Imagination: The Writer as Cartographer*, San Antonio, TX: Trinity University Press, pp. 203 ff., for a range of pictorial versions of Freytag's triangle.

26 See, for example, Edward Said, *Representations of the Intellectual: 1993 Reith Lectures*, London: Vintage, 1994. He cites Turgenev, Flaubert and Joyce as manifesting this trend, which was a contemporary one and a move away from the social world as represented by earlier writers.

27 See Ford Madox Ford *The March of Literature: From Confucius to Modern Times* (1938), London: George Allen & Unwin, 1947, pp. 155, 145.

28 Max Saunders provides a new chronology of *The Good Soldier* in Appendix C of his edition of the novel (see note 24 above), pp. 214-24.

29 Adam Phillips, *Going Sane*, London: Hamish Hamilton, 2005, p. 99.

# THE CASE OF *THE GOOD SOLDIER*

## Max Saunders

**Abstract**

The word 'case' occurs with surprising frequency through *The Good Soldier*, drawing in a range of discourses including pathology, sexology, ethics, jurisprudence, criminology, scandal and gossip. The chapter argues that these competing versions of what kind of 'case' the Ashburnham story is indicates its resistance to being framed in any unitary way, as well as indicating the narrator's difficulty in framing it. Whether it is describable as any or all of these possibilities, the language of the 'case' implies both a form of non-normativity – whether deviant, pathological, excessive, or extreme – and justification for readerly interest.

Sometimes for Ford 'case' is interchangeable with the word 'affair', used for a specific entanglement of characters offering a suitable subject for a novel. The chapter argues that through Dowell's exploration of the aspects of the Ashburnham 'case', Ford is elaborating his impressionist theory of the form of a novel; that, as the term 'affair' puns between the senses of story and liaison, so the term 'case' keeps intimating precisely that there is something problematic or disturbing about Ashburnham's story; and that it is the pressure of sexuality in the story that elicits the medico-philosophical language of the 'case'.

It seeks to relate these ideas of different *discourses* of the 'case' to the novel's curious *imagery* of cases, which itself threads through the plot; such as the glass case containing the Protest document, which Ashburnham is touching when Florence provocatively touches his wrist; and especially 'the profusion' of Ashburnham's pigskin leather cases; and the trunk into which Maisie Maidan falls dead. The logic of the imagery implies containment. As the psychological, medical, moral or legal discourses seek to contain the disturbance of the sexual, the transgressive, the non-normative, so Ford seeks a literary form which can contain the content; a problem he turns inside out, into a question of how a first-person narrative can contain its narrator's garrulity.

'I hope', says John Dowell, 'I have not given you the idea that Edward Ashburnham was a pathological case'.[1] But the word 'case' echoes through *The Good Soldier*, appearing at least seventy times – a high count in such a short book. Its frequency intimates that a 'case' – of some kind – is what we are dealing with. This chapter will trace the trajectory of the word through *The Good Soldier*, arguing that it reveals much about what the novel is doing. If Ashburnham's story is not a pathological one, what kind of case is it? What is at stake in referring to him as a case? And what effect does the language of cases have on the idea of the story; of a story?

Whether or not Ashburnham was 'a pathological case' – and it is characteristic of Ford's cunning in handling his unreliable narrator, that to have Dowell hoping he hasn't given us that idea is both to give it to us, and leave us wondering whether it's Dowell or Ford who means us to have it – the novel certainly has its heart sufferers, whether genuine or metaphorical or feigned, and it certainly includes three deaths. Perhaps, though, Dowell is thinking not of this kind of medical case history, but rather, a less specific medical sense of unwellness; malaise.

Calling someone a 'pathological case' (or introducing the idea only to say you are not calling them one) might suggest something verging on the *psycho*pathological; a lack of control; a compulsiveness or relentlessness. Even if the kind of case Dowell doesn't want us to think of Ashburnham as representing is a *mental* case, does Ford want us to think of Ashburnham is these terms? Or Dowell, who might be a candidate for a diagnosis of *folie du doute*? Again, the novel certainly shows us one incontestable mental case, in Nancy Rufford's eventual insanity; and several examples of characters in psychological desperation: Maisie Maidan distraught; Leonora Ashburnham clutching at her head as if seeing the pit of hell, and then riven by migraine; Edward Ashburnham suicidally depressed; and even Dowell himself, in a state he describes as 'cataleptic' or 'catalepsy' after the shock of his wife Florence's death (*GS* 88, 96, 97).

The term 'case' in *The Good Soldier* is also subject to a pull towards the legal. The novel's story isn't exactly that of a legal case either, though legal cases come into it, such as the Kilsyte case (after Ashburnham assaults a young servant on a train); or divorce cases such as that of the Brands (which has such a devastating effect on young Nancy's conception of marriage), or the potential case of the blackmailing fellow officer. Though not a police case, is the book a form of detective case, with Dowell gradually piecing together not who did what, so much as their motives? Is it a moral case? A social scandal – like the Dreyfus affair, which Dowell invokes, again only to disavow, when discussing how, in the Kilsyte Case, Edward 'saw himself as the victim of the law. I don't mean to say that he saw himself as a kind of Dreyfus' (*GS* 123)?

The ways in which the law bears on *The Good Soldier* are explored in Rex Ferguson's recent study *Criminal Law and the*

*Modernist Novel*. Ferguson sees modernism as responding to a crisis in jurisprudence. He quotes Virginia Woolf's uncle Sir James Fitzjames Stephen's *Introduction to the Indian Evidence Act* (1872), which sought to maintain the Enlightenment rationalist view that:

> the approximate rules which relate to human conduct are warranted principally by each man's own experience of what passes in his own mind, corroborated by his observation of the conduct of other persons, which every one is obliged to interpret upon the hypothesis that their mental processes are substantially similar to his own.[2]

Yet, as Ferguson argues, 'This was precisely what was undermined by the practical functioning of the courts in British India', where 'the commensurability of individuals' minds and, indeed, the simple veracity of their testimony' were continually under suspicion due to assumptions about racial difference (Ferguson 90). He sees this undermining of the legal notions of the 'reasonable man' and the 'responsible individual' as becoming felt in Britain in the early twentieth century, recognizing also that it was a crisis reflecting changes in 'the way that insanity was approached by the judicial system earlier in the nineteenth century' (Ferguson 90). Both aspects of his legal focus here – criminality and insanity – are clearly relevant to *The Good Soldier*'s thematising of legal and mental cases. The increasing uncertainty about the knowability of other minds, about 'character', and about reason and responsibility, and indeed how the experience of British India may weigh on these questions, offer further suggestive contexts for Ford's novel.

Such scepticisms can't be confined to the legal sphere, of course. Ferguson cites the historian Martin Wiener's claim that throughout the Victorian and Edwardian periods there was a growing sense of the individual as subjected to:

> the actions of remote others, actions that became increasingly crystallized into impersonal forces. By the turn of the century, it was becoming widely recognized, as the social analyst Graham Wallas put it, that 'each man's life depends on causes he can't understand'.[3]

According to Ferguson, questions about the nature and origins of crime 'were only being asked because of earlier legal anxiety over the complete "otherness" of those such as native Indians or the clinically insane. By the end of the nineteenth century, the suspicion had grown that everyone but oneself was just such another' (Ferguson 91). Yet, as his references to sociological thought make clear, such anxieties about otherness cannot be confined to the legal sphere either, and reflect broader cultural responses to both empire and specifically capitalist modernity – responses detectable in epistemological and psychological discourses, as well as in literature. Where sociological analyses locate the unknown other outside the self, in other people, economic relations, institutions, or in social systems of class, nation, or empire, psychological analyses – and especially the emerging psycho-analytic versions – internalize it as the unconscious. From this perspective, everyone *including* oneself is an other. The knowability of one's own mind – the ability to understand one's own experience – has become as fraught as judging anyone else's. Ferguson knows this, giving a shrewd account of the way Ford's novel eludes the closure of a (legal) case:

> Dowell only experiences his story as he hears it told, by himself. But as he tells it slightly differently every time, the experience is never quite the same. Even the end of *The Good Soldier* does not, therefore, provide a final *case* because the sense is created that another, different, interpretation would have been proffered by Dowell if he had just kept on writing. (Ferguson 85)

But it is a moot point whether it is the undecidability about others that shakes confidence in autobiographical knowledge, or vice versa.

Often in *The Good Soldier* the use of the word 'case' seems vaguer than such legal or psychological senses: a synonym for an overall situation or predicament. Sometimes it highlights the peculiarity of that predicament, posing it as a curiosity; a 'special case' (*GS* 120). A couple of years before starting to write *The Good Soldier*, Ford said of Galsworthy's play *Joy* that he had 'really enjoyed [it] immensely':

> it was rather valuable in our moralising age because of the governess who wandered through in the play, exclaiming to everybody, 'Yours is a special case', and that is the whole moral of life.
>     That is why all moralisations are ineffectual, and why no morality ever covers any real man or any set of real men [. . . . ] The problem of poverty – the whole problem – can never properly be solved because each poor man, each destitute woman, and every pauper child is a special case [. . . .][4]

This shows Ford locating the notion of a 'special case' precisely in the context of sociological thinking – here about the 'problem of poverty', though the phrase 'all moralisations' makes it clear that he believes other kinds of social and moral problem to be equally resistant to generalisation. In a world in which the intelligibility and commensurability of subjects in in doubt, everyone is a special case; and the novel provides a better means of their presentation than the tract, or the taxonomic systems of law, morality or psychology.

Ford had used the term 'case' to bring together several of these aspects in a story called 'The Case of James Lurgan' two years before *The Good Soldier*.[5] This introduces a more ironic sense of the word which isn't irrelevant to the novel: the story 'does not take itself seriously'. In a facetious tone it combines 'a murder mystery, a buried body, and two cousins named Holmes into an experience finally explained as telepathy [. . .]'.[6]

That phrase 'special case' indicates that one sense of the term 'case' is interchangeable for Ford with the word 'affair'. 'The Dreyfus case was perhaps the most important affair of the modern world [. . .]', he wrote, in an essay published the week he said he began *The Good Soldier*.[7] Ford used the word 'affair' to denote a specific entanglement of characters offering a suitable subject for a novel, defining it as 'one embroilment, one set of embarrassments, one human coil, one psychological progression'.[8] In part, then, what Ford is doing by playing on the associations of the word, through Dowell's exploration of the aspects of the Ashburnham 'case', is to elaborate his impressionist theory of the form of a novel. In this sense, a 'case' is the kind of complex situation too intricate to be categorized or analysed. Something that might correspond to what T. E. Hulme terms an 'intensive manifold', and De Quincey before him an 'involute':[9] a knot or twist or tangle of thought and feeling that couldn't be unfolded or unpicked into two dimensional space, but that could only be apprehended through a complex work of art. For Hulme, a condensed poem; for Ford, a condensed fiction.

The term 'affair' puns between the senses of story, scandal, and liaison. An early example in Ford is the 1899 story 'L'Affaire Ingram', in which an American actress recounts to the narrator how she tricked a young British officer into thinking she loved him and wanted to elope.[10] The term 'case', too, hovers between a neutral description – of a situation or a story – on the one hand, and a sense of something problematic in that situation or story on the other. Again, as with 'affair', the word 'case' might hint at scandal; as in the humiliating '*Throne* case' Ford and Violet Hunt had become embroiled in just before Ford began *The Good Soldier*, when his wife Elsie Hueffer had sued the *Throne* magazine for referring to Hunt as 'Mrs. Ford Madox Hueffer'.[11] As the word 'case' echoes through the novel, it keeps intimating precisely that there *is* something, if not exactly 'pathological', certainly perplexing and disturbing about Ashburnham's story.

Dowell narrates how, after the Kilsyte case, Edward:

> began to indulge in day-dreams in which he approached the nurse-maid more tactfully and carried the matter much further. Occasionally he thought of other women in terms of wary courtship — or, perhaps, it would be more exact to say that he thought of them in terms of tactful comforting, ending in absorption. That was his own view of the case. (*GS* 123)

Which case was that? The particular embroilment on the train? The embarrassments when charged, and tried, and shamed publicly? Or the psychological progression of Edward's views about women, and about his own character? Or the whole situation and story? In Dowell's summing up here, the term 'case' slides from denoting the court case to the fantasies it induced in Ashburnham later on. 'That was his own view of the case' seems to mean not just that that was his view of the Kilsyte case against him, but also that it was his view of his own 'case': of what the trial said about him, and how it made him think differently about himself. In other words, the Kilsyte case doesn't stay confined to the courtroom, but becomes part of the fabric of Ashburnham's inner life; and especially of his sexual life.

Another way of putting this would be to say that the attraction of the word 'case' for Ford was precisely how it reveals the social world as entangled with the legal and the sexual. We can glimpse this in *The Spirit of the People* (1907), where Ford tells the anecdote that appears to be the germ of *The Good Soldier*'s plot, about witnessing a married man, P—, parting at a train station from the ward, Miss W—, with whom he's fallen in love. Reflecting on the episode, Ford adds: 'to quote another of the English sayings, hard cases make bad laws'.[12]

If Ford experienced this entangling of law and sexuality in a particularly bruising way in the *Throne* case, such entanglement was evident more widely in the intense debates in the period about women's rights, divorce law reform, and sex education. For, just as the legal and sociological senses of what constituted a 'case' could be said to have been undergoing a crisis, so too was the other sense which bears most forcefully on the word in *The Good Soldier*: the sexological. In the emerging field of sexology at the turn of the century, in the writings not only of Freud, but also in Britain of Havelock Ellis, sexuality was beginning to be presented in the form of *case histories*; as in Ellis' pioneering book *Sexual Inversion*, the first British study of homosexuality, written with John Addington Symonds, and published first in Germany (where *The Good Soldier*'s 'nerve cures' are set) in 1896, then in English translation the following year.

In one sense, clearly it is the pressure of sexuality in the novel which elicits the uncertainty and disturbance over the nature of the story, and perhaps therefore summons the professional terminology of the 'case' to try to calm that anxiety. The sexuality is very much evident – so much so that hostile early reviewers were outraged by it, and by the suggestion – in a book published in wartime – that British soldiers were philanderers like Ashburnham (*GS* xxv-vi). That very self-evidence of sexual concerns might distract us from noticing that the word 'case' often functioned, in the decades before the war, as an innuendo for the sexual (and for sexual pathology). Consider *The Strange Case of Dr Jekyll and Mr Hyde*, for instance.

Stephen Heath's analysis of Stevenson's tale has now become normative. Heath's article of 1986 was entitled 'Psychopathia Sexualis: Stevenson's Strange Case';[13] its argument that Stevenson's uncanny story of bizarre transformations flipping between professional respectability and vicious monstrosity reflects new ways of writing about sexuality; that its combination of medicalizing discourse and insistence on the strangeness chimes with the emerging sexological discourse (which attempted, precisely, to medicalize sexuality) and especially the debates surrounding homosexuality. (R. Krafft-Ebing, *Psychopathia Sexualis* (1876) had offered some of the first case histories of homosexual men, ten years before the appearance of Stevenson's novella.) According to this reading, the irrupting of Hyde into Jekyll's world is the return of the repressed: sexuality subject to suppression whatever its nature. (*Jekyll and Hyde* manages to intimate not only homosexuality, but also prostitution, and even paedophilia.)

Yet in Ashburnham's case the sexuality isn't suppressed; at least, not until his last, hopeless, and destructive, passion for Nancy. Until then, it is all too evident, both in his conduct and in Dowell's narration. You might say that it's Dowell's nature that represents the repressed; in his continual disavowals of sexual interest or knowledge. But those disavowals have incited critics, including this one, to wonder whether the sexuality at issue in the novel doesn't go beyond

Ashburnham's womanising; either to intimations of a homoerotic bond between Dowell and Ashburnham; or to suspicions of an incestuous or quasi-incestuous feeling between Ashburnham and Nancy.[14]

We might note two odd consequences of this line of enquiry, taking the story as a form of enigma, turning on what is hidden, and subjecting it to a hermeneutics of suspicion. First, that there is another sense in which *The Good Soldier* might read more like *Jekyll and Hyde* than is generally recognized. This would locate the uncanniness less in any repressed sexuality, but in the *transformations* which Ashburnham seems to undergo, at least in Dowell's mind, repeatedly from a vision of gentlemanly perfection to that of a hopelessly immoral libertine. Of course the novel keeps coming up with figures like Peire Vidal, Ludwig the Courageous, and Henry VIII who remind us that that duality is already deeply inscribed in the courtly tradition (though no less damaging for that). But according to this reading Ashburnham is a Jekyll for whom sexuality is the drug that turns him into an object of horror, and which he becomes incapable of controlling.

But the second consequence leads, curiously, to the opposite conclusion: that the enigma of Ashburnham may be not that he contains repressed passions, but that he doesn't; that instead, he may contain – nothing at all:

> Good God, what did they all see in him; for I swear that was all there was of him, inside and out; though they said he was a good soldier. (*GS* 27)

This passage comes after one of the more wonderfully enigmatic impressions in the whole book; and its strangest and most insistent manifestation of the word 'case'. Dowell has described his vivid, if also slightly troubling, first impression of Ashburnham, arriving in the dining room at Nauheim. He gives a few scraps of his conversation over their subsequent friendship – about horses, clothes, investments. Then he comments:

> And that was absolutely all that I knew of him until a month ago – that and the profusion of his cases, all of pigskin and stamped with his initials, E. F. A. There were guncases, and collar cases, and shirt cases, and letter cases and cases each containing four bottles of medicine; and hat cases and helmet cases. It must have needed a whole herd of the Gadarene swine to make up his outfit. And, if I ever penetrated into his private room it would be to see him standing, with his coat and waistcoat off and the immensely long line of his perfectly elegant trousers from waist to boot heel. And he would have a

slightly reflective air and he would be just opening one kind of case and just closing another. (*GS* 27)

The story of the Gadarene swine introduces the disturbing note ironically into this image of immaculate profusion. When Jesus visits the Gadarenes, he casts devils out from a madman (two in Matthew's version), and they enter a herd of pigs who immediately drown themselves.[15] Ford frames the description of the cases between two clauses summing Ashburnham up: 'that was absolutely all that I knew of him'; 'that was all there was of him'. Which gives us the sense that the description of Edward's cases is somehow equivalent to a description of Edward – his 'case history', as it were. There seems to be some kind of equivalent between people looking into Ashburnham – 'Good God, what did they all see in him'? – and Ashburnham himself looking into the cases which bear his initials: 'just opening one kind of case and just closing another'. That, after all, is not a bad description of the way Dowell handles his narrative, looking into one aspect after another.

Ashburnham might seem to be an open and shut case – someone with no content, no substance. But the image Ford gives us of the cases is very puzzling. If the image of Ashburnham opening and shutting his cases is 'all there was of him', what exactly does it tell us about him? At one level it restates the idea that he is an assemblage of clutter. That he amounts to nothing more than a set of stylish accessories; a man of mere surfaces. But the *profusion* of the cases complicates the issue. Is the point that you think you know him, but what you know is just one box, whereas there are many more, and for every one you open another one is closed? Or does it mean that any appearance of complexity is only an appearance? He may seem to have many facets, but each is just a case with an object inside it, nothing more. Or possibly something less: a case without an object.

'[T]hat was all there was of him, inside and out'. Are the cases an image for Ashburnham's outside – the pigskin a second skin, as a pigskin glove conceals a hand; or do they show us something about his inside? Or for the relation between outside and inside? When Dowell says that, he might mean indoors and outdoors: that Edward was like that outside of his private room too. But it might equally mean that Ashburnham's inside and outside are the same; equally superficial. The cases are thus a special kind of thing, with an inside and an outside; which enables them to work as an emblem of emptiness or hollowness, as much as of secret depths.

Ashburnham's cases are signs of class; there for porters to carry, and to enable him to live the life of luxury wherever he goes. But there is also a sense of secret obsession: 'if I ever penetrated into his private room, it would be to see him standing', opening and shutting his cases; as if that's all he ever does. When in Germany he is living out of his cases, certainly. But the prose makes us feel that somehow they *are* his life. Perhaps they have come to represent his feeling of exile from his home at Branshaw, since Leonora had arranged for them to be in India for the eight years before their meeting the Dowells in Nauheim in 1904. That idea of penetration suggests getting to his core; but that core is a profusion of cases; of cases within cases, since the prose connects rooms and cases: the pigskin cases are inside the 'private room', presumably his 'dressing room' (*GS* 131), presumably *en suite* to his and Leonora's bedroom.

If the pigskin cases function, as I am suggesting, as an image of a hermeneutic puzzle – the hermeneutic puzzle as to the nature of Edward Ashburnham – then later in the narrative they become an example of such a puzzle in a different way. True to Ford's avowed impressionist method of giving a strong first impression, then juxta-posing unsettlingly contradictory views,[16] Dowell then complicates Ashburnham's relation to these cases, when he tells us they were Leonora's gift to him, suggesting that her taste was not his:

> She was always buying him expensive things which, as it were, she took off her own back. I have, for instance, spoken of Edward's leather cases. Well, they were not Edward's at all; they were Leonora's manifestations. He liked to be clean, but he preferred, as it were, to be threadbare. (*GS* 130)

What does this information do to the earlier image of Edward's 'slightly reflective air' as he opens one kind of case and shuts another? If Dowell is right – and that of course is in itself an increasing source of uncertainty throughout the novel – then if 'they were not Edward's at all', it might problematize any sense of his attraction to the cases, or identification with them. Even so, if that reflective air doesn't reflect his sense that the cases reflect him, it might instead hint at Leonora's view of Edward as all reflective surface – or as someone who might be easily distracted by reflective surfaces. Again, the glare of the narrative's self-reflection makes the cases hard to diagnose.

The nineteenth-century novel is haunted by enigmas, mysteries. But where classic 'case' stories like *Bleak House* or *The Moonstone* work towards solutions to core mysteries, Ford multiplies the enigma. Ashburnham's story, that is, is not one case, but a whole set. This relates to the emerging sense in the broader period that the self is not one integral thing but multiple. 'My name *is* Legion: for we are many'. But if many, many what? Ford's radical sense of the self as fragmentary, a collection of aspects, a matter of surfaces, rather than an essential and coherent personality, is parallel to the Freudian model of the mind as opaque to itself and divided against itself; and his detective-like history of Ashburnham's 'case' is contemporaneous with Freud's famously detective-story-like case histories. Though, arguably, Ford is more radical – at least, more radical than an ego-psychological reading of Freud that sees analysis as solving the enigma by identifying a repressed desire – in that Ford poses the self as not one enigma but many.

These parallels are easily made, and easily made of almost any literary text of the long turn of the century. I make them mainly to outline the context for what I think is truly distinctive about what Ford does. And this is my main point: that, in *The Good Soldier*, these different senses of the word 'case'; different *discourses* of the 'case' – relate to the novel's curious *imagery* of cases, which itself threads through the plot; pre-eminently in this image of 'the profusion' of Ashburnham's pigskin leather cases. It is because Edward had lent Maisie Maidan 'one of his fascinating cases containing fifteen different sizes of scissors' that she is caught by Leonora coming out of his room. Maisie innocently 'having seen from her window, his departure for the post-office [. . .] had taken the opportunity of returning the case' (*GS* 55). More bizarrely, it is her own case – a large trunk – which serves as her death-bed or coffin, when she falls into it after her heart fails (*GS* 62).[17]

Etymologically a 'case' (from the Latin *cadere*) is a fall; whether a tragic one, or a fall into degradation (remember those poor Gadarene swine). But the logic of the imagery implies containment; Maisie's uncanny trunk, which 'had closed upon her, like the jaws of a gigantic alligator' (*GS* 62) perhaps alluding to Emma Bovary's three-layered coffin. The psychological, medical, moral, philosophical or legal language of 'the case', that is, purports to contain the disturbance of the sexual, the transgressive, the non-normative. And *The Good Soldier* is not only concerned with continence in those physical and social senses, but in the literary sense too: of how the form can contain the content; how Ford's delimiting of the story can contain his narrator's garrulity.

It is hardly surprising – a piece of realism – that a story of so much travel and tourism contains a number of suitcases. There are the trunks Florence mentions when Dowell is on the rope ladder outside her window; she makes him swear he's actually got tickets to Europe, telling him '"I wanted to know, so as to pack my trunks."' (*GS* 69). Then there's the 'very precious leather grip' supposedly containing her heart medicine, which Julius drops and for which Dowell attacks him.

But most of the other instances of the word 'case' in the novel refer to things other than suitcases or trunks. Lest you think Ford was a casual user of the word – Ford whose first novel published after the war would be *The Marsden Case*; and who would end *No More Parades* with General Campion inspecting the kitchen lockers of one Sergeant Case, who claims his mistress is his sister – in case you doubt Ford's self-consciousness in using this word; I shall consider a few of the more salient examples.[18]

There are the 'cases of oranges' – 'I don't know how many', says Dowell – that Florence's uncle takes on their European tour, together with 'half-a-dozen folding chairs in a special case that he always kept in his cabin' (*GS* 22). A special case? In that family?

There is the 'large glass case' containing the Protest documents, which 'Captain Ashburnham had his hands upon' just before Florence so provocatively and ominously puts her hand upon him, touching his wrist (*GS* 39).

'So I do set down a good deal of Leonora's mismanagement of poor dear Edward's case to the peculiarly English form of her religion' says Dowell, his repetition again drawing attention to the word: 'her English Catholic conscience, her rigid principles, her coldness, even her very patience, were, I cannot help thinking, all wrong in this special case' (*GS* 51). But then, as Ford the novelist and Galsworthy's governess knew, everyone is a special case: 'I do not know where the public morality of the case comes in', says Dowell: 'and, of course, no man really knows what he would have done in any given case' (*GS* 74). Indeed, 'one cannot be certain of the way any man will behave in every case – and until one can do that a "character" is of no use to anyone' (*GS* 122), he says, after recounting another tale of sex, crime and enigma:

> Once, however, at our Paris flat we had a maid who appeared to be charming and transparently honest. She stole, nevertheless, one of Florence's diamond rings. She did it, however, to save her young man from going to prison. So here, as somebody says somewhere, was a special case. (*GS* 120)

Sometimes Dowell's harping on the term seems designed to draw attention to it:

> That at any rate was the case with Edward and the poor girl. It was quite literally the case. It was quite literally the case that his passions – for the mistress of the grand-duke, for Mrs. Basil, for little Mrs. Maidan, for Florence, for whom you will – these passions were merely preliminary canters compared to his final race with death for her. (*GS* 93)

'And, now', he says, wearily, 'I suppose I must give you Leonora's side of the case. . . .' (*GS* 136). But just as a case this complex has many sides, so it is composed of many cases, many affairs – a whole Gadarene herd of them. Leonora knows, from certain changes in Edward's demeanour, that:

> in the affair of the poor girl, this was a case in which Edward's moral scruples, or his social code, or his idea that it would be playing it *too* low down, rendered Nancy perfectly safe. (*GS* 156)

Ford isn't playing language games for their own sake. He intuits how the multiplicity of senses and nuances of these words can help him find his way through the labyrinth of this narrative so tortuous Dowell doesn't know how to categorize it: saying 'I call this the Saddest Story, rather than "The Ashburnham Tragedy"' (*GS* 128), but then going on anyway to describe 'the closing scenes of the Ashburnham tragedy' (*GS* 181). What is striking about these examples is how they occur around crucial episodes or ideas in the novel, and often in clusters at those points of maximum intensity; indicating, as they do so, how the Ashburnham story isn't simply tragedy or comedy, sad story or moral tale, but is instead a special case (which needs a superlative to do justice to its uniqueness: the *saddest* story). And that its special quality is conveyed in part by the way the mention of the word 'case' then sparks off other senses and uses. Which is to say that what makes the case of *The Good Soldier* special is not just the intricacy of what Ford called its 'intricate tangle of references and cross-references',[19] but also the poetry of their often enigmatic hints and echoes. Such as the image of Edward's study just before he asks Dowell to accompany him and Nancy for their agonising farewell at the station the next day: 'The candles glowed in the green shades; the reflections were green in the glasses of the book-cases that held guns and fishing-rods' (*GS* 189). At first glance everything is unobtrusively as one might expect in such a county gentleman's habitat. Yet Ford has Flaubert's genius for the unobtrusively bizarre objects that express the pathos of a life (as in the auction of Mme Arnoux' possessions at the end of *L'Education sentimentale*). The things are in the wrong place. The book-cases hold not books but sports gear. The notion of hunting and fishing won't stay in its container. The green light turns the subdued domestic interior eerily into field and water. The predator is about to become the prey.

Yet there's something else in those *book*-cases. How does Dowell survive the sadness and perplexity of his story? He writes. As he explains:

> You may well ask why I write. And yet my reasons are quite many. For it is not unusual in human beings who have witnessed the sack of a city or the falling to pieces of a people to desire to set down what they have witnessed for the benefit of unknown heirs or of generations infinitely remote; or, if you please, just to get the sight out of their heads. (*GS* 12)

The slight awkwardness of that phrase 'quite many', together with the hint of a kind of exorcism in needing to exteriorize a vision of disaster, may suggest that Dowell hasn't got the Gadarene swine quite out of his head; and that, to do so, he needs to put the Ashburnham case into words, into writing; just as Ford closes it into a book.

## NOTES

1   Ford, *The Good Soldier*, ed. Max Saunders, Oxford World's Classics: Oxford University Press, 2012 – henceforth *GS*; p. 119.
2   James Fitzjames Stephen, *Introduction to the Indian Evidence Act*, London: Macmillan, 1872, p. 31. Rex Ferguson, *Criminal Law and the Modernist Novel: Experience on Trial*, Cambridge: Cambridge University Press, 2013 – henceforth 'Ferguson'; p. 90.
3   Ferguson 85. Martin J. Wiener, *Reconstructing the Criminal: Culture, Law and Policy in England, 1830–1814*, Cambridge: Cambridge University Press, 1990, p. 160.
4   Ford, 'Mr. Galsworthy and the Problem of Poverty', *Bystander*, 33 (6 March 1912), 502, 504.

5   Ford, 'The Case of James Lurgan', *Bystander*, 32 (6 December 1911), 535-45.
6   Mary S. Millar, *Dictionary of Literary Biography, Volume 162: British Short-Fiction Writers, 1915-1945*, ed. John H. Rogers, Detroit: Gale Group, 1996, pp. 93-105 (p. 101).
7   Ford, 'Literary Portraits – XIV: M. Anatole France and "L'Affaire Dreyfus"', *Outlook*, 32 (13 Dec. 1913), 826-7. In the 'Dedicatory Letter to Stella Ford', written for the 1927 reissue of *The Good Soldier*, Ford said he sat down to write the novel on 17 December 1913 – his fortieth birthday: *GS* 3.
8   Ford, *Thus to Revisit*, London: Chapman and Hall, 1921, p. 44. Also see *The Critical Attitude*, London: Duckworth, 1911, p. 89, and *A Call*, London: Chatto and Windus, 1910, p. 299.
9   De Quincey, 'Autobiography', *The Collected Writings of Thomas De Quincey*, ed. David Masson, 14 vols, Edinburgh: A. & C. Black, 1889-90, vol. 1, pp. 39, 43. T. E. Hulme, *Speculations*, ed. Herbert Read, London: Kegan Paul, Trench, Trübner, 1924, pp. 171-214.
10  Ford, 'L'Affaire Ingram', *Outlook*, 3 (1 July 1899), 709-10.
11  See Saunders, *Ford Madox Ford: A Dual Life*, 2 vols, Oxford: Oxford University Press, 1996, vol. I, pp. 366-90.
12  See Ford, *England and the English*, ed. Sara Haslam, Manchester: Carcanet, 2003, p. 315. I am very grateful to Sara Haslam for drawing my attention to this conjunction.
13  Stephen Heath, 'Psychopathia Sexualis: Stevenson's Strange Case', *Critical Quarterly*, 28 (1986), 93-108.
14  See Dewey Ganzel, 'What the Letter Said: Fact and Inference in *The Good Soldier* ', *Journal of Modern Literature* , 11 (July 1984), 277–90; Saunders, *Ford Madox Ford*, I, pp. 406, 420-6; and John Sutherland, 'Whose Daughter is Nancy', in *Can Jane Eyre Be Happy?: More Puzzles in Classic Fiction*, Oxford: Oxford University Press, 1997, pp. 210-14.
15  See Matthew 8: 28–32, Mark 5: 1–13, and Luke 8: 26–33.
16  See Ford, *Joseph Conrad: A Personal Remembrance,* London: Duckworth, 1924, pp. 129–30. I'm indebted to Catherine Belsey for suggesting (in discussion) that these cases say more about Leonora than Edward.
17  In the popular Victorian ballad 'The Mistletoe Bough' (1884) by Thomas Haynes Bayley, a young bride disappears during a game of hide-and-seek in her castle. Years later her mouldering skeleton is found, still wearing her bridal wreath: she had accidentally got locked inside an old trunk. The reason for thinking Ford may have known of this story is that the husband is referred to twice as 'Young Lovell', so it may provide a source for Ford's novel immediately preceding *The Good Soldier, The Young Lovell* (1913); and also for the situation at that novel's ending, in which Lovell becomes a hermit, immured in a cave, as haunted by his vision of a goddess as the Lovell in the ballad is haunted by the disappearance of his 'fairy bride'. If so, it may also have provided a source for Maisie's death in *The Good Soldier*, discovered by the Ashburnhams on their return from the castle of M—. See *Everyman's Book of British Ballads*, ed. Roy Palmer, London: Dent, 1980, pp. 78-9.
18  See also Ford, 'The Case of James Lurgan', *Bystander*, 32 (6 December 1911), 535-45.
19  Ford, 'Dedicatory Letter to Stella Ford', *GS* 4.

Bad Nauheim: statue on the fountain steps.

# AFFAIRS OF THE HEART: ILLNESS AND GENDER SUBVERSION IN *THE GOOD SOLDIER*

## Elizabeth Brunton

**Abstract**
While Ford's *The Good Soldier* is set in a spa town for heart patients, the only troubles among the text's central characters are metaphorical: the illnesses of Edward Ashburnham and Florence Dowell are entirely feigned as a means of pursuing extra-marital affairs. This chapter explores the relationship of gender, illness and subversion in the text; while Florence uses feminine, passive suffering as a ruse for her 'unfeminine' sexual desires, Ashburnham's appropriately masculine presentation of a 'heart' caused by hard sportsmanship allows him to follow his sentimental longings. Ford's novel is not the only modernist text to make reference to heart diseases, with Woolf and Joyce also incorporating it into their novels. In *Ulysses,* Paddy Dignam's death of a sudden heart 'breakdown' is in keeping with the hard-drinking, aggressive masculinity of his friends in Dublin, whereas the eponymous heroine of *Mrs Dalloway*'s recent heart trouble has left her white, frail and virginal in convalescence. In Ford's work, I argue, whereas 'true' illness remains in line with gender binaries, the appropriate present-ation of fake illness disguises subversive sexual behaviour. However, the price of such manipulation and transgression in this rigidly gendered society is suicide; Florence and Edward are both victims of uncontrolled passions – their metaphorical hearts – rather than their physical health.

At the very heart of *The Good Soldier* sits that organ itself, with heart patients as protagonists and the spa town of Bad Nauheim as its primary setting.[1] With coronary troubles also found in *Mrs Dalloway*, *Ulysses* and *Howards End*, it seems that modernism more generally could be seen as suffering from sickness of the heart. However, unlike these other novels, the physical illness in Ford's text is entirely fictitious in the two main 'sufferers', feigned in order to pursue sexual liaisons outside of their marriages. Florence Dowell hides her sexual activity behind the smokescreen of a heart requiring rest and calm, avoiding intimacy with her husband while gaining otherwise unthinkable privacy and freedom. Edward Ashburnham comes to Nauheim in pursuit of Maisie Maidan – one in a series of highly sentimental, often imprudent and messy affairs, in which his lack of self-control undermine the 'masculinity' expected of a country landowner and a soldier. Throughout the text, which is concerned with tragic love affairs and unhappy marriages, the word 'heart' is used both physically and metaphorically; affairs of the heart are present in both senses. In this chapter, I will examine the ways in which Ford uses feigned illness in *The Good Soldier*, as his characters find a means of transgressing the sexual codes, and even subverting social norms through their traditionally gendered presentations of sickness. Alongside this, I will briefly look at Joyce's *Ulysses* and Woolf's *Mrs Dalloway* to contrast the gender representation of heart trouble in these texts with Ford's.

At the start of *The Good Soldier*, we learn that Florence and Edward both 'had a heart';[2] their treatment at the spa giving rise to the 'four-square coterie' (*GS* 11) of the friendship between the Ashburnhams and the Dowells. In the opening pages of *Mrs Dalloway*, we learn the eponymous heroine has been recovering from illness, which 'might be her heart, affected, they said, by influenza'.[3] Leopold Bloom's black clothes in his first appearance in 'Calypso' are for his friend Paddy Dignam, who 'died quite suddenly, poor fellow. Heart trouble, I believe'.[4] In all three texts, the importance of the heart as a physical organ, and not merely a metaphorical centre of emotions, is strong. While there are vagaries in the illnesses in these latter two novels, the fact of sickness itself is not in dispute. The revelations that come in *The Good Soldier*, therefore, when the reader learns of Florence's deception and also that 'there was nothing the matter with Edward Ashburnham's heart' (*GS* 41), are disorienting, (further) undermining a narrator who has deliberately fed his reader a series of untruths. These doubts and deceptions underpin the double meaning of the notion of 'having a heart' that runs throughout the text; as Eugene Goodheart has said, the 'diseased heart' is the 'principal conceit' of the novel.[5]

## The Heart at the Turn of the Century

Ford was writing at a time of significant medical advancement, although many of the discoveries leading to modern understandings of coronary heart disease did not come until the two decades following *The Good Soldier*. Understanding of angina pectoris, Florence's supposed diagnosis, had roots in the eighteenth century, when 'the English physician William Heberden described a clinical picture characterised by chest pain and an ominous prognosis'.[6] Illness of the heart was less common as a cause of death; in a comparison of common causes of death between 1909 and 2009, it was reported that:

> The other noticeable feature is the lack of heart disease as a cause of death. The only major cause of death linked to heart disease was "rheumatic fever and rheumatism of the heart," which accounted for only 0.5% of deaths and was itself an infectious disease.[7]

Clearly, this is a complicated picture; Pasteur's germ theory and Lister's antisepsis in the late nineteenth century had reduced the power of the infectious diseases. Later in the twentieth century, the use of antibiotics and the greater access to healthcare in developed countries has meant that non-communicable causes of death (cancer, heart disease and accidents) increased in their prevalence compared with infection. That heart disease was not a leading cause of death in 1909 does not necessarily mean that it was rare, simply that other causes were higher and often caused deaths at a younger age than is common for heart-related fatalities.

Additionally, for the large part, heart illness was for the rich in this era. In 1910, increased activity, less processed food, fewer labour-saving devices, scarcity of automobiles and higher levels of manual labour meant hearts worked harder, more often – if, of course, these factors were applicable to your lifestyle; poorer sectors of society benefitted more than their rich neighbours. In many cases, heart disease was a 'disease of affluence', with increased chances resulting from rich food, alcohol, smoking and a lack of physical exercise.[8] Edward VII's famously self-indulgent lifestyle, including twenty-two cigarettes and thirteen cigars a day, led to three heart attacks on the day of his death.[9]

Other factors were being considered as a reason for this tendency, including heredity: a notion which proves useful to Florence. Aronowitz shows that:

> [William Osler] recognised the much higher frequency of the disease among the 'better classes' [. . .] he did not simply attribute this pattern to greater stress, noting that work and worry are the 'lot of the poor' [. . .] arguing that 'it is as though only a special strain of tissue reacted anginally so to speak, a type evolved amid special circumstances or which existed in certain families'.[10]

To have, as Ford says, 'a heart', implies wealth, leisure, even good breeding; to treat it means the ability to pamper the troublesome organ in spas like Bad Nauheim. The opening page of *The Good Soldier* aligns the reader with these wealthy sufferers, as Dowell states, 'Nauheim always received us from July to September. You will gather from this statement that one of us had, as the saying is, a "heart", and, from the statement that my wife is dead, that she was the sufferer' (*GS* 9). Dowell assumes that his reader will know what the words 'Nauheim' and 'a heart' mean, and while changing medical language may make this more obscure in the twenty-first century, there is an understanding that his readers, like the protagonists, are 'good people'.

## The Gender of Illness

Even where men and women are equally susceptible to illness, social codes govern the experience and presentation of those illnesses in very different ways. Lorber suggests that 'as a social phenomenon, illness has to be gendered because gender is one of the most important statuses in any society'.[11] As a result, the social construction of gender permeates society in all ways, including diagnosis, treatment and even the presentation of suffering. Edward and Florence do not fake their conditions in cahoots; these two 'patients' do not meet until they are both in Nauheim. Ford shows them both as using traditionally gendered presentations of illness to pursue sexual liaisons outside of the marriage vow; furthermore, both use this mask in order to act in ways that question, if not contravene entirely, the gender expectations of their day.

When their heart troubles are introduced, we learn:

> Captain Ashburnham also had a heart. But, whereas a yearly month or so at Nauheim tuned him up to exactly the right pitch for the rest of the twelvemonth, the two months or so were only just enough to keep poor Florence alive from year to year. The reason for his heart was, approximately, polo, or too much hard sportsmanship in his youth. The reason for poor Florence's broken years was a storm at sea upon our first crossing to Europe, and the immediate reasons for our imprisonment in that continent were doctor's orders. They said that even the short Channel crossing might well kill the poor thing. (*GS* 10)

Their illnesses align perfectly with the conventional gender ideals of the age. Edward, a military man, has a damaged heart resulting from 'hard sportsmanship', from overexertion on the polo field: a sign not only of physical prowess but also of social and financial status. In an age where muscular weakness and degeneracy were feared, his medical condition is sufficiently in keeping with the notions of 'muscular Christianity' and healthy virility which dominated late Victorian notions of masculinity. Significantly, while allowing him to retire, neither the record of his military service nor his manliness is disgraced by such an injury. Florence, however, has suffered the onset of her heart's delicate condition as a result of the strain of a storm at sea, in keeping with contemporary belief that 'angina pectoris was frequently observed to follow emotional upset'.[12]

Diane Herndl writes that 'the figure of the invalid woman at once unites the romantic ideology of woman as "body" (as opposed to man as "mind") [and] the Victorian stereotype of woman as weak and delicate'.[13] Furthermore, the passive suffering of the invalid, the delicacy and the submissiveness to (male) doctor's orders, makes the long-term illness fitting for a woman, but ill-suited to a man. For Joyce's Paddy Dignam, there is no passive suffering, given the sudden nature of his death. We are told: 'Breakdown, Martin Cunningham said. Heart.'[14] Death is strangely active in its sudden flurried appearance, and, as I will demonstrate later, serves to amplify his masculinity. It is appropriate then, that Ashburnham's fictional illness only needs his two months of 'rest'. Herndl adds that the female invalid also invoked 'the bourgeois ideal of woman as "conspicuous consumer" (who passively consumes since as an invalid she must be served at all times)'.[15] This plays out in the text as Florence, always beautifully dressed, uses her ongoing suffering to maintain the service of her male-nurse husband, and her position in his eyes as 'poor dear Florence'. Ashburnham, however, prefers to serve rather than be served and is happy showering attention on the true invalid, Maisie Maidan, on the ship from India, where he 'was wrapped up, completely, in his girl – he was almost like a father with a child, trotting about with rugs and physic and things, from deck to deck' (*GS* 50-1). In both the cause and presentation of their pseudo–sicknesses, Edward and Florence fit the gender model.

**Femininity and Illness**
Much of this notion of the female invalid is drawn from nineteenth-century models, and yet, in spite of changing gender roles in the Edwardian era, the 'modern woman' and the 'invalid' do not completely part company, as can be seen in Woolf's *Mrs Dalloway*. At the very start, we are informed that there is 'a touch of the bird about [Clarissa Dalloway], of the jay, blue-green, light, vivacious, though she was over fifty, and grown very white since her illness' (*Mrs D* 3). The ongoing visual reminder of her illness, combined with her bird-like and bright qualities, presents both a feminine nature (the word 'vivacious' is rarely applied to a man), but also the hint of ongoing suffering. There are similarities between Clarissa Dalloway and the character of Maisie Maidan; Dowell suggests she is a woman 'whom other women will allow magnetism. She was very pretty; she was very young; in spite of

her heart she was very gay and light on her feet' (*GS* 124). Like the touch of the bird – the jay – she is presented as vivacious and charming; although there is a suggestion that she poses so little threat to other women that they can 'allow' such compliments. The delicacy of Mrs Dalloway's femininity can be contrasted with Woolf's portrayal of Lady Bruton, who 'seldom did a graceful thing' and whose 'movements were always angular' (*Mrs D* 89). She is eccentric, and able to be so as a result of her status and wealth. Furthermore her behaviour progressively rejects femininity: she 'ha[s] the reputation of being more interested in politics than people', and also for 'talking like a man' (*Mrs D* 89). In her appropriation of the 'masculine' in order to be taken seriously, she appears to reject the 'feminine'; in saying 'she detested illness in the wives of politicians' (*Mrs D* 152), Woolf presents a character who aligns illness with femininity and therefore with weakness.

The emphasis on Mrs Dalloway's whiteness continues throughout the novel, and is equated with an enduring purity. The notion of Mrs Dalloway as a sexual being is denied; she has a 'virginity preserved through childbirth' which clings to her. Her illness, however, erases her sexuality further:

> The sheets were clean, tight stretched in a broad white band from side to side. Narrower and narrower would her bed be. The candle was half burnt down and she had read deep in Baron Marbot's Memoirs… Richard insisted, after her illness, that she must sleep undisturbed [. . .] the room was an attic; the bed narrow; and lying there reading, for she slept badly. (*Mrs D* 27)

Her narrow attic with its tight white sheets leave a ghostly figure lying between them as we know that 'since her illness she had turned almost white' (*Mrs D* 31). Her purity and her illness are connected, leaving femininity in tune with prevailing attitudes. While Clarissa has had moments of passion with Peter and with Sally, she has since retreated into a largely passionless life. In both Woolf and Ford, real illness of the heart in women results in fragility, delicacy and a regression to a state of sexual purity.

The same cannot be said of Florence, although like Mrs Dalloway, she is saved from her husband's embrace by her heart. Dowell says 'it was the ship's doctor who discreetly suggested to me that I had better refrain from manifestations of affection' (*GS* 65); the later part of the paragraph, 'I wonder, though, how Florence got the doctor to enter the conspiracy—the several doctors', may perhaps hint towards the non-marital uses towards which Florence puts her sexual charms. Unlike Mrs

Dalloway, however, in permitting her to spend the hours from ten at night to ten in the morning behind closed doors, Florence's 'heart' grants her a license to pursue not her interest in historical reading, but her adulterous sexual liaisons. The pretence of the passive feminine suffering of long-term illness allows her an active expression of sexual desire, unacceptable for women in the society of her time. Her affair with Jimmy before and after her marriage, also transgresses social and class boundaries, meaning she achieves a freedom that Edward, her lover of nine years, is thwarted in when he kisses a servant-girl on a train. The locked doors to her bedroom open up avenues of sexual opportunity.

Without her marriage to Dowell, Florence would simply not be able to achieve her desires; a woman could not easily start a new life in Europe alone. Furthermore, following her liaison with Jimmy, her Uncle's financial generosity comes only after Dowell's assurances of her 'virtue and constancy' (*GS* 67). As Pines notes, 'When Florence decides to marry, for example, she does so in order to escape the circumscribed world inhabited by her prudish aunts and to gain access to the world at large; her marriage signals the beginning rather than the end of her sexual freedom'.[16] As 'infamous' as her actions may be, they stem from a desire to pursue paths – socially and sexually – unavailable to women, yet equal to those of her male counterparts. Dowell says that 'an overmastering passion' is a 'good excuse for straight action' (*GS* 64), suggesting Florence should have 'bolted' with Jimmy. However, he would not face the same options of 'cut[ting] his throat or spong[ing] on [his] family' should he do the same, as, indeed he does not when he becomes 'one-minded' in his desire to marry Florence (*GS* 65). As his knowledge increases, Florence is judged in social, if not sexual, terms, by Dowell and also Leonora. She is 'vulgar' (*GS* 125) due to her social ambitions; being an 'unstoppable talker' (*GS* 126); and in her willingness to use marriage as a means to further her ends. Double standards make her a villain; Ashburnham, her lover, is also committing the same sins and yet is not risking ostracisation by society. Mr Bagshaw's readiness to disclose her 'shameful' sexual past to a complete stranger (*GS* 75) uncovers the extent to which female sexuality is policed. In the Kilsyte case, Dowell describes Ashburnham as 'following [his] natural but ill-timed inclinations' (*GS* 42), and yet the emergence of Florence from Jimmy's bedroom at 5 a.m. in the house is not judged to be natural at all. Florence's real 'sin' is to be a sexually desiring woman (and an American seeking the recovery of her family's estate), and her 'vulgarity' is simply not to hide it well enough.

By feigning sickness, Florence is using the very patriarchal structures that contain her as the means of subverting them. Herndl writes that 'the woman who becomes sick is portrayed as a figure with no power, subject to the whims of her body or mind, or as a figure of enormous power, able to achieve her desires through the threat of her imminent death, or her disability'.[17] It is this dual role that lies at the heart of Florence's deception; at the start of the text, Dowell describes his late wife in terms of the former figure: a 'poor, frail corpse', barely clinging to life, that he sees 'die ten times a day' (*GS* 66). However, as Dowell comes to realise, she is actually the latter, using precisely this fear of her 'imminent death' as a means to ensure her husband would 'as soon have thought of entering her room without her permission as of burgling a church' (*GS* 66). Dowell is under the illusion that he has an element of power to keep his wife alive. In cases of angina 'therapeutic regimens specifically included avoidance of emotional tension'[18] and here Dowell believes he keeps tight control:

> If she became excited over anything or if her emotions were really stirred her little heart might cease to beat. For twelve years I had to watch every word that any person uttered in any conversation and I had to head it off what the English call "things"—off love, poverty, crime, religion and the rest of it. (*GS* 18)

Florence talks incessantly, but remains within the realms of historical facts and fashion. It seems that the feminised illness of her heart must dominate the contents of her head; it is not coincidental that 'things' she is to be kept away from amount to 'unfeminine' subjects.

The increasingly vicious anger that Dowell displays towards his wife as the novel unfolds seems to result not so much from his cuckolding – indeed he suggests he was 'ready enough' to refrain from sexual passion (*GS* 65), even that she might have been a 'proper wife' had he 'shown warmth' (*GS* 63) – as from the realisation of his true powerlessness. In his interest in Nancy, and his lack of 'sex-interest' for the strong Leonora (*GS* 29), there is a suggestion that Dowell is drawn to vulnerability and helplessness, which offers a rare opportunity for power in a man 'that not even the youngest child [will] pay heed to' (*GS* 43). To be duped by his wife's use of feminine powerlessness as power, therefore, is much more than sexual betrayal. His initial determination to marry Florence results from his vision of her as a victim of a controlling family who intend her never to marry (*GS* 62). His focus on rescuing his damsel in distress leaves him blind to her agenda. If she wasn't a real damsel, he could not have been her knight in shining armour. Instead, he is (to use American slang of the era) a 'patsy', and ultimately, her male nurse. The gender codes by which he is able to maintain a self-image based on a chivalric masculinity are destroyed.

Florence's understanding of the structures of power, and her manipulation of them through the gendering of illness, seem to intensify her culpability for her sexual and social transgressions in Dowell's narrative. Herndl writes that 'a woman's manipulation of that powerlessness is an act that we may understand, but that we have learned to distrust and disapprove of.'[19] Florence's actions lead to radical consequences. Belsey suggests:

> Women as a group in our society are both produced and inhibited by contradictory discourses. Very broadly, they participate both in the liberal humanist discourse of freedom, self-determination and rationality, and at the same time in the specifically feminine discourse offered by society of sub-mission, relative inadequacy and irrational intuition. The attempt to locate a single and coherent subject-position within these contradictory discourses, and in consequence to find a non-contradictory pattern of behaviour, can create intolerable pressures. One way of responding to this situation is to retreat from the contradictions and from the discourse itself and to become 'sick'.[20]

While, as Rob Hawkes notes, this occurs in the novel, with Nancy 'retreating into a catatonic state',[21] Florence instead pretends to be sick, and then retreats dramatically into suicide when her ruse is discovered. She is doubly guilty of transgression in terms of the patriarchal structures of her society; she doesn't just transgress social structures, but actively uses them against those who impose them.

### Masculinity and the Sentimental Heart

While it is certain that Ashburnham uses his 'heart' as a means of pursuing his affair with Maisie Maidan, and then Florence, it is less clear on the surface how this 'excellent magistrate, first rate soldier, one of the best landlords, so they said, in Hampshire' (*GS* 14) subverts gender expectations in the process. His sexual appetites, his military record and his very physique point to him being manly in every respect. If Dowell is described by Levenson as being led by his nose,[22] many readers may agree that Ashburnham is led by another organ entirely. However, this is at best only partially true; his fatal flaw lies in sentimental rather than purely sexual passions. Judging 'masculinity' is complex; it is not a construct with a single form of presentation; the masculine ideal for Ford's 'good people' is a far cry from that of Bloom's Dublin. However, there are underlying similarities; Brannon and Juni's measures of masculinity, which include subscales of '(a) avoiding femininity, (b) concealing emotion, (c) [being] the breadwinner, (d) [being] admired and respected', among others,[23] give common principles whether interpreted by the criteria of Joyce's hard–drinking Citizen, or the 'good people' of Nauheim.

Ashburnham's affairs are not all sexually consummated – indeed this does not seem, in several cases, to even be the desired result. Saunders demonstrates that:

> Counting the women Ashburnham becomes entangled with – Leonora, the Kilsyte girl, La Dolciquita, Mrs Basil, Maisie Maidan, Florence, and finally Nancy Rufford – he could be more polygamously inclined than even Henry VIII. Yet there is little hard evidence that Edward actually committed adultery with more than two of these, La Dolciquita and Florence.[24]

While with the mistress of the Grand Duke, 'he kissed her passionately, violently, with a sudden explosion of the passion that had been bridled all his life [. . .] and he passed the night in her bed' (GS 110), this is not typical of his dalliances. Dowell informs us that '[Ashburnham] had thrown up his commission and had left India and come half the world over in order to follow a woman who had really had a "heart" to Nauheim' (GS 41). The prompt for his feigned heart trouble is Maisie Maidan, with whom he has a romantic, but not sexual, affair as her 'heart was really so bad that she would have succumbed to anything like an impassioned embrace' (GS 44). Concerning Mrs Basil, Dowell tells us, 'I suppose she was his mistress, but I never heard it from Edward, of course' and that 'they carried it on in a high romantic fashion [. . . .] Edward wanted long passages of deep affection kept up in long, long talks' (GS 116). There are suggestions that the relationship had sexual moments – more by accident than design – we are told 'every now and then they "fell," which would give Edward an opportunity for remorse' (GS 116). These two great loves, for Edward, are not based on the gratification of sexual desires, but high romantic ideals. Levenson says he 'violates the duties of his station only to place him at the mercy of his loins',[25] yet this sentimentality is not all sexual passion.

Edward's sentimental yearnings chime more with the turn-of-the-century view of the uncontrolled, emotional woman than the man. Dowell's famous description is that:

> he would pass hours lost in novels of a sentimental type—novels in which
> typewriter girls married Marquises and governesses Earls. And in his books,
> as a rule, the course of true love ran as smooth as buttered honey [. . . .] I have
> seen his eyes filled with tears at reading of a hopeless parting. And he loved,
> with a sentimental yearning, all children, puppies, and the feeble generally. . . .
> (*GS* 26).

Edward's reading material is that of Joyce's Gertie, not the reading of the military man. Hawkes suggests that Ashburnham is driven by 'adherence to the rules of a particular discourse, this time to one of explicitly literary origins, that of the "sentimentalist" lover'.[26] He may be harking back to an earlier, less 'muscular' masculinity, that of the late eighteenth-century Romantic, but even then 'sensibility's unstable relationship with masculinity resulted in rather ambiguous advice about whether, and under what circumstances, a male should give expression to his innermost feelings'.[27] Ford seems to have taken pains in editing to cast Edward as not a 'promiscuous libertine but a sentimentalist', as seen in the revisions to the text. The phrase 'committing rapes' was removed, the active assault on female sexuality replaced by 'having, perhaps, chance love affairs on the highways' (*GS* 48, n 9), in which these things happen while he is passive. His much talked-of virility leaves behind no progeny.[28] Like Dowell, he can be duped: Florence is sufficiently canny about his qualities as to play them to her strengths. Despite being her lover of nine years, he does not know her heart disease was feigned, 'Florence had never undeceived him on that point. She thought it made her seem more romantic' (*GS* 93). The text is unclear as to whether she knows the truth about him. Neither does he know of her suicide; we are told 'why, not even Edward Ashburnham, who was, after all more intimate with her than I was, had an inkling of the truth. He just thought that she had dropped dead of heart disease' (*GS* 78).

In terms of masculinity, much depends on the codes of specific sectors of society, as can be seen in Joyce's Dublin. Dignam's sudden death is able to help restore his good – masculine – name. In Brannon and Juli's analysis, being the 'breadwinner' plays a significant part, whereas Dignam has lost his job due to his heavy drinking (*U* 129). Dignam's death leaves his wife behind with five young children and a heavily mortgaged insurance policy, showing a desire and healthy reproductive function, even if the desire to support and protect his family is lacking. In terms of the specific masculine ideals of working-class Dublin society, this is not a problem; it is those who take responsibility who are feminised. In 'Cyclops', Bloom is mocked by the Citizen and

his cronies with the question, 'do you call that a man?' as a result of
being seen buying baby food before his son, who later died, was born (*U*
439). For this group of men, being a man is about much more than
biological sex, or even the ability to produce children. Tracey Teets
Schwartze suggests: 'To J. J. O'Molloy, Jack Lambert, and the Citizen,
being a man evidently has something to do with fathering children and
then disregarding them.'[29] Bloom is emasculated further in his
unwillingness to drink heavily and buy rounds: something Dignam did to
excess. Paul Lin shows that, in Joyce's Dublin, acting '"like a man"
requires one to put [...] up a pint of stuff whereas Bloom will neither
drink nor buy'.[30] While losing his status as breadwinner may undermine
his masculinity, the act of drinking itself, alongside fathering (but failing
to provide for) five children shows that Dignam is a true man in the
society he inhabits. His sudden heart breakdown and instant death only
bolsters this masculinity.

    Ashburnham's behaviour emasculates him in terms of his own
social status. Recent work on masculinity in the landed gentry
demonstrates the 'significance of self-control in both indicating and
projecting elite masculine authority and status'.[31] Financially extravagant, sentimental and incautious in his dealings, Ashburnham has very
limited self-control. His passion for La Dolciquita leads him to 'drink
like a fish after Leonora was in bed and [. . .] spread himself over the
tables [. . .] for about a fortnight [. . . ] he would have thrown away every
penny that he possessed' (*GS* 112). His debts resulting from this folly of
all-consuming passion (a result of a single night of acquaintance) would
have cost him his estate and his position in society, were it not for the
work of his careful, rational, capable, and self-controlled wife. For the
landed elites:

> Their position as the 'natural rulers' of the country depended on their fitness to
> rule, which emphasises gendered qualities of personal autonomy, independent
> judgement, and self-command. In the words of the Norfolk clergyman and
> tutor, Patrick Sinclair (paraphrasing Lord Shaftesbury), this required them to
> learn to 'govern ourselves, & then to govern others'.[32]

Ashburnham seems incapable of self-governance. While his wife
restores their fortunes, he pines for Mrs Basil (resulting in further
blackmail) and Maisie Maidan. Even his most notable physical passion
(for La Dolciquita) very quickly turns to something less embodied,
'when [she] was at last asleep in his arms he discovered that he was
madly, was passionately, overwhelmingly in love with her. It was a

passion that had arisen like fire in dry corn. He could think of nothing else; he could live for nothing else' (*GS* 110-11). Afterwards, La Dolciquita is businesslike – exchanging sexual favours only for money – and Dowell notes that 'he took it all to be love. Poor devil, he was incredibly naïf' (*GS* 112). When considering separation from Maisie, he becomes ill, 'the sweat poured from him and he trembled with cold [. . .] he had no minute's rest; his bowels turned round and round within him'. He follows Maisie, 'radiantly happy when he carried cups of bouillon to [her]' (*GS* 121-2), in order to make gurgling sentimental noises at her and to call her his little 'rat' (*GS* 57). As Dowell says, 'that was the sort of sentimental ass he was' (*GS* 41). Edward follows his heart in the most traditional sense: he is led by instinct, by passion, and by love. While this behaviour may make him a 'sentimentalist lover' in the Romantic fashion, it isn't fitting for the codes of masculinity of his social station.

If he initially feigns his heart troubles to pursue Maisie Maidan, he uses them for different purposes as the tragic attraction to Nancy – and the ensuing inner struggle – unfolds. Instead of getting him closer to the one he loves, his heart allows him to absent himself from her presence: 'he turned his heavy head and his bloodshot eyes upon his wife and looked full at her. "Doctor von Hauptmann," he said, "has ordered me to go to bed immediately after dinner. My heart's much worse"' (*GS* 93). Whether or not she is, as Saunders contemplates, his biological child, his role as a father figure is enough finally to engender the need for self-control (Saunders 421-3). However, instead of facing up to his feelings, his only instinct is to hide behind the illness that Leonora knows to be fake. As with Florence, the only way out proves to be suicide.

In conclusion, Saunders' claim that '*The Good Soldier* is thus more ambiguous in its sexual politics than has been recognized' can be expanded to thinking about gender politics more broadly (Saunders 426). Ford's novel contains complex gender structures, and these allow transgressive behaviour to play out in the text as a result of feigned illness. While wearing the mask of a soldier and a landed gentleman with strong sexual appetites, Edward's sentimental yearnings, obsessive passions and financial profligacy are more in line with the picture of hysterical femininity than the self-controlled gentleman of the governing class. Unlike Edward, Florence cannot exercise her actively sexual desires or social ambitions and thus uses marriage and the sick-role – two of the very structures controlling femininity in her patriarchal society – as a means of gaining the freedom to do so. Ford lets these two characters explore their trangressive sexual positions through the feigning of illness, but in order to maintain the fiction, it is vital that the expression of their illnesses is presented in a traditionally gendered way. That the characters must both die shows how the freedom of transgression must always come with a cost.


## NOTES

1   Bad Nauheim, around 35km north of Frankfurt, is a spa where 'patients experienced a regimen of saline baths and mostly static exercises'. See C. A. Pierach, S. D. Wangensteen and H. B. Burchell, 'Spa therapy for heart disease – Bad Nauheim (circa 1900)' *American Journal of Cardiology,* 72: 3 (1993) 336-42.
2   Ford Madox Ford, *The Good Soldier*, Norton Critical Edition, ed. Martin Stannard, New York and London: W. W. Norton & Company, 1995; revised 2012 – henceforth *GS*; p. 9.
3   Virginia Woolf, *Mrs Dalloway,* Oxford World Classics, ed. David Bradshaw, Oxford: Oxford University Press, 2000 – henceforth *Mrs D*; p. 4.
4   James Joyce, *Ulysses*, London: Penguin, 1992 – henceforth *U*; pp. 67-8.
5   Eugene Goodheart, 'What Dowell Knew', in Stannard, pp. 382-91, p. 390.
6   Robert A. Aronowitz, *Making Sense of Illness: Science, Society and Disease*, Cambridge: Cambridge University Press, 1998, p. 85.
7   Ian N. Gregory, 'Comparisons between geographies of mortality and deprivation from the 1900s and 2001: spatial analysis of census and mortality statistics', *BMJ* 339: b3454 (2009): http://www.ncbi.nlm.nih.gov/pmc/articles/PMC2741565/ [accessed 18th January 2014].
8   T. McKeown, *The origins of human disease*, Oxford: Blackwell, 1988, p. 233.
9   Christopher Hibbert, *Edward VII: The Last Victorian King*, New York: Palgrave Macmillan, 2007, p. 226.
10  Aronowitz, p. 90.
11  Judith Lorber, *Gender and the Social Construction of Illness*, Thousand Oaks, CA: SAGE, 1997, p. 4.
12  Aronowitz, p. 88.
13  Diane Price Herndl, *Invalid Women: Figuring Feminine Illness in American Fiction and Culture 1840–1940*, Chapel Hill, NC: University of North Carolina Press, 1993, 1997, p. 10.
14  Joyce, p. 119.
15  Herndl, p. 10.
16  Davida Pines, 'Irony and the Marriage Plot in *The Good Soldier*' in *Ford Madox Ford's Modernity,* ed. Robert Hampson and Max Saunders, IFMFS 2, Amsterdam: Rodopi, 2003, pp. 73–83 (p. 75).
17  Herndl, p. 4.
18  Aronowitz, p. 88.
19  Herndl, p. 2.
20  Catherine Belsey, 'Constructing the Subject: Deconstructing the Text', in *Feminist Criticism and Social Change: Sex, Class and Race in Literature and*

*Culture,* ed. by J. Rosenfelt and D. Newton, London: Methuen, 1985, pp. 45-64, (p. 50).

21 Rob Hawkes, *Ford Madox Ford and the Misfit Moderns: Edwardian Fiction and the First World War*, Basingstoke: Palgrave Macmillan, 2012, pp. 9, 49.

22 Michael Levenson, 'Character in *The Good Soldier*', in Stannard, pp. 368-78, p. 377.

23 Vicki S. Helgeson, 'Masculinity, Men's Roles and Coronary Heart Disease' in *Men's Health and Illness: Gender, Power, and the Body*, ed. by Donald Sabo and David Frederick Gordon, Thousand Oaks, CA: SAGE, 1995, 68-104, p. 70.

24 Max Saunders, *Ford Madox Ford: A Dual Life*, 2 vols, Oxford: Oxford University Press, 1996, vol. I – henceforth 'Saunders'; p. 421.

25 Levenson, p. 372.

26 Hawkes, p. 47.

27 Christopher E. Forth, *Masculinity in the Modern West: Gender, Civilisation and the Body*, Basingstoke: Palgrave Macmillan, 2008, p. 47.

28 At least on the surface of the text – Max Saunders has argued convincingly for the possibility of Ashburnham's true status as Nancy Rufford's father. See Saunders, pp. 421-3.

29 Tracey Teets Schwartze, '"Do You Call That a Man?": The Culture of Anxious Masculinity in Joyce's Ulysses', in *Masculinities in Joyce: Postcolonial Constructions*, ed. by Christine van Boheemen and Colleen Lamos, Amsterdam: Rodopi, 2001, pp. 113-36 ( p. 117).

30 Paul Lin, 'Standing the Empire: Drinking, Masculinity and Modernity in "Counterparts"', in *Masculinities in Joyce,* pp. 33-58 (p. 34).

31 Henry French and Mark Rothery, *Man's Estate: Landed Gentry Masculinities, 1660-1900*, Oxford: Oxford University Press, 2012, p. 62

32 French and Rothery, *Man's Estate*, p. 3.

This 1934 advertiser had presumably not read Ford's novel.

# CARING TO KNOW: NARRATIVE TECHNIQUE AND THE ART OF PUBLIC NURSING IN *THE GOOD SOLDIER*

## Barry Sheils

**Abstract**

John Dowell's narrative voice in *The Good Soldier* is suffused with the language of professional care. Not only do many of the novel's major scenes take place in the vicinity of a health institution, but Dowell also designates himself a sick nurse or carer several times throughout the text. In one respect, this conforms to his role as onlooker and cuckold: Dowell is a perennial third party whose dramatic power resides in his apparent facility for abidance and observation. However, as this essay suggests, the nursing metaphor extends beyond Dowell-as-character, to Dowell-as-narrative-device. Through a close reading of Florence Nightingale's 1859 seminal handbook *Notes on Nursing: What it is and what it is not*, I show the remarkable extent to which Nightingale's healthcare prescriptions for nurses were also directed at novelists. The Victorian novelists had got illness completely wrong as far as Nightingale was concerned; and since nursing was equally a question of representing illness, it behoved a good nurse to record and, where necessary, revise in writing whatever the patient or the 'Victorian' figure of the doctor might say. I argue that Dowell's narrative reflects the hermeneutic predicament as well as the power of Nightingale's modern nurse. Within the context of an historical affiliation between novelistic technique and the social technologies of care, this essay examines the tight bond between nursing and writing as it is identified in Ford's novel.

It is a critical truism that the narrative technique of *The Good Soldier* cultivates a sense of epistemological uncertainty. While narrator John Dowell's not-knowing *then* but knowing *now* establishes the basic retrospective framework for the novel, the reader is simultaneously confronted with the possibility that Dowell retains his ignorance up to the present moment of his 'actually writing'.[1] 'I don't know', he tells us, or warns us, several times in the opening few pages of the novel: he doesn't know whether at Nauheim he was stepping out a minuet or standing in 'a prison full of screaming hysterics' (*GS* 13); or whether, when 'only this afternoon' she recounted to him her abortive affair (14), Leonora spoke with the exceptional boldness of a harlot or with ordinary hypocrisy. 'And, if one doesn't know as much as that about the first thing in the world, what does one know and why is one here?'

he concludes in exasperation (15). Dowell's apparent difficulty knowing the meaning of Leonora's words can only anticipate the reader's difficulty knowing the meaning of his narrative; and in this fashion, his self-confessed obtuseness demonstrates the reflexivity of a narrative device. His succeeding questions, sliding from the epistemological 'what does one know?' to the existential 'why is one here?', accord with this witting unreliability, since they remind us of the perils of pure invention. Indeed, 'why is one here?' echoes the 'you may well ask why I write' of just three pages earlier (12), which Dowell attempts to answer several times over the course of the novel, but most memorably in its enigmatic opening line: 'This is the saddest story I have ever heard' (11). Here we have the formative attempt to justify on affective grounds what cannot be justified epistemologically.

In this essay I want to consider why John Dowell's unreliable narration in *The Good Soldier*, most often considered as a technical and meta-fictional device, also exemplifies a problem of care. I suggest that as we address our epistemological queries to the novel – do I know the truth of what happened or not? – a further question is implied: why do I care to know? But care in this context is both the care to know the truth of what happened and, notwithstanding truth content, the care to know what Dowell will write next. Novelistic affect can *make* the reader care – to a fault: a fact reflected within *The Good Soldier* through serial philanderer Edward Ashburnham's promiscuous reading habits. Ashburnham, we recall, is 'a sentimentalist, whose mind' according to Dowell, 'was compounded of indifferent poems and novels' (*GS* 193). On the one hand we can allow that the essential difficulty of Dowell's narrative, torn by interjections and ambivalences, is a strategic disavowal of Ashburnham's sentimentality. Although Dowell's legend 'this is the saddest story' certainly promises sentimental satisfactions, as a discursive, even moralistic, exaggeration, it is hardly in itself a spur to strong feeling. Consequently, the irony of a reader not being able to feel sad once she knows she is expected to feel sad might be deemed a performative feature of *The Good Soldier*'s various prevarications and, indeed, indicative of its difference from definitively sentimental poems and novels. On the other hand, the longer Dowell's narrative remains unstable, at varying degrees of remove from 'actual' events and knowable characters, the longer it remains open to the accusation of novelistic unreality. In this light it is significant that Dowell ends his narrative by considering the admission that he too, like Ashburnham, *is* a sentimentalist (193). Dowell's unreliable narration, so-called, is a device through which the modernist novel can reflect on its novelistic heritage and comment on the history of sentiment as it attached itself to the writing of fiction. In this vein, it also reveals the novel form as an intricate structure of care, even when it is not clear what or who is being cared about.

Dowell advertises the fact that he *cares* – in the first instance for Florence, but also for Edward, Leonora and Nancy – most flagrantly by using the language of nursing. He fulfils several times over the function of a nurse. In Part One, chapter one, recalling Florence's infidelities, he describes himself as leading the life of 'a sedulous, strained nurse' (*GS* 14). In chapter six, after revealing the intricacies of Florence's early involvement with the Ashburnhams over the Maisie Maidan affair, he complains: 'For all that time I was just a male sick nurse' (57). And again, a page later, developing the extent of Florence's infidelity with Edward Ashburnham, he excuses his historical obtuseness as follows: 'You cannot, you see, have acted as nurse to a person for twelve years without wishing to go on nursing them, even though you hate them with the hatred of the adder, and even in the palm of God' (58). Finally, in the fifth chapter of Part Four, after concluding that none among the Ashburnhams and Dowells had gotten what they wanted, he sums up his own case – looking after Nancy – with a precision note of pathos: 'what I wanted mostly was to cease being a nurse-attendant. Well, I am a nurse-attendant' (181).

In fact, Dowell's whole narrative is suffused with the language of professional care. Many of the novel's major scenes take place in the vicinity of a health institution, albeit a resort frequented almost exclusively by haut-bourgeois decadents of the kind found in a Thomas Mann or Arthur Schnitzler story. In Bernard Bergonzi's memorable coinage, Nauheim is the perfect scene for the 'consumptive cosmopolitans' of the early twentieth century to register with appropriate foreboding the imminent catastrophe of the First World War.[2] On the group's famous outing from Nauheim to M[arburg], as Dowell witnesses from the window of the train a black and white cow doing 'just what one doesn't expect of a cow' and uncharacteristically laughs, he describes himself as 'relieved to be off duty' (*GS* 38). His duty, we infer, is to nurse his wife Florence. Florence, he describes elsewhere, as 'a thin-shelled pullet's egg' which he has been charged to carry on his palm. Dowell also presents a reflective affinity with other auxiliary staff in the novel, noting 'the authority' of the bath-attendants and remarking on how correct his first impressions of waiters and chambermaids have generally been (*GS* 120); after all, they lack the deceptive complexity of a character with 'a heart', of a patient like Edward Ashburnham. The most peculiar instance of this kind of identification between Dowell and the auxiliary class is the one he makes with his 'darky servant', Julius. Dowell is so enraged at Julius having dropped the leather grip, containing – we are told – Florence's medication, that he determinedly takes on Julius's nursing duties himself. The manner of this exchange is most telling however since it reveals the coincidence between his subservience to Florence's needs and the menacing extent of his desire for control:

> I saw red. I saw purple. I flew at Julius. On the ferry, it was, I filled up one of his eyes; I threatened to strangle him. And, since an unresisting Negro can make a deplorable noise and a deplorable spectacle, and, since that was Florence's first adventure in the married state, she got a pretty idea of my character. (*GS* 75)

The plot point, most simply, is that henceforth, having seen the occasion of Dowell's murderous rage, Florence will exercise extreme caution when trying to conceal from Dowell her affairs. This provides a convenient excuse for Dowell's subsequent ignorance. But the language is more interesting than this – reminding us that it is only ever a plot point plotted by Dowell – especially the phrase 'an unresisting Negro can make a deplorable noise' which strikes the reader as critically ambiguous. Even allowing that the subject here is supposed to be Julius, who on account of his loyalty refused to fight back, or even protect himself from Dowell's punches, it is surely the 'unresisting' Dowell who was actively responsible for the deplorable spectacle as Florence witnessed it. There is a brief moment of linguistic confusion in which Dowell can be read as 'an unresisting Negro [. . .] [making] a deplorable spectacle' at the same time as he is pummelling 'an unresisting Negro' – a confusion which briefly formalises his character's identification with Julius's nursing duties, as well as the power he expects such duties to confer, namely the power of holding the leather grip and whatever it contains. The spectacle of Dowell's aggression born of his desire to serve is transferred from the revelation of his character to the organisation of his narrative through the double edge of a linguistic ambiguity.

All of these various incidents give Dowell visibility as a nurse through his apparent subordination to the medical requirements of Florence and Nancy. But nursing also helps account for his psychological condition. Readers of the novel often point out how unlikely it is that Dowell truly knows so little of the sex-instinct as he claims, how unlikely that a man so betrayed by the passions of others would render his tale in such extraordinarily passionless terms, averring that he 'feels just nothing at all' (*GS* 58). And yet, in all of this, Dowell only conforms to a behaviour pattern which Freud in *Studies on Hysteria* found to be typical among those who nursed the sick: a condition he termed the 'retention hysteria' in which the nurse's identification with the patient's suffering is so complete that he inhibits or actually cedes his own affective existence.[3] It seems safe to say that Dowell's nursing function is not only basically descriptive of what he does, but that it also helps to explain the psychological motivations of his character; that is, as long as we choose to believe that Dowell remains readable as a character in the traditional sense, his incapacity for feeling anything over Florence's betrayal or his understanding of himself as a 'eunuch' can indeed be characterised as pathologically hysterical (16).[4] There is, however, a broader claim to make, namely that his status as nurse with its implications of gender confusion is inextricable from the narrative ambitions of *The Good Soldier:* the novel's formal and technical accomplishment is somehow consonant with the gendered techniques of nursing. Although it may appear as little more than a felicitous metaphor designed to indicate his auxiliary status behind the principal actors of the sad drama, I suggest that Dowell's peculiar and repetitive self-designation as a 'male sick nurse', especially given the surrounding language of duty, observation and abidance, attributes a particular cultural power to the role of his narration which, in turn, helps determine the complexity of the novel's narrative technique.

The case is strengthened when we consider that Ford had nursed his wife Elsie in the years following 1902; in other words, in the period when much of the action of *The Good Soldier* takes place. As well as biographically foreshadowing an important theme in the novel, several consequences of dealing with Elsie's illness – frequent separations, European travel in search of rest cures, and mutual suspicion between the carer and the cared-for – percolated for Ford as problems of novelistic representation. Before Elsie was diagnosed with a tubercular kidney in 1908, he had suggested that her symptoms might be 'purely hysterical'.[5] But as a writer, whose care was seldom administered without an accompanying reflection on whatever animosity or desire it concealed, he had equal cause to question the sincerity of his altruism. Max Saunders has pointed out that in his 1905 novel *The Benefactor* Ford used 'the idea of altruism as a means of exploring the nature of his own art'.[6] George Moffat, the protagonist of that novel, is, like Ford, a writer; and George's altruism, like his writing – and for that matter Dowell's writing in *The Good Soldier* – is a drug: palliative perhaps, but also addictive, and, at certain dosages, toxic.

## Nursing: What It Is and What It Is Not

Nurses have long been judged indicators of cultural as well as physical health. Goethe's neatly expressed fear that 'in the long run [. . .] the world will have turned into one big hospital and everybody will be everybody else's humane nurse' is by no means untypical in the annals of cultural criticism for its association of the primitive, nutritional ministration of the mother substitute with a futuristic state of sinister dependency.[7] Goethe was writing in the 1780s, before the advent of nursing as a public profession. His decadent nurses therefore, heralding a culture gone in the tooth, could only have been modelled on private volunteers or adjuncts to private households: nursemaids, nannies, wet nurses and such like. By contrast, when Ford was writing *The Good Soldier* in 1913 there was a standing reserve of public nurses – Voluntary Aid Detachments – numbering over fifty thousand in Britain alone.[8] The development of nursing as a public practice in the mid-to-late nineteenth century had two necessary conditions. The first was the emergence of women into the public sphere and the work of public service. Most prominently, it was the profession of 'typist' which, well in advance of suffrage, provided a means of social legitimation for the 'new' women in Britain around the turn of the century; but social histories suggest that the service of public nursing may have played an equal role in encouraging middle-class women to take up, or demand, visible work roles outside the home. The second condition for the development of nursing was the progressive militarisation of civil society. It is indisputable that public nursing and modern warfare went hand in hand, and that the military escalations from the Crimean war to the Boer wars and then to the First World War were in direct proportion to the growth of the nursing infrastructure of Britain – a trend reflected across Europe. If we wish to celebrate the emancipation of women into Victorian and Edwardian workplaces, we must also acknowledge the imperial ideology such emancipation inevitably served. Indeed, we should emphasise the exemplary modernity of nursing in this respect: a standing reserve of fifty thousand nurses was equivalent to a standing reserve of fifty thousand good soldiers, their 'goodness', much like Edward Ashburnham's, derived from their placement at one remove from the act of killing. The military nurse – the auxiliary – was an exemplary sign of the modern bureaucratic state in action.

This bureaucratic character is exemplified in one of the seminal texts of modern nursing practice, Florence Nightingale's *Notes on Nursing: What it is and what it is not* (1859).[9] The historical importance of this work for understanding the construction of gender roles in Victorian Britain needs hardly to be stated – it provides a view of nursing productively at odds with one based upon the mothering instinct or a woman's natural kindness. However, the literary character of its prescriptions has seldom been acknowledged. Not only does Nightingale delight in exposing the fallacies of her novelist contemporaries in the 1850s – how they get it wrong when it comes to matters of reading character or narrating death – but she also proposes a nursely guardianship over modern narrative. For Nightingale, care is foremost a principle of composition in which the air, the light, the ambient sound of the room, and the nutritional intake of the patient, are all to be perceived and reordered; not shy of correcting cooks, architects or town planners, she conceives the hospital ward as an aesthetic totality (*NN* 12-34). Her oft-quoted boast that nursing is 'the finest of Fine Arts' may justly be complemented by the remark that it is the most total of all total arts, being the artwork of the everyday conditions of life. The aesthetic practices which comprise a nurse's routine are not reliant upon natural sympathy, but rather on the demand for a hermeneutic capacity to read and re-interpret given scenes of suffering. Indeed, Nightingale considers defects of novelistic representation as failures in the kind of readerly aptitude she demands of her ideal nurse.

In what follows, I shall determine a resemblance between the nursing strategies as delineated by Nightingale and the narrative strategies of *The Good Soldier* on the grounds that there is a necessary relation between the development of cultural technologies and that of literary technique.[10] More specifically, because the nurse strikes such an anomalous figure within the canon of modernist writing – doubling as a notionally contemptible and feminised figure of sentimental care *and* as a paragon of bureaucratic record keeping – developing this relation will help account for the archly veiled registers of Dowell's voice, which shifts from the elegiac, to the stoically realist, to what Saunders has termed the 'futurological'.[11] This is not to make the claim that Ford paid any particular attention to Nightingale's work, or indeed to the Victorian art of nursing; rather it is to isolate one hitherto under-examined means by which the novel concretises its own representational predicaments.

## The Relation Between Nursing and Narrative

The nurse orders space in the service of discretion, insists Nightingale, yet importantly this is a discretion facilitated by overhearing other peoples' indiscretions. So, for example, nurses should be careful to listen in to what visitors say to patients: if the visitor is giving the patient false hope or an excessively grim prognosis, then the nurse should ready herself to intervene. In fact, she should be suspicious of everything that is said on the ward, including that which is said by the patient himself, since he is almost certainly the least reliable witness to his own illness. This obligation to observe and overhear means that the nurse confronts head on, and often, the problem of fabrication, a subject upon which Nightingale provides the following acute disquisition:

> It is a much more difficult thing to speak the truth than people commonly imagine. There is the want of observation, *simple*, and the want of observation compound, compounded, that is, with the imaginative faculty. Both may equally intend to speak the truth. The information of the first is simply defective. That of the second is much more dangerous. The first gives, in answer to a question asked about a thing that has been before his eyes perhaps for years, information exceedingly imperfect, or says, he does not know. He has never observed. And people simply think him stupid.
>
> The second has observed just a little, but imagination immediately steps in, and he describes the whole thing from imagination merely, being perfectly convinced all the while that he has seen or heard it; or he will repeat a whole conversation, as if it were information which had been addressed to him; whereas it is merely what he has himself said to somebody else. This is the commonest of all. These people do not even observe that they have not observed, nor remember that they have forgotten. (*NN* 106)

That modern nurses are tasked with considering such epistemological old chestnuts as these has consequences for the kind of narrative they are obliged to present: one in which each reported speech act is necessarily italicised, re-interpreted, and scribbled over with marginal notes. The relevance of the final sentence of this passage in particular to Dowell's narration is striking; 'one goes back, one goes forward', he tells us while excusing the 'rambling way' of his narration: 'One remembers points that one has forgotten and one explains then all the more minutely since one recognises that one has forgotten to mention them in their proper places and that one may have given, by omitting them, a false impression' (*GS* 143). As his own first reader, Dowell begins to suspect his capacity for communicating the truth: this while professing, both that his is 'a real story' and that his digressions and doubts will make his story '*seem* most real' (143: my italics). Consequently, the reader can only share Dowell's suspicions: does he endeavour to tell a difficult truth or only an imagined 'truth' we are liable to believe? Has he truly remembered what he has forgotten? This bind is given another twist as his self-professed unreliability becomes a paradoxical spur to narrative rigour. He has 'explained everything' he assures us, 'from the several points of view that were necessary' (143). This accumulative, multi-perspectival, if not quite tireless (Dowell admits to his exhaustion) work of narration stands in stark contrast to the two major incidents he has attempted to recount: the apparent suicides of Maisie Maidan and Florence. It is only to be expected that Dowell does not 'know' for certain that these were indeed suicides – 'Who knows?' (96) he asks with typical knowing-ness. Nevertheless, both scenes, as he depicts them, involve a betrayal of intimacy: Maisie Maidan overhears Edward refer to her by her pet name 'poor little rat' when talking to Florence (60); Florence sees Edward with Nancy 'under the dark trees of the park' adjacent to the Casino (89). In both, it is an unfortunate proximity which allows the indiscretion to be perceived and the illusion of a privileged intimacy to be dispelled. Maisie and Florence fall into suicidal distress because neither is equipped to occupy the position of the third person – the one who overhears or observes. Dowell, by contrast, appears as an expert *third*, a strategic cuckold we might say, whose most remarkable characteristic is his seeming lack of expectation for true intimacy. Where Maisie and Florence confront what they see or hear with an effective lack of suspicion – it is their sincerity (their 'heart') which kills them – Dowell, the eternal survivor, is suspicious at all times, even of himself, his apparent aptitude for the role of onlooker or eavesdropper due to his nurse's eye and ear for prolonged indeterminacy.

Significantly, for Nightingale, it is not only a patient's speech acts which are to be suspected, a patient's physiognomy can also mislead. Like Joseph Conrad in his Preface to *The Nigger of the 'Narcissus'*, she wants to *make* her reader see. But to see is to see as a nurse; and part of seeing as a nurse is to learn of the human face's essential unreliability. '[P]eople never, or scarcely ever, observe enough to know how to distinguish between the effect of exposure, of robust health, of a tender skin, of a tendency to congestion, of suffusion, flushing, or many other things' she instructs, adding the warning that 'the face is often the last to shew emaciation. I should say that the hand was a much surer test than the face, both to flesh, colour, circulation, &c.' (*NN* 116). The menace of literary cliché, Nightingale suggests, is that it privileges the complexion of the face, to the extent of fixing both character and incident to what can be seen there: 'it is generally supposed that paleness is the one indication of almost any violent change in the human being, whether from terror, disease, or anything else. There can be no more false observation [. . . .] de rigueur in novels, but nowhere else' (120). There is an element of the nurse's training, then, in Ford's celebrated technique, developed along with Conrad, of using a character's face as a palimpsest, something which can be noted by the narrator, but then written over, revised and contradicted by further acquaintance, and brought into relief by different physical signs. The Ashburnhams look like 'quite good people', Edward's face is 'light brick-red', his moustache 'yellow as a tooth brush' and so forth (*GS* 26-7); Dowell's narrative comes and goes from these initial observations, and in particular goes nurse-like in pursuit of the hands – knowing full well that hands are always chattering – but finds in his way those 'three hardened gamblers' as he calls them determined to prevent him from seeing their cards.[12] The shift from accepting the conceit of the face to interrogating the parapraxes of the hands is suggestive of a corresponding move from novelistic self-evidence (sentimentalism) to the self-conscious task, constantly imperilled by the problems of dissemblance, of reconstructing 'actual' events.

Time is an important factor in this work of reconstruction. Nightingale's nurse is concerned with recording everyday reality, noting the small inconsistencies of a patient's character, and understanding the vicissitudes of disease: 'I have often seen really good nurses distressed, because they could not impress the doctor with the *real* danger of their patient; and quite provoked because the patient 'would look' either 'so much better' or 'so much worse' than he really is 'when the doctor was there' (*NN* 123 my italics). The doctor who does not listen to the nurse is liable to be fooled by semblance; his surgical interventions and punctual consultations are necessarily fallible without the supreme managerial competence of the nursing project to patiently observe and record pathologies. This same preference for reading the character of illness across time underlies Nightingale's suspicion of climactic death-scenes: 'In writings of fiction, whether novels or biographies, these death-beds are generally depicted as almost seraphic in lucidity of intelligence [. . .] Indifference, excepting with regard to bodily suffering, or to some duty the dying man professes to perform, is the far more usual state' (99). In accordance with Dowell's nursely character, the deaths in *The Good Soldier* present open enigmas in the place of the sentimental spectacle. Maisie, trapped by her own portmanteau as if by 'the jaws of a gigantic alligator'; Florence, 'looking with a puzzled expression at the electric-light bulb that hung from the ceiling'; and Ashburnham, encountered in postscript in the stables with 'a little neat penknife' with which to kill himself, are all far from the copybook of Dickens's Little Nell in *The Old Curiosity Shop*, whose climactic death, according to Ada Leveson, could make Oscar Wilde cry only tears of laughter (*GS* 62, 96, 193).[13] Anti-climax is both a subversion of those Victorian novelistic tropes critiqued by Nightingale, and the consequence of a narrative logic which attempts to explicate a character's death across the extent of his or her life. Such a representational motive, working 'backwards and forwards' over a character's past, necessitates a generalisation of the fatal malaise, as clues to its aetiology are sought out in conditions of apparent health. This is a telling example of how the modern practices of medical care, including the pathologisation of everyday life, and the aesthetic developments of modernism were to converge.

Ford writes appositely in the following well known passage on literary impressionism:

> You meet an English gentleman at your golf club. He is beefy, full of health, the moral of the boy from an English Public School of the finest type. You discover, gradually, that he is hopelessly neurasthenic, dishonest in matters of small change, but unexpectedly self-sacrificing, a dreadful liar but a most painfully careful student of Lepidoptera and, finally, from the public prints, a bigamist who was once, under another name, hammered on the stock

exchange... Still, there he is, the beefy, full-fed fellow, moral of an English Public School product.[14]

If the heroic and punctual figure of the Victorian doctor would likely have proclaimed this gentleman fit as a fiddle and left it at that, thus preparing the way for an unexpected reversal of fortune in the form of the gentleman's tragic demise, Ford's nurse-like narrator, for whom the gradual unfolding of character in all of its many facets is imperative, can only diminish the possibility of any such turn of events. While not absolutely precluding the unexpected incident (there is still room for 'just exactly what one didn't expect' (GS 38)), the duty to care for the complexity of a character over time emphasises processes of narrative revision over and above the clear chronology of a tragic arc. At the same time, however, the implied claim to verisimilitude which accompanies such scrupulous revision – this is how people really strike us, first with a strong impression then with a plethora of supplementary and contradictory details – does not remain solely as a faithful rendering of subjective perception, but is also 'an account' of character, and beyond that points to a generalising record of human characteristics. Through this double sight (subjective *and* objective) we find not only the paradoxical link between impression and abstraction in modernist art, but also the further connection between artistic abstraction and the bureaucratic forms of modern care.

### Petty Management, or Being in More Than One Place at Once

As a narrator who pedantically describes the intimacy of two people as being played-out 'under those four eyes' (GS 46), it is hardly a stretch to conceive Dowell in terms of modern bureaucratic surveillance. To be sure, such an imagined multiplication of a private scene into four single-organ perspectives demonstrates a scopophiliac's desire for knowledge. But it also coheres with the novel's more impersonal ambition to show how particular scenes are structurally overdetermined. For the critic Michael Levenson, Dowell functions as a 'bare ideal' of narrative generation: his character blends imperceptibly into technique.[15] David Trotter has characterised *The Good Soldier*'s search (which is also Dowell's search) for formal abstraction as Cubist in nature, while Saunders has emphasised the impersonality of its formalism.[16] As Levenson suggests, Dowell is a theorist of literary impressionism who embodies the contradictions of his method. In other words, there is understood to be a necessary confusion between

Dowell's voice and Ford's technique, so that even in those cases where Dowell the character seems to err, his narrative capacity is only strengthened.

For example, despite an early boast of competence – of never having let Florence out of his sight ('except when she was safely tucked up in bed') – Dowell subsequently admits that Florence was 'out of his sight most of the time' (GS 72). In a fashion unfitting to a nurse, he has allowed a combination of the patient's guile and a doctor's ill-informed advice to stand in the way of his surveillance. However, at the level of narrative technique this only effectuates a powerful duplication of perspective: by first observing Florence, and then observing his failure to observe her, Dowell manages to present and absent himself from the dramatic action at the same time. In this way, he not only engenders what he calls his new world faintness, but also becomes the Fordian subject of literary impressionism for whom seeing is always, at the same time, a form of not seeing – underwritten by the consideration that given time there is always more to see. This is where Dowell's apparent unreliability and the prescriptive reliability of Nightingale's nurse most clearly crossover: they are equally preoccupied with exceeding a single perspective. The following two quotations – the first from Nightingale advising on the techniques of petty management, the second, an excerpt from Ford's essay on literary impressionism – help demonstrate this paradoxical affinity:

> All the results of good nursing, as detailed in these notes, may be spoiled or utterly negatived by one defect [. . . .] by not knowing how to manage that *what* you do when you are there, shall be done when you are not there. The most devoted friend or nurse cannot be always *there*. Nor is it desirable that she should. (*NN* 35)

> It is, I mean, perfectly possible for a sensitised person, be he poet or prose writer, to have the sense, when he is in one room, that he is in another, or when he is speaking to one person he may be so intensely haunted by the memory or desire for another person that he may be absent-minded or distraught [. . . .] we are almost always in one place with our minds somewhere quite other.[17]

Both quotations, we can safely say, are involved with the fantasy of multiple selves, or the dislocated self, though perhaps at first glance they seem to be taking opposite perspectives. Isn't it the case that Nightingale wants eternal presence of mind – managerial vigilance –

while Ford describes the psychological inevitability of absent-mindedness? And yet it is all too easy to overstate this difference as that between the technocratic and the artistic. We should be careful to note, for instance, that though Ford ends this extract with what appears to be a description of 'our' natural state – and he says that impressionism exists 'to render the queer effects of *real* life' (my italics) – he begins it with reference to a specific class of people: namely the 'sensitised person, be he poet or prose writer'. In other words, he is at pains to point out that the capture of the impression of a moment requires a special training or sensitisation – a technique. Literary impressionism is not naïve; conversely, nurse management is not without its imagination. Indeed, hidden within Nightingale's prescription that the nurse think of herself as not there – for it is impossible to be always there – is the demand for a managerial imagination: an imagination capable of thinking of the spaces the self is absent from. The nurse manager when she occupies a single space must think both of all those spaces she is not occupying as well as of the space she is occupying when she is no longer occupying it; otherwise, how can she organise the ward according to her own sensitive standards? The manager duplicates the self in order to be in more than one place at the same time, and to be in the same place for more time than it's physically possible to be there.

This convergence between literary impressionism and the offices of a modern nurse manager return us to the epistemological ambitions of the modernist novel. Dowell's ambition 'to know', combined with his recurrent doubt that anything can truly be known, surely points the way towards Joyce's doubt-haunted ambitions to capture a single time period from multiple perspectives in 'Wandering Rocks', or to replace personal response with the scientific impersonality of a catalogue of conversations and things in 'Ithaca'.[18] But it also marks a midway point of literary self-reflection. In his attempt to reconstruct the last day of his 'absolute ignorance', beyond his own singular horizon, Dowell incorporates Ashburnham's perspective, which we are told was delivered to him as part of a 'final outburst' (*GS* 89). On the day in question, 4 August 1913, Dowell had already learnt from Bagshawe of Florence's past indiscretions with Jimmy in Ledbury; but that was knowledge from *inside* the Casino. Ashburnham's virtue was that he could explain what was going on *outside* at the same time, and why, in particular, Florence had come running into Dowell's and Bagshawe's sightlines 'with a face whiter than paper'.

'But the fellow talked like a cheap novelist' he says of Ashburnham's report, 'Or like a very good novelist for the matter of that if it's the business of a novelist to make you see things clearly' (89). Ironies abound in this statement, not least in the fact that as Ashburnham makes him see things clearly, Dowell tells us he was yet unaware that Ashburnham was having an affair with his wife. But more significant than this further example of Dowell's strategic obtuseness is how 'the cheap novelist' becomes in the space of a single sentence 'the very good novelist': the literary impressionist who makes you see things clearly is offered no categorical protection from the sentimentalist. We can read Dowell's uncertainty here as expressive of a greater Fordian ambivalence with respect to the fate of sentimental fiction, and of those 'hearts' with which Dowell seems constitutionally incapable of connecting.[19]

It is paradoxical that Ashburnham's taken-for-granted 'English' masculinity is attached to his sentimentalism, a quality often associated with the feminised consolations of reading fiction, while Dowell's handmaid qualities determine his qualified distance from sentimentalism and his obdurate survival as the narrator of this 'saddest story'. Although standing on the cusp of joining Ashburnham in the ranks of the sentimentalists, Dowell ends the novel with a strategic discretion, by holding his tongue and 'trotting off' with a telegram for Leonora, with which we are told she was 'quite pleased' (*GS* 193). The displacement effect of the telegram moving away from the *mise en scène* of Ashburnham's suicide into the non-dramatic register of a qualification – the ironic emphasis on 'quite' – contradicts the sentimental imperative for emotional identification. And yet, if this suggests a superior measure of realism above and beyond the conventions of sentimental fiction, it also indicates a further pathos based on equivocation, displacement, deferral, and a demand for knowledge that can never be fully satisfied. This is reflected by the novel's abrupt shifts in register from the elegiac reconstruction of the past into open 'futurology'; from Dowell's apparent attempt to render character and event in all of its living complexity we are led into an indeterminate image of life support:

> No one visits me, for I visit no one. No one is interested in me, for I have no interests. In twenty minutes or so I shall walk down to the village, beneath my own oaks, alongside my own clumps of gorse, to get the American mail. My tenants, the village boys and the tradesmen will touch their hats to me. So life

peters out. Nancy will sit opposite me with the old nurse standing behind her. (*GS* 192)

Dowell's recurring fantasy of telling his story beside a fire in a country cottage to a sympathetic listener is conspicuously inadequate cover for this futural scene of his 'actually writing', where it is clear that there are no such sentimental givens. The abstract, even catastrophic, weather – 'the great black flood of wind', the 'bright stars', 'the great moon' (18) – with which he imagined at the beginning of his writing project, combines now perhaps two years later with the distant transmissions of an American mail system to render the familiar pastoral of the English countryside (tenants, village boys, tradesmen) as little more than a kitsch apparition. In addition, it is telling that his peregrinations return him to an image of 'the old nurse'. It is not only that the nurse is a reflection of Dowell himself, but also that she en*genders*, dialectically, both the past convention of novelistic consolation in which a character is nursed carefully to his death *and* the bureaucratic and technological structures of care designed to prolong life, no matter how dismal that life is.

Friedrich Kittler has pointed out an almost too-perfect cultural parapraxis of the late nineteenth-century in which a futuristic machine and the woman who operated it were given the same name: 'the typewriter'.[20] What this betrayed – and it was betrayed once more by T. S. Eliot in 1922 when in *The Waste Land* he had his typist become her gramophone 'with automatic hand' – is just how odd an idea it seemed that femininity and the material forces of modernity could be deemed identical, and that the new woman could engender the spirit of technology, of supplementation itself, rather than remain the measured effect of a series of stage-managed political concessions.[21] I suggest that the nurse, as much as the typist, is capable of provoking such a profoundly gendered anxiety: that within the consoling image of an auxiliary who *cares* for a human character resides the germ of a dystopian prosthesis with the capacity to supplant human character altogether. In this respect, writing and nursing have a historically structured bond. Accordingly, it is more than adventitious that Dowell, 'the eunuch' (16), the enduring supplement to others' passions, a character-becoming-technique who has never been a patient or had a 'heart' (24), but who nonetheless strives to write attentively from multiple perspectives, should refer to himself with frequency as someone who *nurses*.

# NOTES

1  Ford, *The Good Soldier*, Oxford World's Classics ed. Max Saunders, Oxford: Oxford University Press, 2012 – henceforth *GS*; p. 12.

2  Bernard Bergonzi, 'Fiction and History: rereading *The Good Soldier*' in Robert Hampson and Max Saunders (eds), *Ford Madox Ford's Modernity*, IFMFS 2, Amsterdam and New York: Rodopi, 2003, pp. 149-58 (p. 151).

3  See Sigmund Freud, 'Fräulein Elisabeth von R', in *Case Histories from Studies on Hysteria* in James Strachey, Anna Freud, Alix Strachey and Alan Tyson (trans. and eds) *The Standard Edition of the Complete Psychological Works of Sigmund Freud*, vol. II, London: Hogarth Press and the Institute for Psychoanalysis, 1955, pp. 135-181. As well as attributing a large degree of importance to sick nursing as a cultural pathology, Freud's following remarks in *Studies on Hysteria*, questioning what it means *to have* 'an impression', anticipate the critical problem throughout *The Good Soldier* in which Dowell's pathological character proves indistinguishable from Ford's narrative technique:

> Anyone whose mind is taken up by the hundred and one tasks of sick-nursing which follow one another in endless succession over a period of weeks and months will, on the one hand, adopt a habit of suppressing every sign of his own emotion, and on the other, will soon divert his attention away from his own impressions, since he has neither time nor strength to do justice to them. Thus he will accumulate a mass of impressions which are capable of affect, which are hardly sufficiently perceived and which, in any case, have not been weakened by abreaction. He is creating material for a 'retention hysteria.' (p. 162)

4  For a smart discussion of the fate of 'character' in *The Good Soldier*, see Michael Levenson, 'Character in *The Good Soldier*' in *Twentieth Century Literature*, 30:4, 1984, pp. 373-87.

5  Max Saunders, *Ford Madox Ford: A Dual Life*, 2 vols., Oxford: Oxford University Press, 1996, I, p. 235.

6  Saunders, *op. cit.*, p. 201.

7  Goethe, Johann Wolfgang von, *Italian Journey* in T. P. Saine and J. L Sammons (eds) and R. R. Heitner (trans.), *Goethe: The Collected Works*, vol. 6, New Jersey: Princeton University, 1989, p. 262.

8  Anne Summers introduces the historical relation between public nursing and the military in *Angels and Citizens: British Women as Military Nurses 1854-1914*, London: Routledge, 1988, pp. 1-11; 237-91.

9  Florence Nightingale, *Notes on Nursing: what it is and what it is not*, New York: Dover Publications, 1969 – henceforth *NN*.

10  What Michel Foucault calls the 'apparatus' [*dispositif*] denotes this interaction, between heterogeneous technologies, techniques and discourses, which produces modern subjectivity. See Graham Burchell (trans.) *Security, Territory, Population: Lectures at the Collège de France: 1977-78*, Basingstoke: Palgrave Macmillan, 2009.

11  Saunders, 'Empire of the Future: *The Inheritors*, Ford, Liberalism and Imperialism' in Laura Colombino and Max Saunders (eds), *The Edwardian Ford*

*Madox Ford*, IFMFS 12, Amsterdam and New York: Rodopi, 2013, pp. 125-40 (p. 128).

12  Dowell exemplifies another Freudian wisdom here: namely, that '[i]f [someone's] lips are silent, he chatters with his finger-tips; betrayal oozes out of him at every pore.' Freud, 'Fragment of an Analysis of a Case of Hysteria', in *A Case of Hysteria, Three Essays on Sexuality and Other Works*, in *The Standard Edition of the Complete Psychological Works of Sigmund Freud*, vol. VII, 1953, p. 88.

13  Wilde's quip as recorded by Leveson has no tears in it: 'One must have a heart of stone to read the death of Little Nell without laughing'. Ada Leveson, *Letters to the Sphinx from Oscar Wilde and Reminiscences from the Author*, London: Westminster Press, 1930, pp. 39-40.

14  Ford, *Joseph Conrad: a Personal Remembrance*, London: Duckworth and Co., 1924, pp. 129-30.

15  Levenson, *op. cit.*, pp. 383-5.

16  David Trotter, *Paranoid Modernism: Literary Experiment, Psychosis and the Professionalisation of English Society*, Oxford: Oxford University Press, 2001, p. 218; Saunders, *Ford Madox Ford: A Dual Life*, I, pp. 429-38.

17  Ford, 'On Impressionism' in Frank MacShane (ed.) *Critical Writings of Ford Madox Ford*, Lincoln: University of Nebraska Press, 1967, pp. 40-1.

18  James Joyce, *Ulysses*, London: Penguin Books, 1992, pp. 280-328; 776-870.

19  Although enduringly associated with the masculinist masquerade of those writers including T. E. Hulme, Ezra Pound and Wyndham Lewis who denigrated sentimental fiction for its soft, consoling qualities, in *The Good Soldier* Ford seems less disposed to jettison sentiment than to hold it close in dialectic relation to his own writing. See Jeffrey Mathes McCarthy, '*The Good Soldier* and the War for British Modernism', in *Modern Fiction Studies*, 45:2 (1999), 303-39.

20  Friedrich Kittler, *Gramophone, Film, Typewriter*, Geoffrey Winthrop-Young and Michael Wutz (trans.), Stanford, CA: Stanford University Press, 1999, pp. 183-265.

21  T. S. Eliot, *Selected Poems*, London: Faber and Faber, 1964, p. 60.

# 'RABBITING ON': FERTILITY, REFORMERS AND *THE GOOD SOLDIER*

## Paul Skinner

**Abstract**

In *Some Do Not. . .*, Sylvia Tietjens accuses her husband of 'immorality', quoting views of his that bear unmistakeable traces of the nationwide concerns with degeneration and the language of eugenics prevalent in Edwardian England, specifically, the proposal to consign to 'the lethal chamber' the sickly and feeble-minded. A decade earlier, the same themes are aired in Ford's *Critical Attitude*, where he seems to write *in propria persona*. In 1910, Winston Churchill had written to Asquith of the 'terrible danger to the race' posed by the 'multiplication of the feeble-minded' and he was among the 400 delegates at the First International Eugenics Congress held in London two years later. In fact, such concerns and prejudices were found across the whole political – and cultural – spectrum, cropping up in various guises in the writings of Wells, Shaw, D. H. Lawrence and Sidney Webb. This chapter revisits Ford's *The Good Soldier* in the light of these concerns about the worrying fertility of the underclass, the declining birth-rate among the middle and upper classes, and the health of a nation already widely seen as heading inevitably towards war, and considers the extent to which the language and metaphors of such debates, together with Ford's hostility towards 'reformers', are inscribed in the pages of the novel.

In Ford Madox Ford's *Some Do Not . . .*, Sylvia Tietjens seeks to counter the assertions of her mother and of Father Consett, that her husband Christopher is 'a good man' and 'perfectly sound':

> "you don't know. . . . Look here. Try and be just. Suppose I'm looking at the *Times* at breakfast and say, not having spoken to him for a week: 'It's wonderful what the doctors are doing. Have you seen the latest?' And at once he'll be on his high-horse—he knows *every*thing!—and he'll prove . . . *prove .* . . that all unhealthy children must be lethal-chambered or the world will go to pieces. [ . . . ]"[1]

This conversation takes place, we surmise, a couple of years before the world-out-there *did* go to pieces, a great many of other people's children expiring in a wide but surely lethal chamber. We may recall that the Tietjens' child 'had been a seven months' child, rather ailing', about whom Christopher is 'perfectly soppy' and whose life he may

have saved by plunging the sick child's body into a bath of ice to
bring his temperature down (*SDN* 21, 52).[2]

In Ford's *The Critical Attitude*, essays first published in the
*English Review*, we find:

> But that, logically speaking [ . . . ] these degenerates should be either executed
> or relegated to pest colonies as in mediaeval times the lepers were—that this
> is the logical corollary of the modern commercial state, no thinking person
> could very well deny. But imagine the dislike that would be felt even by the
> normal, the prosperous, and the perfectly healthy for the constructive critic
> who first seriously enunciated this doctrine, or for the statesman who
> attempted to enforce a Poor Law based upon it.[3]

He foresees the coming of 'advocates [ . . . ] for the extinction, painless or otherwise, of the physically weak, of the unemployed, or even
of the merely unfortunate', and the endless expression of opposing
views, which would risk producing 'in the public mind a weariness, a
confusion that leads in the end to something amounting almost to
indifference' (*CA* 119-20).

How seriously should we take such statements? What is there
here to flag up satirical intent? The phrase 'constructive critic' surely
has positive associations for Ford, if not for his friend Ezra Pound
(then getting into *Blast* mode), whose 'An Essay in Constructive
Criticism. With Apologies to Mr F—d M–d–x H—ff–r in the
"Stoutlook"', appeared in the *Egoist* in February 1914.[4] Perhaps the
stress on logic, particularly 'the logical corollary of the modern
commercial state' hints at mischief but, certainly, from this distance,
there's a marked degree of risk-taking. So, characteristically, there
was with George Bernard Shaw's speech to the Eugenics Education
Society in March 1910 which prompted the headline 'Lethal Chamber
essential to Eugenics' in the *Daily News* and the *Birmingham Daily
Mail*. Apart from G. K. Chesterton in the *Illustrated London News*,
there were very few other papers that, in Dan Stone's words, 'also
recognised it as a skit on the dreams of the eugenicists'.[5] Clearly, not
everyone was in on the joke.

The theme of 'degeneration', as Venetia Abdalla recently
reminded us,[6] runs through much of the later nineteenth century and
romps into the twentieth. Following the Boer War and the realisation
that barely a third of the volunteers were sufficiently fit to join the
army, 'the conviction that the British race was degenerating physically
became increasingly prevalent.'[7]

In 1884 the Battersea Dogs' Home had begun to use carbonic acid gas to put down unwanted animals, following Dr Benjamin Ward Richardson's patenting of his 'Lethal Chamber for the Painless Extinction of Lower Animal Life'. The term made its way into popular use, as did suggestions that it be used on humans.[8] At polite London dinner parties, guests 'discussed the threat of the "unfit" and the virtues of the "lethal chamber."'[9] 'If I had my way', D. H. Lawrence wrote jauntily to Blanche Jennings in October 1908:

> I would build a lethal chamber as big as the Crystal Palace, with a military band playing softly, and a Cinematograph working brightly; then I'd go out in the back streets and main streets and bring them in, all the sick, the halt, and the maimed; I would lead them gently, and they would smile me a weary thanks; and the band would softly bubble out the "Hallelujah Chorus". [10]

In *Anticipations*, H. G. Wells writes of 'the merciful obliteration of weak and silly and pointless things', for whom 'the men of the New Republic will have little pity and less benevolence'.[11] In *A Modern Utopia*, he discusses the 'obvious devices by which' the future State 'will achieve the maximum elimination of its feeble and spiritless folk in every generation with the minimum of suffering and public disorder'.[12]

Following reports on Physical Deterioration and on the Feeble-Minded, the Mental Deficiencies Act was passed in 1913, representing, in Daniel Pick's view, 'a complex compromise with eugenic alarmism'.[13] Such phrases as 'race suicide' had begun to circulate. Sidney Webb's 1907 Fabian publication, *The Decline of the Birth Rate*, expressed fears about decreasing British fertility set against the fact that children were being 'freely born' to Irish Catholics, Jewish immigrants, the thriftless and the irresponsible. One outcome might be 'this country gradually falling to the Irish and the Jews'.[14] By 1911, 'even such relatively moderate eugenicists' as Dr. F. W. Mott 'deplored the "neuropathic taint"' carried by children born to 'alien' Jews and Irish Catholics but also to 'the feeble-minded, to the pauper [. . .], to the thriftless casual laborers, to the criminals and . . . the denizens of one-roomed tenements of our great cities.'[15] Two years before Winston Churchill attended the First International Eugenics Congress in London, one of 400 delegates that included a couple of lords and several European ambassadors, he wrote to the Prime Minister: 'I am convinced that the multiplication of the Feeble-Minded, which is proceeding now at an artificial rate, unchecked by any of the old restraints of nature, and actually fostered by civilised conditions, is a very terrible danger to the race.'[16] Concern was growing that 'the feeble-minded were far more fertile than the rest of the population'[17] and the 1911 census confirmed the sharp fall in middle-class married fertility in contrast to the marked rise among the unskilled.[18] There were diverse reasons advanced to account for this: the rising cost of living, women's educational, economic and social aspirations, the wider availability of contraception. Whatever the cause, the fertility rate of the professional classes was diminishing appreciably. The feckless, the unemployed, the sick, the feeble-minded, on the other hand, were, it seemed, breeding like rabbits.

### The Good Soldier

> Bramshaw Manor lies in a little hollow with lawns across it and pine-woods on the fringe of the dip. The immense wind, coming from across the forest, roared overhead. But the view from the window was perfectly quiet and grey. Not a thing stirred, except a couple of rabbits on the extreme edge of the lawn. It was Leonora's own little study that we were in and we were waiting for the tea to be brought. I, as I said, was sitting in the deep chair, Leonora was standing in the window twirling the wooden acorn at the end of the window-blind cord desultorily round and round.[19] She looked across the lawn and said, as far as I can remember:
>
> "Edward has been dead only ten days and yet there are rabbits on the lawn."
>
> I understand that rabbits do a great deal of harm to the short grass in England. And then she turned round to me and said without any adornment at all, for I remember her exact words:
>
> "I think it was stupid of Florence to commit suicide."[20]

Rabbits in conjunction with death by suicide will be followed, in due course, by rabbits in conjunction with pregnancy:

> Edward was the normal man, but there was too much of the sentimentalist about him; and society does not need too many sentimentalists. Nancy was a splendid creature, but she had about her a touch of madness. Society does not need individuals with touches of madness about them. So Edward and Nancy found themselves steamrolled out and Leonora survives, the perfectly normal type, married to a man who is rather like a rabbit. For Rodney Bayham is rather like a rabbit, and I hear that Leonora is expected to have a baby in three months' time [. . . .] Yes, society must go on; it must breed, like rabbits. (GS 158, 168)

Here, then, are the rabbits. Where are the children?

Although Edward and Leonora 'never had a child' (*GS* 103), there are many children in *The Good Soldier*. Yet somehow, like Groby Hall in *Parade's End*, they are never quite *there*. Edward Ashburnham 'loved, with a sentimental yearning, all children, puppies, and the feeble generally. . . .' but this is disappointingly indefinite (*GS* 26) as is the generic 'child crying in the street' (*GS* 69), to which he also responds. There is Maisie Maidan, an object of sexual desire, one might think, presumably to her husband, if not to Captain Ashburnham but she is, rather, 'the child' (*GS* 43, 57, 58, 127), 'the poor child' (*GS* 50, 56, 57), to whom Leonora is almost a mother, not least when she is 'hitting a naughty child' (*GS* 51) and to whom Edward, again, is 'almost like a father with a child' (*GS* 51). She is even, we gather, 'submissive' to John Dowell, 'that not the youngest child will ever pay heed to' (*GS* 43). Leonora listens to Florence like a mother to the child at its knee (*GS* 41), while Nancy will eventually speak to Leonora as if the older woman were 'a tiny child' (*GS* 144). In the wake of the Kilsyte case, Leonora seemingly accepts that Edward was just administering 'fatherly comfort to a weeping child' (*GS* 108). There are allusions to Nancy Rufford's childhood (*GS* 89, 90) and to Colonel Rufford's child (*GS* 156, 157) but we see Nancy essentially as an adult: young but nevertheless as focus of adult male desire. Dowell is, he says, in love with her: yet she is mad and he is in love, rather, with 'the poor child's memory' (*GS* 87), yet another ambiguous phrase, since her memory is apparently blank. Even those children directly presented are, somehow, still not *quite* there. Though longstanding friends, it 'happened that the Ashburnhams had never seen any of the Powys girls': fittingly, of the seven daughters, Edward will choose Leonora because her face is rendered almost invisible in the photograph that her parents send to Edward's (*GS* 96, 97). The adulterous Mr Brand is pictured playing with his children; but this is in Nancy's recollection and, oddly, they were not *seen*. Not, at least, by Mr Brand, because he was playing Blind Man's Buff with them at the time (and kissing his wife when he caught her: *GS* 146). Leonora is, Dowell remarks, the normal woman, 'desiring children' (*GS* 159) – a slightly worrying phrase in some contexts, not least because of the lingering possibility that Edward is Nancy's true father[21] – but her giving birth is still prospective, though it is already clearly settled that 'the child is to be brought up a Romanist' (*GS* 168).

In the autumn of 1913, just before Ford began work on *The Good Soldier*, Chatto and Windus published *The Desirable Alien: At*

*Home in Germany*, ascribed to Violet Hunt but with a preface, two chapters and a number of extensive footnotes by Ford.

For those with rabbits on their mind, there are several passages of interest to be found in one of Ford's chapters: 'We lay quite still, the dog stood perfectly still and barked. It seemed to resemble the result of several crosses between a rat, a rabbit, and a wire-haired terrier'.[22] Warm sun, blue sky:

> the dog-rabbit-rat entertains us with the queer sound of its two hundred and forty barks a minute. But are we, English-Westphalian-Hessian—a queer mixture like that of the rat-rabbit-dog—are we going to get up and do anything about it? Not a bit of it. We shall not be even as energetic as the triple quadruped. We have not got so much as a bark in us. (*DA* 213)

Despite or, perhaps, because of, being far from home, 'home politics' preys upon their minds: 'we say once more, "It is the will of God." Rat-dog-rabbit; English-Westphalian-Hessian; one of three will rule us in the end, Prussian, Jew, or hungry tradesman. And for ourselves we say as we get up and go down the hill: "Please God that it will be the Prussian"' (*DA* 217). Finally, another canine encounter:

> Pushing through the hawthorn hedge of the first house in the village there comes another dog. But it is a puppy; it is smaller than a rat; it resembles a brown cloth child's toy. It is the child of the rat-dog-rabbit, and it is more absurd than any creature reported by Sir Richard Mandeville or by Gulliver. It plants its four legs in the warm turf, and it barks, and it barks. We stand and look at it, and it continues to bark. It does not move; nothing will move it. It is administering. That breed will not die out, you see. (*DA* 218)

The oddly repeated tripartite clusters recall, of course, both Ford's difficulties with at least one-third of the Holy Trinity and his relaxed views of race and nationality expressed in his preface to *The Spirit of the People*: 'The author can claim to be a quite ordinary man, with the common tastes and that mixture in about equal parts of English, Celtic and Teutonic bloods that goes to make up the usual Anglo-Saxon of these islands.'[23] They also prepare us for the innumerable such repetitions in *The Good Soldier* itself.[24]

But what precisely is the 'breed' that Ford refers to? Might it be related to that 'rabble' in Ezra Pound's 1913 poem 'The Garden'?

> Like a skein of loose silk blown against a wall
> She walks by the railing of a path in Kensington Gardens,
> And she is dying piece-meal

of a sort of emotional anaemia.

And round about there is a rabble
Of the filthy, sturdy unkillable infants of the very poor.
They shall inherit the earth.

In her is the end of breeding.
Her boredom is exquisite and excessive.[25]

Boredom among high-born women was no doubt on Pound's mind just then: he was working on Arnaut Daniel and 'Troubadours—Their Sorts and Conditions' would appear that October ('There was unspeakable boredom in the castles. The chivalric singing was devised to lighten the boredom; and this very singing became itself in due time, in the manner of all things, an ennui.')[26] But fertility was also on his mind in the season of *Blast*, as is made clear by his letter to John Quinn about the phallic and literally seminal element of Vorticism, 'enough to repopulate the island with active and vigorous animals'.[27] This is the backdrop to Ford's memory of that time, in which 'Those young people had done their best to make a man of me'.[28] Another element may be the terms of Pound's attack on Amy Lowell and what he saw as her dilution of Imagism, the implied idea of an excessive fluidity, of unstoppable talking as incontinence – as *The Good Soldier* has it: 'and talk. And talk! My God!', and again, 'talking, talking, talking' (*GS* 135, 159). A *talked* novel. Rabbiting on, so to speak.

**Reformers**
But is it, perhaps, another breed that Ford is thinking of? That puppy, that child, that absurd child's cloth toy was, we recall, 'administering'. Though we are not quite yet, historically, under the thumb of those minor officials only too happy to administer the Defence of the Realm Act, 'the unlovely DORA' (*IWN* 84), we already have those reformers to whom Ford so often alludes – and with whom he had been long familiar.[29] None of them, surely, would want too many sentimentalists or individuals with a touch of madness. And to a great many people, the admirable, worthy, practically progressive gas-and-water socialism of the Fabians and their allies threatened a levelling down, an imposed conformity, a rubbing away of oddities and eccentricities.

*High Germany* (1912) included Ford's 'Süssmund's Address to an Unknown God', in which he imagined, neither for the first nor the last time, a heaven in which he might find some peace:

> with treachery
> Of the sword and dagger kind to keep it sweet
> – Adultery, foul murder, pleasant things,
> A touch of incest, theft, but no Reformers.[30]

Satirical, yes; coat-trailing, deliberately provocative, no doubt; but recognisably the Ford who would, shortly afterwards, write: 'I think that what we want most of all in the literature of to-day is religion, is intolerance, is persecution, and not the mawkish flapdoodle of culture, Fabianism, peace, and good will. Real good religion, a violent thing full of hatreds and exclusions!'[31] Or this: 'But I do want anger; I do want fury; I do want either to burn or to be burnt at Smithfield.'[32]

In the same month, writing of Gilbert Cannan, Ford remarked: 'He is not a satirist like—but we have no satirist; not an ironist like Mr. Galsworthy. He is not a social reformer like Mr. and Mrs. Webb, or a preacher like myself.'[33] And four months later:

> I do not mean that a writer of novels should hate governments, or institutions, or organized cruelties. Such a man is a Social Reformer. But a certain hatred for certain types, a certain cynical dislike for the imbecile, gross, and stupid nature of things, for the meannesses of the human, for want of imagination, and for the measure of hypocrisy that is necessary to keep us poor human things all going on—that sort of hatred is an almost necessary motive power for the artist.[34]

In October 1913, Ford wrote of the writers he had recently treated in the columns of *The Outlook*: 'It is remarkable to observe how the virus of French influence has "taken" in this land. It has produced sociologists.' And he concluded that: 'the work that is being turned out for us by our novelists who now "count" suggests nothing so much to me as a modern Anglican church with a brass-railed pulpit, and an active vicar directing with energy "social endeavour" amongst the respectable poor.'[35]

I make no new and adventurous claims for what *The Good Soldier is* – I merely emphasise what it is *not*: and that is *not* isolated from, or raised fastidiously above, the political and social issues and controversies of its day. However idiosyncratically or elliptically, it engages with them and uses, at least in part, their language, their terms of discourse and their weapons. So that when Ford writes of: 'the purely economic school, the imbecile Fabian Society, the Rationalist Press Association, and all that cretinism';[36] or refers to 'Mr. Lloyd George, holding quite honestly doctrines that are the merest imbecility',[37] such choices as 'cretinism' and 'imbecility' are very much in tune with the discussions and provisions related to The Mental Deficiency Act. The debates of 1912-13 which preceded the passing of the bill were, Michael Freeden notes, 'One of the rare occasions on which eugenics actually occupied the national political stage'.[38]

Nor do I wish to provoke the suspicion that I'm foisting onto Ford a burdensome architecture of rabbity symbolism. He had spent many years in the country and refers to rabbits dozens of times in a quite unexceptionable manner – but a few occasions may warrant closer scrutiny. His story of being made to give his pet rabbit to his brother Oliver, Oliver having accidentally stepped on his own rabbit and killed it, hints at his complex familial relations, not least with his mother (*IWN* 122).[39] In the course of his fascinated recollections of anarchists he has known, he remembers Prince Kropotkin opposing – 'in low tones' – Tom Mann's excited urgings to destruction by suggesting that '"we must take example of the rabbit and found communistic settlements."'[40] In *The Heart of the Country*, 'the scampering profusion of wild rabbits' is a part of the rural plenty that renders the poor slum child 'absolutely breathless' (*EE* 124) and, by 1914, rabbit-pie has become a symbol of 'the whole tragedy of life' – the life, at any rate, of Mr Jones, the character used by Ford to serve as vehicle for discussion of the tenets of impressionism.[41]

But perhaps the most germane example is that of John Galsworthy, a man whom Ford viewed with a warm and lasting affection, and a novelist whom he saw in increasingly dispirited terms. In 1907, he wrote reassuringly that 'the English reader need not be alarmed. Mr Galsworthy is English: he is not the man to stop at Art; he will go on to being useful to the Republic'.[42] Elsewhere he recalled the amazement with which he saw Galsworthy at work: 'the grim persistence [ . . . ] the dog-like tenacity'. He would, Ford writes, 'ponder for hours and hours. Then the little rabbits would creep out to die after the battues' and the screws would be tightened until 'the cruel stupidity of men and their institutions was shown at its apogee' (*IWN* 36, 37). In *Return to Yesterday*, he discusses Galsworthy's *The Country House*, in which the battue is described, particularly the 'poor little wounded rabbit' creeping out 'into the twilight open to die', and the correspondence that resulted from Ford's review (*RY* 213). That rabbit can stand for the sentimentality, the reforming or crusading impulse, which Ford saw as increasingly damaging Galsworthy's work. And Galsworthy will stand, I think, for reformers in general, or rather, the ulterior motives that divert the author from his or her art, as Ford sees it. Ford's enthusiasm for the early work of both Kipling and Lawrence persisted; but he saw in their later writings a worrying tendency to urge their personal political or philosophical views. Discussing the temptation for the 'mere writer' to become dissatisfied with that role and so attempt to become 'a social reformer, a man of action or a censor of the State', Ford commented: 'The most dismal instance of this last tendency is Mr Rudyard Kipling' (*CA* 106). For his part, Lawrence could not, Ford thought, resist adding his own clamorous voice to those of his characters: 'he indulges his moods too much - at the expense of his subject'. In a rare reference to Lawrence's postwar work, Ford observed that, 'in *Women in Love*, a recent novel, Mr Lawrence gives us in all seriousness, during a discussion of Love-in-Liberty and Liberty-in-Love the most ridiculous sentence that was ever set down by the human pen. I regret that it is too indecent to be quoted in this context'. Ford acknowledged the importance of sex ('along with eating and other physical processes') and remarked that the novelist in particular should 'regard it with composure', adding 'But so few do' (*CE* 215). The clear implication is that Lawrence is not among those few.

The Good Soldier concerns those 'good people' whom all those reformers would surely wish to *breed*. Yet Ford gives us a narrator often regarded as both a eunuch and a deluded fool; a hero who is a serial adulterer and a suicide; a wife who is also both adulterer and suicide; a young woman who is crazy. The fifth major character is cold, manipulative, Irish and Catholic! She is also, of course, the novel's most dedicated reformer, certainly of her husband and of the Ashburnham finances. But she'll have a child with a man like a rabbit which *does*, perhaps, bode well for the 'modern commercial state' and even its future military might. And this *is* a fiction, after all, albeit one with restless Fordian ghosts and shadows, not least those of lost daughters. Modernist masterpiece, yes; triumph of form and structure, yes. But *The Good Soldier* is also undeniably, one might even say, ineluctably, a novel of its time and place.

# NOTES

1 Ford Madox Ford, *Some Do Not . . .*, 1924; edited by Max Saunders, Manchester: Carcanet, 2010 – henceforth *SDN*; p. 52.

2 See also Ford Madox Ford, *No More Parades*, 1925; edited by Joseph Wiesenfarth, Manchester: Carcanet, 2011, pp. 176-7.

3 Ford, *The Critical Attitude*, London: Duckworth, 1911 – henceforth *CA*; p. 20. The first chapter, 'On the Objection to the Critical Attitude', was first published in February 1910, the fifth, 'The Passing of the Great Figure', in December 1909.

4 Brita Lindberg-Seyersted suggests that 'it may have been sparked off by one of the installments in Ford's series of "Literary Portraits" in the Outlook': *Pound/Ford: The Story of a Literary Friendship*, London: Faber & Faber, 1982, p. 22. The offending word, 'constructive', crops up in several 'Literary Portraits' but a likely candidate, preceding Pound's piece by a little over three weeks, is 'Literary Portraits – XX. Mr. Gilbert Cannan and "Old Mole"', *Outlook*, 33 (24 January 1914), 111: 'Perhaps we, all of us, having lost the Teutonic habit of slogging through and damning the expense, have become a sort of hybrid between men of action and contemplative moralists without definitely constructive creed.' For a subsequent use of 'constructive criticism', see Ford's *Thus to Revisit*, London: Chapman & Hall, 1921, p. 104.

5 See Dan Stone, *Breeding Superman: Nietzsche, Race and Eugenics in Edwardian and Interwar Britain*, Liverpool: Liverpool University Press, 2002, pp. 127, 128. Also G. K. Chesterton, 'Our Notebook', *Illustrated London News* (12 March, 1910), 372.

6 See Venetia Abdalla, '"That Neurasthenia Joke": Degeneration and Eugenics in the Work of Ford Madox Ford and Violet Hunt', in *The Edwardian Ford Madox Ford*, IFMFS 12, edited by Laura Colombino and Max Saunders, Amsterdam and New York: Rodopi, 2013, pp. 141-58.

7 Joanna Bourke, *Dismembering the Male: Men's Bodies, Britain and the Great War*, London: Reaktion Books, 1999, p. 171.

8 Angus McLaren, *Reproduction by Design: Sex, Robots, Trees, and Test-Tube Babies in Interwar Britain*, Chicago: Chicago University Press, 2012, p. 73.

9 Stephen Garton, review of Mark Jackson, *The Borderland of Imbecility* (2000), in *Victorian Studies*, 54:3 (Spring 2003), 575.

10 *The Letters of D. H. Lawrence, Volume I: 1901–1913*, edited by James T. Boulton, Cambridge: Cambridge University Press, p. 81.

11 H. G. Wells, *Anticipations*, London: Chapman & Hall, 1901, pp. 298-99, 300.

12 H. G. Wells. *A Modern Utopia*, 1905; edited by Krishan Kumar, London: J. M. Dent, 1994, p. 83.

13 Daniel Pick, *Faces of Degeneration: A European Disorder, c. 1848 – c. 1918*, Cambridge: Cambridge University Press, 1989, p. 179, n.15.

14 See Lucy Bland, *Banishing the Beast: English Feminism and Sexual Morality, 1885-1914*, Harmondsworth: Penguin Books, 1995, p. 225.

15 Mott, 'Heredity and Insanity', *Lancet*, 177, No. 4576 (1911), 1259, 1251: quoted by Elaine Showalter, *The Female Malady : Women, Madness and English Culture, 1830-1980*, London: Virago Press, 1987, p. 110.

16 Quoted by Richard Toye in *Churchill's Empire*, London: Pan Macmillan, 2011, p. 126.

17 Jose Harris, *Private Lives, Public Spirit: Britain 1870-1914*, Harmondsworth: Penguin, 1995, p. 244.

18 Donald Read, *Edwardian England 1901-15: Society and Politics*, London: Harrap, 1972, p. 22.

19 On the possible erotic implication of this acorn, see John Espey's *Ezra Pound's Mauberley: A Study in Composition*, Berkeley: University of California Press, 1974, p. 80.

20 Ford, *The Good Soldier*, 1915; edited by Martin Stannard, second edition, New York and London: W. W. Norton & Co., 2012 – henceforth *GS*; p. 76.

21 See Max Saunders , *Ford Madox Ford: A Dual Life*, Oxford: Oxford University Press, 1996, 2 vols, I – henceforth Saunders; pp. 420ff.

22 Ford, with Violet Hunt, *The Desirable Alien: At Home in Germany*, London: Chatto & Windus, 1913 – henceforth *DA*; p. 211.

23 See Ford Madox Ford, *It Was the Nightingale*, 1933; edited by John Coyle, Manchester: Carcanet Press, 2007 – henceforth *IWN*; p. 99 on the Trinity. *England and the English*, ed. Sara Haslam, Manchester: Carcanet Press, 2003 – henceforth *EE*; p. 232.

24 Among many examples, Nancy repeats 'Shuttlecocks!' three times (*GS* 167) and Edward says, three times, 'I don't want it' (*GS* 161). The word 'carefully' (itself of three syllables) is repeated six times (twice three times) in four lines early in the third chapter (*GS* 22).

25 Published April 1913: see Ezra Pound, *Poems and Translations*, edited Richard Sieburth, New York: Library of America, 2003, p. 264.

26 Ezra Pound, 'Troubadours: Their Sorts and Conditions', in *Literary Essays*, edited by T. S. Eliot, London: Faber, 1960, p. 101.

27 Ezra Pound to John Quinn, 10 March 1916, *Selected Letters of Ezra Pound to John Quinn, 1915-1924*, ed. Timothy Materer, Durham and London: Duke University Press, 1991, p. 66.

28 Ford Madox Ford, *Return to Yesterday*, 1931; ed. Bill Hutchings, Manchester: Carcanet Press, 1999 – henceforth *RY*; p. 312.

29 Before Fabians, there were Garnetts and Rossettis – and a sister. The first chapter of Juliet Soskice's *Chapters from Childhood*, London: Selwyn & Blount Ltd., 1921, is entitled 'Social Reformers': 'I had four cousins, who, though they were young, were social reformers [. . . .] I was eight, and I became a social reformer too'; p. 1.

30 See Ford, *Selected Poems*, edited by Max Saunders, Manchester: Carcanet Press, 1997, p. 66. Elsewhere, Saunders remarks that 'Ford's satire on "Reformers" continues with different degrees of bitterness until after the war (when his advocacy of the small producer and self-sufficiency begins to turn him into his own reformer).' He notes that *An English Girl* was originally to be called 'The Reformers', commenting: 'the title would have done as well for *The Simple Life Limited*, *The Panel*, or *The New Humpty-Dumpty*': see Saunders 416.

31 Ford, 'Literary Portraits—XVII. Nineteen-Thirteen and the Futurists', *Outlook*, 33 (3 January 1914), 15.

32 Ford, 'Literary Portraits—XXIII. Fydor Dostoievsky and "The Idiot"', *Outlook*, 33 (14 February, 1914), 206.

33  Ford, 'Literary Portraits—XX. Mr Gilbert Cannan and "Old Mole"', 111.
34  Ford, 'Literary Portraits—XXXIV. Miss May Sinclair and "The Judgment of Eve"', *Outlook*, 33 (2 May, 1914), 599.
35  Ford, 'Literary Portraits—VII. Mr. Percival Gibbon and "The Second-Class Passenger"', *The Outlook*, 32 (25 October 1913), 571.
36  Ford, 'Literary Portraits—XXXI. Lord Dunsany and "Five Plays"', *Outlook*, 33 (11 April, 1914), 495.
37  Ford, 'Literary Portraits—XLIV. Signor Marinetti, Mr. Lloyd George, St. Katharine, and Others', *Outlook*, 34 (11 July, 1914), 46.
38  Michael Freeden, 'Eugenics and progressive thought: a study of ideological affinity', *Historical Journal*, 22 (1979), 658.
39  See Saunders 267.
40  Ford, *Ancient Lights and Certain New Reflections*, London: Chapman & Hall, 1911, p. 284. In an earlier version, Kropotkin 'found his fellow men always predatory, so he based his theories of mutual help, scientifically, upon the rabbits': 'Nice People', *Temple Bar*, 128:5 (November 1903), 564-78 (p. 570). Kropotkin attended the First International Eugenics Conference in London in 1912.
41  Ford, 'On Impressionism: Second Article', *Poetry and Drama*, 2 (December 1914), 324-6.
42  Ford, *Critical Essays*, edited by Max Saunders and Richard Stang, Manchester: Carcanet Press, 2002 – henceforth *CE*; pp. 34-5.

# THE GOOD SOLDIER: A TALE OF POISON. LETHAL LITTLE BOTTLES IN THE WORK OF FORD MADOX FORD AND VIOLET HUNT

## Venetia Abdalla

**Abstract**

As a deceptive and elusive entity within a complex network of historical, literary and cultural associations, poison is ideally suited to the slippery sophistication of Fordian discourse. Although an interest in poison was one of Ford's many eccentric obsessions, it has so far evaded critical attention. This chapter suggests that a critical analysis of poison's place in *The Good Soldier* is essential to understanding not only his masterpiece but also a much wider selection of his works. Through the prism of the poison bottle, Ford focuses on topics as diverse as female duplicity, adulterated food, toxic texts and dangerous doctors. His confident claim that his 'observations' are as valid as the 'evidence' presented by an analytical chemist in the court room is not an example of Fordian hubris, but an indicator of how his impressionism is predicated firmly on the process of bringing what is hidden to the surface, of making you see.

Ford's relationship with Violet Hunt, who had a keen interest in poison herself, gave him new hope that the era of the poison bowl was not quite over. It was a matter, perhaps, of seeing prussic acid instead of aqua tofana. It was all 'just possible'.... Hunt's own toxic contributions to *The Good Soldier* are considered in the second half of this chapter.

> Bottles add a layer of ambiguity to poisons by bestowing on chemicals a definitive and easily observed identity but also by destabilizing this identity, because there is no guarantee that the bottles will be used as expected.[1]

Half-way through *The Good Soldier* Florence runs to her hotel bedroom, her pallid face 'contorted with agony'.[2] It would appear that her heart is playing up and that she is in desperate need of her 'little brown flask' of heart medicine (*GS* 87). But Florence does not use her glass phial as expected. When we next encounter her, she is the 'little, pale, frail corpse' (*GS* 72) that Dowell, her nursemaid husband, has dreaded for so long, but her alleged angina is not to blame – Florence has drunk prussic acid.

Poison is deceitful and secretive and its destructive presence may be difficult to detect within the body. In the *Lancet* in 1843,

Thomas Wakley admitted that the majority of poisons 'leave no mark or sign of the dreadful work that has been going on internally on the external surface of the body'.[3] Poison may masquerade either as a medicine, love potion or household substance and any attempt to define poison must acknowledge its multivalence:

> There is hardly any active medicine which may not be so; and on the other hand, there is hardly any poison which may not, in certain qualities, and in certain circumstances, be salutary.[4]

It is elusive, hard to pin down, like Florence, the 'gay tremulous beam' (*GS* 19), who flickers apparently almost to extinction after running for the German Express train, 'one hand to her side and her eyes closed' (*GS* 43), yet is miraculously restored to life in the closed bedroom.

The imaginative and emotional appeal of poison is derived from its unique position within a complex network of historical, cultural, and literary associations in the public imagination. Its indeterminacy and tantalising complexity, the fact that, as Ian Burney explains, it manages to evade being 'fully contained within a framework of rational procedures',[5] is surely indicative of its appeal for Ford. Its evanescence is a recognisable part of 'the complexity, the tantalisation, the shimmering, the haze, that life is'[6] and is simultaneously suggestive of those two Fordian pre-requisites, mystery and romance.

The prevalence of poison in Ford's work is a testimony to the peculiar power it exerted over him. It played a leading role in both his first published novel, *The Shifting of the Fire* (1892), and in his masterpiece, *The Good Soldier*. He also responded enthusiastically to its portrayal in the work of fellow writers. As editor of the *English Review*, Ford placed poison in a startlingly prominent position – Thomas Hardy's poem 'A Sunday Morning Tragedy' in which a young woman is poisoned by a toxic herbal abortifacient, opened the first issue which also contained a welcome antidote to this poisonous prelude. A remedy was only a few pages away, in Wimblehurst, somewhere in amongst all those bottles of patent medicine in Uncle Ponderevo's chemist's shop, situated in H. G. Wells's *Tono-Bungay*, serialized in the same magazine.

Poison was not simply a fictional entity for Ford. In an *Outlook* article of 1914, he described a personal encounter with poison which had a traumatic and lasting effect upon him. Aged nine, he was sucking the end of a matchstick in bed when he suddenly remembered that phosphorus was poisonous and began screaming. He described this incident as 'the most important, the most far-reaching, the most agonizing event of my life' and declared it to be the source of all his future anxiety. Fear of death? Fear of darkness palpable? He said it was 'as if I had been beneath a thin soft curtain'.[7] It is a brief second of monochrome terror, far removed from the multi-coloured reality of life reflected in the window of the Fordian train, and it corresponds to that moment in *The Good Soldier*, when Dowell is horribly frightened by Florence's performance at Marburg and Leonora's angry response "'Don't you see?", she said, "don't you see what's going on?"'(*GS* 40). Dowell does not see and he does not know what is going on. Paralysed in the headlamp-like glare of Leonora's bright blue eyes, 'like a wall of blue that shut me off from the rest of the world' (*GS* 40), he is as helpless as young Ford in his nursery, under that imaginary curtain. But the most enduring fictional legacy of Ford's poisonous match is surely the fact that the eyes of serial-adulterer Edward Ashburnham are 'as blue as the sides of a certain type of box of matches' (*GS* 29).

Something much worse happened when, as a young married man, Ford experienced a poison tragedy in his own family. On 2 February, 1902, his father-in-law, Dr. William Martindale, an eminent pharmaceutical chemist, drank prussic acid in his laboratory. Ford's response to the tragedy was characteristically double-edged. In his fiction, he exorcised Martindale's ghost in a cavalcade of dead or distant father figures led by the Reverend Brede in *The Benefactor* (1905), but in his own life, he found the presence of a little fluted bottle in his jacket pocket (Rossetti's old brown velvet jacket, actually!), rather re-assuring, and at times, positively exciting. It offered instant escape from writing and his constant financial worries but surely it was also a comforting reminder of his artistic heritage, a link to the colourful world of Pre-Raphaelite romance which he characteristically managed both to despise, and admire. Happily for Ford (and us, his readers), the allure of the little glass bottle was no match for the robust reality of Violet Hunt. As she advanced on Ford and boldly extracted it from his pocket, intent on offering what she later coyly referred to as 'the old traditional way of comfort',[8] all thoughts of suicide magically evaporated into the oleaginous blue haze that rose from their shared meal of lamb cutlets. What actually occurred on this memorable evening in the offices of the *English Review* will, of course, never be known. These are Violet's flurried reminiscences and from Ford, there is only the admission in his 1913 deposition: 'I was actually on the point of committing suicide by means of prussic acid, when Miss Hunt came into my office'.[9] Yet it all makes a good story, a tale of poison.

Despite the fact that *The Good Soldier* is predicated on an instantly recognizable poison metaphor, 'a goodly apple that is rotten at the core' (*GS* 13), the significance of poison in this novel and others by Ford, has evaded critical attention. Yet *The Good Soldier,* in particular, is saturated with poison. Its creeping power extends across the text like the 'grey lichen on the raddled trunk' (*GS* 108) of the apple tree against which Leonora and her sisters are photographed, an ominous blot, indicated by 'the black shadow from one of the branches of the apple tree' (*GS* 109) that blacks out Leonora's face. The novel is over-run by a complex network of poison capillaries, numerous instances of poison's pervasive presence in a multitude of guises. These range from the historical and exotic, as in mention of Edward's own personal enchantress, La Dolciquita, who, as 'his Circe' (*GS* 44*)* offers him a herbal balm, 'Eau de Melisse' (*GS* 108), to the rather more prosaic, Edward's cynical definition of the D.S.O.: 'It's a sort of thing they give grocers who've honourably supplied the troops with adulterated coffee in war-time' (*GS* 77).

*Ancient Lights* (1911) contains an illuminating anecdote that goes some way to explain poison's imaginative hold over Ford. In a discussion about the power of music as an accompaniment to conversation, Ford states: 'there is nothing that so makes irresistibly interesting topics bubble up in the mind as a pianissimo movement in the strings'.[10] What are these 'interesting topics' that 'bubble up' so suggestively? Ford's answer foreshadows his well-known explanation of his impressionist method: 'the queer effects of real life that are like so many views seen through bright glass. You are aware that on its surface it reflects a face of a person behind you'.[11] The difference is that now, it is an aural, as opposed to a visual, process that Ford describes when he remembers being in a crowded room at a wedding reception:

> My vis-a-vis was telling me something that did not interest me, when the voice of a person behind me said: 'So they left him there in prison with a broken bottle of poison in his pocket.' And then the music stopped suddenly and I never heard who the man was or what he had done to get into prison or why he had broken the bottle of poison. (*AL* 104)

This is intriguing because it is essentially a story untold, a series of questions involving a poison bottle, to which Ford can never know the answer. It is the opposite of 'the saddest story [...] ever heard' (GS 11), John Dowell's fire-side narration, which also involves a poison bottle. Yet, in quite another sense, it is the same as Dowell's story which is 'fundamentally concerned with its own crisis of knowing'.[12]

Within an area of creative tension, the Fordian narrator is faced with the challenge of bringing what is hidden to the surface, of making you see. A similar demand faced the toxicologist, the expert in poisons, called upon to produce tangible evidence of things unseen, something which in the early days of toxicology often demanded considerable imaginative input in the absence of definitive analytical tests. The process could become dangerously subjective as there are so many different versions of reality and a simile cannot be used as an argument. 'What a variety of different hues come under the denomination of blue, green and brown!' Joseph Adams wrote in an article about poison in 1807,[13] words which foreshadow Dowell's Pre-Raphaelite-inspired response to the panorama before him:

> The country isn't really green. The sun shines, the earth is blood red and purple and red and green and red. And the oxen in the ploughlands are bright varnished brown and black and blackish purple[.] (GS 38)

Dowell is speaking here from a position of authority, in his self-appointed role as strategically-positioned Fordian impressionist gazing through a train window. Ford, in his role as impressionist, sought the gravitas which the use of medico-legal language implied, and set himself up as the equivalent of the toxicologist's voice of expertise. His war-time propaganda work Between St. Dennis and St. George: A Sketch of Three Civilisations (1915) includes a spirited discussion of the 'relative bellicosities' of the Germans and the English after which Ford is compelled to admit that his impressions cannot be accepted as 'direct evidence', of the kind submitted in a murder trial by a man who has seen a revolver fired off. But because Ford has spent the greater part of his life 'recording impressions with an extreme exactitude', his observations are of as much value 'as the evidence in a case of murder by poison, of the analytical chemist who finds traces in the body of a victim of poison difficult of analysis'.[14]

This re-iterates his proud boast in Ancient Lights that his 'accuracy as to impressions is absolute' (AL xv) but also has a wider resonance as evidence of Ford's scientific approach to impressionism.

In *The Critical Attitude* (1911) he insisted that the novelist should be a 'scientific observer' who would present the result of their 'observations'[15] to the reader and later, in 'Techniques', he postulated that writing was an investigative process in which (like the toxicologist, again) 'you will forever be questioning and re-questioning and testing and re-testing the device you will have evolved' so that the reader's interest 'may be inevitably and scientifically aroused'.[16] Ford's equation of his own art with the work of the 'analytical chemist' simultaneously draws attention to the limitations of toxicology and 'confines' his own impressionism. Ford's chemist knows that poison has been used but cannot readily identify it, a situation that is reflected in Ford's impressionism which is 'about what is perceived, not what can be subsequently proved'.[17]

The poisonous potential, the lurking instability of that London crowd 'like a section of dark and troubled fluid in a test tube'[18] in *Mr. Apollo* (1908) is explicit but this does not mean that the crowd will become a baying mob. It is, however, 'just possible'...

This constant sense of possibility was important to Ford, possessed of a child-like yearning for novelty. His ideal reader possessed a receptive brain, open to all possibilities, but this Fordian requirement, is of course, a description of himself as an impressionist writer. The endless supply of 'queer facts' that this greedy intelligence requires begins innocently with mention of frosts and 'fantastic icicles' but culminates in a tale of poison that is itself precisely positioned: 'the other fact that a certain man murdered his wife by the use of a packet of sheep dip which he had stolen from a field where the farmer was employed at lamb washing'.[19] It is a strange story, a 'queer' story, yet as a collection of facts, restrained, disciplined and therefore, credible.

*The Shifting of the Fire* (1892), Ford's first published novel, is an unbelievable tale of poison. It is as if the poison bottle has been tilted too much in one direction and everything is hopelessly magnified, perhaps because it follows Ford's fairy tales. Edith is the only girl in the world lucky enough to possess a love token in the form of a little bottle of 'the strongest poison in the world',[20] a poison more sudden in effect than prussic acid, which she kisses a hundred times in her bedroom. Poison and passion are linked but only in playful display – in *The Good Soldier* they are incestuously entwined, impossible to differentiate, both 'a flame, a thirst, a withering up of the vitals' (*GS* 170). The centre of a morbidly melodramatic plot, it is Edith's bottle that is the real focus of the story because it magically changes from love token and dark glass poison vessel to become a sparkling crystal trinket. It is one of those wonderful Fordian co-incidences that this metamorphosis should occur in a railway carriage, just outside St. Denis, a peculiar harbinger of Ford later locating his 'toxicologist's impressionism' within the pages of *Between St. Dennis and St. George*. It is all too easy, perhaps, to dismiss this novel as jolly juvenilia, but the origins of Florence's little phial are here, within its pages, and Edith is 'a stupid little chatterbox' (*SF* 5), so it is quite possible to get a glimpse of *The Good Soldier* rising phoenix-like from the shifting of its fictional flames.

A tale of poison written in 1909, which has been described as 'a feebly self-indulgent story'[21] would appear to back-up Ford's claim that he had written *The Good Soldier* in his head, a decade before he actually reached for his pen. An analysis of English sang-froid, 'all secrecy and lying and concealment', 'A Silence' (1909)[22] is the story of Henry Penred who is married to Isabel, a volatile South American, but like the Ashburnhams, they are not on speaking terms. Henry loves his best friend's wife Brenda, but she is dead, and like Edward, deprived of Nancy, he cannot live without her. His 'bookcase', a miniature pharmacy, holds the solution, a certain little bottle in amongst 'a number of bottles of cleaning oils, of embrocations, patent medicines, of phials, of pills' ('Silence' 681) – unlike Florence, who feigns invalidism, Penred is a genuine hypochondriac. As in *The Good Soldier*, poison manifests as medicine, its 'pungent and sickly odour' makes the room smell 'like a drug store' ('Silence' 681, 682). Yet it equally can appear totally harmless and it is then at its most dangerous as 'the transparent liquid that might have been water' ('Silence' 681). Poison now transforms swiftly from fluid state to physical reality with the entrance of Isabel, who has just found her husband's love-letters to Brenda. Poison personified, she appears as if poisoned, 'her hand was upon her throat, as if its muscles had failed and she could neither speak nor swallow' ('Silence' 682). Unfortunately, she regains her voice and goads Henry, whom she regrets not shooting on their wedding night: 'this is not a quarrel: this is an execution. I am thrashing you with a raw hide whip, as my father's men do when their broncos jib' ('Silence' 682). Fast-forward to *The Good Soldier*, in which Ford re-wrote this scene (and, perhaps, further still, to *Parade's End*, in which Sylvia revels in both her verbal laceration of Christopher and her physical thrashing of the white bulldog, poisoned with red lead) and it becomes immediately evident that Ford had managed to discipline his writing, to 'contain' the poison. Leonora repeats Isabella's performance, 'lashing, like a cold fiend, into the unfortunate Edward' (*GS* 162), inert in his armchair, 'because he was so silent' (*GS* 163) yet her words are largely absent from the text: 'She began spiritedly, but she could not find any ending for the sentence' (*GS* 163). Unseen, they exert a more deadly power than Isabel's ranting, evident in the fact that Leonora feels compelled to check that Edward has not killed himself after her onslaught. Her unfinished sentences are the verbal equivalent of those 'traces' referred to in *Between St. Dennis and St. George*, traces of that particularly elusive poison which confronted the Fordian impressionist in his dual role as toxicologist, traces of toxic talk.

And so to the death of that ghastly, garrulous Florence, under a sordid, naked light bulb. In a sense, her death does not matter at all; the Nauheim *Totentanz* can continue with different partners, Dowell can marry his girl. Florence's exit is a modulation, a change of key, echoed in the 'silly old tune' (*GS* 170) that Nancy picks out on the piano, in which the 'cheerful insistence' (*ibid.*) of the major notes is representative of Florence's bright chatter, melting into minor sounds, in anticipation of Nancy's sad 'Shuttlecocks!' (*GS* 191).

Yet Florence's death is central to making sense of *The Good Soldier*. Rushing past Dowell, on her way to her death, 'with a face whiter than paper and her hand on the black stuff over her heart' (*GS* 81) (that terrifying, palpable curtain of blackness in Ford's nursery, again), it is as if she has quite literally taken over the function of the text. Dowell is momentarily displaced, and just as in his earlier moment of panic at Marburg, he almost goes into cardiac arrest: 'I tell you, my own heart stood still' (*GS* 81). Florence's frantic actions tell the story at this point as all the pieces of the plot start to come together. The process is very similar to that which Ford described in an *Outlook* article in which he wrote about the role of the artist in a cinematograph show who gives you:

> A black triangle in the centre of the sheet, a space of black in shape like a sausage to the right of the triangle, and then, with one swift and uniting line presents to the beholder's gaze an unmistakable bulldog.[23]

What is actually happening, of course, is that everything is converging on the little glass bottle. Ford, as creative artist, is in the process of putting together the fragments of the unnamed prisoner's broken poison bottle that had captured his imagination at the wedding party in *Ancient Lights*, which is why, after Florence's death, Dowell's eye focuses on her little phial. He does not know that she has killed herself, he believes that in running for her medicine, she over-strained her heart. What matters is that he recognises the importance of the bottle and he gets straight to the hub of Ford's impressionistic method when he remarks: 'in such circumstances, it is some little material object, always, that catches the eye and that appeals to the imagination' (*GS* 87).

Florence's corpse is a conduit from which poison flows back into the larger body of the text, which is now saturated with the idea of destructive passion. The inexperienced Nancy reads about the Brand divorce case, another tale of passion, and it is as if she has drunk poison: 'the whole effect of the reading upon Nancy was mysterious, terrifying, evil. She felt a sickness – a sickness that grew as she read' (*GS* 167). Like Nancy, we too are reading a sad story, a story far more toxic than that 'poisonous' novel, *Ann Veronica*,[24] but, unlike Nancy, and several outraged contemporary reviewers,[25] we are not sickened as we read. We have to admit that mention of a 'raging stallion forever neighing after his neighbour's womenkind' (*GS* 16) is infinitely more exciting than all those rabbits nibbling the grass at Branshaw Teleragh. We are seduced by the quiet voice of the fireside storyteller who is also relating one of the most exciting types of story, a tale of passion, which is also a poison story. As Dowell's narrative oscillates between the country cottage by the sea and 'the circumstances of clamour, of outcry, of the crash of many people running together' (*GS* 87) after Florence's death, we are in a position similar to that of readership referred to in an article in *Blackwood's Edinburgh Magazine* in 1864, which discussed the popular appeal of poison trials:

> [...] interest vacillates between the most powerful passions and the pangs of arsenic and the listener is alternately carried from the domestic hearth to the laboratory and back again'.[26]

Perhaps Florence has seduced all of us, which is another way of saying that like Ford we are all susceptible to the imaginative power of poison. She is inextricably a part of that complex network of historical, literary and cultural associations that surrounds poison – a woman who desires to be 'like one of the great erotic women of history' (*GS* 95). Her very name is suggestive of Renaissance intrigue, an association strengthened by her habit of bidding Dowell good-night 'as if she were a cinque-cento Italian lady saying good-bye to her lover' (*GS* 72) and the fact that she meets Dowell at a Browning Society tea links her to that painted laboratory world of enclosed illicit passion that so enticed Ford. Rossetti's picture 'The Laboratory' (1849), inspired by Browning's dramatic monologue, which depicted an alchemist preparing a poisonous drop for a woman, obsessed him. Its status as Ford's 'Wonderland' is confirmed by the fact that in *A Mirror To France* (1926) he was still hoping that as a reflecting mirror to his times, he could gain entrance to this looking glass world, be a part of its poisonous historical drama:

> you will see yourself as someone dimly villainous, come to make nefarious purchases of wicked white-hatted merchants who writhe over alchemisms in the shadowy depths behind you.[27]

Florence dwells in her own closed world; she is defined by her suspicious interiority, her predilection for locked bedrooms, closed bathing places and most significant of all, by her medicine grip, 'the symbol of the existence of an adored wife of a day' (*GS* 75). While she is busy packing her prussic acid in this, Dowell is being given a lecture by her elderly uncle on the immoral character of Parisian women, a particularly poisonous breed, a threat to the unwary, 'snakes in the grass' (*GS* 71). The inseparable association of Florence with her medicine/poison case accounts for Dowell's exaggerated reaction, his fury, when poor old Julius lets it fall to the floor. In Dowell's mind, this must appear as if he has dropped Florence, the precious 'thin-shelled pullet's egg' (*GS* 74) with which he, Dowell, is entrusted.

Violet Hunt picked up all the pieces of poor Florence and put her together again, if we are to believe her account in *The Flurried Years* of how she salvaged the torn-up manuscript of *The Good Soldier* from the dustbin. Violet may also have suggested the manner of Florence's suicide, by poison. In 1897, she wrote *Unkist, Unkind!*, a lurid Gothic romance, which featured the witch-like alchemist, Sibella. Secretary to an antiquary, she is introduced in his study: 'I saw three green-shaded candles on the middle of a shining oak table, and a woman's eager face bent down between them':[28] a room which anticipates Ashburnham's gun room with its candles 'hidden by green glass shades' (*GS* 162). She talks in a manner which would have resonated with Hunt's late Victorian readers, many of whom were becoming increasingly worried about the professionalization of science and medicine. At a time when death by poison was on the increase, this carried with it the terrifying possibility that medical men, entrusted with the care of the body, might choose to hasten its demise, an anxiety apparently justified by several high-profile poison cases involving doctors, among them Dr. William Palmer (1856), and Dr. Thomas Cream (1892). Sibella boasts:

> I know the secrets of the modern scientific chemists which are in deadly earnest [. . . .] I know how Italian mediaeval doctors concocted the slow poisons [. . .] aqua Tofana that anticipated the secret of the deadliest poisons of modern science. (*UU* 161-2)[29]

But her proudest achievement is the fact that she has concocted a deadly poison and put it into a glass capsule, 'the kind that one uses for nitrite of amyl' (*UU* 196), the heart medicine that is prescribed for Florence in *The Good Soldier*. Like Florence, she will commit suicide with this toxin, in the guise of a medicinal remedy. It is easy to see how this behaviour appealed to Ford's imagination and contributed to the manner of Florence's exit from *The Good Soldier*. Ford, despite sometimes being a hopeless hypochondriac, dependent on sleeping draughts and Adalin, 'that nice new German drug' (*FY* 211), a hypnotic/sedative into which a worried Violet drafted bread pills, nurtured a deep distrust of doctors and boldly accused them of killing his father in an unpublished typescript with a most provocative title – 'What Do Doctors Know?'.[30] So, perhaps, Dowell is right and Florence does not matter. We should be more worried about all those doctors, those 'cool, quiet men' (*GS* 73) who are quite possibly the most dangerous of all the '"good people"' (*GS* 87).

*Unkist, Unkind!* like Ford's early novel, *The Shifting of the Fire*, is essentially poison pantomime but Hunt had a serious interest in poison and knew a lot about it. Her enthusiasm re-inforced Ford's own interest in the subject. Poison was a part of her literary heritage – her mother, Mrs Alfred Hunt, a prolific three-decker novelist, was the author of *Mrs Juliet* (1893) in which the heroine is suspected of arsenic poisoning. As Mrs Hunt grew older and more eccentric she imagined herself as a victim of poison in cups of tea handed out by Ford and Violet at their tennis parties at South Lodge.[31]

Unlike Ford, Hunt was not interested in poison's subtle qualities, its porous boundaries which seem to slide so effortlessly into the complex labyrinths of Fordian discourse. She was interested in poison per se and confronted it fearlessly in both her fiction and her own life. She used arsenic for her complexion and in 1892 wrote a short dialogue 'The Green Carnation' in which she responded with characteristic aplomb to the Aesthetic Movement's fascination with flowers dyed green with arsenic. She likened this unnatural process to the production of foie gras when Isabel St George tells Billy: 'I don't want your horrid pate de foie gras flower!'[32]

Hunt devoured poison novels such as Robert Hichens' phenomenally successful 'Bella Donna', deriving considerable pleasure from using her growing knowledge of poison as a weapon against her rivals for Ford's affection. One of her 'victims' in *I Have This To Say* (1926), the American edition of *The Flurried Years,* was Rebecca West who had entered into correspondence with Hunt about Edith Thompson, famously convicted of trying to kill her husband. West saw pathos in the fact that Edith, in a desperate attempt to impress her lover, had likened herself to fictional poisoners, such as Hichens's appropriately named Bella Donna. Hunt, wary of Ford's growing interest in Rebecca, tartly implied that she was obviously another of Edith's victims, her personality had appealed to the novelist in Rebecca. She concluded her onslaught by tartly suggesting that Edith's poisoned husband had obviously paid a stiff price for his library subscription![33]

Hunt may never have owned a wedding ring but, like Sibella in *Unkist, Unkind!,* she was the proud possessor of a poison ring, 'like the head of an enamelled toad with the bolt that shot and the lid that lifted, disclosing a cavity just big enough to hold a mere pinch of nitrate of amyl' (*FY* 217). She made sure that Ford knew of its existence and it became an integral part of their shared poison games, the equivalent of that little brown bottle in Ford's jacket pocket. While Ford dictated *The Good Soldier* to another of Hunt's rivals, Brigit Patmore, Hunt stomped over the stony Selsey beaches but later recalled with pleasure how Ford had run anxiously down the street, searching for her 'wanting to know if I had committed suicide' (*FY* 217). He need not have worried – this was figure-conscious Violet Hunt and her ring contained nothing more than a pinch of Saxine, the artificial sweetener of the day.

'She just went completely out of existence, like yesterday's paper' (*GS* 96) – how often Ford must have longed to say that about Hunt after all those poisonous outbursts of hers which characterised their relationship. Although he wrote her out of his reminiscence she saw that her curious jewellery had manipulative possibilities he could use. The narrator of *The Nature of a Crime* owns a similar ring, 'with a bulging, greenish stone'[34] and makes sure that the woman he loves knows of its existence. He is equally obsessed with the love- philtre in Wagner's 'Tristan and Isolde', with the idea of succumbing fatally to passion 'madness justified with a concrete substance, a herb, a root' (*NC* 46) but sadly has to content himself with thoughts of rather more mundane liquids. He is weaning the husband of the women he loves off chloral:

> 'I have persuaded your chemists to reduce very gradually the strength of chloral so that the bottles contain nearly half water [...] it must be carefully seen to that instead of pure chloral he obtains the exactly diluted mixture. In this way he may be brought gradually to drinking almost pure water' (*NC* 87).

Ford is once more playing with his bottles. . . .

So Fordian poison takes many forms, a match stick, a heart remedy, a Wagnerian love philtre, or plain old Saxine. It is nearly always inextricably linked with passion so we are all at risk because 'every human being knows what it is to act, irrationally, under the stress of some passion or other' (*NC* 46). We have all heard the saddest story, that 'deadly story' related in that cold-blooded manner of Dowell's which was likened by C. E. Lawrence to the style of the Borgias, who 'could kiss and slay, smile, and at the same time, poison'.[35] And then behind Dowell, there is another face in the glass, that of Dr Ford, who as a medical man really cannot be trusted. His knowledge of medicine is suspect, actually very dangerous. He has several heart patients including Don Kelleg's father in *An English Girl* (1907), and the bed-ridden Lady Ada, with her 'squat, violently green, small bottle' in *The Marsden Case* (1923).[36] He should have pre-scribed amyl nitrite, a vasodilator, for their angina pectoris, but he has given them amyl nitrate, which is an ignition agent and used in gunpowder.[37] He has poisoned them all!

**NOTES**

1   Sylvia Pamboukian, *Doctoring the Novel: Medicine and Quackery from Shelley to Doyle,* Athens: Ohio University Press, 2012, p. 104.

2   Ford, *The Good Soldier*, ed. Max Saunders, Oxford World's Classics, Oxford: Oxford University Press, 2012 – henceforth *GS*; p. 94.
3   'Inquest on Which The Absurd Dictum of Lord Ellenborough was Pronounced', *The Lancet,* I (1842-3), 362-4 (p. 364).
4   'What is a "Noxious Thing?"', *The British Medical Journal*, Vol. 1, (1002), (13 March 1880), 407.
5   Ian Burney, *Poison, Detection and the Victorian Imagination*, Manchester: Manchester University Press, 2006, p. 173.
6   Ford, *Joseph Conrad: A Personal Remembrance,* London: Duckworth, 1924 – henceforth *JC;* p. 204.
7   Ford, 'Literary Portraits – XLV.: Mme Yo Pawlowska and "A Child Went Forth"', *Outlook*, 34 (18 July 1914), 79. The poisonous (incestuous?) relationship between Edward and Nancy is shown in a poisonous green light in *The Good Soldier*. Nancy's dress glimmers 'like a phosphorescent fish in a cupboard' (*GS* 89), and later, when she rises up at the foot of his bed, Edward associates her ghostly appearance with 'a greenish sort of effect as if there were a greenish tinge in the shadows of the tall bedposts that framed her body' (*GS* 184).
8   Hunt, *The Flurried Years*, London: Hurst and Blackett, 1926 – henceforth *FY*; p. 57.
9   Max Saunders, *Ford Madox Ford: A Dual Life*, 2 vols, Oxford: Oxford University Press, 1996 – henceforth 'Saunders'; I, p. 285.
10  Ford, *Ancient Lights and Certain New Reflections*, London: Chapman and Hall, 1911 – henceforth *AL*; p. 104.
11  Ford, 'On Impressionism', *Poetry and Drama,* 1 (June 1914), 167-75 (p. 174).
12  Carey J. Mickalites, '*The Good Soldier* and Capital's Interiority Complex', *Studies in the Novel*, 38:3 (Fall 2006), 288-303 (p. 290).
13  Joseph Adams, 'Observations on Morbid Poisons, Chronic and Acute', *Edinburgh Medical and Surgical Journal*, 3, (1807), 333-46 (p. 335).
14  Ford, *Between St. Dennis and St. George: A Sketch of Three Civilizations,* London: Hodder and Stoughton, 1915, p. 34. The chronological relationship of this book to *The Good Soldier* is uncertain. 'He did a long literary article every week and at the same time was engaged on a novel, *The Good Soldier* and his propaganda book *Between St. Dennis and St. George.*' If Richard Aldington, Ford's wartime amanuensis, writing long after the event, can be believed, these two books are linked by a toxicological thread, His account does not tally with Ford's claim in his 'Dedicatory Letter' that he had finished *The Good Soldier* before the war began. Mizener points out that Ford would actually have been writing his first propaganda book *When Blood Is Their Argument* and dismisses Aldington's claim as 'somewhat inaccurate'. Arthur Mizener, *The Saddest Story: A Biography of Ford Madox Ford*, London: The Bodley Head, 1972, p. 251. Martin Stannard acknowledges that 'Aldington's account of his period as Ford's secretary after the declaration of war has often been thought by Ford scholars to be vitiated by inconsistencies'. 'A Note on the Text', in *The Good Soldier* ed. Martin Stannard, New York: W. Norton. (1995) – henceforth 'Stannard'.
15  Ford, *The Critical Attitude*, London: Duckworth, 1911 – henceforth *CA*; p. 97.
16  Ford, 'Techniques', *Southern Review*, 1 (July 1935), 20-35 (pp. 22, 35).

17  Max Saunders, 'Ford and Impressionism' in *Ford Madox Ford: Literary Networks and Cultural Transformations,* IFMFS 7, ed. Andrzej Gasiorek and Daniel Moore, Amsterdam: Rodopi, 2008, pp. 151-67 (p. 151).

18  Ford, *Mr. Apollo: A Just Possible Story,* London: Methuen and Co., 1908, p. 41.

19  Ford, 'On Impressionism', *Poetry and Drama,* 2 (December 1914), 323-34 (p. 334).

20  Ford, *The Shifting of the Fire,* London: T. Fisher Unwin, 1892 – henceforth *SF*; p. 15.

21  See Saunders I, 262, n. 555.

22  Ford, 'A Silence', *Bystander,* 24 (29 December 1909), 681-4 – henceforth 'Silence'; p. 681.

23  Ford, 'Literary Portraits: XL.: Vernon Lee and "Louis Norbert"', *Outlook,* 33 (13 June 1914), 815-16 (p. 816).

24  See 'A Poisonous Book', *Spectator* (20 November 1909), pp. 846-7.

25  The *Daily Telegraph* issued a health warning, informing readers that if they read the novel in its entirety, they could expect to feel 'more than a little nauseated'. 'Current Literature', *Daily Telegraph* (6 April 1915), 4.

26  'The Modern Crichtons', *Blackwoods Edinburgh Magazine,* 96 (1864), 282-6 (p. 284).

27  Ford, *A Mirror To France,* London: Duckworth, 1926, p. 8.

28  Hunt, *Unkist, Unkind!,* London: Chapman and Hall, 1897 – henceforth *UU*; p. 109.

29  For a Fordian reference to Aqua Tofana see Ford, 'Literary Portraits: XL.: Vernon Lee and "Louis Norbert"', p. 816. Ford praises Vernon Lee's technique in *Louis Norbert*: 'So with touch upon touch, does Vernon Lee evolve for you the figure of Louis Norbert, with the background of Italy of the seventeenth century – the Italy of torches shining upon the facades of palazzo, of assassins, of libidinous cardinals, of dangerous priests, of grand dukes of Tuscany, of Englishmen going on the grand tour – an Italy not of many courtesans, but much besprinkled with aqua tofana'.

30  Ford, 'What Do Doctors Know?', unpublished typescript (no date), six pages, Carl A. Kroch Library, Cornell University Library. Probably the rough draft of 'O Hygeia!', *Harpers,* 156 (May 1928), 768-76.

31  See Grace Lovat Fraser, *In The Days of My Youth,* London: Cassell, 1970, p. 128: 'Once, on being handed a cup of tea, the old lady sniffed it suspiciously and then in a deep and tragic voice said: "What is this, poison? Well, never mind, I'll drink it if you like", downing it all in a single hearty gulp [...]'.

32  Hunt, 'The Green Carnation', *Black and White,* 3 (12 March 1892), 350-1 (p. 351). See Karl Beckson, 'Oscar Wilde and the Green Carnation', *English Literature in Transition,* 43:4 (2000), 387-97.

33  Hunt, *I Have This to Say: The Story of My Flurried Years,* New York: Boni and Liveright, 1926. For more on the trial of Edith Thompson, see John Wilson Foster, 'Poison and Romance: Oscar Wilde and the strange case of Edith Thompson', *Irish Studies Review,* 20:4 (2012), 353-65.

34  Ford and Joseph Conrad, *The Nature of a Crime,* London: Duckworth, 1924 – henceforth *NC*; p. 19. The story originally appeared in Ford's *English Review* in 1909.

35  C. E. Lawrence, 'Passion and People: The Old Story in New Settings,' *Daily Chronicle* (28 April 1915), 4. Quoted Stannard; p. 227.
36  Ford, *The Marsden Case,* London: Duckworth, 1923, p. 237.
37  See Saunders, ed., *The Good Soldier*, p. 242, n. 87.

Bad Nauheim: Pump Room in the New Spa Facility

# 'EARLY KIPLING TOLD BY HENRY JAMES': A READING OF *THE GOOD SOLDIER*

## Harry Ricketts

**Abstract**
This essay explores how far *The Good Soldier* can be read as a homage to, and critique of, two of Ford's great literary predecessors, Kipling and Henry James. If at all, these three writers are usually linked via Ford's famous rendition in *Return to Yesterday* of James's hilarious account of the breakdown of Kipling's expensive motor car. *The Good Soldier* however suggests closer literary ties. The subject matter of the novel (infidelity) is a frequent one in James's work, but also in Kipling's early Indian stories, particularly those set in Simla or dealing with Station life. Ashburnham is a typically Kiplingesque army officer, home 'on sick leave from India'. Like many Kipling characters, he is given little interiority and is mostly knowable by his pet subjects, such as 'the spreading power of number three shot before a charge of number four powder'. By contrast, the apparently timorous, ineffectual American narrator Dowell seems a recognizably Jamesian figure, and the story itself to be told in a distinctly Jamesian manner, characterized by delay, deflection and the minute dissection of detail. Ford gives the reader several nudges about his literary intentions, including Dowell's description of Ashburnham as talking 'like quite a good book'.

My title comes from a remark the late John Bayley made to me forty years ago when he was supervising my B.Litt. on Kipling's short stories. 'Read *The Good Soldier*,' he said one afternoon in New College, holding a not very clean cup under the tap and pouring hot water straight on to the grains of instant coffee; 'it's early Kipling told by Henry James.' So I read the novel, vaguely saw what he meant and tucked away the aphorism. I have written a good deal on Kipling since then, including on his literary influence and legacy, but only now tried to test out Bayley's *bon mot*.

Ford, James and Kipling are rarely thought of together, except perhaps via Ford's hilarious version of what might be called 'The Tale of Kipling, Henry James and the Motor Car'. This is Ford's reminiscence in *Return to Yesterday* (1931) of James recounting at great length the breakdown of Amelia, Kipling's extremely expensive motor car (costing 1200 guineas, according to Ford), and the consequent abandonment of Kipling's highly elaborate motoring plans. This bravura performance is a double Ford joke, simultaneously poking fun at the rich, brash, philistine Kipling and at the periphrastically orotund James. However, in fairness, it should be pointed out that when James originally delivered his peroration thirty years earlier in October 1902, Kipling himself was a delighted spectator. 'Henry James's monologue over [Amelia's] immobile carcase', he told their mutual friend Charles Norton, '– with all the machinery exposed and our engineer underneath growing progressively blacker – would have been cheap at the price of several wrecked cars.'[1]

This story, also collected in *The Oxford Book of Literary Anecdotes*, is all the better for being substantially true, and offers a useful reminder, if one were needed, of Ford's talent for literary ventriloquism and pastiche. (I shall have more to say later about his literary playfulness.) Not that James's extensive influence on the Edwardian Ford probably needs much demonstration. In 1910, Ford himself told the now-forgotten novelist Edgar Jepson in parodicly Jamesian tones:

> I am very glad, very glad, indeed that you accuse me of imitating the brother of William James [. . .] nothing gives one a greater pleasure than to discover in one's most cherished and penetrating friends [. . .] a capacity for uttering the purely obvious.[2]

As for *The Good Soldier*, Brita Lindberg-Seyersted's claim in 1987 that 'James's influence on [the novel] is something readers in general agree about' was already by then something of a truism.[3] And it is the case, particularly early in the novel, that the reader is constantly tripping over Jamesian features, Jamesian turns of phrase, echoes, delays, deflections and non-digressive digressions.

One obvious example is Ford's frequent repetition of that favourite James adjective 'queer', here often used with reference to Nancy Rufford and her situation. Another is the way that Leonora is described as 'extraordinarily fair and so extraordinarily the real thing'.[4] The phrase both mimics James's habit of repeating a qualifier (here 'extraordinarily') and of course overtly evokes his story 'The Real Thing' about another model couple, who are also too good to be true and won't do (though for rather different reasons). By the end of *The Good Soldier*, the only word Nancy will or can say is 'Shuttlecocks!', repeated three times and referring presumably to the way she has been batted to and fro between her quasi-parents Edward and Leonora, and even perhaps between them and Dowell (*GS* 191-2). This, as has often been pointed out, alludes to the description, early in

James's *What Maisie Knew*, of the young Maisie as a 'little feathered shuttlecock' whom her egregious parents 'fiercely [kept] flying between them'.[5] Furthermore, James's protagonist's name is itself reprised by Ford in that of Maisie Maidan, one of Edward's mistresses and an earlier 'shuttlecock'. On a larger scale, in *The Good Soldier* as in *What Maisie Knew*, serial adultery is a central preoccupation. Equally, the apparently timorous, ineffectual narrator Dowell and his wife Florence are recognizably Jamesian figures – 'leisured Americans' (Dowell's phrase) floating around Europe (*GS* 11).

So *The Good Soldier* is undeniably full of Jamesian traits. But can it, in Bayley's phrase, be described as 'told by Henry James'? Philip Horne in 'The Master and the "Queer Affair" of "The Pupil"' vertiginously describes James's 'practice' of 'creating epistemological abysses round which one warily treads – gaps one may imagine filling in a multiplicity of ways, temptations to the over-confident guesser'.[6] That seems to fit *The Good Soldier* which also hints at such abysses and gaps, most alarmingly the possibility that Edward's relationship with Nancy is potentially or actually incestuous, a sounding persuasively taken by Max Saunders in his biography of Ford. Equally suggestive is Julian Barnes's elegant characterization of the 'dividedness' of Dowell's narration as 'a creak under the foot as we put our weight on it'.[7] Which could as aptly apply to, say, the governess's creaky narration in 'The Turn of the Screw', a story Ford often mentions. He, in his not very critical study of James, commends James's ability to 'convey an impression, an atmosphere of what you will with literally nothing' – what Tony Tanner calls James's 'characteristic pregnant vagueness'.[8] But 'pregnant vagueness' is not really, or not consistently, Ford's way in the novel. Dowell's manner does occasionally gesture towards James's late style, but his characteristic habit of switching openly and abruptly between mutually contradictory views of people and his reaction to them, and bursting out with a 'Who knows?' or 'I don't know' is distinctly un-Jamesian. So too, as Kathryn C. Rentz spiritedly argues in 'The Question of James's Influence on Ford's *The Good Soldier*', is the novel's structure. As Rentz puts it: 'James's novels, except for an occasional flashback, characteristically develop in chronological order, moving the main character(s) from an initial state to a different final state.'[9] Hardly the case with the splintering, spiralling structure of *The Good Soldier*.

But for any Fordwise reader that is probably more than enough on the Jamesian and non-Jamesian qualities of *The Good Soldier*. In what sense can the novel be thought of as 'early Kipling'? As far as I know, Robert L. Caserio's 2003 essay 'Ford's and Kipling's Modernist Imagination of Public Virtue' remains the only concerted attempt to read Ford and Kipling together, and then not in relation to *The Good Soldier*; so what follows is at least original.

The poet-painter David Jones, looking back from 1961 to his turn-of-the-century upbringing, told a friend: 'One lived in a kind of Kipling-conditioned world without knowing it.'[10] The comment also holds good for Ford, born twenty-two years earlier. In *Return to Yesterday*, as a prelude to his story about Kipling, Henry James and the motor car, Ford recalls (perhaps not entirely reliably) his 'oldest literary recollection'. He is eighteen, has just published his own first book, is on a train to Rye, knocking out his clay pipe and reading in a blue-grey booklet the words '*So you see, darling, there is really no fear* ...'[11] These are part of the conclusion of a love letter in Kipling's 1888 story 'Only a Subaltern'. Sara Haslam in *Fragmenting Modernism: Ford Madox Ford, the Novel, and the Great War* (2002) convincingly presents Ford's whole reminiscence here as a quintessential modernist moment in which Ford's 'writing of the memory becomes a way of balancing, controlling and explaining the access he has achieved to an older self, to the past'.[12] A simpler point is that Ford's reminiscence shows how he too, and very specifically, developed in 'a Kipling-conditioned world'. 'You have no idea', Ford goes on, 'how exciting it was then to be eighteen and to be meditating writing for the first time "there is really no fear" ... And to know that those blue-grey booklets were pouring from the press and all England buzzing about them' (*RY* 4).

'Only a Subaltern' comes from Kipling's mini-collection *Under the Deodars*, first published in India in 1888. The story itself portrays in highly sentimental terms how Bobby Wick, a young English army officer in India and in love, dies of cholera self-sacrificingly caring for his adoring men. Bobby is in all the most obvious ways a 'good soldier' and, both publicly and privately, everything he ought to be. However, most of the other 'pukka sahibs' in the stories in *Under the Deodars* are not. 'A Wayside Comedy', for instance, is an isolated Station version of the second circle of Dante's hell or Sartre's *Huis Clos*. The tiny Anglo-community comprises Captain (Ted) Kurrell, Mr. and Mrs. Boulte and Major and Mrs. Vansuythen. Kurrell has been having an affair with Mrs. Boulte, but then he and Boulte both fall for Mrs. Vansuythen, whom Mrs. Boulte tells about her relationship with

Kurrell. At which point, things become complicated. 'The Hill of Illusion' and 'At the Pit's Mouth' are both set in Simla, and both involve adulterous couples out riding and discussing running away together. In the first story, the couple end by realizing, sickeningly, that they can no longer trust each other; in the second, the Tertium Quid (as the cuckolding lover is insouciantly called) falls to his death when his horse slips off the rain-rotted Himalayan-Tibet Road.

The point to notice is that the Kipling which Ford was reading so assiduously and adhesively at eighteen was Kipling the chronicler of the army and of infidelity in British India. Ford's reminiscence adds further fuel to a sometimes forgotten detail of literary history, which is that, for the English-reading public of Ford's generation and at least the next two generations to follow, Kipling's early stories and poems in effect invented India as a literary subject, and particularly what was then known as 'Anglo-India', i.e. the British in India. (So, for instance, E. M. Forster's portrayal of the Turtons and Burtons in *A Passage to India* (1924) is thoroughly Kiplingesque; it is just that, unlike Kipling, Forster shows his Anglo-Indians as thoroughly unlikeable.)

Set in this Anglo-Indian context, Captain Edward Ashburnham in *The Good Soldier* emerges, I think, as a recognizably Kiplingesque figure. So, when, early on, Dowell describes Ashburnham as 'talk[ing] like quite a good book', the 'quite a good book' could be imagined as one by Kipling, *Under the Deodars* perhaps (*GS* 28). Indeed, Ashburnham can be seen as a composite of Kipling's professional 'good soldiers' like Bobby Wick – whose name 'Wick' the more obviously incendiary 'Ashburnham' subliminally evokes – and Kipling's philandering officers and civilians who, in a slyer *Much Ado About Nothing* sense, are, like Ashburnham, 'good soldiers to a lady'.[13]

To take this line a bit further: like most of Kipling's army officers, Edward Ashburnham is a 'sentimentalist' (*GS* 28, 49, 119, 181, 183, 192, 193). Like them too, he is given little interiority and less capacity to articulate his thoughts. We are told that, occasionally late at night during the two couples' nine-year intimacy, he 'blurted out' to Dowell 'something that gave an insight into the sentimental view of the cosmos that was his' (*GS* 28). But that is more or less it. For the rest, Ashburnham is mostly knowable, as Captain Gadsby is, say, in Kipling's 1888 novella *The Story of the Gadsbys* by his pet subjects, his patch of special knowledge. Gadsby's pet subject is trying to develop 'lighter' saddlery for his hussars.[14] Ashburnham's pet subjects, given by Dowell in a very Kiplingesque list, also include

horse-talk: 'Martingales, Chiffney bits, boots; where you got the best
soap, the best brandy, the name of the chap who rode a plater down
the Khyber cliffs; the spreading power of number three shot before a
charge of number four powder . . . by heavens, I hardly ever heard him
talk of anything else' (*GS* 27). Captain Ashburnham's career is a kind
of distorted mirror image of Captain Gadsby's. Leonora makes her
semi-aristocratic, land-owning husband serve in India to economize
and, as she unrealistically hopes, to save their marriage – only for
Ashburnham to carry on philandering in Simla, in other hill stations
and elsewhere. In Kipling's novella, the aristocratic, land-owning
Gadsby, we come to learn, has also been a committed philanderer –
with at least two women, including his future wife's mother – but his
real mistress (this is Kipling, after all) is the army which Gadsby must
renounce, and then return to England in order to preserve his marriage.
Both Ashburnham and Gadsby are faithful, in their fashion, though
not to duty but to passion.

One of the clear Jamesian hints in *The Good Soldier* is Maisie
Maidan's Christian name with presumably an ironic pun on her
surname: maidan/maiden. But her full name is also a double nudge to
Kipling. Maisie is the name of the heroine of Kipling's 1890 novel
*The Light That Failed* (of which a famous stage version was
performed in 1903), and 'maidan' is the Hindi word for an open field,
a space used for meetings and sports – evoking obvious Kiplingesque
Indian associations, but perhaps also suggesting something of Maisie's
open nature and her emotional treatment by Ashburnham.

A quick further digression on names here – or 'isn't it
digression?', as Dowell might say (*GS* 19). Ford, like both Kipling
and James, likes to use oddly pitched, character-indicative names. (For
instance, Wick, Boulte and Gadsby in the Kipling stories I have
referred to, and Moddle, Miss Overmore and Beale Farange in *What
Maisie Knew*.) I have already pointed out the incendiary properties
inherent in Ashburnham's name ('ash', 'burn 'em'), but the narrator's
name, John Dowell, also flickers with possibilities, as John Meixner
and Sara Haslam have suggested. Most obviously, Dowell splits into
'Do Well', suggesting some minor character from *Pilgrim's Progress*
or a Restoration comedy, encouraging us to wonder whether, morally,
the narrator, cuckolded husband of Florence, would-be husband of
Nancy, admirer and friend of Ashburnham, really does in any sense
'do well'. At the same time, the name offers other inflections,
depending on whether we pronounce it Dowell to rhyme with 'Lowell'

or Dowell to rhyme with 'towel'. If the former, the name suggests 'dole' as in suffering (certainly one way of looking at the character) and is close to John Doe (as in Everyman), which is sometimes how he likes to present himself. But there is also 'dowl' as in 'a barb of a feather, down, fluff', which emphasizes the narrator's drifting quality, his insubstantialness. His unfaithful wife's name Florence perhaps recalls the Italian city Maisie's mother absconds to with Sir Claude in *What Maisie Knew* but Dowell's recollection of his initial encounter with Florence also allows Ford to slip in a neat literary joke. 'First I had drifted in on Florence at a Browning tea,' Dowell remembers, while the alert reader recalls that Robert and Elizabeth Browning famously eloped to live in Florence (*GS* 20). And, like other writers before and since, Ford has quietly worked his own name into the text by choosing Fordingbridge as the village 'where the Ashburnhams' place is' (*GS* 12).[15]

A notable element in the opening pages of *The Good Soldier* – discussed elsewhere in this volume – is the recurrence of references to Florence and Ashburnham both having 'a heart', as in having a heart condition (*GS* 11).[16] Dowell soon reveals, however, that in both cases this was just a convenient ploy. For Florence, it helped her keep the upper hand over her husband, including keeping him out of her bedroom. For Ashburnham, it allowed him to quit the army and follow his current mistress Maisie Maidan back to Continental health resorts like Nauheim. On first encounter, the repeated references briefly mislead the reader into sympathy for Florence and Ashburnham before typically complicating this response when we discover the real motive for their imaginary complaints. A further point, of course, is metaphorically to point up just how 'heartless' Florence and Ashburnham are in contrast to Maisie Maidan, who really does have a heart and a heart condition, from which she dies.

This device of significantly repeated words or phrases ('good people' would be another obvious example) is an acknowledged Jamesian technique, but is equally characteristic of Kipling's stories from *Traffics and Discoveries* (1904) onwards. So, while James was probably the principal technical influence here, it is also credible to argue for Kipling's influence. Why? Because *The Good Soldier* provides clear evidence that Ford had continued to be a Kipling reader, if perhaps a sporadic one. The novel, for instance, contains passing echoes (among others) to the polo story 'The Maltese Cat' and to 'The Brushwood Boy', both in *The Day's Work* (1898). (The echoes I have

in mind here are the description of Edward Ashburnham swinging his
polo pony round 'like a cat dropping off a roof' (*GS* 29), which recalls
'The Maltese Cat', and the moment when Edward's mother has with
him 'one of those conversations that English mothers have with
English sons' (*GS* 110), which directly recalls a comparable mother-
son conversation in 'The Brushwood Boy', where George's mother
'sat down on the bed, and they talked for a long hour, as mother and
son should, if there is to be any future for our Empire'.)[17] More
strongly recalled is 'An Habitation Enforced' in *Actions and Reactions*
(1909). Here a rich childless American couple in pursuit of the
husband's health 'drift [. . .] about Europe' from resort to resort,
including Nauheim.[18] Eventually, like Florence, they locate the wife's
ancestral roots in an English village where they settle and where they
experience, like Dowell but more happily, the difficulties of really
understanding the English character. One villager even dies of heart-
failure. So it is plausible to suggest that Kipling's turn-of-the-century
and later experiments with formal fragmentation, absence of privileged authorial viewpoint, intense literary self-consciousness, sub-
merged narrative, and narrative indeterminacy (the latter brilliantly
teased out by David Lodge in his 1989 essay '"Mrs. Bathurst":
Indeterminacy in Modern Narrative') contributed to the technical
aspects of *The Good Soldier* – once one is prepared to accept
Kipling's presence in and behind the novel. To do so is in no sense to
diminish Ford's extraordinary achievement, but to recognize more
fully the subtle, synthesizing, impressionistic nature of that achievement, to add to *The Good Soldier* a further (and less obvious) literary
layer, to be reminded just how wide-ranging and unavoidable
Kipling's influence was at the time.

A final glance to Kipling. In his letter to his publisher John
Lane about a gentleman from Liverpool's objections to *The Good
Soldier*, Ford observed: 'after all, what is chaste in Constantinople
may have the aspect of lewdness in Liverpool, and what in Liverpool
may pass for virtue in Constantinople is frequently regarded as vice'.[19]
Compare this to Kipling's 1892 poem 'In the Neolithic Age' (a poem
Ford certainly knew and misquotes elsewhere): 'And the wildest
dreams of Kew are the facts of Khatmandhu / And the crimes of
Clapham chaste in Martaban.[20]

So, is John Bayley's encapsulation of *The Good Soldier* as
'Early Kipling told by Henry James' anything more than a donnish
*bon mot*? Yes, it does usefully draw attention to Kipling's (still)

unacknowledged presence in and behind Ford's novel. But, as this essay demonstrates, a considerably larger claim can also be made and sustained. Ford's allusions do much more than strongly evoke, in general and in particular, the milieu of Kipling's early Indian stories of the army and adultery; his allusions constitute an act of criticism, an act of literary self-assertion. They encourage the reader to recognise what else – and how much more – can be drawn out of such rich, emotionally resonant material.

## NOTES

1   *The Letters of Rudyard Kipling*, ed. by Thomas Pinney, 6 vols, London: Palgrave-Macmillan, 1990-2004, III (1996), p. 115.

2   *Letters of Ford Madox Ford*, ed. by Richard M. Ludwig, Princeton University Press: Princeton, 1965, p. 45.

3   Brita Lindberg-Seyersted, *Ford Madox Ford and His Relationship to Stephen Crane and Henry James*, New Jersey: Humanities Press International, 1987, p. 89.

4   Ford Madox Ford, *The Good Soldier: A Tale of Passion*, ed. by Max Saunders, Oxford: Oxford University Press, 2012 – henceforth *GS* with references inserted parenthetically in the text; p. 14.

5   Henry James, *What Maisie Knew*, London: Penguin Modern Classics, 1966, p. 24.

6   Philip Horne, 'The Master and the "Queer Affair" of "The Pupil"', in *Henry James: The Shorter Fiction: Reassessments*, ed. by N. H. Reeve, London: Macmillan, 1997, p. 119.

7   Julian Barnes, *Through the Window: Seventeen essays (and one short story)*, London: Vintage, 2012, pp. 46, 48.

8   Ford, *Henry James: A Critical Study*, New York: Octagon Books, 1972, p. 153; Tony Tanner, '"The Birthplace"', in *Henry James: The Shorter Fiction: Reassessments*, p. 82.

9   Kathryn C. Rentz, 'The Question of James's Influence on Ford's *The Good Soldier*', in *English Literature in Transition, 1880-1920*, 25:2 (1982), 104-14 (p. 109).

10  *Dai Greatcoat: A Self-portrait of David Jones in his Letters*, ed. by René Hague, London: Faber and Faber, 1980, p. 184.

11  Ford, *Return to Yesterday*, London: Victor Gollancz, 1931 – henceforth *RY*; p. 4.

12  Sara Haslam, *Fragmenting Modernism: Ford Madox Ford, the Novel and the Great War*, Manchester: Manchester University Press, 2002, p. 191.

13  William Shakespeare, *Much Ado About Nothing*, ed. by Sheldon P. Zitner, Oxford: Oxford World's Classics, 1993, I, i, 52 (p. 99).

14  Rudyard Kipling, *Soldiers Three and Other Stories*, London: Macmillan, 1895, p. 182.

15  It is probably no coincidence that Fordingbridge is the Hampshire village where Ford had a breakdown in 1904.

16  See the essays by Catherine Belsey and Elizabeth Brunton.
17  Rudyard Kipling, *The Day's Work*, London: Macmillan, 1898, p. 365.
18  Rudyard Kipling, *Actions and Reactions*, London: Macmillan, 1909, p. 4.
19  Quoted in Max Saunders, *Ford Madox Ford: A Dual Life*, 2 vols, Oxford: Oxford University Press, 1996, I, p. 403.
20  *The Cambridge Edition of the Poems of Rudyard Kipling,* ed. by Thomas Pinney, 3 vols, Cambridge: Cambridge University Press, 2013, p. 400.

# ANGLO-GERMAN DILEMMAS IN *THE GOOD SOLDIER*, OR: EUROPE ON THE BRINK IN 1913[1]

## Julian Preece

**Abstract**

*The Good Soldier*, which was written either side of the outbreak of World War One in August 1914, becomes a political novel through its portrayal of the diminishing understanding between individuals and their affiliated identities, especially those provided by nation and religion. The narrator John Dowell sees the world in terms of binary oppositions, such as those between British and Irish, Catholic and Protestant, while collapsing a number of these in his own person through his self-advertised Anglo-American and, though he keeps it much quieter, German-American heritage. The novel contains too elements of Ford's critique of Wilhelmine Germany, expressed in contemporaneous literary journalism and books such as *The Desirable Alien* (1913) and *When Blood is their Argument* (1915), in which he blamed Prussia for usurping the gentle spirit of the southern German Catholics. While Nancy Rufford is read as a new version of Goethe's Mignon, the degenerate colonial aristocrat Edward Ashburnham is the villain who can no longer assume society exists for his benefit and it soon crumbles on top of him. At the end of the novel the Irish Leonora has broken free, while Dowell and Rufford sit in the shell of Ashburnham's country seat, multiple ciphers for the end of British and German imperial culture.

As has often been remarked, one would surely assume that a novel entitled *The Good Soldier* which was published in March 1915, would be set in the trenches of the Western Front. That was presumably Ford's publishers' expectation in adopting his second choice of title, which was somewhat to his surprise. Taken metaphorically, as a comment on 'good soldiering' in war-time, the novel, which was largely completed before the outbreak of the war itself, is anything but morale-boosting, of course, and contemporary reviewers were not slow to recognise its potentially unpatriotic import. Ford's approach to the British officer class through his depiction of the behaviour of the eponymous good soldier Edward Ashburnham was decried at the time in one quarter as 'despicable'.[2] His portrayal of loose sexual morals in the higher social echelons is still shocking. But Ford's preferred title 'the saddest story' would be overblown if it referred merely to an account of double adultery amidst a moneyed elite in pre-1914 Europe, albeit an account which narrates the suicides of both adulterers (the good soldier himself and the narrator's wife Florence Dowell), as well as the death of a second woman (Maisie Maidan) and the mental breakdown of a third (Nancy Rufford, usually known as 'the girl'). These three women are all romantically involved in one way or another with Edward. Both Mrs Dowell and Miss Maidan are would-be correspondents in a potential divorce case. The narrator John Dowell does let on at the outset that he is writing from his deceased friend's country estate in Hampshire, Branshaw Teleragh, but not that he has recently purchased this property, which makes him an American sitting inside the shell of former British grandeur. His New World naiveté in not noticing that he spends nine years chaperoning Florence to her trysts with his friend would have to be ascribed to saintly innocence (or holy folly) were it not up to a point meant to be taken as a metaphor, even if he is deliberately deluding himself or is having us on when he claims not to have known the truth.

My argument proceeds from the premise that the war is the great unspoken presence in *The Good Soldier*, acknowledged not only in the title and his use of the date 4 August, on which day in 1914, around six months before the novel was published, the United Kingdom declared war on Germany. The war was the final expression and culmination of a civilisational crisis which Ford was already exploring in his novel when it began, both through its thematic contents and, perhaps more radically, by means of its form. Ford, until 1919 known as Ford Madox Hueffer, had come to know contemporary Germany and German culture intimately, even attempting to acquire German citizenship during his prolonged stay in 1910-11. But he developed an acutely critical appreciation of the land of his father's birth in the run-up to the war, which is evident in his literary journalism and, most forcefully, the memoir-cum-travelogue, co-written with Violet Hunt, *The Desirable Alien: At Home in Germany*. This is also the source for the German settings (Nauheim and Marburg) and some of the German characters (the Grand Duke) in *The Good Soldier*. Ford's own distinct contributions to this book are on points of political history and philosophy or consist of social comment, such as his account of suicides among young men in German secondary schools (one of the great scandals in the Second Empire).[3] His basic view, which again is evident in *The Good Soldier* and which he held for the rest of his life, is that the 'good Germany' which he loved had been taken over by unimaginative and authoritarian Protestant Prussians.

Ford's use of narrative form is undoubtedly more original. Dowell has great difficulty containing his story within the aesthetic parameters which he assigns himself. The elaborate narrative patterns which exceed his control can be argued, however, to articulate the political context which indeed led to Europe's 'saddest story'. Content challenges form in his repeated assertion of an imagined community with a listener, as he avers towards the beginning: 'So I shall just imagine myself for a fortnight or so at one side of the fireplace of a country cottage, with a sympathetic soul opposite me' (*GS* 18). *Wuthering Heights*, which recounts a tale of equally destructive passions, makes use of just such a 'frame'. Boccaccio had proceeded in the same way in *The Decameron*, which was emulated in Germany by novella writers through the nineteenth century from Johann Wolfgang von Goethe in *Conversations of German Emigrés* (1795) to Theodor Storm in *The Rider on the White Horse / Der Schimmelreiter* (1888). Ford may be recalling this classic ghost story set on the North German coast when he continues: 'And I shall go on talking, in a low voice while the sea sounds in the distance and overhead the great black flood of wind polishes the bright stars' (*GS* 18).[4] Nature may be threatening, mysterious, and unpredictable, but for Storm the cosmos retained its moral order. In 1935 Walter Benjamin wrote in a celebrated essay about the devastating effects of the First World War on the human capacity for experience, which he saw to be the basis for traditional story-telling:

> A generation that had gone to school on a horse-drawn streetcar now stood under the open sky in a countryside in which nothing remained unchanged but the clouds, and beneath these clouds, in a field of force of destructive torrents and explosions, was the tiny, fragile human body.[5]

Ford may not have known in late 1914 as he finished *The Good Soldier* about the true horrors of trench warfare, though the poem *Antwerp* written in October that year shows that he already had a pretty good idea, but as a novelist he sensed enough. Orality was certainly as passé as the verse epic or the epistolary novel. For this reason the narrative arrangement of *The Good Soldier* is no more than a proposition. Dowell does not even attempt to simulate the traditional story-telling set-up, as there is no listener in the novel itself, as there is with Boccaccio, Goethe, Brontë, and Storm.[6]

Dowell covers up for his incapacities by trying a number of tactics. He ignores, pretends, dissembles, refuses to get to the point, and contradicts himself. As he cannot give us a full picture, he passes on redundant information, relaying the four characters' ages in two different formats on the first page, for instance. He repeatedly professes an inability even to describe what he has seen. By the end, he is either deliriously confused or has veered into a dystopian fantasy because, if we follow his otherwise precise chronological markers, his narration post-dates the novel's publication. Given the events in the world outside, which had already hurtled into an abyss, it is not inappropriate that he should career ever further into an uncertain future. From the point of view of narratology, he has lost control of the story teller's most important dimension: time itself.

If Dowell's own behaviour before he puts pen to paper can be connected to the causes of the war, then he sleepwalks to disaster, to borrow Christopher Clark's metaphor in the title of a recent book on the war's origins, one of a slew which marked the centenary.[7] *The Sleepwalkers* was also what the Austrian novelist Hermann Broch called his trilogy on the same theme published in 1931. The Anglo-German Ford Madox Hueffer either echoes or anticipates a number of key metaphors from other ambitious Central European novels (by such as Robert Musil, Jaroslav Hašek, Franz Kafka, Elias Canetti, Arthur Schnitzler and Thomas Mann), some of which are set retrospectively at this apparent end point of European civilisation.[8] *Faux-naiveté* was turned to devastating satirical effect by Hašek, whose 'good soldier Švejk' subverts the established order through the simple expedient of taking official pronouncements literally. Thus Švejk is arrested for expressing his patriotic joy as a loyal subject of the Emperor when he hears that war is declared; as an ethnic Czech the authorities assume that he must be faking his enthusiasm. Dowell is also both myopic and more or less incapable of emotional warmth and communication with a fellow human being, much like Peter Kien in Canetti's *Auto-da-Fé* (1935) or the aristocratic hero of Schnitzler's *The Road into the Open* (1911). Ford greatly admired the latter, even referring in 1938 to 'the polished Mediterraneanism of [his] late friend Arthur Schnitzler'.[9] In November 1913 he also praised *The Road into the Open* but did not appear to notice its recurrent theme of casual anti-Semitism, calling it instead 'a sort of Pilgrim's Progress of a poet's soul', which it no doubt is, though the soul in question is more callous and arguably as rotten as Ashburnham's.[10] The heroes' failure either to connect or to take responsibility for words and deeds results in moral catastrophe in both *The Road into the Open* and Canetti's *Auto-da-Fé* . What links both Florence Dowell and Edward Ashburnham with Mann's Hans Castorp in *The Magic Mountain* (1924), who spent seven years in a sanatorium in the Swiss Alps before being released to join the army in 1914 when the novel ends, is that none of them is really ill. Ford's use of illness, hypochondria and repressed eroticism as metaphors for feverish ethical short-sightedness also anticipates Mann's great novel of cultural cataclysm. Ford sees this behaviour as typically German. He wrote in January 1914, just after beginning *The Good Soldier*, in a review of Gerhart Hauptmann's *Atlantis* that 'Germany is the best of all asylums for the really neurasthenic', which he sees, metaphorically, to be Hauptmann's real subject, as it was becoming his.[11]

Emptiness and lack are also recurrent motifs in *The Good Soldier*. Dowell lives from rents that he earns from his New England properties, having no need to work and no inclination to practise a profession. Economically, he is a superfluous man. At least Ashburnham would have used up his fortune (which is also derived from rents) on the casinos and courtesans of Monte Carlo had he not been saved from his own appetites by the offices of his long-suffering wife. As he acknowledges towards the end, Dowell is a mirror or inverted image of Ashburnham. The full initials of the serial seducer, gambler, drinker, 'sentimentalist' and upholder of the feudal ideal who lusts after his adopted daughter (who may even be his *own* daughter) are E.*F*.*A*. As we do not get to hear what the middle 'F' stands for, its inclusion is redundant unless the habitually elegant FMF is lapsing into the Anglo-Saxon vernacular to make an uncharacteristically coarse joke at Edward's expense. This is how Dowell recalls glimpsing him for the first time, as he entered the dining room at the Hotel Excelsior in Nauheim:

> His face hitherto had, in the wondrous English fashion, expressed nothing whatever. Nothing. There was in it neither joy nor despair; neither hope nor fear; neither boredom nor satisfaction. He seemed to perceive no soul in that crowded room; he might have been walking in a jungle (*GS* 26).

Like Dowell himself, Ashburnham is another 'man without qualities', as Musil would entitle a much bigger multi-volume novel project which he sets in Vienna in the twelve months leading up to August 1914, and which also features brother-sister incest.

On 2 August 1914 Franz Kafka wrote in his diary: 'Germany has declared war on Russia. — Swimming in the afternoon'.[12] Some readers have seen in the entry a lack of interest in world affairs. But in

what remained of the summer and through the autumn Kafka wrote
*The Trial*, his best known novel, which, like *The Good Soldier*, is
about a disruption to the settled patriarchal and bourgeois order. As
Elisabeth Boa notes, it begins when a woman fails to bring the novel's
hero his breakfast in bed.[13] On the same day, which is also his thirtieth
birthday and thus traditionally associated with the assumption of adult
responsibility, Josef K's advances to Fraulein Bürstner, his room
neighbour in Frau Grubach's pension, are rebuffed. He has wrongly
thought to himself that Fraulein Bürstner is 'a little typist, who would
not keep up her resistance [. . .] for long', but has tragically misread
her and his superiority over her.[14] K.'s first audience with the court is
held in a working-class area of the city that he has not visited before,
suggesting that his trial has something to do with his unacknowledged
bad social conscience. Edward's world is similarly under threat, which
is expressed through challenges to his sexual and social supremacy.
He was found guilty of importuning a nineteen-year-old nursemaid on
a train. However, she not only fended him off, she pulled the communication cord and showed the strength of resolve to take him to
court. Dowell reflects that: 'All her life, by her mother, by other girls,
by schoolteachers, by the whole tradition of her class she had been
warned against gentlemen' (*GS* 118). The law then backs her up and
her assailant is punished. Is this not as fantastic as anything in Kafka?
Dowell typically denies both the young woman agency and her
assailant ill intent, blaming Edward's debacle on the maid's employer,
the leader of the local anti-Tory Nonconformists who wants to ruin
Edward as the local landowner. Dowell's social discourse is unreflect-
ively apologetic. The English gentleman is always in the right. In this
respect he is his friend's alter ego.

A case can be made against Josef K. He is haughty, snobbish,
arrogant, largely oblivious to the needs of others, and interested in
furthering his own self advancement and satisfying his sexual needs,
but his values are also those of the society which surrounds him,
which is thus on trial alongside him. Similar charges could be made
against Edward. His other escapades are no more edifying than the on-
train assault. Out of his league with La Dolciquita, he lays himself
open to blackmail through his affair with Mrs Basil and relies on his
wife to 'pimp' (the narrator's term) Maisie Maidan.[15] As a scion of an
ancient family and owner of a country estate, Captain Ashburnham
DSO is a representative figure, associated closely with the British
Empire. In addition to the suspicions that he was intimate with 'the

girl' Nancy Rufford's mother,[16] one of his last, apparently kindly and sentimental actions is to pay the legal fees of a young woman accused of infanticide. They amount to some £200. In earlier versions of the novel Ford referred directly to Edward's illegitimate children. The most horrifying element here may be that Dowell insists to the end that Edward's actions were always motivated by the noblest sentiments.[17] His sentiments of *noblesse oblige* cover up 'the horror'.

Ford could not have known most of these German or Austrian novels when he wrote *The Good Soldier* because (except for Schnitzler's) they were published in the two decades after the war ended. My point is thus not that he borrowed from them, but that, working essentially with the same material, he identified some of the same pathological symptoms and turned them into metaphors.[18] Ford did, however, know Goethe's *Wilhelm Meister's Apprenticeship*, a draft version of which (*Wilhelm Meister's theatrical Mission*) was published for the first time in 1911.[19] Poems included in the novel were set to music over the nineteenth century by composers such as Beethoven, Schubert, Liszt, Schumann, and Wolf, becoming part of the classical repertoire. The most famous of these 'Kennst Du das Land?' (Do you know the land?) is sung in Italian by an enigmatic figure called Mignon, who is thirteen years old when she enters the novel.[20] Mignon is associated with art, mystery, and sexuality. Her own sexual and even gender identity are indeterminate but at the end she dies of a broken heart when Wilhelm, who has acted as a surrogate father to her, announces that he will marry another woman. While Mignon's background is never entirely explained, she appears to be the victim of abuse and is revealed to be the product of an incestuous marriage between brother and sister. Characters resembling Mignon appeared in numerous works by German, French and English writers over the next one hundred years. In a detailed comparative study Terence Cave lists texts in English by Thackeray, George Eliot, and Ford's contemporary and friend, Henry James.[21] Nancy Rufford, whom Dowell refers to as 'the girl' or 'the poor girl', is surely another such 'Mignonesque' figure. She has lived with Edward and Leonora since the age of thirteen. She comes from an abusive family: we are told that her father Major Rufford beat his wife and even once struck Nancy so hard 'that she had lain unconscious for three days' (*GS* 101). While she has no association with art, on her last journey she travels through Italy, to where Mignon longed to return, cabling from Brindisi to say that she is well. The next that we hear from her after she has heard about Edward's suicide she has suffered a breakdown which robs her of her mind.

Nancy is the most allegorical character in the novel. Dowell professes to finding her 'queer' and 'very difficult to describe', eventually capitulating to what he regards as her contradictions:

> She was tall and strikingly thin; she had a tortured mouth, agonised eyes, and a quite extraordinary sense of fun. You might put it that at times she was exceedingly grotesque and at times extraordinarily beautiful [. . . .] She was just over twenty-one and at times she seemed as old as the hills, at times not much more than sixteen. (GS 99)

Once she has gone mad, he calls her appearance 'a picture without meaning' (GS 192). For Cave, Mignon is a threshold figure because she mediates between cultures and languages: hers is 'at its core [. . .] the reiterated story of vulnerability and severance, the story of an arrest at the threshold', all of which could apply to Nancy.[22] Ford deploys her as an unacknowledged intruder from the German tradition which, like the tradition she intrudes upon, is in the process of going to the bad. Whereas the recognition or 'anagnorisis' in *Wilhelm Meister* contained tragedy (Mignon's incestuous origins) and preceded her demise, in *The Good Soldier* it is simply horrific: it may well be that Edward, who slits his own throat after becoming infatuated with her, is her own father. Dowell senses the true monstrousness of the tale he sits down to recount at the beginning of one of his early paragraphs with a sentence which readers have sometimes found a touch melodramatic. Reflecting on the meaning of his story, he compares it to the greatest event in ancient history which sealed the end of an epoch and the destruction of a civilisation: 'Some one has said that the death of a mouse from cancer is the whole sack of Rome by the Goths, and I swear to you that the breakup of our little four-square coterie was such another unthinkable event' (GS 12). Ford is aware that the circumstances of this breakup express, however indirectly, some of the causes of the First World War, which sealed the end of the epoch that he knew.

A more tangible clue about Ford's intentions may be contained in the date – 4 August – which, by a set of coincidences which even the studiedly unobservant Dowell finds remarkable, is the day on which, by his own lights at least, everything of note occurs in his wife Florence's brief life. While this is well known in writing on *The Good Soldier*, it will be useful for my argument if I summarise the information once again. 4 August is Florence's birthday; on 4 August 1899 when she turned twenty-five she set out on a world tour with 'her kindly uncle' (who may also be her father) and 'a young man called Jimmy', who certainly became her lover (65). Exactly one year later, she agreed to marry Dowell and eloped with him one year after that in 1901. On her thirtieth birthday in 1904 Maisie Maidan suddenly died (for which, according to Leonora Ashburnham, Florence was co-responsible) and the Ashburnhams and the Dowells made the fateful excursion to the Castle at M—. It is at this Prussian location which was the site of the original 'protest' setting in motion the Reformation that Florence insults Leonora's Irish Catholicism and flaunts her liaison with Edward, Leonora's husband. On 4 August in 1913, either because she realises that her husband has heard that she was Jimmy's lover before they got married, as Dowell at first wants us to believe, or because she has overheard Edward express his love for Nancy, which is more likely, Florence takes her own life. Between 4 August 1904 and 4 August 1913 Dowell claims that there are nine years of 'nothing'. Florence thus takes a wrong turn at the threshold age of thirty in 1904 which ensures her failure to arrive at the next threshold age of forty in 1914 (Ford began to write his novel on 17 December 1913, which happened to be his own fortieth birthday). In German modernist literature, failure to pass these threshold ages and to settle down into adulthood, secure in one's identity and integrated into a social environment, is a central trope.[23]

4 August 1914 was the day that Britain declared war on Germany, after German troops marched through neutral Belgium en route for France. Austria-Hungary had declared war on Serbia a week earlier as a consequence of the assassination of the Archduke Franz Ferdinand by a Bosnian Serb nationalist a month before that. Serbia was allied to Russia which was allied to France which was allied to Britain. Germany declared war on Russia on 1 August (as Kafka noted in his diary the following day). For Ford's British readers 4 August 1914 marks the beginning of what came to be called the First World War, which is commemorated on different days across the Continent, as is, more bizarrely, its end. If, as seems highly likely, Ford had chosen this 'pivotal date' before 4 August 1914 in ignorance of what the future held, he was certainly aware of its full range of significances as he finished the novel.[24] In the book on Germany that he wrote immediately after finishing *The Good Soldier*, he gives the impression that all hostilities between the various powers began pre-

cisely on 4 August, which then assumes even greater symbolic significance. Explaining how, in his interpretation of events, German public
opinion was manipulated against her future enemies, Ford writes:

> the great bulk of the population of Germany seriously imagined before August
> 4th, 1914, that the French nation was so enfeebled as to be unable to offer any
> armed resistance to the legions of William II, the English so sunk in sloth,
> decadence, and the love of comfort as to be incapable of armed resistance or
> the power of commercial organisation in war time; and the Russian Empire a
> horde of negligible and impoverished barbarians.[25]

In Ford's memoir *Return to Yesterday*, which ends with the
assassination of the Archduke Franz Ferdinand, C. F. G. Masterman
predicted the outbreak of war one full year before it happened. As he
and Ford holidayed on the Rhine, Ford recalls him announcing on 2
August 1913: 'By this date next year we shall be at war with
Germany', his reason being that Germany would be bankrupt by the
following summer. As Ford reminds his readers, Masterman, was just
'two days out'.[26] For the author of *The Good Soldier*, 4 August 1914
is thus undoubtedly the key date.

The relationships between the major characters and their sat-
ellites in *The Good Soldier* are not wholly dissimilar to the tangled
military alliances between the Great Powers. Both engender unintend-
ed outcomes. In the novel there are two reasons for the significance of
4 August 1904 (Maisie Maidan's sudden death and the visit to the
Castle at M—.) Similarly, there are two explanations for Florence's
suicide on 4 August 1913: either she killed herself because she realises
that her husband has been told that she was not a virgin when they
married or she has overheard Edward's advances to 'the girl' and fears
her own affair with him is over. The causes of the events unleashed on
4 August 1914 are being debated to this day. The deceptions of the
Ashburnhams and the Dowells do not directly reflect or represent the
relations between states in the pre-1914 era. The novel's style is
oblique and metonymic rather than allegorical. But behind the facade
of good manners (Edward and Leonora only talk to each other when
others are present), this quartet of 'quite good people' (12) is morally
corrupt to a degree which beggars belief. That was certainly also true
of Great Power Europe.

There is a series of binary oppositions in *The Good Soldier*
which set individuals against each other in ways which do mirror the
mechanisms of enmity between states. Dowell divides the characters

into mutually uncomprehending camps: British and American; Anglo-Saxon and Continental European; Protestant and Catholic; English and Irish; even white and black, thinking of Dowell's servant Julius, as well, more generally, given the novel's imperial settings, as subaltern and colonial.[27] The narrative gains much of its power from Dowell's misapprehension of gestures and motives as he assigns people to their faith, class, political allegiance (for Americans: Democrat or Republican; or which side their family supported in the War of Independence), country or culture, while not naming the difference which quite possibly drives the whole story: his own homosexuality. As an Anglo-German Ford collapsed at least one of these false binaries in his own person, which must be one reason that he announces it to be a chimera a year before the war: 'there is no such thing as Germany as distinct from England; no such thing as England as distinct from the wide lands from the Rhine to the Elbe'.[28]

The Great War pitched most of these camps against each other, ending the leisured cosmopolitan world inhabited by the two married couples at the centre of the novel. All four principal characters have multiple affiliations. The Ashburnham marriage emblematically captures an idea of the British Empire as an unworkable sham. Both spouses are from military families, Edward is a Protestant Englishman and Leonora, née Powys an Irish Catholic. Rob Doggett has recently written that Leonora is the unknowable 'Irish other', but for this 'eminently perplexed narrator', as he calls Dowell, I would argue that all such 'others' are equally unknowable, which is why Dowell is such an inveterate 'otherer' in the first place.[29] British relations with Ireland are another subterranean theme. In a satirical article on the Irish Question written in 1911, Ford makes two comparisons with Germany and Anglo-German relations.[30]

If there is hope (to paraphrase George Orwell) it lies with the subalterns: the Irish Catholic Leonora temporarily saves her husband by whisking him away from European fleshpots to colonial Burma and taking over the management of Branshaw Teleragh and his finances. According to Dowell, she wants her husband back for the sake of her religion and the integrity of a vanished order. Like the Dowells, the Ashburnhams have no children, but once Edward is dead Leonora immediately becomes pregnant on remarrying. One index of a novel's historical optimism is its ratio of births to deaths. In the German and Austrian list that I have enumerated, babies are few and far between. Only Irish Catholics are fertile in *The Good Soldier*.

The other paper marriage is between a couple of wealthy New Englanders, the narrator John Dowell and Florence, née Hurlbird, who is descended from the original owners of Branshaw Teleragh. While Dowell introduces himself as no less English in origin than his wife ('the first Dowell [. . .] left Farnham in Surrey in company of William Penn' (*GS* 12), making him an aristocrat among settlers) and he succeeds, where she fails, by ending up as owner and occupier of her ancestors' country seat, there is another ingredient to his identity which he brags about less and which is not usually accorded the prominence it surely deserves by critics. Dowell is also of German stock. He reveals on the trip to the Castle at M— that he speaks the language better than his wife, though without being able to rid himself of 'the accent of the Pennsylvania Duitsch of my childhood' (*GS* 39). This 'Duitsch' is still spoken, but today, as in the latter part of the nineteenth century when Dowell grew up, only by members of the language community. Dowell is as coy about his German roots as he is about his sexuality. While he and Florence are both American, through their ancestors their union represents an Anglo-German alliance, which makes the novel into a kind of round dance of the Anglo-Irish and the Anglo-Germans.

Branshaw Teleragh is the novel's point of origin and its point of return. *The Good Soldier* nevertheless begins properly in the cosmopolitan German Spa town of Nauheim where Dowell is alienated by his surroundings. Before the Ashburnhams' entrance he describes his detachment as he stands on the steps of the Englischer Hof or 'English Court': 'Natty, precise, well-brushed, conscious of being rather small amongst the long English, the lank Americans, the rotund Germans, and the obese Russian Jewesses' (*GS* 25). By birth or heritage, Dowell is English, American, and German but he does not fit in amongst any of them any more than he does amongst the fat Russian Jewish women. Petra Rau sees the hotel as a counterpoint to Branshaw Teleragh:

> The novel's sexual and epistemological crises, however, are also constructed as crises of Englishness, denoted through the loci of its melodrama, the Hotel Englischer Hof and the English country house, both of which fail to contain transgressive desire as if it were some heinous German bacillus that has infected the social fabric.[31]

Yet the English are also Irish, American and German. The name of the establishment indicates a kind of German Anglophilia and stands in the novel as a piece of England on foreign soil. (The hotel in Nauheim which bore this name in 1913 is now called the Bayrischer Hof or 'Bavarian Court'.)

There are four further episodes in Germany involving German figures either living or dead which I would now like to interpret in the light of the calamity of 4 August 1914. These are: the brief account of Edward's polo match against a German team (*GS* 29), which shows the archetypal military Englishman and British imperialist triumphant in mock battle with the future foe; the visit to M— on 4 August 1904; the annual dinner at Nauheim for the Grand Duke of Nassau Schwerin hosted jointly by the Dowells and the Ashburnhams (*GS* 33); and Florence's death from an overdose of 'nitrate of amyl' on 4 August 1913 (*GS* 82). The Castle at M— is where Luther, Zwingli, Martin Bucer, and the 'trigamist' Ludwig the Courageous signed the 'protest' which, as Florence triumphantly informs the assembled company, 'is why we were all called Protestants' (*GS* 39). Her announcement has the intended effect of upsetting Leonora, as Florence calculated that it would, but Maisie Maidan is also Irish. But if Leonora is thus marginalised, the Anglo-American trio of Protestants is allied with their German or rather Prussian confrères. Ford blamed the war not on Germany itself but on Prussia, tracing its origins to the Reformation, which he interpreted to have been a Prussian affair. He argued that 'The religious struggle [. . .] that began in Germany in the days of Holbein has impoverished Germany from that day to this, and is, I think I can prove, one other direct cause of the war at whose hands to-day we are all suffering'.[32] M— is not only identified with Luther's protest as, according to Dowell, it 'has the disadvantage of being in Prussia; and it is always disagreeable to go into that country' (*GS* 36).[33] Dowell appears to share Ford's antipathy to the dominant force in the German Reich while retaining a positive attitude towards other non-Prussian (and Catholic) regions of Germany. Ford's father was born in Münster in the northern part of the Catholic Rhineland, which became part of Prussia at the Congress of Vienna in 1815. Ford himself ascribes all that is good and likeable about Germany to the southern parts of the country, while blaming Prussia for everything that set the Reich on a collision course with Britain. As political or cultural history, this is more or less nonsense, though became an influential view during the Second World War, at the end of which Prussia was officially dissolved by the Allies. On Ford's part, it is a strategy for dealing with his split loyalties. In the metaphorical scheme of *The Good Soldier* it collapses the 'German' part of any binary opposition, since 'German' itself divides into 'good' and 'bad'.

At Nauheim the two couples find themselves playing the role of impromptu diplomats inviting the Grand Duke 'and a good many of his suite and any members of the diplomatic bodies that might be there' to a dinner, which 'became a sort of closing function for the season, at any rate as far as we were concerned' (*GS* 33). The Grand Duke reminds Dowell of the British King, 'the late Edward VII' (*GS* 34), who like Ford had a German father and English mother, in his pleasantness and affability.[34] These are attributes which were never attached to the Grand Duke's nephew the Emperor Wilhelm II about whom we are told the Grand Duke would occasionally talk. Once again there is a split, this time between the good Germany of the old nobility which is anglicised in its manners and the bad Germany of the Prussian Hohenzollerns, which is in the ascendancy. Another Grand Duke assisted by a chief of police and a hotelier officiate over Florence's corpse. Ford here paints a tableau vivant of the German state: there is an ineffectual but charming leader, an aggressive policeman, and a representative of commerce reminiscent of a clergyman with poor personal hygiene or worse. Dowell remembers only their faces, which 'seemed to bob into my consciousness, like floating globes':

> At times one head would be there alone, at another the spiked helmet of the official would be close to the healthy baldness of the prince; then M. Schontz's oiled locks would push in between the two. The sovereign's soft, exquisitely trained voice would say, 'Ja, ja, ja!' each word dropping out like so many soft pellets of suet; the subdued rasp of the official would come: 'Zum Befehl Durchlaucht,' like five revolver shots; the voice of M. Schontz would go on and on under its breath like that of an unclean priest reciting from his breviary in the corner of a railway-carriage. (*GS* 88)

Nauheim is beyond the border of Prussia, which situates it in the 'better' southern Germany whose inhabitants have a natural inclination, according to Ford, 'towards the French language and French forms of culture'.[35] This must be why the hotelier is a 'monsieur' rather than a 'Herr'. Comparing him with a sinful priest further aligns him with a waning Catholicism which will not be strong enough to mediate between other two forces let alone support the Grand Duke against the military mannered chief of police. Though the *Pickelhaube* was worn throughout Germany by the late nineteenth century, the police chief's signature phrase ('At your command, your highness') indicates that he belongs with the Prussianised Germany that Ford reviled and blamed for the war.

This is the last reference to Germany or Germans. There remains the German-American Dowell himself, who at the close occupies the grand but empty house of England with only his terminally damaged Mignon for company, between them representing two cultures in ruins.

## NOTES

1   I am very grateful to the editor for his generous and detailed advice on Ford's German literary interests, which greatly enhanced the scope of this essay.

2   J. K. Prothero, quoted by Max Saunders, in 'Introduction', Ford Madox Ford, *The Good Soldier*, Oxford: Oxford University Press, 2012, Oxford World Classics, new ed. – henceforth *GS*; pp. vii-xliii, here xxvi. All references are to this edition. An anonymous reviewer affected disbelief in the journal *Outlook*: 'Captain Ashburnham [...] is described to us as a typical specimen of the best kind of Englishman, an officer and a gentleman, a good landlord, a staunch friend. It is therefore inconceivable that he should have behaved as [. . .] Mr Hueffer tells us he did behave', in Ford Madox Ford, *The Good Soldier*, London/New York: Norton, 1995, ed. Martin Stannard, pp. 226-7, here p. 226. On the choice of title and the shocked reactions to the novel, see also Max Saunders, *Ford Madox Ford: A Dual Life*, Oxford: Oxford University Press, 2012, 2 vols, I, pp. 417-19. First published 1996.

3   *The Desirable Alien: At Home in Germany by Violet Hunt. With a Preface and two additional chapters by Ford Madox Hueffer*, London: Chatto and Windus, 1913, pp. 112-14. See Ford's chapter 'How it Feels to be Members of Subject Races', pp. 210-19.

4   He must have known *Der Schimmelreiter*, but did not rate it highly if he was referring to it in this characterization of a recent phase in German fiction: 'Every second novelist was giving you the history of strong passionate engineers, wrestling with dykes against the sea, and forming affinities with superwomen not their wives'. See 'Herr Schnitzler and Bertha Garlan' (first published November 1913), in *Ford Madox Ford, Critical Essays*, selected, edited and introduced by Max Saunders and Richard Stang, Manchester: Carcanet, 2002, pp. 122-5, here p. 124.

5   Walter Benjamin, 'The Story Teller. Reflections on the Work of Nikolai Leskov', *Illuminations*, edited and with an introduction by Hannah Arendt, London: Fontana, 1973, tr. Harry Zohn, pp. 83-107, here p.84.

6   Denis Donoghue suggests that Dowell is initially thinking of Nancy, but gives up the talking paradigm once he realizes she's unable to comprehend: 'Listening to the Saddest Story', *Sewanee Review*, 88 (1980), 557-71, esp. 561.

7    Christopher Clark, *The Sleepwalkers. How Europe went to war in 1914*, Harmondsworth: Penguin, 2013.

8    Bergonzi notes the similarities with the novels by Mann and Musil. See Bernard Bergonzi, 'Fiction and History: Rereading *The Good Soldier*', in *Ford Madox Ford's Modernity*, International Ford Madox Ford Studies 2, ed. Robert Hampson and Max Saunders, Amsterdam and New York: Rodopi, 2003, pp. 149-58, esp. p. 151. In 1938 Ford mentions Mann, including *The Magic Mountain*, and reveals that he bought a copy of *Buddenbrooks* in Marburg on publication in 1901: *The March of Literature. From Confucius' Day to Our Own*, New York: Dial Press, 1938, p. 793.

9    *Ibid.*, p. 794.

10   'Herr Arthur Schnitzler and Bertha Garlan', p. 123.

11   'Literary Portraits—XIX. Gerhart Hauptmann and *Atlantis*', *Outlook*, 33 (17 January 1914), 77-9.

12   *The Diaries of Franz Kafka 1910-23*, edited by Max Brod, Harmondsworth: Penguin, 1964, trs. Joseph Kresch and Martin Greenberg with the cooperation of Hannah Arendt, p. 301.

13   Elizabeth Boa, *Kafka: Gender, Class and Race in the Letters and Fictions*, Oxford: Oxford University Press, 1996, p. 188. The novel's second sentence reads: 'Frau Grubach's cook, who brought him his breakfast at around eight o'clock every day, did not appear'. Franz Kafka, *The Trial*, Oxford: Oxford University Press, 2009, tr. Mike Mitchell. With an Introduction and Notes by Ritchie Robertson, p. 5.

14   *The Trial*, p. 172.

15   One can also argue that Dowell pimps his wife Florence to Edward in a similar fashion. See Rose de Angelis, 'Narrative Triangulations: Truth, Identity, and Desire in Ford Madox Ford's *The Good Soldier*', *English Studies*, 88:4 (2007), 425-46, esp. p. 434.

16   Saunders, *A Dual Life*, I, pp. 421-3.

17   Saunders recognises the contradiction in the novelist's own allegiances: 'Ford's nostalgic admiration for the paternal landowner is unmistakeable, even as he reminds us that the droit de seigneur involves not only being a father to your tenants, but fathering their children', *ibid.*, p. 427.

18   Saunders acknowledges that the novel 'comes out of many of the same tensions and forces which produced the war', *ibid.*, p. 431.

19   *Wilhelm Meisterstheatralische Sendung*. Nach der Schulthess'schen Abschrift-zumersten Male herausgegeben von Harry Maync (Berlin / Stuttgart: 1911). A central chapter of Ford's very next book *When Blood is Their Argument: An Analysis of Prussian Culture*, London: Hodder and Stoughton, 1915, is on the subject of 'Goethe as Superman', pp. 270-90.

20   In *The March of Literature* he discusses *Wilhelm Meister* and quotes 'Kennst Du das Land?', pp. 544-6.

21   Terence Cave, *Mignon's Afterlives: Crossing Cultures from Goethe to the Twenty-First Century*, Oxford: Oxford University Press, 2011.

22   *Ibid.*, p. 265.

23   See Theodor Ziolkowski, 'The Novel of the Thirty-Year-Old', in *Dimensions of the Modern Novel. German Texts in European Contexts*, Princeton: Princeton University Press, 1969, pp. 258-88.

24 The textual and circumstantial evidence for Ford having chosen the date for his novel in advance of its acquiring its historical resonance is fairly overwhelming. See Bergonzi, pp. 150-1.

25 Ford, *When Blood is their Argument*, p. 213.

26 Ford Madox Ford, *Return to Yesterday*, edited and with an introduction by Bill Hutchings, Manchester: Carcanet, 1999, p. 315. First published 1931.

27 Initially, Dowell was aggressively anti-Belgian, but after the German invasion which prompted Britain's declaration of war, Ford deleted these sentiments. See Bergonzi, p. 150.

28 *The Desirable Alien*, pp. xi-xii.

29 Rob Doggett, '"Those were Troublesome Times in Ireland, I understand": Ireland, the Limits of knowledge, and Ford Madox Ford's *The Good Soldier*', *Modern Fiction Studies* 53:4 (2007), 697-721, p. 698. He continues that 'the novel explores a set of issues that are fundamentally intertwined with the Irish Question: the viability of the British Empire; the decay of the old aristocracy; and the decline, at both the colonial periphery and the imperial center, of a political, economic, and cultural system based on land ownership', p. 699.

30 'By our senseless opposition to Napoleon we gave life to Prussia, the flail of the world. By our senseless opposition to Home Rule we flooded the party with Whigs that spawned upon us Democratic ideas'; 'In the German Empire, Catholics are to Protestants as two to five. Yet it was the German Catholics alone in the world who brought Bismarck to his knees, and the German Catholics have ruled Germany ever since'. From 'A Tory Plea for Home Rule' (1) and (2), in Saunders and Stang (eds.), *Critical Essays*, pp. 98-105, here p.101 and p.105.

31 Petra Rau, *English Modernism, National Identity and the Germans, 1890-1950*, Farnham, Surrey: Ashgate, 2009, p. 108. See esp. her chapter on the use Ford makes of Bad Nauheim: 'Ford's "Tricky German Fashion". Medical Modernity and Anglo-Saxon Pathology', pp. 89-112.

32 *When Blood is their Argument*, p. 8.

33 Cf. also his praise of Hauptmann's *Atlantis* to the effect that 'it gives such a very brave rendering of the good German, as opposed to the atrocious Prussian, spirit'.

34 The Grand Duke that Ford and Violet Hunt encountered at Nauheim, who was apparently also reminiscent of Edward VII, 'preferred Americans, with an occasional incursion into Dutch territory – Americans, probably, because they are still capable of being frankly dazzled by the old order, which is by no means passing away in Germany', *The Desirable Alien*, p. 100.

35 *Ibid.*, p. 271.

Bad Nauheim: Sprudelhof doorway

# 'THE END IS WHERE WE START FROM': SPATIAL ASPECTS OF RETROSPECTION IN *THE GOOD SOLDIER* AND *IN PARENTHESIS*

## Cara Chimirri

**Abstract**

The narrator of Ford's *The Good Soldier*, John Dowell, attempts to explain the motivation behind constructing his narrative by stating that: 'it is not unusual in human beings who have witnessed the sack of a city or the falling to pieces of a people to desire to set down what they have witnessed for the benefit of unknown heirs or of generations infinitely remote; or, if you please, just to get the sight out of their heads'. While Dowell's personal tragedy implies a parallel to the sack of cities and downfall of civilizations, David Jones's chronicle of the First World War, *In Parenthesis*, deals directly with these events. Both texts present retrospective narratives, which while operating on different scales, address the destruction of a previously held sense of order and stability. The act of composing these reflective narratives is an attempt, through textual composition, to achieve a catharsis and a sense of meaning. As journeys into the past and into memory, both display many similar spatial concerns, the most revealing of which are fragmentation and liminal space. Comparing these techniques draws both texts together within a wider sense of fracturing and dislocation surrounding the First World War.

In T. S. Eliot's 'Little Gidding', the speaker informs us that:

> What we call the beginning is often the end
> And to make an end is to make a beginning.
> The end is where we start from.[1]

Eliot's challenge to a standard narrative timeline provides us with an approach to a comparative reading of Ford's *The Good Soldier* and *In Parenthesis* by David Jones. In distinct, yet analogous, ways these two texts engage memory in order retrospectively to render events and experiences. The most interesting parallels between this phenomenon in both texts lies in the spatial qualities involved in recalling a personal history. Analysing fragmentation and liminality in *The Good Soldier* and *In Parenthesis* highlights the spatiality of recollection and the contextual environment both texts engage with. This comparison reveals how Jones and Ford explore the same cultural dilemma in a pre- and post-war situation.

Each text depicts how the human mind employs memory when attempting to understand and resolve traumatic and destabilising events. John Dowell muses upon his reason for writing, stating:

> it is not unusual in human beings who have witnessed the sack of a city or the falling to pieces of a people to desire to set down what they have witnessed for the benefit of unknown heirs or of generations infinitely remote; or, if you please, just to get the sight out of their heads.[2]

We could be tempted to dismiss this as pure hyperbole as Dowell is, essentially, referring to the affairs of two wealthy couples residing at a German spa. But when we consider this statement as part of a comparison with *In Parenthesis*, the implied parallel between Dowell's tragedy and the Great War comes to the fore and offers further insight into Jones's epic. The First World War, as portrayed in *In Parenthesis*, really is the falling to pieces of a people; the violent end of an epoch and start of a new. The collapse Dowell witnesses may not be that of an entire civilizational order but it is that of his own world order or illusion of such. Kenneth Womack summarises the novel as 'Dowell's personal act of narrative therapy'.[3] Although operating on larger cultural and historical scales *In Parenthesis* is as personal a narrative as Dowell's, representing a similar textual therapy, or catharsis.

Both texts navigate a world that has transitioned from the stability of an established tradition into the flux, crisis, and disorder that characterises modern existence. The space of the trenches has abolished a sense of order, form, and coherence. The power of an artillery shell is described as 'barrier-breaking — all unmaking'.[4] In a landscape where 'material things are but barely integrated and loosely tacked together' (*IP* 181) the human mind reaches after something to instill or imply meaning. Jones's narrative presents physical as well as psychological spaces of disorder and flux. Dowell's physical world may be intact but he still laments the loss of permanence and stability, struggling to believe they no longer exist (*GS* 13). The entirety of *In Parenthesis* can be read as a coming to terms with the destruction of permanence and stability and the attempt 'to make order for however brief a time and in whatever wilderness' (*IP* 22).

It is important to distinguish that while it is John Dowell as narrator who engages in the act of recalling in *The Good Soldier* it is David Jones, rather than one of his characters, who does so in *In*

*Parenthesis.* Jones began composing the text a decade after the end of the war, though it was not published until 1937. This means that when comparing these two texts we must speak of Jones and Dowell as reconstructors, keeping in mind that behind Dowell is Ford crafting his character's journey into the past.

Letters written by Jones and Ford add layers of complexity to this distinction. Ford almost casts himself as Dowell in the dedicatory letter added to the text in 1927. Ford writes that he had the novel 'hatching within' himself for a decade, paralleling Jones's gap between active service and putting pen to paper (*GS* 4). Furthermore, Ford declares that 'the story is a true story' which he 'had from Edward Ashburnham himself' (*GS* 4). Ford explains that the story was carried 'about with me all those years' as he had to wait until the others involved had passed away, but never entirely forgot it, as he thought of the narrative 'from time to time' (*GS* 4). Ford's depiction of the origin of the narrative itself suggests an equation of narrator and author and offers the potential for a reading which looks at the doubling between Dowell and Ford as retrospective narrators. This discussion will focus on Dowell's role as narrator, but Ford's letter also opens the possibility for considering the biographical and documentary aspects of the text in relation to those which exist in *In Parenthesis*.

Writing privately in 1965 to critic Bernard Bergonzi, rather than his readers, Jones almost defensively asserted his position on the issue of recollection in the text. Like Ford, Jones appears anxious to state, for the record, the basis of fact upon which the text rests. Reflecting that:

> even some who are inclined to like the book or are enthusiastic about it, tend to feel that I have superimposed or dragged in ideas, feelings, reactions etc that could not have been present during the events described.[5]

Jones here seems to be particularly targeting his use of literary allusion, wishing to affirm that the associations such as that between Shakespeare or Malory and contemporary events did in fact occur in the moments and spaces *In Parenthesis* seeks to distill. Jones emphatically rebuts such a critical stance:

> whatever the faults in *In Parenthesis*, and god knows they are many, this notion that in writing it (beginning exactly a decade after 1918) I superimposed things alien to my actual *experiences* and *feelings* of the war

years [...] is an untrue notion, fundamentally untrue. That in expressing
things in the writing I made *explicit* (sometimes) what was implicit during the
actual events is true enough. But during the writing I was *especially careful* to
think back of [*sic*] concrete instances of actual experiences and feelings [....] I
can say with truthfulness that in writing *I. P* a decade and more after the
events concerned that I introduced *nothing* that had not a foundation in
remembered actualities[.]

Although Jones concedes that he had 'not hesitated to change the
*chronology* where it appeared to serve [his] purpose' he almost
entirely dismisses the influence of memory on his text, while at the
same time displaying an acute awareness of its effects:

I say this taking into account the conditioning of one's own mind during the
decade that intervened between 1918 and 1928. I take also into account the
obvious fact that the memory plays tricks in the minds of all us [word
illegible] and the older we get the more this is so. But bearing these
generalisations *fully* in mind, it remains that the events and the feelings etc of
my period with my unit in France [. . .] made what the theologians in another
connection, call an 'indelible mark' or 'an imprinted character'.

Jones's comments are important to incorporate into our reading of the
text, but it may be necessary to read against them to a certain extent,
just as we read against the unreliable narrator Dowell. Jones's comments should put us on the alert rather than discourage us from finding
instances where the issue of recollection may be of significance to our
reading of the text.

Connected to this issue of memory is another key difference in
the retrospective quality of both texts. Dowell, like Ford in his letter,
makes the recalled nature of his narrative explicit through declarations
to readers. In one such example, Dowell describes how he has 'been
writing away at this story now for six months and reflecting longer
and longer upon these affairs' and that the longer he considers them
'the more certain' he becomes (*GS* 143). Jones supplies a similar
declaration in his preface, where we are told 'this writing has to do
with some things I saw, felt, and was part of. The period covered
begins early in December 1915 and ends early July 1916' (*IP* ix).
Jones's statement is, however, found only in the preface, with no
analogous declaration surfacing in the text itself. As readers we must
constantly bear in mind that the present tense of Jones's text is being
written more than a decade after the fact, meaning there is implicit
retrospection at work throughout. We can choose to read against
Jones's testimony as to the limited extent that memory and hindsight

affected *In Parenthesis*, searching for instances where the recalled events are just as coloured by reflection, hindsight and experience as those in *The Good Soldier*. Two examples include how Jones often depicts the wartime waste as a parallel to a post-war industrial landscape and his cynical characterisation of an ammunitions expert as a 'departing commercial traveller' (*IP* 13).

Although Dowell explicitly embeds within his narrative indications of his act of recalling, there is work for readers to do here also. We can question the reliability of many of his declarations and whether or not these actually constitute transparency, or further obscure what has gone on. We bear witness to Dowell's decision-making about how to order and compose the narrative. He tells us:

> I don't know how it is best to put this thing down—whether it would be better to try and tell the story from the beginning, as if it were a story; or whether to tell it from this distance of time, as it reached me from the lips of Leonora or from those of Edward himself. (*GS* 18)

Here Dowell acknowledges the many options available to an author while at the same time defining his narrative choice in spatial terms. Dowell tells us that the story 'reached' him across a great distance, giving us a sense of a narrative's movement between different spaces. Dowell also offers another decidedly spatial image of his story-telling process. He imagines his audience is a friend seated opposite him in front of the fire to whom he relates these events. Like so much of what Dowell as an unreliable narrator offers us his image of the space his narrative inhabits is misleading. The space of recalled narrative is not the singular, relatively static, space of these two individuals before the fire. There is a dynamic, two-way spatial exchange at work. Retrospective narratives are a recalling, a bringing forth of something from the past to live in the present moment as well as a journey back into the spaces of memory. Dowell does in fact provide an example of this very phenomenon when he states:

> I have been casting back again; but I cannot help it. It is so difficult to keep these people going. I tell you about Leonora and bring her up to date; then about Edward, who has fallen behind. And then the girl gets hopelessly left behind. I wish I could put it down in diary form. (*GS* 169)

He does attempt a rehashing of events in a diary format, but trails off into an ellipsis and returns to his previous narrative track (*GS* 169-70). This is a significant detail, indicating such an approach does not offer the same cathartic power as the spatial engagement of reflection.

It is helpful to think of these movements in terms of two features of Classical epic. There is the *katabasis*, the descent of the living hero into the underworld and the *nekyia*, the summoning of ghosts for questioning. For both Dowell and Jones, interaction with the past means interaction with the dead. Dowell constantly refers to the other characters as the dead – as they are – but it is important to identify how Dowell reiterates this fact at the same time as he is, essentially, bringing them back to life. Dowell also repeatedly refers to a given situation as 'Hell': 'This sweltering hell of ours' (*GS* 161), 'what happened was just Hell' (*GS* 155), 'that Hell that is the abode of broken resolves' (*GS* 157). While referring to something as 'Hell' is a kind of colloquialism, Dowell's repetition flags it as significant. Considering the relationship of the underworld motif to retrospection in *In Parenthesis*, Dowell's references to Hell take on a new kind of resonance.

Jones's wartime wasteland is an underworld. The troops' voyage across the channel is a version of crossing the Styx, a passage over water in order to enter the underworld of the trenches. Once there we encounter 'Lazarus figures' (*IP* 43) and bands of men 'with deadness in their eyes and hands as each to each they / spoke like damned-corpse-gossiping' (*IP* 63). One soldier is a 'fleet passing sound wraith' (*IP* 33) in a ghostly landscape of 'Low sharp-stubbed tree skeletons' (*IP* 44). At the end of Part Three the trenches merge with images of the Celtic Underworld and we see Arthur's harrowing of Hell (*IP* 52).

The dissolution of boundaries between the spaces of living and dead alerts us to the larger disordering forces at work. In the face of this disorder Jones and Dowell recall the dead in an attempt to re-order their worlds, just as Aeneas and Odysseus consult their dead as part of their larger quests to re-establish order in the aftermath of the Trojan War.

Having established the character of each recalled narrative and the overarching spatial dynamics at play I will now turn to a more detailed discussion of what fragments and liminal space can reveal about retrospection in both texts.

Fragmentation is evident in the formal choices both Jones and Ford make. Dowell frequently employs ellipses, dashes, and unfinished statements. Readers are left to decide whether these indicate the limits to his knowledge as a narrator, the purposeful withholding of information, or his inability to deal with some aspects of his own story. Jones, too, makes frequent use of ellipses and favours the exaggerated line of the em dash. But he also utilises line breaks and blank space visually to present pages of gappy text in a more radical formal experiment than Ford's. Certain pages of *In Parenthesis* give the impression that what may once have been whole has been blasted away. Jones once also recalled how finding a few surviving sheets of a pocket calendar he kept in 1916, years later, induced such a vivid recalling of the events of that period.[6]

Fragments also affect the make-up of the recalled narrative. Both texts are not retrospective in the sense that they present a reversal of the kind of chronological narrative Dowell's diary entries attempt to create, but jump back and forth in time. This interaction with time can be thought of as a collage of disparate fragments. Jones presents a chronological narrative on the level of what is occurring within the timeframe of 1915-16, but his fragments of history and literary allusions upset the linear structure pulling us back and forth from past and present spaces, eventually merging the two in a kind of polyvalent vision.

Jones employs fragments to symbolise those things that appear whole and meaningful – myth, literature, history, tradition. The parallels he establishes between present experience and these fragments are an attempt to combat the disintegration occurring. Dowell expresses the same desire. Speaking about relationships between men and women, he states that 'we are all so afraid, we are all so alone, we all so need from the outside the assurance of our own worthiness to exist' (*GS* 93) and that he desires 'to be enveloped, to be supported' (*GS* 92). He imagines he desires support from a sexual relationship, but the meaning of these words extends beyond. The 'assurance of our own worthiness to exist' and the desire for 'support' relate to the more general condition of fragmented modern space. Dowell's crisis is one with the infantry of the First World War. This parallel deepens if we look closer at Florence's symbolic relationship to fragmentation.

Dowell's belief in Florence's fictitious heart condition compels him to protect her from anything too shocking or exciting. In doing so, he attempts to 'keep poor dear Florence onto topics like the finds at Gnossos' (*GS* 20). Florence is also 'singularly expert as a guide to archaeological expeditions and there was nothing she liked so much as taking people round ruins' (*GS* 35). Dowell associates Florence with culture and history but the particular inclusion of 'ruins' in this description presents a significant parallel to what is occurring in *In Parenthesis*. Rather than a harmless topic of conversation, these ruins denote some of the darker forces present in Dowell's and Jones's world. Dowell has a sudden realisation that Florence is not real, she 'was just a mass of talk out of guide-books, of drawings out of fashion-plates' (*GS* 97). Florence becomes one of Jones's textual fragments as Dowell suddenly sees her as 'a scrap of paper' (*GS* 97). Florence's association with fragments of cultural history is unsettling as she is also the force which exposes Dowell's illusions of certainty and meaning. Uniting illusion, deceit, and cultural history in Florence's character has serious implications if we are comparing *The Good Soldier* with *In Parenthesis*. For is cultural history not the savior of *In Parenthesis* while Florence is one of our many villains?

This realisation about Florence prompts us to question the fragments Jones desperately pastes together. Florence forces us to ask to what extent Jones's allusions can re-order chaotic modern space. Critics have struggled to reconcile themselves to the fact that however strongly Jones's fragments strive towards unity and cry out for a realisation of meaning this is never achieved. Paul Fussell has concluded that on this count Jones failed to realise his intent. Such a conclusion overlooks the important message related to the very fact of irreconcilability. The achievement of *In Parenthesis* and *The Good Soldier* is to communicate, through fragments, the tension between our human desire for order and coherence and the impossibility of achieving this.

Towards the end, Dowell surrenders, declaring 'I don't know. I know nothing. I am very tired' (*GS* 186). An admission which contradicts his earlier statement that reflecting upon these events had provided resolution. Dowell's resignation bears a striking resemblance to Pound in the late *Cantos*: 'Tho' my errors and wrecks lie about me. / And I am not a demigod, / I cannot make it cohere'.[7] The ending of *In Parenthesis* offers an analogous affirmation of uncertainty. Adapted from *La Chanson de Roland,* the text closes with John Ball lying wounded and this textual fragment: 'The geste says this and the man who was on the field . . . and / who wrote the book. . . the man who does not know this / has not understood anything' (*IP* 187). Although we are told we may not have understood anything, Jones does not direct readers towards any possible conclusions. Dai's heroic boast has also challenged us to quest after elusive meaning. In the very center of *In Parenthesis* Dai declares 'You ought to ask: Why, /

what is this, what's the meaning of this' (*IP* 84).

Dowell and Jones have searched the spaces of the past for meaning. Their limited success, embodied by fragmentation, results in a challenge to readers to do the same not only with regard to the texts but in relation to our own experiences of flux and transition.

In addition to fragmentation, liminal space is integrally involved with retrospection in both texts. From the Latin *limen* for threshold, the term originates from the field of social anthropology, where it describes the transitory stage in rituals and rites of passage. Arnold van Gennep is credited with first applying the term in *Rites of Passage* (1908) and Victor Turner further developed the concept by broadening the scope of the term. Liminal has become part of the vocabulary of literary criticism, most notably in post-colonial studies, but also surfacing in modernist discourses. Carol L. Yang and Jennifer Fairley, to choose two examples, have applied the term in their readings of Eliot and Jones respectively.[8]

We can imagine a recalled narrative as the threshold space from which we can view both the past on one side and the present on the other. The doorway distinguishes these two spaces but also allows them to intermingle; for an exchange between them to occur. If we think back to Dowell's apology for 'casting back' and forth we see how, as a narrator standing in the threshold space, his vision of events is alternating between and recombining from either side of the lintel.

Jones's very title establishes a liminal space for the text. He explains his choice of *In Parenthesis* by saying that he has written the text 'in a kind of space between' and that the war itself 'was a parenthesis' out of whose brackets he stepped in 1918 (*IP* xv). This 'space between' is also the space that memory constructs, where recalling the past cannot help but be influenced and shaped by the present. For Jones the war and indeed a human life were spatially imagined as parentheses (*IP* xv). We can also perceive how neatly *In Parenthesis* fits into that which existed between each World War and further contextualise it accordingly.

Dowell echoes Jones by employing parenthetical vocabulary. Dowell remarks: 'I have stuck to my idea of being in a country cottage with a silent listener, hearing *between* the gusts of the wind and *amidst* the noises of the distant seas the story as it comes' (*GS* 143, emphasis mine). This positions the narrative in a liminal space parallel to that of *In Parenthesis.*

Fairley notes a variety of examples of liminality in *In*

*Parenthesis*, but particularly emphasises the importance of the epigraph. Taken from *The Mabinogion*, the quotation establishes a liminal premise. The passage describes an enchanted doorway encountered by a band of soldiers returning home:

> Evil betide me if I do not open the door to
> know if that is true which is said concerning
> it. So he opened the door . . . and when they
> had looked, they were conscious of all the
> evils they had ever sustained, and of all the
> friends and companions they had lost and of
> all the misery that had befallen them, as if
> all had happened in that very spot[.]

Jones effectively re-enacts this scene of recollection in the threshold space as he composes his text.

There are at least forty-one individual references to doors and doorways in *The Good Soldier* and doors take on many symbolic resonances within the novel, of which liminal space is one. Branshaw has an upper gallery, out onto which the bedrooms of Edward, Nancy, and Leonora open. Dowell professes that the 'sight of those three open doors, side by side, gaping to receive whom the chances of the black night might bring, made Leonora shudder all over her body' (*GS* 164). Yet he also tells us that Leonora 'hated to be in a room with a shut door', he supposes that she 'liked to have her door open [. . .] so she might hear the approaching footsteps of ruin and disaster' (*GS* 161).

Such half open doors contrast with Florence's perpetually locked one. However, when considering liminal space, there is one particularly important scene involving Florence and a doorway. When Dowell leaves her at the baths each day she pauses in the doorway and looks back at him 'with a little coquettish smile' (*GS* 25). This memory torments Dowell as he cannot make sense of it. He asks:

> For whose benefit did she do it? For that of the bath attendant? of the passers-by? I don't know. Anyhow, it can't have been for me, for never, in all the years of her life, never on any possible occasion, or in any other place did she so smile to me, mockingly, invitingly. (*GS* 25)

These doorway sites are ominous and confusing ones, symbolising the dangerous spaces that exist between the characters. The spaces created by things half said, unsaid, or mis-said. Dowell creates the same space between himself and the reader as his frequent contradictions and incomplete statements crack the door open, but do not allow us to proceed past the threshold. We are left wondering, as he does after Florence, what some of his gestures truly mean kept perpetually in the uncertain, liminal space.

Paul Fussell has argued that 'the Great War took place in what was, compared with ours, a static world, where the values appeared stable and where the meanings of abstractions seemed permanent and reliable'.[9] While Jones's reflection on World War I supports the very shift Fussell here describes, Dowell's narrative act of recalling indicates the cracks already appearing in the pre-war age of assumed stability and concrete realities. As Womack describes it, Dowell 'slowly comprehends the truth about the couples' five year association', which Womack aptly sums up as a 'façade'.[10] Within fragmented and liminal spaces we discover the illusions these pre-war certainties represent; the illusion of a heroic code, the meaningfulness of war, of appearances, and social institutions. Considering the spatial aspects of both of these recalled narratives illustrates how we can situate modernist texts which surround the war into a larger vision. That almost all of the significant and cataclysmic events of *The Good Soldier* take place on the 4th August poses intriguing questions.[11] Textual evidence demonstrates that the presence of the date in the text is coincidental. However, even as coincidence, the fact remains that Ford chose to retain the date after the outbreak of war, allowing for its newfound connotations to enter the novel. As it stands, regardless of authorial intent, it makes a gentle nod to the war and extends the same invitation Jones was to make over twenty years later, to consider the fragmented parenthesis of the War as an extreme embodiment of human experience in the newly unfolding space of the modern world.

## NOTES

1   T. S. Eliot, *Collected Poems 1909-1962*, London: Faber and Faber, 2002, p. 208.
2   Ford Madox Ford, *The Good Soldier: A Tale of Passion*, ed. by Max Saunders, Oxford: Oxford University Press, 2012 – henceforth *GS;* p. 12.
3   Kenneth Womack, '"It is All a Darkness": Death, Narrative Therapy, and Ford Madox Ford's *The Good Soldier*', *Papers on Language and Literature*, 38:3 (Summer 2002), 316- 34 (p. 318).

4   David Jones, *In Parenthesis*, London: Faber and Faber, 2010 – henceforth *IP*; p. 24.
5   Aberystwyth, The National Library of Wales, MS The David Jones Papers CF 1/6. Note that these letters are drafts of the final letter Jones would send to Bergonzi. There are multiple versions in the collection and these extracts are taken from a range of these drafts.
6   This anecdote is found in the same draft letters to Bergonzi detailed above. The loose diary pages survive to this day as part of a collection of Jones's diaries. One of these entries describes Jones's indignation at an administrative error involving the troops' blankets, while another records a raid carried out on an enemy trench. See Box P 1/1/2 of The David Jones Papers.
7   Ezra Pound, *The Cantos*, London: Faber and Faber, 1987, p. 796.
8   Jennifer Fairley, 'David Jones's Thirties', in *Recharting the Thirties*, ed. Patrick J. Quinn, London: Associated University Press, 1996, pp. 40-50; Carol L. Yang, 'Revisiting The *Flâneur* in T. S. Eliot's "Eeldrop and Appleplex – I"', *Orbis Litterarum*, 66:2 (2011), 89-120 (p. 104).
9   Paul Fussell, *The Great War and Modern Memory*, New York and London: Oxford University Press, 1975, p. 21.
10  Kenneth Womack, '"It is All a Darkness": Death, Narrative Therapy, and Ford Madox Ford's *The Good Soldier*', *Papers on Language and Literature*, 38:3 (Summer 2002), pp. 316-34 (pp. 318; 323-4).
11  Max Saunders points out that the 4th August appears in the version published in *Blast* prior to the outbreak of war (*GS* xl), a view supported by Martin Stannard's identification of 4th August in early versions of the text. Saunders suggests, however, that Ford gave the date greater prominence after the war had started in order to capitalise on the association (*GS* xl). James T. Adams certainly interprets the date as alluding to the outbreak of war in 'Discrepancies in 'The Time-Scheme of *The Good Soldier*' *English Literature in Transition, 1880-1920*, 34:2 (1991), 152-64. While Frank G. Nigro also interestingly notes several details in the novel which suggest the world of *The Good Soldier* is very much 'a militarized world': 'Who Framed *The Good Soldier*? Dowell's story in search of a form', *Studies in the Novel*, 24:4 (Winter 92), 381-92 (p. 389).

# GOOD PEOPLE AND CHORUS GIRLS: THE NOTION OF RESPECTABILITY IN *THE GOOD SOLDIER* AND *QUARTET*

## Nagihan Haliloğlu

**Abstract**

This chapter is an examination of the notion of respectability in the textual worlds created in Ford Madox Ford's *The Good Soldier* and Jean Rhys's *Quartet*. Taken together, the two novels provide a literary representation of how respectability is defined and performed in different ranks of the English class system. The article aims to map out the class and gender categories that shape the respectability of their characters. The sanctity of the marriage contract and 'keeping face' reveal themselves as crucial elements of respectability in the English class system both authors are depicting. Respectability is attainable only through knowing both one's own and others' boundaries when it comes to gender and class. These boundaries are to be respected regardless of the emotional carnage depicted in equal measure in both novels. The delinquents who refuse to accept the role that society gives them are punished, as in the case of Marya in *Quartet* and Florence in *The Good Soldier*. The moneyed classes remain respectable so long as their affairs do not become public, as is proven by the lasting epithet of 'good' for the philandering 'good soldier' of Ford's novel.

Jean Rhys met Ford Madox Ford, the editor of the *English Review* and the then ailing *transatlantic review* in Paris in 1924, and after a short while, in the best tradition of Ford's plots, the frail young woman and the established Englishman who was already in a relationship became lovers.[1] The affair started on a literary basis, he encouraged her to write, and then her dependence on him as a mentor and lover grew, at which point he found that he couldn't live up to her expectations of him.[2] Judith Kegan Gardiner, in her quest to find the connections between *Quartet* (1928) and *The Good Soldier* (1915) goes so far as to call *Quartet* a 'countertext' to Ford's.[3] The present article does not set out to trace Fordian influence on Rhys. Rather, it aims to reveal how the authors expose complementary images of the regime of respectability of their period. In different ways, the two novels present very detailed anatomies of marriage and society of their time, and I am particularly interested in how the characters' sense of respectability and class informs their actions. While Ford's characters are drawn from the moneyed classes, Rhys's are those who live in the margins of society and mix with the leisured classes at their peril. I argue that respectability, in both novels, is revealed to be a function of how the characters perform their class and gender: how they perform being the ideal gentleman, the proper wife, the proper mistress, the good soldier and the good chorus girl.

The euphemism 'four-square coterie' used by the narrator Dowell in *The Good Soldier* to refer to the various amorous arrangements between the novel's characters has become a favourite quotation with critics,[4] and it invites us to draw parallels with Jean Rhys's *Quartet*.[5] Rhys, of course, was one of the four of the coterie that Ford managed in his real life. Or rather, she was the member of one of the various coteries that he gathered around him. As in *The Good Soldier*, the love/business entanglements that Ford found himself in had more than four sides. Rhys's own affair with Ford remained largely contained within the circle of Rhys, her husband, Ford and Stella Bowen, Ford's partner. All four involved in the Rhys-Ford affair wrote books about their experience and Rhys's account was related in *Quartet*. All these accounts naturally reflected the writers' sense of respectability and their sense of who was inflicting harm and pain on whom. Ford's contribution was the novel called *When the Wicked Man*, written just as self-pityingly as Rhys's *Quartet*.[6] Rhys was simultaneously 'the other woman', 'the muse' and 'the apprentice' and she was clearly conflicted about how this affected her writing. Although in her letters she said she was 'astonished' to see that everyone treated the novel as *roman-à-clef*, she also added: 'though, some of it was lived of course'.[7]

In Rhys's biography, Carole Angier explains at length how Ford responded to Rhys's drafts and how he honed her skills, advising her to pare down the writing, to translate passages into French and to get rid of what didn't make sense in translation. Ford was, if one may draw a modernist parallel, Rhys's Ezra Pound. If Rhys is indeed responding to, or indeed 'supplanting' and 'besting' Ford as Betsy Draine puts it, she seems at least to have taken Ford's advice to heart in one sense: *Quartet* is much shorter than Ford's novels. In fact, as a mark of a good working writer-mentor/editor relationship, if not a functional emotional one, Rhys's writing bears very little resemblance to Ford's, who seems to have managed to encourage what was typically Rhysian in her writing. There is not a trace of Ford's ironic narrator to be found in Rhys, whose narrators are on a genuine quest to understand what is going on around them, to decipher the social and moral codes with which their upbringing has failed to provide them. Coming from the colonies, or indeed from downwardly mobile families, Rhys's heroines seem to lack both a middle class education that would enable them to speak to the faux-bohemian people that they come into contact with, as they lack the sharp-wittedness of a chorus girl which would enable them to fend for themselves. Rhys's novels depict how the protagonists and narrators learn what others think of them and how different classes are held to account differently when it comes to respectable behaviour.

What seems to have interested both Ford and Rhys is how social mores are constructed and how and in what circumstances people can be exempted from them. They seem to have managed to bring messages from different camps – of men and women, of the privileged and the destitute – to each other. This exchange is very much apparent in Ford's description of Rhys having 'a terrifying instinct and a terrific – almost lurid! – passion for stating the case of the underdog'[8] and it is also apparent in the way Rhys is able to represent the mind script of the men her chorus girls get involved with. She was also, as Bowen put it, through her own experiences with other respectable men and women and with her first husband 'well acquainted with every rung of that long and dismal ladder by which the respectable citizen descends towards degradation'.[9]

'Good' is the adjective under which both Ford and Rhys treat issues of respectability: in Ford, it is the title that invites us to ponder the goodness of the protagonist Edward Ashburnham, and in *Quartet*, the opening poem 'Good Samaritan' by R. C. Dunning prepares us for acts of 'goodness' that will be to the detriment of the heroine:

> ... Beware
> Of good Samaritans – walk to the right
> Or hide thee by the roadside out of sight
> Or greet them with the smile that villains wear. (*Q*, epigraph)[10]

*Quartet,* set between the wars, is the story of Marya, an expatriate British young woman who is trying to survive in Paris after her husband is put in jail. She seeks the company of men for emotional and material help when she is left to look after herself. Society tries to contain Marya in the way in which she will give the least offence to established modes of behaviour and social institutions such as marriage. She is a woman who is perceived as not having higher ambitions, and has forfeited her good name through her marriage to a person who is slowly descending the rungs of respectability. She seems to have no aspirations to acquire qualities that are good and beneficial to society although the Heidlers, who prove themselves to be the good Samaritans of the poem, encourage her to do so.

The 'good' soldier of *The Good Soldier*, Ashburnham is introduced, early on, as a hollow figure like the good Samaritans Marya is to beware of in *Quartet*. After describing his clothes, the narrator says:

> Good God, what did they all see in him; for I swear that was all there was of him, inside and out; though they said he was a good soldier. Yet, Leonora adored him with a passion that was like an agony, and hated him with an agony that was as bitter as the sea. How could he arouse anything like a sentiment, in anybody?
>
> What did he even talk to them about—when they were under four eyes? — Ah, well, suddenly, as if by a flash of inspiration, I know. For all good soldiers are sentimentalists—all good soldiers of that type. Their profession, for one thing, is full of the big words, courage, loyalty, honour, constancy. (*GS* 33)[11]

Thus, Ford allows us to see the good soldier as circumscribed by these big words, able to move only within a certain confine of the 'minuet'[12] the narrator keeps referring to. It is the good soldier's gallantry, his incapability of saying no to women that wrecks the two perfectly 'respectable' marriages. At the very beginning the American, scheming or innocent (depending on which narratological position you find more convincing) narrator Dowell attempts to define a more general idea of goodness that applies to all who were dancing the 'minuet', trying, all in their own capacity, to comply with the big words mentioned in relation to Ashburnham:

> The given proposition was, that we were all "good people." We took for granted that we all liked beef underdone but not too underdone; that both men preferred a good liqueur brandy after lunch [. . .] that sort of thing. It was also taken for granted that we were both sufficiently well off to afford anything that we could reasonably want in the way of amusements fitting to our station—that we could take motor cars and carriages by the day; that we could give each other dinners and dine our friends [. . . .]
>
> I don't in the least mean to say that we were the sort of persons who aspired to mix "with royalty." We didn't; we hadn't any claims; we were just "good people." (*GS* 42-3)

From this introductory passage we understand that 'good' people are people who have money for their leisure, but more importantly, they are people who know and are content with their place in society. Good people are people who do not commit 'delinquencies of space'.[13] They are men and women who keep within their own social category and indeed within the physical space that suits their position. How these categories are delineated and how members of these categories are monitored for any aberration is very important for both Ford's and Rhys's writing.

Both Ford's and Rhys's novels reveal a world in which the institution of marriage is still very much respected. Both in the upper classes of Ford and the supposedly bohemian environment that Rhys depicts a proper good woman is a woman who is very much married.[14] The following is the description of Leonora, the perfect English wife burdened with an adulterous husband, Edward:

> Leonora, as I have said, was the perfectly normal woman. I mean to say that in normal circumstances her desires were those of the woman who is needed by society. She desired children, decorum, an establishment; she desired to avoid waste, she desired to keep up appearances. (GS 275)

This is a passage in which Dowell describes, and indeed recruits Leonora as the 'normal woman', judging her performance of gender to be of the highest standard. Normality is expressed through functionality such as avoiding waste, keeping house, and bearing children in order to ensure the longevity of the establishment, the English house. Children, who do not materialize in either of the two central marriages in *The Good Soldier*, are the prerogative of the wife, and characters like Marya jeopardize this prerogative with their unchecked sexuality and fertility: when she tries to sell a dress she's censured discreetly and told that 'it will be bought by that kind of woman' (Q 31). And it is with comments like these, in turn, that Marya is recruited as a decorative 'petite femme' in a respectable household:

> She learned, after long and painstaking effort, to talk like a chorus girl, to dress like a chorus girl and to think like a chorus girl – up to a point. Beyond that point she remained apart, lonely, frightened of her loneliness, resenting it passionately. (Q 15)

Marya has no immediate family and no fixed address; she passes time in rented hotel rooms, restaurants and cafes. Her sense of identity as a young woman is very much connected to her relationship to space, and it determines her place in the scales of respectability:

> [H]er existence, though delightful, was haphazard. It lacked, as it were, solidity; it lacked the necessary fixed background. A bedroom, balcony and *cabinet de toilette* in a cheap Montmartre hotel cannot possibly be called a solid background. (*Q* 10)

This haphazard quality of unattached young women in the early twentieth century has been conceptualized as the category of the 'amateur',[15] the name denoting the lack of professionalism and legitimacy in gender relations, a name that therefore lacks the respectability of the wife. Professionalism and a solid background are of course the very things that determine the goodness of a person. In a world away from Marya's, in *The Good Soldier* the ideal solid background is a country seat, Branshaw Teleragh, belonging to the Ashburnhams, seemingly coveted by all the other characters. The characters all have various moral quandaries and it will be whoever manages to get the pedigreed country house whose morals will be vindicated. And it is none other than the increasingly manipulative and devious narrator Dowell, whose respectability can never be questioned, who gets the house: history is told by victors.

One of the first conversations that Leonora and Florence have seems to be about the heritage of families in Connecticut that hail from Fordingbridge: 'For it had been discovered that Florence came of a line that had actually owned Branshaw Teleragh for two centuries before the Ashburnhams came there' (*GS* 78). Dowell tells us that even before Edward Ashburnham appeared on the scene, Florence wanted to make the passage to England from the continent, only to be hampered by the illusion of frailty she had created in order to ward off Dowell and keep her then-lover at her side, of whom, Dowell assures us, she gradually became tired:

> the only main idea of her heart, that was otherwise cold – was to get to Fordingbridge and be a county lady in the home of her ancestors [. . . .] Yes, it was a bad fix for her, because Edward could have taken her to Fordingbridge and, though he could not give her Branshaw Manor, that home of her ancestors being settled on his wife, she could at least have pretty considerably queened it there or thereabouts, what with our money and the support of the Ashburnhams. (*GS* 104-5)

In his final analysis of the whole debacle – two deaths and a madness – Dowell states that it was in fact the house that his wife Florence wanted when she started an affair with Edward Ashburnham

'You see, she had two things that she wanted. She wanted to be a great lady, installed in Branshaw Teleragh' (*GS* 138).[16]

While the coterie in *The Good Soldier* starts when Dowell's wife is drawn into an affair with Ashburnham, attracted by his good soldierly qualities and his house, in *Quartet*, the quartet starts when the expatriate community, not knowing quite what to do with Marya – indeed the Bohemian circles themselves do not like waste – is introduced, to Heidler 'who made discoveries' and helped young men' and before long Heidler and she have an affair. Heidler's wife Lois understands her husband's infatuation with Marya, and tries to get her to live with them. It is Marya's carelessness about her body and the consequences thereof that alarm the Heidlers. Rather than let it loose on the stage as a chorus girl, in contact with other 'bodies', Lois tries, subversively, to contain Marya's body within her marriage, almost as a co-wife, rather than let her have a multiplicity of partners.

In *The Good Soldier*, Ashburnham's wife, as the narrator tells us, could not but be aware that both Mrs Basil and Maisie Maidan, with whom Edward has affairs, were nice women. Leonora is ready to see these women's place in the scheme of things.[17] What she really fears is that Edward might become promiscuous, in the same way Lois in *Quartet* fears that if Marya is set loose on the stage, her husband will become promiscuous by proxy. In *The Good Soldier* the liaison that manages to upset Leonora in the most fundamental way is the one with Dowell's wife Florence. Florence is the one woman, of all the women with whom Ashburnham gets involved, including the maid, who is described as vulgar:

> Yes, the mental deterioration that Florence worked in Leonora was extra-ordinary; it smashed up her whole life and all her chances. It made her, in the first place, hopeless—for she could not see how, after that, Edward could return to her—after a vulgar intrigue with a vulgar woman. (*GS* 221-2)

The verdict of vulgarity is one that Dowell repeats a few pages later, confirming Leonora's judgment:

> Florence was vulgar; Florence was a common flirt [. . . . .] Florence was an unstoppable talker. You could not stop her; nothing would stop her. Edward and Leonora were at least proud and reserved people. (*GS* 215)

As the opposite of good, meaning respectable and proper, vulgar is the worst epithet in the book. Dowell's narrative attitude towards his wife gets very complicated towards the end – from the woman he was very happy to have finally managed to marry, he turns her into a common flirt. Things he had narrated with a certain abandon at the beginning – such as her lover in Europe who was the reason why she accepted to marry Dowell to go to Europe with him – start to transform into deceptions and vices in his telling. Also, of course, as much as common flirt, 'unstoppable' talker is a grave accusation, next of kin to hysteria, which is unacceptable in 'good' circles, something that the Heidlers, in *Quartet* fear equally.

The character that allows Ashburnham to be, in Dowell's description 'the fine soldier, the excellent landlord, the extraordinarily kind, careful and industrious magistrate, the upright, honest, fair-dealing, fair-thinking, public character' (*GS* 60) to the full, without Leonora's financial caution and Florence's fixation on Branshaw Teleragh, is Nancy, another, much younger Ashburnham protégé. Indeed, it seems to be because she allows him to have that illusion of himself that he falls in love with her and then expresses his feelings:

> He was for her, in everything that she said at that time, the model of humanity, the hero, the athlete, the father of his country, the law-giver [. . . .] She had her recompense at last. Because, of course, if you come to figure it out, a sudden pouring forth of passion by a man whom you regard as a cross between a pastor and a father might, to a woman, have the aspect of mere praise for good conduct. (*GS* 132-3)

So it is the good soldier's approval that makes Nancy feel that she has been accepted into good society for her good conduct. She does not quite understand what this approval actually involves, and what Ashburnham's affections will set into motion in the supposedly four-square coterie. This aspect of the relationship – of seeking approval and acceptance for 'good conduct' by an authority figure – is similar to that between Rhys and Ford, as that relationship, too, seems to have been founded on the myth of the perfect Englishman, the pinnacle of goodness. This attribution of godly characteristics to the older lover takes on a more sinister note in *Quartet*; and Marya, before they are about to break up, imagines Heidler saying the following to her:

> 'God's a pal of mine,' he said. 'He probably looks rather like me, with cold eyes and fattish hands. I'm in His image or He's in mine. It's all one. I prayed to Him to get you and I got you. Shall I give you a letter of introduction? Yes, I might do that if you remind me. No trouble at all. (*Q* 125)

However, the one condition of the young female lover is the understanding that she gives her love freely, that the affair is not a mercantile affair. At the point where Marya can no longer bear the petite femme role she is expected to play by both the Heidlers, she lashes out, calling their 'goodness' into question:

> 'You have made an arrangement!' said Marya loudly. 'Not in so many words, perhaps, a tacit agreement. If he wants the woman let him have her. Yes. D'you think I don't know?' Heidler got up and said nervously: 'Don't shout. You can hear every single word that's said at Madame Guyillot's next door!' (*Q* 81)

Maisie's reaction to finding out that her passage to Europe was paid for by the Ashburnhams is even more drastic: she decides to leave immediately and the effort proves too much for her 'heart' – the one heart of all the parties involved that really seems to have something physically wrong with it.

As, if not more, important than promiscuity for respectability is the public image of good people, which they feel constantly to be under attack from emotionally or financially blackmailing lower classes. Heidler fears that the neighbours will hear the arguments between himself, his lover and his wife and that their 'good' name will be called into question. Heidler's good name is not tainted while he lives with his wife and mistress under the same roof as long as the mistress is known as a protégée for form's sake and there are no loud scenes revealing the sexual dynamics. Respectability requires a public character without any publicity.

The same fear of scandal is expressed when Dowell speaks of an incident Ashburnham has with a maid: 'For, along with his passions and his shames there went the dread of scenes in public places, of outcry, of excited physical violence; of publicity, in short' (*GS* 40). As all good, respectable people, Ashburnham doesn't like publicity for himself, nor does he approve of others' affairs becoming public. In one scene he snatches a paper from Nancy's hand as she is trying to read about the details of a divorce trial. There is a strong sense of loyalty to one's class, and after the string of relationships he has described, Dowell still cannot bring himself to censure Ashburnham. He sees Ashburnham's love for women as some sort of prerogative of a healthy male of his standing and the last verdict he has of him is the following:

> I suppose that that was the most monstrously wicked thing that Edward
> Ashburnham ever did in his life. And yet I am so near to all these people that I
> cannot think any of them wicked. It is impossible of me to think of Edward
> Ashburnham as anything but straight, upright and honourable. That, I mean, is, in
> spite of everything, my permanent view of him. I try at times by dwelling on
> some of the things that he did to push that image of him away, as you might try to
> push aside a large pendulum. But it always comes back—the memory of his
> innumerable acts of kindness, of his efficiency, of his unspiteful tongue. He was
> such a fine fellow. (*GS* 133-4)

Compared to this adulterer, Marya, adulteress of another class, expects
no such forgiving favours from society. After they break up with
Heidler they see each other one last time and she imagines what he
must be thinking of after all they have been through together:

> Now then, don't be hysterical. Besides, Lois was there first. Lois is a good
> woman and you are a bad one; it's quite simple. These things are. That's what is
> meant by having principles. Nobody owes a fair deal to a prostitute [. . . . ] Intact
> or not intact, that's the first question. An income or not an income, that's the
> second.' (*Q* 125)

So while sexual transgression does not affect Ashburnham's
respectability one bit, Marya's extramarital relationship with Heidler
makes her a prostitute, and this supersedes all the possible other good
characteristics of such a loose woman; no one needs to acknowledge
them, no one owes a fair deal to a prostitute. It appears, in fact, Marya
has *no* characteristics that are recognized as 'good' by society; she is
dispensable, she's not 'needed' by society as Leonora is. Here Marya
has fully grasped the economics of social respectability, and when she
does, she refuses to be recruited by a society whose strings are held by
those like the Heidlers.

In both novels a person's relationship to the institution of
marriage is the crucial factor in one's respectability – you are a good
man or woman if you manage to keep your marriage going even if
there may have been adultery on either side. It is this hypocrisy that
Marya cannot take. While we are not allowed to think of Ashburnham
as wicked, Marya is aware that she will be made into the villain of the
story. Dowell does, though, at the very end acknowledge the hollowness of the 'goodness' of the Ashburnhams and their entourage,
naturally including himself:

> It was a most amazing business, and I think that it would have been better in the eyes of God if they had all attempted to gouge out each other's eyes with carving knives. But they were "good people". (*GS* 286)

Goodness and its attendant, respectability, is defined throughout the novel as coming from good stock, having money, knowing one's place in society and keeping to it, and keeping one's affairs from the public eye. In Dowell's final analysis above, this goodness is shown to be bogus, in fact, the cost of keeping this sense of 'goodness' or respectability comes is described in the most damning terms. The disregard of human emotion that has been played out is equated to the most violent act imaginable. Despite the physical and spiritual damage caused to all parties involved, the coterie remains respectable, 'good' people, as all of them have been prevented, voluntarily or involuntarily, from doing anything to jeopardize the institution of marriage. It is only death that undoes the marriages, but then order is restored again with Leonora marrying someone else and Dowell taking charge of Nancy. Thus Dowell's last verdict acts as the cautionary poem Rhys uses to open *Quartet*.

Thus, respectability comes at the price of keeping to the set norms of social categories in both novels. Dowell allows the reader to understand this state of affairs through his increasingly ironic use of the adjective 'good', and the narrator in *Quartet* reveals the process through which Marya comes to the understanding that one rejects the role society has set for a woman only at one's peril. As the 'chorus girl' who rejects the role of odalisque that has been ascribed to her, she becomes 'the villain of the piece', shunned by society. In Ford's world, as narrated by Dowell of course, no one seems to be reproachable for what has happened, except for Florence, who, like Marya, threatens the strict borders of social categories, by aspiring, 'vulgar' as she is, to become Mrs Ashburnham, the lady of Branshaw Teleragh. Women and the poorer classes are held to account much more strictly: Edward Ashburnham dies without having lost his good name while Marya dies a social death, and is left moneyless and friendless at the end of the novel. The need to preserve respectability proves to be what paves the road to the private hells of the characters.

## NOTES

1   The *English Review* helped launch the careers of writers such as Wyndham Lewis and D. H. Lawrence. It was H. Pearl Adam, a journalist friend, who sent an edited version of Rhys's notebooks under the name *Suzy Tells* to Ford Madox Ford. She explained to Rhys that Ford helped expatriate writers. 'Jean thought: 'Expatriate? Expatriate from where?' Carol Angier, *Jean Rhys: Life and Work,* London: Faber and Faber, 2011, p. 131. Rhys was 34 and Ford 50. Ford had already written *Some Do Not . . .* and after meeting Rhys started with *No More Parades*. The *transatlantic review* published various authors including Joyce, Pound, Hemingway, and Stein. See *Ford Madox Ford, Modernist Magazines and Editing*, ed. Jason Harding, IFMFS 9, Amsterdam and New York: Rodopi, 2010.

2   'He was something more dangerous to her than a real English gentleman: a believer, like her, in the myth of one [. . . .] And he tried to create the Good Soldier in himself as well.' Angier, *Jean Rhys: Life and Work*, p. 132.

3   Judith Kegan Gardiner, 'Rhys Recalls Ford: *Quartet* and *The Good Soldier*' in *Tulsa Studies in Women's Literature*, 1:1 (Spring 1982), 67-81. In her article 'Adulterous Liaisons: Jean Rhys, Stella Bowen and Feminist Reading', Sue Thomas also engages with readings of the novel as a countertext, this time, to Ford Madox Ford's *When the Wicked Man* (1931), pointing to the interpretative pitfalls of such a reductive reading and of theories of privileging 'precursor' texts. See Sue Thomas "Adulterous Liaisons: Jean Rhys, Stella Bowen and Feminist Reading": http://www.australianhumanitiesreview.org/archive/Issue-June-2001/-thomas.html (accessed January 2, 2015).

4   As Julian Barnes puts it: 'Together the couples dance a social "minuet", they make a "four-square coterie", an "extraordinarily safe castle", they are a "tall ship" on a blue sea, proud and safe': http://www.theguardian.com/books/2008/-jun/07/fiction.julianbarnes (accessed 10th July, 2013).

5   Dowell's description in *The Good Soldier* and Rhys's title were indeed deemed so similar that Chatto and Windus insisted that Rhys's title be changed when it was published. Angier, *Jean Rhys: Life and Work,* p. 133.

6   *Ibid.*, 133.

7   Wyndham, Francis and Diana Melly (eds), *The Letters of Jean Rhys*, New York: Viking/Elizabeth Sifton Books, 1983, p. 171.

8   Carol Angier, *Jean Rhys*, Harmondsworth: Penguin, 1985, p. 40.

9   Betsy Draine, 'Chronotope and Intertext: The Case of Jean Rhys's Quartet.' In: Jay Clayton and Eric Rothstein (eds.) *Influence and Intertextuality in Literary History*, Madison: University of Wisconsin Press, 1991, p. 328

10  The page numbers refer to the edition: Jean Rhys, *Quartet*. London: Penguin, 2000.

11  Ford, *The Good Soldier: A Tale of Passion*, Oxford World Classics, ed. Thomas Moser, Oxford: Oxford University Press, 1999 – henceforth *GS*.

12  Dowell described the couples' socially predetermined interaction as follows:
    Upon my word, yes, our intimacy was like a minuet, simply because on every possible occasion and in every possible circumstance we knew where to go, where to sit, which table we unanimously should choose; and we could rise and go, all four together, without a signal from any one of us, always to the

        music of the Kur orchestra, always in the temperate sunshine, or, if it rained, in discreet shelters. (*GS* 10)

13  In his article mapping out the relations between narrative and autobiography 'Autobiography and Geography: A Self-Arranging Question', Frederic Regard speaks of a 'delinquency of the autobiographical narrative', as a narrative that doesn't obey conventions. See http://reconstruction.eserver.org/023/regard.htm, (accessed January 2, 2015) Similarly, since Regard convinces us of the intricate relation between space and narrative, I argue we can speak of 'delinquency of space' when the subject does not agree to stay in the 'space' that the society has prescribed for him/her.

14  The most respectable woman in *The Good Soldier* is of course Leonora, who is a Catholic, and carries the burden of being the symbol of the unbreakable marriage bond. '[Y]ou have also to remember that her getting him back represented to her not only a victory for herself. It would, as it appeared to her, have been a victory for all wives and a victory for her Church [. . . .] She saw life as a perpetual sex-battle between husbands who desire to be unfaithful to their wives, and wives who desire to recapture their husbands in the end. That was her sad and modest view of matrimony' (*GS* 215-16). Ford's other famous Catholic creation Sylvia Tietjens in *Parade's End* is, in contrast, an unfaithful wife. However, throughout the illicit affairs she conducts, she remains the perfectly respectable hostess, as she is of the moneyed classes and is closely connected to figures of power. Sylvia even manages to get the old English house, as her respectability seems to entitle her to it. Leonora decides not to keep Branshaw, however she is the only one in the story who ends up in a functioning marriage, with children. In both Ford novels, the Catholics, as protectors of legal contract of marriage, seem to be doing rather well.

15  Sue Thomas, *The Worlding of Jean Rhys*, Connecticut: Greenwood Press, 1990, p. 200.

16  Dowell describes what being Mrs Ashburnham entails in the following way: 'Her visitors' book had seven hundred names in it; there was not a soul that she could speak to. She was Mrs Ashburnham of Branshaw Teleragh. She was the great Mrs Ashburnham of Branshaw and she lay all day upon her bed in her marvellous, light, airy bedroom with the chintzes and the Chippendale and the portraits of deceased Ashburnhams by Zoffany and Zucchero' (*GS* 236).

17  Dowell explains Leonora's reasoning in the following way:

        Leonora, indeed, imagined that she could manage this affair all right. She had no thought of Maisie's being led into adultery; she imagined that if she could take Maisie and Edward to Nauheim, Edward would see enough of her to get tired of her pretty little chatterings, and of the pretty little motions of her hands and feet [. . . .] Leonora imagined that when poor Maisie was cured of her heart and Edward had seen enough of her, he would return to her. She had the vague, passionate idea that, when Edward had exhausted a number of other types of women he must turn to her. (*GS* 210)

# LOVE'S KNOWLEDGE:
## REALISATION BEYOND DEFENCE:
## DURRELL'S *ALEXANDRIA QUARTET* AFTER, AND
## BEYOND, FORD'S *THE GOOD SOLDIER*

## Omar Sabbagh

**Abstract**

The provenance of this essay is both the common ground and the essential difference in epistemological (and by proxy ethical) stance between Lawrence Durrell's *The Alexandria Quartet* and its putative forbear, in many respects: Ford Madox Ford's *The Good Soldier*. More specifically, I aim to critique the role and value of each author's use of story-telling narrators and/or narrator-characters – in relation, of course, to the overall signifying topography of each novel.

There are three complementary sections on each of the major works, tracing and retracing, in critique, the grounds of both works. I begin with the later work, and then, moving backwards assess the continuity or contrast between the earlier and later work, whether at a biographical level, or at a more objective one. The underlying theme and elicited context by which I permit myself to compare and contrast is, broadly speaking, provided by the epistemological or reflective categories, relating to truth and to knowledge, of subject and object. They are also ethical categories, when related to romantic/erotic or psycho-sexual differentia.

What immediately follows, then, are three thematic broaches at the later work – the first relating to the relativistic aspect of Durrell's major work; the second, by contrast, invokes the work's signal use of, and enactment of a certain kind of 'objectivity' shared with other, earlier modernists; the third section is, in a manner, an attempt to see how both poles interact and put each other into relief. After these three opening gambits, there are three (roughly) corresponding ripostes within one final section relating to Ford's celebrated novel, and going beyond it. In a sense, the discussion of Durrell is the (more extensive) vehicle, and that of Ford, the (intensive) tenor. If more time is spent on the first than the second, it is because the former works as it were as descriptive ground, and enabling context, for a critical appraisal of the contrasts and correspondences between both works.

---

when something untoward happens, some trauma or damage, whether inflicted by the commissions or omissions of others, or some cosmic force, one makes the initially unwelcome event one's own inner occupation. You work to adopt the most loveless, forlorn, aggressive child as your own, and do not leave her to develop into an even more vengeful monster, who constantly makes you ill in ill-health as in unhappy love. It requires taking in before letting go.

> To grow in love-ability is to accept the boundaries of oneself and others, while remaining vulnerable, woundable [. . . .] Acknowledgement of conditionality is the only unconditionality of human love.[1]

## I: The Paradox of Being in Time

In *The Alexandria Quartet* Lawrence Durrell attempts to apply relativity theory to the novel form. The first three novels aim to represent the three dimensions of Space, with the fourth, the only one to move forward in time, representing the fourth dimension of Time. One of the ways this intention shows up in the novel(s) is the way they illustrate the paradox of being in time.

At the beginning of his *The Logic of Sense,* Deleuze writes of this paradox, illustrating it using the character of Alice in Lewis Carroll's fiction. He takes the incident of Alice shrinking. She shrinks in time, but at any moment during this shrinkage reason is eluded by the antinomian movement, the conjunction and contradiction of opposing senses or directions produced by the fact that it happens in time. At any moment during her shrinking Alice is both smaller than she was and larger than she is going to be. Another version of this paradox is illustrated by Zeno's paradox of the race between Achilles and the tortoise. Because of its comparative slowness the tortoise is given a ten metre head start, say. But once Achilles starts running it turns out, quite rationally, that he will never be able to catch up to the tortoise. For to close the gap he must first close half the gap. To close half the gap he must first close half that. And so on in an infinite regress: the problem is vertiginous. In both instances, motion, movement, embodied action, plain living, defy reason because reason works to create static relations, classifying, whereas life and living are in time and therefore in flow. Reason aims to break down this flow, creating boundaries between one moment and the next, cause and effect, and yet in reality things just feed into each other osmotically, as endlessly dynamic as music. Hence, perhaps, both Bergson's and, before him, Augustine's use of music as a heurism to escape this paradox, to put the only truthful flesh on fluid time.[2]

At one point in *Justine,* Durrell's unreliable narrator, the innocent Darley, calls himself a 'poet of the historic consciousness'. This of course alludes to the central theme of memory and its vagaries in the novel(s) – also a key to their form. Across the *Quartet,* the narrative builds itself like a patchwork and then palimpsest of scenes, shifting and sliding backwards and forwards in time. At one point Darley says that he will not record his story chronologically, for that would be to render it as history, but rather give it poetic or heraldic form, writing his story as the events became significant for him. For in imagination resides 'reality prime'; only in fiction can one produce the meaning of the pattern and realise character (another recurrent theme in the novel(s)), against the chaos of experience and of living in time, which continues to flow and continues to change the significance of each moment in retrospect, and endlessly. And so these 'sliding panels of the human heart', the *Quartet*, serve to illustrate the relativity of truth, as against the pretensions of any rational history, or any notional 'end of history'. It does this firstly in the sense that at every point in space (for every different person) the story is different; and secondly, because of being in time. It is the very nature of historical research to keep reinterpreting the past, not only as gaps are filled in the historian's knowledge, through new perspectives, new evidence, but also because the relation of the historian's present to the past is continuously changing. And not only this, but also, as expressed in Walter Benjamin's anti-Hegelian 'Theses on the Philosophy of History', because at each moment the counterfactual 'if' suggests that the world could have gone in an infinity of directions (a theme that is eventually developed in *Balthazar*). Thus the (historical) object is illusory. What is left is a heraldic universe, a personal universe. (Indeed, the retreat onto his Greek 'island' to write is the very symbol of this.) (Re)interpretation is all that is left, and becomes one of the central reading directions to emerge from Durrell's novel(s). In this sense Durrell is a late-romantic, an epigone of the Nietzschean critique of objectivity or transcendence.[3]

## II: The Mythoi of Eros and Thanatos: An Objective Pattern
The 'historic consciousness' and 'the Capitol of Memory' also suggest in true modernist fashion a mythological backdrop to the events re-lated in the novel(s). This backdrop is a precursor which acts, in slight contradistinction to the suggestions of radical relativity (above), as (metaphysical) anchor. One thinks, of course, however facilely, of the earlier exemplars of *Ulysses* or *The Waste Land*; or indeed the pivotal role of notions of objectivity in the work of T. E. Hulme or, later, Wyndham Lewis.[4]

Just as Darley reflects on the untimely death of Pursewarden, the main fictional 'artist/writer' character – that the man has been replaced by his writings, his fiction, and has become the mythos that emerges from it, so the novel(s) as a whole have a distinctive mythologizing function. Which is to say, a gambit aimed at stilling time. The backdrop to the fictional Alexandria of *Justine* is the city of Myth, the 'Capitol of Memory'. This suggests a certain changeless stability as opposed to the inveterate process of change and newness already adverted to. The epiphanic or ecstatic rhythm of the writing, the series of 'realisations' reached by the characters usually after experiences of sex or death are both ciphers of hermeneutic sealing and hermeneutic openness. (Indeed, if one reads these points of 'realisation' closely it will be seen that the imagery surrounding the description is often identical or very similar, which suggests the intentional nature of this epiphanic rhythm.) But there is in fact a tension in the novel(s) between the vertiginous process of discovery, most overtly suggested by the 'Workpoints' at the end of the novel(s), and the concomitant and periodic reaction of stillness and resignation. The tension is a motive equilibrium between *Eros* and *Thanatos* deliberately made to regulate the rhythm and pacing of the story-telling. Durrell of course was a strident aficionado of Freud, and not only makes use of him within the tetralogy, but makes use of a passage of his (from a letter to Fliess), as epigraph to the latter. 'I am accustoming myself to the idea of regarding every sexual act as a process in which four persons are involved.'[5]

Assessing the mythic element in *Justine*, George Fraser saw more of the myth of the Quest than of the Foundation.[6] True, there is a sense of endless questioning, of maeutic in these novel(s), made poignant by the Socratic irony produced by the role of the unreliable narrator, Darley. But this sense of movement and discovery, of *Eros* is crossed with a spiritual calm, evoked by another repeated rhythm in the writing: mini-narratives invariably followed by passages of reflection, judgment and conclusion – the still reactionary countermovement of death, *Thanatos*. The prismatic, refracted layering of both plot and character are set off by an elegiac tone. One reads passages like the following,

> If she ever knew me at all she must later have discovered that for those of us who feel deeply and who are at all conscious of the inextricable tangle of human thought there is only one response to be made – ironic tenderness and silence. (*AQ* 40)

and despite knowing it to be fiction, relative and potentially falsified by perspective, *in extremis*, one can't help sensing the presence of something transcendent, if *via negativa*. What it is in fact is 'acceptance'. Durrell called his *Quartet* from the beginning of its inception almost twenty years before it was completed, 'The Book of the Dead'. In his first serious fiction *The Black Book* the 'little death' is derided. The writing starts with bleak perspectives of winter and deadness, and it evokes the sense of a young man's angst, ennui and melancholy: the *'agon'*. And yet in the far more mature work of the *Quartet*, although Death again is a central theme, the elegiac tone and the sweeter rhythms of the prose create a sense of healthy grieving or mourning, as if something is truly being worked out and resolved. 'In the midst of winter', again, 'you can feel the inventions of spring'. Durrell would eventually see the earlier work, the *Quartet* and his final major work, *The Avignon Quintet*, as representing three phases in his spiritual development: the first as the *agon*, the struggle to be (re)born as an artist; the second, most popular work as the *pathos*, the suffering and the uniting of the artist with his calling, and the defeat of death; and the third as the *'anagnorisis'*, the recognition.[7]

### III: Platonic Modernism: A Rum Tallying of Subject and Object

> And, indeed, the symbols themselves seem almost to be used in a way similar to the mathematician; as when a set of letters may stand for any numbers of a certain sort, and you are not curious to know which numbers are meant because you are only interested in the relations between them.[8]

One of the more recent pieces of myth that lies as backdrop to Durrell's fictional city is Cavafy's Alexandria. The opening passages of *Justine* refer obliquely to Cavafy's 'The City' (quoted in the appendix of *Justine*) by suggesting in passage after passage the determination produced by the spirit of place on its 'exemplars'. Darley writes, for instance, of the 'iron chains of memory', how the city has used him and all the other characters as its 'flora', and stresses how he has 'escaped' onto his Greek island. Indeed, at one point he talks of this 'escape' as a 'remission'. Not only is space then a determinant of time, but the body itself seems to be given centre stage. In fact it is really the boundless flow of desire itself that inspirits the dynamic maeutic of discovery in the novel's epiphanic movement, and satiation of desire that results in the alternate passages of conclusion and still reflection. Like the rhythm of the ocean itself, there is a checkered movement, continuous between life and death.

One of these pieces of reflection and conclusion reached early on in *Justine* suggests that reality is that of the imagination and that only the artist can give us access to reality, giving meaning to the pattern as (s)he does. One revealing pattern which rises almost to a mathematical purity is that of 'Justine' herself. Directly after we read this short reflection about the artist and reality, we learn that the name of the child on the island with Darley is Justine. Justine the elder was Darley's most central and most fateful love, if not his truest, in the *Quartet*. But the child Justine is Nessim and Melissa's baby. Melissa was Darley's partner and Nessim and Justine are married. An asymmetrical symmetry arises. There is something almost algebraic about the pattern of these relationships; that is, there is something ratiocinative in the vagaries of desire.

At one point, Arnauti, Justine's ex-lover, one of Darley's precursors, also a writer, tells us in his diary that he would like to 'contain' Justine in a book, quite literally. And Darley goes on to fulfill this wish. *Justine* and the whole *Quartet* are not only about the many faces of love, but turn out to be also the very lineaments of the lover's body itself. Darley praises Arnauti for recognizing Alexandria as being the 'City of the Soma'. But the city turns out to be also the body of one's lover. 'When one loves one of its inhabitants, a city becomes a world.' Indeed right at the end of Part II of *Justine* we find a fabulous metaphorical passage from Pursewarden (the major writer-character) comparing the insides, rhythms and dynamics of the body with the circulation and organism of the city itself. Suggesting ranging desire, as well as numerical identity and determination, the body is where subject and object coalesce, in a kind of dance.

As suggested above, there is a partial identification between Arnauti and Darley. This introduces another almost mathematical or objectivist element to the fiction. In the first chapter of *Ulysses* we learn that Stephen Dedalus has proven that Hamlet was Shakespeare's grandfather, proven it algebraically. And there is something of this algebraic and generational porousness in some of the relationships in the *Quartet*. We get this generational osmosis especially in the relations of the three authors in the novel, Arnauti, Darley and Pursewarden. Sometimes they coexist in time, sometimes they exist genealogically. The paradox is that of fiction or textuality itself. In the writing we have all three as characters in their own right, speaking to us. And yet, both Arnauti and Pursewarden exist chronologically before Darley, both having been earlier lovers of Justine. At one point Darley reading Arnauti's *Moeurs* feels the identification so great that he says he feels like one of its characters, only intensifying the generational primacy of Arnauti.

> Indeed so fascinating did I find his analysis of his subject, and so closely did our relationship echo the relationship he had enjoyed with Justine that at times I too felt like some paper character out of *Moeurs*.

But it is Darley who fathers them in turn, as we only have access to their voices through the prism of his writing. And finally, of course, we have Durrell himself, begetter of all these fictional writers. The author-character relationships both within and without the fiction act as a symbol for the ubiquity of fiction or textuality itself; fact and fiction, object and subject, merge through the very process of writing. The paradox can be best expressed by saying that these are not only written novels we are reading, objects in our hands, but that they are also novels being written *as we read them*. Nabokov produced the same metaphysical *mise-en-abyme* in his *The Real Life of Sebastian Knight*, by also making (the elliptical) writing itself one of the pivotal themes of his (elliptical) novel.

But the osmotic or porous qualities of the relationships in the *Quartet* are not limited to the writer-characters alone. At times it feels like all the characters flow into and out of each other, repeating and adapting each other's statements. Like Lawrence, Durrell is essentially concerned with oneness, his link to the eastern metaphysics he wanted to conflate with western physics. This idea of a transcendental collect-ivity, giving the lie to the discrete ego and the individual self, some-times crops up thematically, but is most apparent in the overall form of the novel(s). One of the great successes of *Justine* and the whole *Quartet* is how consistent the parallel between some of the themes and the form itself is. To give two thematic examples, we have Clea near the end of Part II talking about the rationing of love, how we each have our own special portion for life, one united portion that is just working itself out in relation to different people throughout our lives.[9] At the heart of this idea is a collective rather than an individual pattern. And then if we look backwards a little bit, earlier Darley had visited the dying Cohen (Melissa's ex-lover) in hospital, primarily to compare his love for Melissa, as in a mirror, with Cohen's. Just like the idea that comes later of Justine committing adultery with Darley *for* Nessim, Darley, visiting Cohen for Melissa, in her stead, seems to be committing another more narcissistic form of adultery. What strikes one in these examples and throughout *Justine* and the *Quartet* is the way everyone is connected with everyone else, even in death, everyone leaving traces in each other's lives. These themes and happenings are symbolic, that is, a deeper version, of the very plotting in the novels, the espionage that everyone in the end seems to be involved in at some level.

In what is a very impressionistic biography of the great Victorian, Chesterton once wrote of Dickens that we shouldn't consider his literary output as a group of separate novels, but rather as the continuous outpouring of the essence of Dickensness itself. There is something of this authorial flood in the way Durrell's characters relate to their author. In this respect too Durrell resembles Lawrence quite closely. Not only is there the continuous checkered movement between life and death, as in, especially, Lawrence's *The Rainbow*, but we get the feeling that the very repetition or difference in repetition that is at work in and amongst the characters, is both authors' rabid denial of an outdated realism. It is the modernist and late modernist's emphasis on self-expression-and-discovery through his literary art. And this self-expression of Durrell's, we will now see, is more direct and immediate than that elicited at the last by Ford. Even if Durrell's prose is overtly baroque, it is Ford's use of narrator and yarning voice which renders the more illusionistic effect.

### IV: A Reckoning: With, and Against, Ford's *The Good Soldier*

> Undertaken in this evasive mood, confessional writing degenerates into anti-confession. The record of the inner life becomes an unintentional parody of inner life.[10]

Interviewing Durrell in 1959, Kenneth Young reveals that Durrell claimed never to have read Ford's pivotal work.[11] Unlike, say, Alan Judd, some of whose work is self-consciously an epigone of Ford, or, perhaps, Kazuo Ishiguro, Durrell's seeming ignorance of *The Good Soldier* is, if not suspect, open to question. Below I show some aspects, thematic and formal, in which Durrell is in continuity, un-canny at times, with Ford. I conclude, however, with some reflections regarding the signal difference between the two works, from the (broadly speaking) epistemological perspective, and irrespective of any biographical context. In effect, Dowell is just as much a relativist or subjectivist as Darley; however, it is his (implicit, as I see it) *attempt* at a more stable, objectivist garnering of value from his tale, that fails resolutely. And that failure is *exemplified* by the calculus of his take on love (the major motif of both works) – which, it will be seen, is eminently rum. So . . .

The sexualization of knowledge and language, the unreliability (the shiftiness) of character and/or of memory, are basic facets that unite both novels. Indeed, after in part alluding to these latter features of signifying perspective, but with specific relevance, I will end with the idea of transcendence, the different results in relation to 'recognition'. That latter closure is Durrell's and Darley's, potentially; and Ford's, but *not Dowell's*.

To begin, then, in line to a certain extent with my suggestions regarding Durrell's mathematicity (akin to mythologizing), Dowell, Ford's unreliable narrator, calls his and the main protagonists' relations a 'minuet', a dance of four, however rigid or waylaid. Striking, in this respect, is the epigraph to Durrell's *Justine*, already mentioned. Just above a short passage from De Sade, Freud, as we've seen, suggests that every erotic or psycho-sexual relationship is actually a relationship of four, rather than two – each person having both a feminine and masculine side. Thus, though it is thematized, and glaringly so, in Durrell, one only has to think of the paradoxical gendering in Ford's major work to see the (potential) seed of Durrell's elaboration.

A second (though selective, as ever) correspondence lies in the simultaneously formal and substantive ideality, if you will, of the two works. As noted with Durrell, the theme of transcending the individual, bordered ego-self is mirrored to a certain extent in the time-shiftiness and the scenic method. These latter two techniques are of course the very underpinnings of Ford's architectonic. However, where it gets suggestive and interesting is to find a passage, like that alluded to in Durrell, in *The Good Soldier*: evoking the same ancient Idealist motif, regarding the Oneness of Love. Dowell is discussing the fleetingness of love affairs for men. And so:

> With each new woman that a man is attracted to there appears to come a broadening of the outlook, or, if you like, an acquiring of new territory. A turn of the eye-brow, a tone of the voice, a queer characteristic gesture—all these things, and it is these things that cause to arise the passion of love—all these things are like so many objects on the horizon of the landscape that tempt a man to walk beyond the horizon, to explore. He wants to get, as it were, behind those eye-brows with the peculiar turn, as if he desired to see the world with the eyes that they overshadow. He wants to hear that voice applying itself to every possible proposition, to every possible topic; he wants to see those characteristic gestures against every possible background. Of the question of the sex-instinct I know very little and I do not think that it counts for very

much in a really great passion. It can be aroused by such nothings—by an
untied shoelace, by a glance of the eye in passing—that I think it might be left
out of the calculation [. . . .] But the real fierceness of desire, the real heat of a
passion long continued and withering up the soul of a man is the craving for
identity with the woman that he loves. He desires to see with the same eyes, to
touch with the same sense of touch, to hear with the same ears, to lose his
identity, to be enveloped, to be supported. For, whatever may be said of the
relation of the sexes, there is no man who loves a woman that does not desire
to come to her for the renewal of his courage, for the cutting asunder of his
difficulties. And that will be the mainspring of his desire for her. We are all so
afraid, we are all so alone, we all so need from the outside the assurance of
our own worthiness to exist. [12]

The correspondence of motif (and perhaps its tallying with technique)
is quite clear here. However, this correspondence leads me, via an in-
terlude of Lacanian-inspired analysis, to the contrast between the
effects and the style of mind implicit in and emergent from the two
novels.

What is so fascinating about the above passage is that it is rife
with self-contradiction, symbolically and generically speaking. The
first sentence outlines what Lacan would call masculine structure,
which is capable only of 'phallic *jouissance*': the acquiring of 'new
territory' is equivalent of treating the other as 'object a', that is to say
as a partial object, to be used, to have sex with (just what Dowell does
not intend at this stage of the passage). It is 'phallic *jouissance*' – the
phallus, for Lacan, being the signifier of signification as such, thus
indicative of the incompleteness and elusiveness of satisfaction.[13] The
next sentence, however, clearly describes feminine structure, in so far
as Lacan states that it is usually such singularities that attract feminine
structure. And walking 'beyond the horizon' is suggestive of the
ineffability, the inarticulacy Lacan reads as feminine structure's
capacity for 'Other *jouissance*', which is not positive and existent, like
'phallic *jouissance*', and thus doomed to never-ending slippage and
thirst, the physical act of sex in short, but 'ex-sists' for Lacan.[14] In
another context he describes this modality as 'neither being nor non-
being, but the unrealized'.[15] It is associated by Lacan, as against
physical sex, with the concept of 'making love'. Hence perhaps the
rather bizarre sentences (being suggested about men) about wanting to
be at one with the other. And then Dowell seems to contradict himself
by using the singularities, the same quiddities, as leading also to what
he terms 'the sex-instinct', meaning the physical act. Finally, he
returns to feminine structure by speaking of the desire to 'lose one's

identity', to be 'enveloped'. Finishing with that typically Fordian cadence, a dying fall.

Due to what I have construed as the rampant self-contradictions of this passage, at least with the aid of Lacanian insight, Dowell remains evidently guilty of defensiveness, ultimately, the imaginary with its 'identificatory processes' being a mask over the symbolic as over the real, which may be accessed and activated by the former. The sense of his narcissistic (and abject) identification is the product, not of the sentences referring to 'Other *jouissance*', but rather of his split intentions, *which therefore are none.* And intentionality is the index of agency, which is to say, a hale subjectivity: the possibility as it were of integral action, as opposed to (an unknowing or self-occluded) reaction.

I would like to suggest that there is a basic contrast in the epistemological grounds of the two works, which is shown up especially well by the difference between the two novelists' use of this (just-cited) motif. There is a sense, much-noted, that Dowell ends his 'saddest story' in inchoate meaninglessness, effecting a distinct lack of closure. He has none of T. S. Eliot's 'historic sense' or Durrell's 'historic consciousness',[16] but rather is a 'hollow man' in direct continuity with his 'horror.' Perhaps the distinct lack of election, or discretion between past and present, character and narrator, is the source of his novel-wide *pan*-ic. In fact, I want to suggest that Dowell ends up being sightless, unlike Ford, by aiming for a static, pre-modernist, or strictly referential truth – when we know how dialectical truth to reality is, both in general and in Ford's various discussions of 'superimposition', 'vibration', 'haze', 'homo duplex' and so on. In a way, Dowell's (*epistemic*) gentility is being mocked by Ford; very similar in effect to the latter's critique of Thackeray, as exemplar of an outdated Victorian didacticism and moralism.[17]

However, Durrell's character seems to be more at one with the manipulations of the artist himself. Perhaps because, unlike Dowell, Darley realises (and realises that he 'realises') that there is a vital distinction between cognitive knowing and that more visceral kind of knowing that is 'realisation'. In the first of the five novels that would make up Durrell's *Avignon Quintet, Monsieur*, we find the following distinction:

> "But how to realise?" It was Piers' sad voice now that interrogated the sea-hushed silence and Akkad sighed, though he remained smiling still. He said:

> "A rather cruel paradox centres about the two notions which we express by the
> words 'knowing' and 'realising'. You can know something and yet not realise
> it, not having lived it, as we say, for in our inarticulate way we are aware of
> the distinction. Realisation is a real sigil conferred upon an experience...[18]

Indeed, in *Clea*, the final instalment of Durrell's *Quartet*, Clea says,
"'Yes, but it *hurts* to realise!'" And it is that which I believe
distinguishes the two works, in the purview and brief of this chapter.
Dowell, simply put, whether an innocent or a wily character, won't let
himself be hurt. Mourning, like love, is a process, essentially healthy,
which involves recognizing the objectivity of the other, either elsewhere or within oneself, and both/either temporally or spatially.
Dowell is far more blind, and blinded, than Darley. Even if Darley,
now alone on his island, has lost in passion, both his display of control
over the contents of memory, however elliptical, and the bare
objective datum of the child on the island with him, render him more
humanely fertile than Dowell's aimless echolalia, his babble, his
'many tongues'. The textual dispersal follows as a direct consequence
(we realise by the end) of a poignantly-rendered 'authorial' dispersal.
Indeed, Dowell's quagmire is aptly (if serendipitously) voiced by
Darley, empathizing, but sadly, with a type of pathetic failure – a
victim of experience rather than its proprietor – the now-dying Cohen
(Melissa's ex-lover).

> It was as if now that the flesh was dying the whole funds of his inner life, so
> long dammed up behind the falsities of a life wrongly lived, burst through the
> dykes and flooded the foreground of his consciousness. (*AQ* 92)

Another novelist who made use of the Idealist motif of the
thoroughgoing Oneness of Love was Graham Greene, in his *The End
of The Affair* (1951). He was surely influenced by Ford. After all, he
edited some of Ford's work posthumously. In his introduction to *The
Good Soldier* he writes:

> A novelist is not a vegetable absorbing nourishment mechanically from soil
> and air: material is not easily or painlessly gained, and one cannot help
> wondering what agonies of frustration and error lay behind *The Saddest
> Story*.[19]

However, while Darley shares Durrell's efficient distance to a certain
extent, Dowell is more like a peripatetic foil for the mastery of Ford.

As another illustration of this distinction regarding the two differently-deployed narrator-characters, witness the different modes or attitudes implicit in the following two passages of belated recognition, or if you will, 'delayed decoding'.[20] Darley writes of his affair with Justine:

> When I discovered, for example (what I knew) that she had been repeatedly unfaithful to me, and at times when I had felt myself to be closest to her, I felt nothing sharp in outline: rather a sinking numbness such as one might feel on leaving a friend in hospital, to enter a lift and fall six floors in silence, standing beside a uniformed automaton whose breathing one could hear. (*AQ* 65)

On reaching a similar retrospective stance on his own affair, Dowell, by turns, evokes and evinces a far more desperate and evidently defensive approach to what should be a more thoroughbred perspective of recognition:

> For, if for me we were four people with the same tastes, with same desires, acting – or, no, not acting – sitting here and there unanimously, isn't that the truth? If for nine years I have possessed a goodly apple that is rotten at the core and discover its rottenness only in nine years and six months less four days, isn't it true to say that for nine years I possessed a goodly apple? (*GS* 13)

Or, as a potential forbear to the last-cited passage from Durrell, note how Dowell *reacts* to Florence (his cuckolding wife's) death. The sentiment is similar. But to have to decide between a biographical borrowing and a merely objective coalescing of insight in relation to human loss is perhaps a too exigent desideratum.

> And I thought nothing; absolutely nothing. I had no ideas; I had no strength. I felt no sorrow, no desire for action, no inclination to go upstairs and fall upon the body of my wife. I just saw the pink effulgence, the cane tables, the palms, the globular matchholders, the indented ashtrays. (*GS* 88)

That tangent duly noted, and for all the other circumstantial (or not) tallying here and there – Dowell remains on the whole a very different type (and expressive tool) from Darley. Similar vehicles serve very different tenors.

Thus, relating their respective rationales (or indeed rationalizations) for narrating their yarns of loss, Darley, again, is the bolder in rhetoric, Dowell giving off the sense of a more feeble special pleading. Darley writes, early on: 'I simply make these notes to record a block of my life which has fallen into the sea.' There's some striding *hilaritas*, for all the mood of elegy. Dowell writes:

> You may well ask why I write. And yet my reasons are quite many. For is it not unusual in human beings who have witnessed the sack of a city or the falling to pieces of a people to desire to set down what they have witnessed for the benefit of unknown heirs or of generations infinitely remote; or, if you please, just to get the sight out of their heads. (*GS* 12)

The sack of a 'city' is a poignant image, which, of course, is at the operative heart of many of Durrell's allusions and metaphoric burdens. And yet, not so much in the substantive choice of simile, but in the mode in which such hyperbole come across, having been expressed, the 'voice' of Darley is more resolute, more honed, and far less abject than that of Dowell's. While the one is declarative, the other shapes the expression of his loss in a far more passive mood. Darley's sacked city, or indeed self, is evocative of realisation, hale recognition, rather than Dowell's self-occluded and waylaid wondering:

> It was as if the whole city had crashed about my ears; I walked about in it aimlessly as survivors must walk about the streets of their native city after an earthquake, amazed to find how much that had been familiar was changed. (*AQ* 77)

One way of putting the distinction (again, in terms of the categories of reflection), is to say that the 'objective' inchoateness of *The Good Soldier* is a result of the subjectively confused and thus *pan*-icking narrator-character writing, *by hearsay*, of 'The Saddest Story.' Whereas in the later novel(s), the subjective unreliability is due to the objective embracing of a modern(ist) relativity. In other words, because Durrell's narrator, Darley, embraces the illusionism of reality, he allows fate to happen to his characters. In a way, he owns the story in a manner on a par with his creator. After all, Darley is quite unlike the purportedly self-deprecating Dowell, being (within the text or without) *a self-professed* writer. Why else would he be overtly capable of talking of the 'historic consciousness' or 'reality prime' as the product of the imagination?

Darley, then, has (more) 'character' – as well as eliciting character(s) of course. Dowell, as Levenson has noted, represents, or, better, reflects, a kind of writerly, or 'authorial', *dis-integration*.[21] Unlike Darley's performance on behalf of his near-twin and *impresario*, Dowell's is a product of a structure of feeling more suggestive of what Coleridge called (as opposed to 'imagination') 'fancy'. That Ford was using Dowell's *ethical* gentility as a foil for a storied criticism of moralistic herd-mentality goes without saying. In the end, however, it is this sham, ethical propriety *tied-in with* Dowell's genteel *epistemology* that, because equally outdated, renders him (quite unlike his creator) blind – in a world where we would rather be *'made* to see'.[22]

# NOTES

1   Gillian Rose, *Love's Work*, London: Chatto and Windus, 1995, pp. 90-1 and 98.
2   See, for instance, Henri Bergson, *Time and Free Will,* trans. F. L. Pogson, London: George Allen and Co, 1913, pp. 103-13.
3   See, for instance, Friedrich Nietzsche, *The Genealogy of Morals,* trans. Horace B. Samuel, Mineola, New York: Dover Publications, 2003, p. 93.
4   Durrell shares his over-determinant opening gambit of the tetralogy (an ominous mythic backdrop), with two preceding colonial novelists, the Conrad of *Nostromo* and the Forster of *A Passage to India.* Indeed, Forster makes mention of Durrell in the 1961 3rd edition of his Alexandria travel guide. In that latter, Forster discusses Alexandria as the city of the 'Soma', meaning, historically, the mausoleum of Alexander. Durrell does so as well, but plays on the term as well, meaning something more generically (psycho)sensual. See E. M. Forster, *Alexandria: A History and a Guide,* Garden City, New York: Anchor Books, 1961, pp. xvii and 11, 22. See T. E. Hulme, *Selected Writings,* ed. Patrick McGuinness, Manchester: Carcanet, 1998, pp. 68-83 & 180-222. See also, Wyndham Lewis, *Time and Western Man*, ed. Paul Edwards, Santa Rosa: Black Sparrow Press, 1993.
5   See Lawrence Durrell, *The Alexandria Quartet,* London: Faber & Faber, 2012 – henceforth *AQ*; p. 15.
6   See George Fraser, *Lawrence Durrell: A Study*, London: Faber and Faber, 1968, pp. 132-3.
7   Ian MacNiven, *Lawrence Durrell: A Biography*, London: Faber and Faber, 1998, p. 662.
8   William Empson, *Seven Types of Ambiguity,* London: Penguin Books, 1995, p. 145.
9   Indeed, this Oneness of Love is an ancient Idealist motif, to be found in Plato's *Symposium.*
10  Christopher Lasch, *The Culture of Narcissism: American Life in an Age of Diminishing Expectations,* New York & London: W.W. Norton and Co., 1991, p. 20.
11  *Lawrence Durrell: Conversations*, ed. Earl G. Ingersoll, Madison, Teaneck: Farleigh Dickinson University Press, & London: Associated University Presses, 1998, p. 49.

12  Ford, *The Good Soldier*, ed. Max Saunders, Oxford: Oxford University Press, 2012, pp. 92-3.

13  See Jacques Lacan, 'The Signification of the Phallus', in *Écrits*, trans. Bruce Fink, New York and London: W.W. Norton, 2006, pp. 575-84.

14  For a detailed rendering of Lacan's views on what he called 'sexuation', 'phallic *jouissance*' and 'Other *jouissance*' and the impossibility of a sexual relationship, which is analogous to the impossibility of closure of signification, rendered: 'copula(tion)', see Bruce Fink, *Lacan to the Letter: Reading Écrits Closely*, Minneapolis and London: University of Minnesota Press, 2004, pp. 141-66. The term 'ex-sists,' as distinct from 'exists' is there to highlight the concept's negativity; which is to say, like the larynx to the (positive or phallic) voice: the absence whose only positivity is as blank ground of the existent or that which is susceptible to indefinite slippage and association.

15  Jacques Lacan, *The Seminar of Jacques Lacan: Book XI: The Four Fundamental Concept of Psychoanalysis*, trans. Alan Sheridan, New York and London: W. W. Norton, 1998, p. 30.

16  The idea of a 'historic sense' is also central to Ford's critical and creative itinerary. 'In the domain of History there is no such thing as Time.' See Ford, 'Creative History and the Historic Sense,' in *Critical Essays,* ed. Max Saunders and Richard Stang, New York: New York University Press, pp. 12-13.

17  See Ford Madox Ford, 'On Impressionism' in *Critical Writings of Ford Madox Ford,* ed. Frank MacShane, Lincoln: University of Nebraska, 1964; see also Ford Madox Ford, *The English Novel; From the Earliest Days to the Death of Joseph Conrad,* Manchester: Carcanet, 1999, pp. 64-105.

18  Lawrence Durrell, *The Avignon Quintet,* London: Faber and Faber, 2004, pp. 141-2.

19  Greene, 'Introduction', *The Bodley Head Ford Madox Ford*, I, London: The Bodley Head Ltd, 1962, pp. 7-12 (p. 12). Indeed, tallying with the central theme of this essay, the epigraph to Greene's novel, from Leon Bloy, runs: 'Man has places in his heart which do not yet exist, and into them enters suffering in order that they may have existence.' I am indebted to Sara Haslam for alerting me to this significant detail.

20  This central term in Conrad criticism was first introduced by Ian Watt in his *Conrad in the Nineteenth Century,* Berkeley and Los Angeles: University of California Press, 1981.

21  See Michael Levenson, *Modernism and the Fate of Individuality: Character and Novelistic Form from Conrad to Woolf,* Cambridge: Cambridge University Press, 2004, pp. 102-20.

22  This celebrated phrase (adapted here), regarding the desideratum of making the reader 'see' – in both senses, viscerally or imaginatively and epistemologically – derives from Conrad's early literary manifesto, the "Preface" to his *The Nigger of the "Narcissus."* See Joseph Conrad, *The Nigger of the "Narcissus,"* ed. Robert Kimbrough, New York: W. W. Norton, 1979, pp. 145-8.

# 'DON'T YOU SEE?': SURVEILLANCE AND UTOPIAN TRANQUILLITY IN *THE GOOD SOLDIER*

## Peter Marks

**Abstract**

This chapter considers *The Good Soldier* through the intersection of recent surveillance theory – with its concentration on the ability of institutions and individuals to monitor each other – and utopia, something that John Dowell craves desperately. Taking at its starting point Ford Madox Ford's appreciative if nuanced response to H. G. Wells's *A Modern Utopia*, the chapter reads John Dowell's first meeting with Edward Ashburnham, when he is able to name the putative 'good soldier' even before being introduced, as revealing underlying surveillance processes at work at Bad Nauheim working to identify and reduce risk. Ironically, these very processes inaugurate the calamitous relationship between the two couples that Dowell belatedly tries to comprehend. This institutional surveillance is looked at in contrast to the various and variously successful ways in which the main characters see or (consciously or unconsciously) fail to see what is happening over nearly a decade of deceit. Dowell's apparent blindness to the obvious is read in terms of his search for a 'shock-proof world', a world of utopian tranquillity that he achieves and is forced to endure.

---

'Don't you see,' she said, 'don't you see what's going on?' The panic again stopped my heart. I muttered, I stuttered—I don't know how I got the words out:
'No! What's the matter? Whatever's the matter?'[1]

'Surveillance studies is about seeing things and, more particularly, about seeing people.'[2]

Ford Madox Ford read H. G. Wells's *A Modern Utopia* when it first appeared in 1905. Wells had tried to revivify the utopian genre, which he felt presented 'perfect and static states, a balance of happiness won for ever against the forces of unrest and disorder that inhere in things'.[3] A modern utopia, he argued, energised by science and technology, must be dynamic and endlessly creative, at a constant 'hopeful stage, leading to a long ascent of stages'. Aesthetically, too, previous utopias tended to be 'comprehensively jejune', full of 'characterless buildings' and 'generalised people' (*MU* 7). To combat these flaws,

Wells created an inquisitive narrator who is enthusiastic about what he finds in the utopia (but who, Wells makes clear, is *not* to be read as Wells himself), as well as a companion, a sceptical Botanist less taken by the utopian world to which they travel. Their different assessments create a certain argumentative dynamic often missing in utopias. The world they discover – a planet 'out beyond Sirius' (*MU* 9), identical to Earth except that it has developed along utopian lines – is overseen by an ascetic, intellectual class called the Samurai, a group enthusiastically admired by the 'not-Wells' narrator. Ford wrote to Wells in May 1905, telling him that 'I've read you with pleasure – & I hope and believe, with profit', before noting that he sympathised with the Botanist rather than with the narrator. He consciously provoked Wells further by declaring, 'To the stake with your Samurai!' before adding the backhanded benediction: 'God bless you and turn you into a Samurai when you're tired of writing'.[4] Ford's consequent aside – 'I mean that one reads to disagree' – seems somewhat redundant.

H. G. Wells read *The Good Soldier* when it first appeared in 1915. He called it a great book, and cancelled his subscription to G. K. Chesterton's brother Cecil's *New Witness* because of the negative review the novel received there. But the key intersection considered in what follows is not the mutual admiration the writers had for each other, nor the fact that that admiration later cooled. Instead, I want to focus on an incident in *A Modern Utopia* that has an illuminating analogue in *The Good Soldier*, and which allows me to start considering Ford's novel in terms of recent surveillance theory. The narrator and the Botanist, newly transplanted to the parallel planet, and having rested the night at an inn, go to the Public Office to register their arrival. When asked for his identity number and papers, the narrator, realising that there will be no record of him on this planet, plays for time: 'A vision of that confounded visitors' book at the inn comes into my mind' (*MU* 92), but he cannot fudge an identity. He and the Botanist have their fingerprints taken, and these are sent to a central bureau in Paris for identification. In *The Good Soldier*, Dowell sees a man in the Hotel Excelsior, and observes that his lips form three syllables (which readers in hindsight might assume to enunciate 'Ashburnham'). From this, Dowell tells us, 'immediately I knew that he must be Edward Ashburnham, Captain, Fourteenth Hussars, of Branshaw House, Branshaw Teleragh' (*GS* 24). This is startlingly precise information to know about someone whom he has never seen before. The explanation for Dowell's magical perception comes immediately:

> I knew it because every evening just before dinner, whilst I waited in the hall I used, by the courtesy of Monsieur Schontz, the proprietor to inspect the little police reports that each guest was expected to sign upon taking a room. (*GS* 24)

Dowell is usually reckoned to be the 'ignorant fool' of his own definition. But in the vital moment that precedes first contact with the man who will play such a consequential role in the next decade of his life, Dowell has superior information, perhaps the only time he has the upper hand. What he lacks is the capacity to turn information into accurate knowledge.

One might see surveillance in various forms, as well as quest-ions of confused or uncertain identity, in a range of Ford works and in his life. There is of course his own name change that raised questions about allegiance, the many affairs that required concealment while they remained secret, accusations that Ford was a spy, and his know-ledge of anarchists that fed into Joseph Conrad's *The Secret Agent*. Institutionalized spying and counter-spying pervades the court of Henry VIII in *The Fifth Queen* trilogy (1906-8), while in *The Marsden Case* (1923) George Heimann is gaoled as a British spy when he travels to Germany in search of his true identity just as war breaks out, and then is accused of being a German spy when he returns to England. The American Henry Martin passes himself off as the Englishman Hugh Monckton in *Henry for Hugh* (1934), an act which Max Saunders reads as 'the universal desire for experience of the other: Wishing to exchange identities'.[5] Something similar could be said of Dowell's attitude to Ashburnham, especially once he wrongly classifies Edward as the good soldier.

Dowell, though, is not the only character on that momentous night who inspects the police reports. Leonora Ashburnham does, as well. She uses them to initiate that first meeting between the Dowells and the Ashburnhams, calling Edward in 'quite a loud voice and from quite a distance: "Don't stop over by that stuffy old table, Teddy. Come and sit by these nice people!"' Her assessment causes Dowell to comment:

> And that was an extraordinary thing to say. Quite extraordinary. I couldn't for the life of me refer to total strangers as nice people. But, of course, she was taking a line of her own in which I at any rate—and no one else in the room, for she too had taken the trouble to read through the list of guests—counted as any more than so many clean, [well-behaved] bull terriers. (*GS* 28)

And so the police reports bring the couples together, if we accept Dowell's account about Leonora and the lists, assuring the normally hyper-vigilant wife of a serial adulterer that the unknown American couple are nice people. Dowell, by contrast, makes no overt assumption about the quality of the Ashburnhams, although the information about Edward might mark him as the eponymous good soldier. Within the confines of the Excelsior, the police reports serve other functions, signalling that guests have been scrutinized and validated, are part of a moneyed elite that also includes the Guggenheimers, whose reserved table sits adjacent to that of the Dowells. The list also advertises the hotel's surveillance regime, its elimination of potential risks. Yet Leonora's overly enthusiastic confidence is shattered almost immediately by Edward's 'appreciative gurgle', a reaction that causes the usually inattentive Dowell to become 'perfectly aware of a slight hesitation—a quick sharp motion in Mrs Ashburnham, as if her horse had been checked' (GS 29). He does not decode this motion, nor can he, for it incorporates Leonora's painfully-acquired knowledge of Edward's repeated sexual deceptions that have found a new target in Florence Dowell.

Seen through the lens of surveillance studies, the police lists provide an example of what Nikolas Rose has termed the 'securitization of identity',[6] whereby identifying documents enable or deny access to particular spaces or zones. For H. G. Wells, the mobility he associated with a creative, energetic modern utopia inaugurated a world 'awash with anonymous stranger men' (MU 95; sic) that required an easily transmittable record for every person. He imagines a central bureau in Paris with transparent index cards 'so contrived as to give a photographic copy promptly whenever it was needed'. From this bureau would issue 'an incessant stream of information . . . of births, of deaths, of arrivals at inns. . . . of tickets taken for long journeys, of criminal convictions, marriages. . . and the like' (MU 96). This, he argues, 'is inevitable if a modern Utopia is to be achieved' (MU 97). While the system at the Excelsior is far less comprehensive, it is possible to see police lists as part of a surveillance system that maintains the hotel and the spa town of Bad Nauheim as a utopian space. Certainly Dowell understands them in this way in the immediate aftermath of the first meeting, announcing, 'So began those nine years of uninterrupted tranquillity' (GS 30). By the time we read this sentence, though, we already know from Dowell that the utopian world has been destroyed: 'Permanence? Stability! I can't believe it's gone. I can't believe that that long tranquil life, which was just stepping a minuet, vanished in four crashing days at the end of nine years and six weeks' (*GS* 11). The dynamic tension between Dowell's desire for utopian tranquillity and the fear and ultimate experience of dystopian upheaval runs through *The Good Soldier*, powerfully realised late in the novel when he plaintively asks:

> Is there then any terrestrial paradise where, amidst the whispering of the olive-leaves, people can be with whom they like and have what they like and take their ease in shadows and coolness? Or are all men's lives like the lives of us good people . . . broken, tumultuous, agonised and unromantic lives, periods punctuated by screams, by imbecilities, by deaths, by agonies? (*GS* 158)

Utopian tranquillity for Dowell entails eliminating surprise and risk. At one point he acknowledges 'evolving my plans for a shock-proof world' (*GS* 41), a revelatory personal credo that readily approximates what surveillance agencies and processes labour to bring about, equally without success.

Dowell's failure to create a shock-proof world results, to an enormous extent, from his inability to do what the second quotation at the start of this article deems central to surveillance; he fails to see. As David Lyon, a leading scholar of surveillance, declares at the beginning of his authoritative *Surveillance Studies: An Overview*, quoted at the outset of this chapter, surveillance studies is about seeing things and, more particularly, people. These aspects are also captured in the title of Lyon's *The Electronic Eye* (1994), and more recent accounts of surveillance, including *The New Politics of Surveillance and Visibility* (2006), *iSpy: Surveillance and Power in the Interactive Age* (2007) and *SuperVision: An Introduction to the Surveillance Society* (2013). Contemporary surveillance involves an array of ways and means of seeing, most obviously through cameras and computers that enable the rapid transmission of personal information (Wells's Paris bureau seems particularly prescient). The intersection between surveillance and utopian and dystopian worlds has a longer history. Thomas More's *Utopia* (1516) expressly has no privacy, on the grounds that all its citizens are engaged in good deeds, while the great modern dystopia, George Orwell's *Nineteen Eighty-Four*, is a surveillance hell, where, famously, 'You had to live – did live, from habit that became instinct – in the assumption that every sound you made was overheard, and except in darkness, every movement scrutinised'.[7] With its telescreens, Thought Police, and Big Brother, *Nineteen*

*Eighty-Four* is the surveillance dystopia *par excellence*. But to some degree the novel skews our thinking about surveillance towards totalitarian state control, when at least some of the monitoring that takes place in Oceania is what we might call peer surveillance, where individuals regularly scrutinise each other. The first quotation at the top of this article instances a peculiarly traumatic example of this personal surveillance, when Florence places her finger upon Edward's wrist. 'Don't you see?', Leonora says, 'don't you see what's going on?' Dowell replies with a confused ignorance 'No what's the matter? Whatever's the matter?' To which she responds:

> 'Don't you see,' she said, with a horrible bitterness, with a really horrible lamentation in her voice. 'Don't you see that that's the cause of the whole miserable affair; of the whole sorrow of the world? And of the eternal damnation of you and me and them. . .' (*GS* 39)

Dowell's stuttering response suggests a fundamental inability to 'see' in several senses that marks him out for contempt, including by himself. But is his failure not so much an inherent deficiency as – on occasions – an act of will, a conscious effort not to see. At times does he, to use a term I consider later, actively 'unsee' what is before him?

Before considering that possibility in more detail, Laura Colombino's statement that 'Vision pervades Ford Madox Ford's work'[8] reminds us of vision's power, and the necessary consequences of absent or faulty vision, not only in terms of characters but at the level of artistic practice. As she notes at the start of her own investigation of vision and visuality in Ford's writing: 'At the cross-roads of Ford criticism is the Conradian idea that all writing should "make you see"'.[9] Colombino's interest lies in vision in terms of various art forms, but Sally Bachner gets closer to vision in *The Good Soldier* as akin to surveillance by investigating links between the novel and Sherlock Holmes stories in '"The Seeing Eye": Deception, Perception and Erotic Knowledge In *The Good Soldier*'.[10] For Bachner, Dowell's statement that 'I guess Florence got all she wanted out of one look at a place. She had the seeing eye. I haven't, unfortunately' (*GS* 16-17) offers a way understanding his ocular failings. 'The rhetoric of "the seeing eye"', she comments, 'concentrates all empirical power onto sight. The eye is like a camera, recording all it sees for posterity and for the satisfaction of the viewer'.[11] Bachner states that Florence, Edward and Leonora all possess the seeing eye, and certainly the relationship between vision and erotic gratification is important throughout the novel.[12] Leonora's anguished 'Don't you see' and the association of seeing with understanding 'the whole sorrow of the world' also points to the potential damage seeing can bring about, her conviction perhaps, that as a Catholic she is under the seeing eye of God. This connection between religion and seeing has a more mundane, pragmatic aspect, for as Leonora struggles to deal with Edward's financial and sexual deceptions, Dowell speculates that she 'would have spied on Edward's bank accounts in secret. She was not a Roman Catholic for nothing' (GS 131). And having opened one of Edward's letters and finding that he 'was paying a blackmailer of whom she had never heard something like three hundred pounds a year', she claims 'the right to open [his letters] when she chose . . . [and] the privilege of having his secrets at her disposal' (GS 44-5). As well as the seeing eye, Leonora might be seen to have the surveillant eye, one that regularly monitors Edward in an attempt to control him. For a while, at least, she is partially successful. And she uses the power of surveillance to her great if fatal advantage. It is she who suggests casually to Florence that Florence follow Edward and Nancy, assuming correctly that, as Edward later admits to Dowell, he had led Nancy 'not up the straight allée that leads to the Casino but in under the dark trees of the park' (GS 79). Traumatised by what she sees, Florence kills herself with nitrate of amyl, a telling instance when surveillance power damages the monitor rather than the monitored. But it is Leonora, who witnesses Edward's innumerable affairs or infatuations over many years, who perhaps suffers most from her capacity to see.

Dowell might not have the seeing eye, but in his regular inspection of the police lists, he does occasionally employ the surveillant eye. We can interpret his actions in several ways – as simple inquisitiveness, or as the actions of an American anxious about his 'place' in genteel European society. But given Dowell's desire for a shock-proof world, checking the lists also assures him that the tranquil life he searches for is being maintained by appropriate forces. His acute anxiety gets exposed in what almost descends into a rant about the loss of permanence and stability, where his belief that the Ashburnhams and Dowells were 'just stepping a minuet' collapses into the fevered admission that 'It wasn't a minuet that we stepped; it was a prison—a prison full of screaming hysterics'. This is immediately replaced with the hyperbolic, though comforting, claim: 'And yet I swear by the sacred name of my creator that it was true. It was true sunshine; the true music; the true plash of the fountains from the mouth of stone dolphins' (*GS* 11). In this passage we hear competing utopian and dystopian notes of desperate intensity. Bad Nauheim itself functions as a utopian healing place for those with 'a heart,' and simultaneously as a dystopian site where the sick congregate. Worse, it provides the opportunity – almost to the point of endorsement – for seasonal adultery and high-end hypochondria. Of the three substantial characters who visit the spa town for treatment, two commit suicide – Edward, admittedly, well beyond its borders –while Maisie Maidan, the only one genuinely ill, winds up dead, in tragi-comic disarray, falling into her trunk, that 'closed upon her, like the jaws of a gigantic alligator' (*GS* 58). No utopia that. Even Dowell, though he in many ways experiences Bad Nauheim positively, confesses that it gave him 'a sense—what shall I say?—a sense almost of nakedness that one feels on the sea shore or in any great open space' (*GS* 22). He recalls standing:

> upon the carefully swept steps of the Englischer Hof, looking at the carefully arranged trees in the tubs upon the carefully arranged gravel whilst carefully arranged people walked past in carefully calculated gaiety, at the carefully calculated hour. (*GS* 23)

The planned arrangement of space is a recurrent feature of utopias, but the 'carefully swept steps' leading to the repetition of 'carefully arranged' and 'carefully calculated' linguistically creates an ominous and oppressive sense of monotony and standardization more analogous to dystopias and surveillance regimes.

Dowell's 'sense of nakedness' raises a key topic for surveillance scholars, that of privacy. They explore the complexity of the term, distinguishing, for example, bodily privacy, communication privacy, information privacy, and territorial privacy. Leonora's monitoring of Edward's letters and bank accounts provide examples of the invasion of communication and information privacy, but in *The Good Soldier* territorial privacy is critical, especially the privacy of the bedroom. Bedrooms are vigorously patrolled zones in the novel, where access is promiscuously allowed to some and aggressively denied to others. The sexual symbolism is inherent, the most obvious person denied entry being Dowell. After climbing by a ludicrous rope ladder into Florence's bedroom on August 4, 1901, he does not enter her bedroom again until August 4, 1913, when, in a perverse anniversary, he finds her dead. Ford's dark humour gets pushed almost beyond endurance when Dowell admits that from the outset he is convinced that he must never enter Florence's room without knocking; that because she is nervous about thieves the door is always locked after 10pm, and that he 'was provided with an axe—an axe!—great gods, with which to break down the door in case she ever failed to answer my knock' (*GS* 66). He never gets to use the axe. But, as he finds out eventually, Florence often unlocks her door for others. The maintenance of territorial privacy is crucial to the narrative, to the control different characters assert over their lives and those of others, as well as to notions of propriety and power. A clear instance of that power, because it goes against Edward's usual amorous successes, comes after his liaison with La Dolciquita; although initially he spends the night in her bed (*GS* 110), eventually: 'Her rooms were closed to him' (*GS* 112). In the novel as a whole, we are more likely to be told about people *leaving* bedrooms than entering them. And we are told, rather than see, because Dowell himself is not around when Jimmy leaves Florence's bedroom at 5am (Bagshawe sees that), or when Edward leaves Florence's bedroom (Leonora sees that), or when Maisie leaves Edward's bedroom (Leonora again is the observer). Each of these viewed exits has telling effects, even when (as in the case of the innocent Maisie) nothing illicit takes place. Despite or because of the essentially sexless marriages of the Ashburnhams (after the La Dolciquita incident) and the Dowells, much of what goes on between two people in a bedroom is adulterous, but Dowell himself apparently fails to see or suspect any of it.

Can we blame him? As he pleads:

> what chance did I have against those three hardened gamblers who were all in league to conceal their hands from me? What earthly chance? They were three to one—and they made me happy. Oh god, they made me so happy that I doubt if even paradise, that shall smooth out all the temporal wrongs, shall ever give me the like. (*GS* 54)

Again, we hear Dowell's palpable and determining desire for utopian tranquillity, for happiness, that partly explains his failings. Surveillance scholar Gary T. Marx might sympathise, for he comments that '[m]ost surveillance systems have inherent contradictions, ambiguities, gaps, blindspots and limitations'.[13] Marx also understands that, 'The strategic actions of both watchers and the watched can be thought of as moves in a game, although unlike traditional games, the rules may not be equally binding on all players'.[14] Here we grasp the asymmetrical situation Dowell later understands, whereby Edward, Leonora and Florence consciously execute moves to deceive him. (Not a difficult task given Dowell's recognised and enervating preference for utopian paradise.) Marx lists eleven responses to different forms of surveillance, including 'blocking' and 'masking'. Blocking defies the surveillant's 'desire to read the signals given off by the subject', who, as a counter-measure, seeks 'to physically block access to the communication'. Its most obvious manifestation in *The Good Soldier* is Florence's barring of Dowell from her bedroom. 'Masking' involves 'deception in respect to the identity, status, and/or location of the person or material of surveillance interest'.[15] Crucially, with masking, information is seen, but the actual significance of the viewed act remains hidden, so that the monitored subjects retain a degree of invisibility, their actions not being correctly interpreted. So, Dowell regularly *sees* Florence demanding that Edward kiss her, and allows Edward to join them in Paris, but apparently fails to understand the implications of these actions. In the game of surveillance, Dowell seems destined to lose because he does not realize that he is in a game; or if he does realise, he is never skilful enough to compete successfully.

Marx comments elsewhere that, rather than understand surveillance simply in relation to seeing things, we need a spectrum of monitoring that encompasses everything from the visible to the invisible.[16] In a recent article I have argued we might usefully extend this spectrum to include the 'unvisible'.[17] I take this term from China Miéville's speculative 2009 novel, *The City & The City*. In Miéville's invented world, two peoples from two city-states inhabit the same space simultaneously – are, in the novel's creative terminology, 'topolgangers'. In order to accommodate this fraught and fragile dystopia, citizens of both cities are taught to 'unsee' each other, on pain of arrest. Unseeing is necessary to maintain social stability both within and between the cities. I think it possible to apply the concept of unseeing to Dowell, to argue that rather than being repeatedly and stupendously ignorant of what is happening over nearly a decade, sometimes literally before his very eyes, he consciously unsees in order to maintain the state of utopian happiness he patently desires. And he does so from the beginning of his relations with Florence. Her aunts implore him not to marry her, but he has already declared: 'I don't care. If Florence had robbed a bank I am going to marry her and take her to Europe' (*GS* 62). And when Florence embraces him, the first time a woman has ever done so, he acknowledges that 'I was in such a hurry to get the wedding over and was so afraid of her relatives finding me there that I must have received her advances with a certain amount of absence of mind' (*GS* 63). Whatever we make of Dowell's motives for marrying Florence in such haste, his courtship, such as it is, requires several consequential instances of unseeing, in the sense of consciously not taking account of what is obvious.

Florence, by massive contrast, whose seeing eye gets all she wants 'out of one look at a place', immediately recognises that Dowell can and will satisfy her desire for a husband, an income, a European establishment, and not much physical passion. Better still, in the promise that he will take her away from the United States, Dowell offers her respite from the monitoring eyes of her aunts, and access to her former lover, Jimmy, in Paris and the utopian Fordingbridge of her English ancestors. But before she commits to Dowell at one in the morning of August 4, 1901, she asks him two vital questions: 'it is determined that we sail at four this afternoon? You are not lying about having taken berths?' (*GS* 63). His assurance is crucial for Florence's plans of immediate escape, but their ability to leave thirteen hours later is a function of the fact that, in 1901, people with sufficient funds could easily travel to Europe, and freely within it. As John Torpey argues in *The Invention of the Passport: Surveillance, Citizenship and The State*,[18] this mobility would not outlast the end of the narrative – which Vincent Cheng dates to late 1915 or early 1916, with Dowell and Nancy in Branshaw Teleragh.[19] World War I, Torpey shows, led to the imposition of new administrative checks and paper barriers that, in his intriguing and suggestive term, increased the state's 'embrace' of its citizens. Once those were in place, the speed and facility with which Florence and Dowell leave the United States and enter Europe would not have been possible. Nor would they have been as able to travel within Europe. Indeed, the Ashburnhams' and Maisie Maidan's passage from India to Bad Nauheim also would have been far more difficult. The surveillance processes of 1916 would have meant that the main characters might never had met, making impossible Dowell's 'saddest story'.

In 1901, though, Dowell's wealth and naivety make him (almost literally) just the ticket for Florence's European dreams. Torpey places this casual mobility in a larger context in 'The Great War and the Birth of the Modern Passport System', observing that 'economic liberalism' underpinned 'an unprecedented trend toward the relaxation of passport controls on the movement of late nineteenth century Western Europe, a period that has been called "the closest approximation to an open world in modern times"'.[20] He adds, though, that:

> The booming of the guns of August 1914 brought to a sudden close the era during which governments viewed foreigners "without suspicion or mistrust" and allowed them to traverse borders relatively unmolested. . . . In pursuit of the objective of greater control over the movements of the national and the alien alike, passport controls that had been eliminated or had fallen into desuetude were reintroduced across the Continent.[21]

An extremely relaxed bureaucracy in 1901, then, enables the newlywed Dowells to escape to Europe, their wealth enabling easy travel. Ironically, Florence's lie about her 'heart', which requires that she not take another sea voyage after leaving the United States, traps her within the boundaries of Europe. She will eventually have assignations with Edward in Paris, but can never go to Branshaw Teleragh without admitting the truth. The Ashburnhams also benefit from the easy international movement possible in the late nineteenth and early twentieth century. But while the Dowells travel because they are well off, Leonora and Edward are forced to India. Their relative poverty – the result of Edward's excesses – means that they must rent out Branshaw Teleragh for eight years. The move to India naturally stems from British imperial control of which Edward is a part, and once Leonora has judiciously managed their finances back into order, they can return to England and to Europe. The intimate relationship between economics and mobility also allows them to bring Maisie back with them to Bad Nauheim. Without that journey she probably would have died in India, but, ironically, Leonora's duplicitous generosity, coupled with Maisie's inadvertent surveillance (when she overhears Florence and Edward), brings about her death in the very place supposed to cure her. Edward packs off the problematic Nancy in the opposite direction, again the result of easy mobility. Remember, too, that Nancy's mother is spirited away to Italy, enabled by Edward White's money, while Mr Hurlbird pays Jimmy *not* to return to the United States, powerful signs that money not only enables travel, but can also control or otherwise restrict it.

Torpey explains that the 1914 Aliens Restrictions Act reversed Britain's previous lax system. That had begun to change with the 1905 Aliens Bill, a response to the rise of 'immigrants', a code word for

East European Jews. He quotes Aristide Zolberg, who observes that this was 'a group so undesirable that they were compared unfavourably with the despised Irish . . . and categorized [in the popular mind] as close to the Chinese'.[22] The 1914 Act, Torpey notes, put 'the onus of proving that a person is not an alien on that person and thus making documentary evidence of one's nationality largely unavoidable',[23] something that might have proved problematic given Leonora's 'despicable' Irish ancestry. Passports function as critical mechanisms for monitoring the movements of aliens, however defined. For all that, both Leonora and the American Dowell are safely ensconced in England in 1916. The Ashburnhams, as well as Dowell and Nancy Rufford, had left Bad Nauheim in September 1913. On July 13, 1914, Torpey notes, Germany implemented a 'temporary passport restriction' for those entering from abroad, and by the end of 1914 required that 'anyone who wished to enter *or leave* (sic) the territory of the empire was to be in possession of a passport'.[24] Between these dates a procession of journeys takes place: Edward, Leonora and Nancy return to Branshaw, before Edward decides that Nancy should go to India; Dowell settles accounts back in the United States before accepting Edward's invitation to help ease tensions in England, and then helps take Nancy to the station; her letter to Edward telling him that she is having a 'rattling good time' (GS 169) causes him to commit suicide, which prompts Nancy to go mad; Dowell agrees to go an retrieve her from India and does so. This final journey, Victor Cheng suggests, would be sometime in mid-1914'[25], just before The Great War begins. At that time Dowell can still travel through Europe, Africa and Asia to retrieve Nancy, but the type of free movement the main characters have enjoyed over the preceding decades becomes far more restricted.

For H. G. Wells, swift global travel was essential to his modern utopia, an index of the freedom at the heart of his vision (*MU* 20-22). Interestingly, in terms of events in *The Good Soldier*, he concedes that the 'question of marriage is the most complicated and difficult in the whole range of Utopian problems' (*MU* 117). Ford, and perhaps many of the characters in his novel, would be likely to agree. Part of Wells's solution to the chance of mismatches is a masterpiece of surveillance thinking: potential couples would have access to the identity card of the:

projected mate, on which would be recorded his or her age, previous
marriages, legally important diseases, offspring, domiciles, public
appointments, criminal convictions, registered assignments of property, and so
forth. (*MU* 115)

'There would', he adds, 'be a reasonable interval for consideration and
withdrawal on the part of either spouse'. One wonders what good this
might have done for the Ashburnhams and the Dowells. Perhaps not
surprisingly for a writer known for a considerable number of affairs,
Wells advocates a wide range of triggers for divorce. Tellingly, of
Ford's two married couples, the more 'Wellsian', liberated pair –
Edward and Florence – both commit suicide. Leonora, the frustrated
Catholic, and the neutered Dowell, survive, exemplifying distinct
aspects of surveillance – Leonora, in part because her regular if
tortured monitoring of Edward's actions, and her cynical encourage-
ment of Florence to spy on Edward and Nancy. Ultimately, she gets
what she desires: 'children, decorum, and establishment; she desired
to avoid waste, she desired to keep up appearances. She was utterly
and entirely normal' (*GS* 159). While he may not entirely understand
all the implications of what he writes, Dowell makes one of his few
astute observations in suggesting that 'Conventions and traditions I
suppose work blindly but surely for the preservation of the normal
type; for the extinction of proud, resolute and unusual individuals' (*GS*
158). Surveillance in many forms works to delineate and, if possible,
eradicate the unusual, to maintain conventions and traditions.

Dowell means Edward, of course, when he lionises the proud,
resolute and unusual. In doing so he forgets that such individuals are
existential threats to the shock-proof world he admits to planning, and
to those nine years of uninterrupted tranquillity for which he yearns.
Whether or not he understands it, or can admit it, that peace was based
on years of 'unseeing' the affair in front of his eyes. This practice
enables him to continue contact over nearly a decade with those whom
he takes clear and sensuous pleasure in seeing, Edward and (to a lesser
extent) Leonora. Ultimately, he functions in an overtly surveillant
role, that of nurse to Nancy, someone he professes to love and would
marry, were she not mad. 'I am the attendant', he laments, 'not the
husband, of a beautiful girl who pays me no attention' (*GS* 157) – an
attendant, then, to someone who not so much 'unsees' him, or fails to
see him, but who is incapable of seeing him, having been shocked into
madness. While Dowell's own willed disconnection sustained a utopian fantasy, her imposed disconnection from the world produces a

low-level dystopia for him that, given her youth, will last the rest of his days:

> I sit here, in Edwards' gun room, all day and all day in a house that is absolutely quiet. No one visits me, for I visit no one. No one is interested in me, for I have no interests (*GS* 168).

Monitoring the beloved Nancy, Dowell is trapped in the hell of a shock-proof world, forced to endure a future of uninterrupted tranquillity.

## NOTES

1   Ford Madox Ford, *The Good Soldier*, edited by Martin Stannard, Second Edition, New York: W. W. Norton, 2012 – henceforth *GS*; p. 39.

2   David Lyon, *Surveillance Studies: An Overview*, Cambridge: Polity, 2007, p. 1.

3   H. G. Wells, *A Modern Utopia*, London: Everyman, 1994 – henceforth *MU*; p. 5.

4   *Letters of Ford Madox Ford*, edited by Ludwig, Richard M., Princeton N.J.: Princeton University Press, 1965, p. 21.

5   Max Saunders, *Ford Madox Ford: A Dual Life*, 2 vols, Oxford: Oxford University Press, 1996, I, p. 401.

6   Nikolas Rose, *Powers of Freedom: Reframing Political Thought*, Cambridge: Cambridge University Press, 1999.

7   George Orwell, *Nineteen Eighty-Four*, London: Secker and Warburg, 1998, p. 5.

8   Laura Colombino, 'Introduction', in Colombino (ed.), *Ford Madox Ford and Visual Culture*, International Ford Madox Ford Studies 8, Amsterdam and New York: Rodopi, 2009, pp. 17-26 (p. 17).

9   Laura Colombino, *Ford Madox Ford: Vision, Visuality and Writing* Peter Lang, Bern, 2008, p. 15.

10  Sally Bachner, '"The Seeing Eye": Detection, Perception and Knowledge in *The Good Soldier*', in Robert Hampson and Max Saunders (eds), *Ford Madox Ford's Modernity,* International Ford Madox Ford Studies 2, Amsterdam and New York: Rodopi, 2003, pp. 103-16.

11  Bachner, p. 110.

12  *Ibid.*, p. 111.

13  Gary T. Marx, 'A Tack in the Shoe: Neutralizing and Resisting the New Surveillance', *Journal of Social Issues*, 59:2 (2003), 369-90 (p. 372).

14  *Ibid.*, p. 374.

15  *Ibid.*, p. 380.

16  Gary T. Marx, 'What's New About the "New Surveillance"? Classifying for Change and Continuity', *Surveillance and Society*, 1:1 (2002), 9-29 (p. 14).

17  Peter Marks, 'Monitoring the Unvisible: Seeing and Unseeing in China Miéville's *The City & The City*', *Surveillance and Society*, 11:3 (2013), 222-36.

18  John Torpey, *The Invention of the Passport: Surveillance, Citizenship and the State*, Cambridge: Cambridge University Press, 2000.
19  Victor Cheng, 'A Chronology of The Good Soldier', in Stannard, (ed.), *GS* 391-5.
20  John Torpey, 'The Great War and the Birth of the Modern British Passport System', in Jane Caplan and John Torpey (eds), *Documenting Individual Identity: The Development of State Practices in the Modern World*, Princeton NJ: Princeton University Press, 2001, pp. 256-70 (p. 256). Torpey quotes from Alan Dowty, *Closed Borders: The Contemporary Assault on Freedom of Movement*, New Haven: Yale University Press, 1987, p. 54.
21  Torpey, *op. cit.*, p. 257.
22  Aristide Goldberg, 'The Great Wall Against China: Responses to the First Immigration Crisis, 1885-1925', in *Migration, Migration History, History. Old Paradigms and New Perspectives*, edited by Jan Lucassen and Leo Lucassen, New York: Peter Lang, 1997, pp. 312-13.
23  Torpey, *op. cit.*, p. 258.
24  *Ibid.*, p. 259.
25  Cheng, p. 395.

# CONTRIBUTORS

VENETIA ABDALLA is an independent scholar who completed a PhD on Ford and the Pre-Raphaelites. She has given papers on Ford at conferences organized by both the Ford Madox Ford and the William Morris Societies. She has a particular interest in Ford's early writing and in the life and work of Violet Hunt. She is working on a study of Ford's neglected short stories.

CATHERINE BELSEY is Professor Emeritus, Swansea University and Visiting Professor in English at the University of Derby. Her books include *Critical Practice* (1980, 2002), *Poststructuralism: A Very Short Introduction* (2002) and *A Future for Criticism* (2011). She is also author of *Desire: Love Stories in Western Culture* (1994) and *Culture and the Real* (2005), as well as *Shakespeare and the Loss of Eden* (1999), *Why Shakespeare?* (2007) and *Shakespeare in Theory and Practice* (2008).

ISABELLE BRASME is Senior Lecturer in British Literature at the University of Nîmes, France, and a member of the EMMA research team at the University of Montpellier. She has written articles on Ford Madox Ford and is currently completing a monograph on *Parade's End.*

ELIZABETH BRUNTON is an associate tutor at Queen Mary, University of London and at Middlesex University, whose research considers modernist works in relation to medicine and gender. She is currently working on her first monograph, *Modernism and the Death of the Baby,* which examines the importance of stillbirth and neonatal death in modernist fiction by Joyce, H.D., Hemingway and Rhys.

CARA CHIMIRRI completed her Master of Arts with Distinction at Victoria University of Wellington in 2014. Her research focuses on David Jones and his relationship to other modernist writers such as Eliot, Ford, and Pound. Her Master's thesis looked at liminal spaces in the poetry of Eliot and Jones.

MELBA CUDDY-KEANE is Emerita Professor, University of Toronto-Scarborough and an emerita faculty member of the University of Toronto's Graduate Department of English. Her areas of specialization are modernism, narratology, and book history/print culture; her publications include *Virginia Woolf, the Intellectual, and the Public Sphere* (2003), the Harcourt annotated edition of Woolf's *Between the Acts* (2008), and, co-authored with Adam Hammond and Alexandra Peat, *Modernism: Keywords* (2014). Some of her recent essays are 'Ethics' in *Modernism and Theory: A Critical Debate* (2008); 'Narration, Navigation, and Non-conscious Thought: Neuroscientific and Literary Approaches to the Thinking Body' (*UTQ* 2010); 'Virginia Woolf and the Public Sphere' in the *Cambridge Companion to Virginia Woolf*, 2nd ed. (2010); and 'Movement, Space, and Embodied Cognition in *To the Lighthouse*' in the *Cambridge Companion* to that novel (2015). She has served as President of both the Modernist Studies Association and the International Virginia Woolf Society.

NAGİHAN HALİLOĞLU is an Assistant Professor at the Alliance of Civilizations Institute in Istanbul where she teaches courses on multiculturalism and orientalism. She has an MSt in Oriental Studies from the University of Oxford, and a PhD in English from the University of Heidelberg. Her doctoral thesis on Jean Rhys was published in 2011 by Rodopi. She has also published articles on cosmopolitanism, travel writing and contemporary Turkish literature. She is currently working on a project on memory in Orhan Pamuk and Vladimir Nabokov.

JANET HARRIS is an award winning documentary producer/director, who has worked for many years at the BBC and as a freelancer with experience of working in Iraq in war and in post-war. Her latest documentary was for BBC2, This World: 'Iraq: Did my son die in vain?' for the 10th anniversary of the invasion of Iraq in March 2013. Janet holds a PhD on the media coverage of the British military in post-war Iraq from Cardiff University and is now a lecturer at the Cardiff School of Journalism, Media and Cultural studies, teaching modules in international journalism and documentaries.

SARA HASLAM is Senior Lecturer in English at the Open University. She is the author of *Fragmenting Modernism: Ford Madox*

*Ford, the Novel and the Great War* (Manchester University Press, 2002), and editor of Ford's *The Good Soldier* (Wordsworth Classics, 2010), and *England and the English* (Carcanet Press, 2003), as well as *Ford Madox Ford and the City* (Rodopi, 2005) and, with Seamus O'Malley, *Ford Madox Ford and America* (Rodopi, 2012). Further publications include *Life Writing* (Routledge, 2009, with Derek Neale), and chapters and articles on Henry James, Thomas Hardy, the Brontës, modernism, and the literature of the First World War, most recently in the *Journal of First World War Studies*, 4:2 (2013). She was a founder member of the Ford Madox Ford Society, and has been its Chair since 2007. Her annotated critical edition of Ford's *A Man Could Stand Up –* was published in 2011 (Carcanet Press).

ROB HAWKES is Senior Lecturer in English at Teesside University. He is author of *Ford Madox Ford and the Misfit Moderns: Edwardian Fiction and the First World War* (Palgrave Macmillan, 2012). His essays include: 'Personalities of Paper: Characterisation in *A Call* and *The Good Soldier*' (in *Ford Madox Ford: Literary Networks and Cultural Transformations*, Rodopi, 2008); 'Visuality vs. Temporality: Plotting and Depiction in *The Fifth Queen* and *Ladies Whose Bright Eyes*' (in *Ford Madox Ford and Visual Culture*, Rodopi, 2009); and 'Trusting in Provence: Financial Crisis in *The Rash Act* and *Henry for Hugh*' (in *Ford Madox Ford, France and Provence*, Rodopi, 2011). With Ashley Chantler, he is co-editor of *Ford Madox Ford's Parade's End: The First World War, Culture, and Modernity* (Rodopi, 2014), *Ford Madox Ford: An Introduction* (Ashgate, forthcoming), and *War and the Mind: Ford Madox Ford's Parade's End, Modernism, and Psychology* (Edinburgh University Press, 2015).

Associate Professor PETER MARKS teaches in the English Department at the University of Sydney. He is interested in connections between literature, cinema and politics, and has published articles and book chapters on George Orwell, surveillance, British and American literary periodicals, and utopias. He is the author of the monographs *British Filmmakers: Terry Gilliam* (2009), *George Orwell the Essayist: Literature, Politics and the Periodical Culture* (2011) and *Imagining Surveillance: Eutopian and Dystopian Literature and Film* (2015).

JULIAN PREECE has been chair of German at Swansea since 2007, after lecturing stints at Kent, Huddersfield and Queen Mary and

Westfield College, London. He took his BA and DPhil at Oxford. He is the author of three monographs, on Günter Grass (2001/2004), Veza Canetti (2007) and *Baader-Meinhof and the Novel* (2012) and has edited more than a dozen collections, including *The Cambridge Companion to Kafka* (2002). He is currently completing the critical edition of Grass's 1992 novel *Unkenrufe / The Call of the Toad* for the Göttingen Edition of Grass's complete works due for publication on his ninetieth birthday in 2017 and has lately been commissioned to write a biography of Grass for Reaktion Books' Critical Lives series. He is also developing interests in cinema and is editing a volume on the director Andreas Dresen, who was a guest of the Swansea Centre for Contemporary German Culture in 2014.

HARRY RICKETTS is a professor in the English Programme at Victoria University of Wellington, New Zealand, and also teaches creative writing. He has published over 25 books. These include two biographies – *The Unforgiving Minute: A Life of Rudyard Kipling* (1999) and *Strange Meetings: The Poets of the Great War* (2010), nine collections of poems (mostly recently *Just Then*, 2012), several anthologies of New Zealand poetry, and a number of personal essays. He has written extensively on Kipling. In addition to his biography, he has published essays on Kipling's poetry, his autobiography, *Debits and Credits*, and his wide-ranging literary legacy and influence.

OMAR SABBAGH is a widely published poet and critic. His poetry and prose have appeared in such venues as: *Poetry Review, PN Review, Poetry Ireland Review, The Reader, Warwick Review, POEM, Kenyon Review Online, Agenda, Poetry Wales, Stand, Wasafiri, The Wolf, Banipal, The London Magazine, The Moth, Lighthouse, Rusted Radishes,* and *Envoi*. His three extant poetry collections include: *My Only Ever Oedipal Complaint* and *The Square Root of Beirut* (Cinnamon Press, 2010/12). A fourth collection: *To the Middle of Love,* is forthcoming with Cinnamon Press in late 2016.

In January 2014 Rodopi published his monograph: *From Sight through to In-Sight: Time, Narrative and Subjectivity in Conrad and Ford*. He also has a novella set in and about Beirut, *Via Negativa,* forthcoming with Cinnamon Press's new Imprint, Liquorice Fish, at the start of 2016. He has published, in a more 'academic' vein, on George Eliot, Ford Madox Ford, Joseph Conrad, Lawrence Durrell, G. K. Chesterton and Robert Browning.

For the years 2011-13 he was Visiting Assistant Professor at the American University of Beirut (AUB). In Fall 2014 he took up an Assistant Professorship in English at the American University in Dubai (AUD). Website: www.omarsabbagh.me

MAX SAUNDERS is Director of the Arts and Humanities Research Institute, Professor of English and Co-Director of the Centre for Life-Writing Research at King's College London, where he teaches modern literature. He studied at the universities of Cambridge and Harvard, and was a Fellow of Selwyn College, Cambridge. He is the author of *Ford Madox Ford: A Dual Life*, 2 vols (Oxford University Press, 1996) and *Self Impression: Life-Writing, Autobiografiction, and the Forms of Modern Literature* (Oxford University Press 2010); the editor of five volumes of Ford's writing, including an annotated critical edition of *Some Do Not . . .* (Carcanet, 2010), and has published essays on life-writing, on impressionism, and on a number of modern writers. He was awarded a Leverhulme Major Research Fellowship from 2008-10 to research the To-Day and To-Morrow book series; and in 2013 an Advanced Grant from the ERC for a 5-year collaborative project on Digital Life Writing.

EYAL SEGAL is a Research Fellow in the Porter Institute for Poetics and Semiotics, Tel Aviv University. He is the author of *The Problem of Narrative Closure: How Stories Are (Not) Finished* (2007, in Hebrew) and *The Decisive Moment is Everlasting: Static Time in Kafka's Poetics* (2008, in Hebrew). His articles and book chapters appeared in *Amsterdam International Electronic Journal for Cultural Narratology*, *Poetics Today*, *Current Trends in Narratology*, ed. by Greta Olson (2011), and *Theoretical Schools and Circles in the Twentieth-Century Humanities*, ed. by Marina Grishakova (2015).

BARRY SHEILS is a Government of Ireland Postdoctoral Research Fellow at University College Dublin. His current project focuses on the linked development of psychological and ecological discourses of care in the early twentieth century and their effect on literary representation. His publications include 'Poetry in the Modern State: the example of W. B. Yeats's "new fanaticism" and "late style"' in *New Literary History* and 'Tragedy and Transference in D. M. Thomas's *The White Hotel*' in *Psychoanalysis and History*. His monograph, *W. B. Yeats and World Literature: the Subject of Poetry* is published with Ashgate in 2015.

PAUL SKINNER edited Ford Madox Ford's *No Enemy* for Carcanet Press (2002) and *Ford Madox Ford's Literary Contacts* (Volume 6 of International Ford Madox Ford Studies, 2007). His annotated critical edition of *Last Post* was published by Carcanet Press in 2011. He has published essays on Ezra Pound and Rudyard Kipling; and essays on Ford in several volumes of *International Ford Madox Ford Studies*, the latest being 'Tietjens Walking, Ford Talking' in *Ford Madox Ford's 'Parade's End': The First World War, Culture, and Modernity* (Rodopi, 2014). He lives in Bristol, where he now works in publishing.

# International Ford Madox Ford Studies

## Other volumes in the series

13. *Ford Madox Ford*'s Parade's End: *The First World War, Culture and Modernity*, ed. Ashley Chantler and Rob Hawkes (2014)


Please contact the General Editor if you would like to contribute to future publications by the Ford Madox Ford Society.

# THE
# FORD
# MADOX
# FORD
# SOCIETY

This international society was founded in 1997 to promote knowledge of and interest in Ford. Honorary Members include Julian Barnes, A. S. Byatt, Hans-Magnus Enzensberger, Mary Gordon, Samuel Hynes, Alan Judd, Bill Nighy, Ruth Rendell, Michael Schmidt, Sir Tom Stoppard, John Sutherland, and Susanna White. There are currently over one hundred members, from more than ten countries. Besides regular meetings in Britain, we have held conferences in Italy, Germany, the USA, and France. A North American Chapter was launched in 2014.

Since 2002 we have published International Ford Madox Ford Studies, a series of substantial annual volumes distributed free to members. The full list of titles is given towards the end of this volume; all of them are still available. If you are an admirer, an enthusiast, a reader, a scholar, or a student of anything Fordian, then this Society would welcome your involvement.

The Ford Madox Ford Society normally organises events each year and publishes news on its website. The Society also inaugurated a series of Ford Lectures. Speakers have included Alan Judd, Nicholas Delbanco, Zinovy Zinik, A. S. Byatt, Colm Tóibín, Hermione Lee, Mary Gordon, and Michael Schmidt.

To join, please see the website for details:

**www.fordmadoxfordsociety.org**

For further information please contact Dr Sara Haslam (Chair) by e-mail at: Sara.Haslam@open.ac.uk

For membership queries please contact one of the following:

UK: Dr Paul Skinner: email: p.skinner370@btinternet.com

North American Chapter: Dr Seamus O'Malley: email: seamus_omalley@hotmail.com

Eurozone: Dr Isabelle Brasme: email: isabellebrasme@gmail.com